Anthony Trollope

McFarland Companions to 19th Century Literature

Alfred Tennyson: A Companion
by Laurence W. Mazzeno (2020)

Anthony Trollope: A Companion
by Nicholas Birns and John F. Wirenius (2021)

Herman Melville: A Companion
by Corey Evan Thompson (2021)

Jane Austen: A Companion
by Laura Dabundo (2021)

Thomas Hardy: A Companion to the Novels
by Ronald D. Morrison (2021)

Anthony Trollope

A Companion

NICHOLAS BIRNS *AND* JOHN F. WIRENIUS

McFarland Companions to 19th Century Literature

Series Editor Laurence W. Mazzeno

Associate Editor Sue Norton

McFarland & Company, Inc., Publishers

Jefferson, North Carolina

McFarland Companions to Nineteenth-Century Literature is a series of scholarly monographs designed as guides to the work of important British, American, and Continental writers whose work appeared during the long 19th century. Each volume is prepared by an experienced scholar-teacher and focuses on the writer's most frequently read fiction, poetry, or nonfiction. Written to aid students and teachers, each companion contains a biography, an Introduction explaining the writer's importance, a list of major publications, an alphabetical listing of entries that discuss the writer's works and provide information on people, places, events, and issues that affected the author's literary career, and a selected bibliography of recent criticism.

ISBN (print) 978–1–4766–7769–9
ISBN (ebook) 978–1–4766–4425–7

Library of Congress and British Library
cataloguing data are available

Library of Congress Control Number 2021045976

Front cover image: Anthony Trollope, 1878 (British Library)

Printed in the United States of America

McFarland & Company, Inc., Publishers
Box 611, Jefferson, North Carolina 28640
www.mcfarlandpub.com

Table of Contents

Acknowledgments   vi

Preface   1

Abbreviations   2

Introduction   3

Anthony Trollope: A Brief Biography   9

Chronological List of Trollope's Major Publications   14

Anthony Trollope: A Companion   19

*Appendix: General Secondary Bibliography
of Anthony Trollope*   225

Works Cited   229

Index   233

Acknowledgments

John Wirenius has been a wonderful, knowledgeable, and resourceful collaborator and it has been a pleasure to experience his encyclopedic knowledge of Trollope, British literature, and the Victorian age. I would like to thank my lovely wife, Isabella Smalera Birns; my mother and longtime fellow Trollopian, Margaret Boe Birns; as well as colleagues Lauren Goodlad, Doug Gerlach, Steven Amarnick, Michael Williamson, Elizabeth Howard, Randy Williams, and Ellen Moody. The Trollope conference at Leuven in 2015 was vital to making this book possible and I thank Frederik van Dam, Ortwin de Graef, and all the other conveners and organizers, as well as the Trollope Society in both the UK and US. I would also like to thank all those who worked on Trollope in the decades when doing so was not prestigious in academia, for keeping discussion of his work alive and providing the ground for efforts like this that transpire in more fruitful times.

—*Nicholas Birns*

To begin, it is a genuine pleasure to collaborate with Nicholas Birns on this volume, and I thank him for inviting me to join him on this ramble through Trollope Country. The late Walter Kendrick, who taught English literature at Fordham College, was a marvelous, witty professor. His own work on Trollope, *The Novel Machine: The Theory and Fiction of Anthony Trollope* (1980) introduced me to Trollopean criticism. Ellen Moody's *Trollope on the Net* (1999) and her other essays, whether in journals, books, or online, always raise interesting challenges to traditional views on Trollope and invite further investigation. The first complete edition of *The Duke's Children* and its scholarly apparatus offer a whole new vista of Trollope at work, and the building blocks of his world. Steven Amarnick, Robert F. Wiseman, and Susan Lowell Humphries have not just restored a classic to its full power, they have given us new insights into Trollope's commitment to his characters and his readers. My beloved wife Catherine has endured weekends, vacations, and ordinary time with me hunched over my old laptop, searching through old (and new) journal articles on Trollope and all things Victorian. I couldn't do it without her generous support, and her occasional arched brow at my less plausible readings.

—*John F. Wirenius*

Preface

This book seeks to combine the enthusiasm of the general reader with the scholarship of the academic reader to give both students and a wider ring of devotees access to and information about Anthony Trollope and the people and contexts important to him. Trollope is an entertainer writing in a commercial genre, but this does not mean that he is not also a major novelist whose achievement is an artistic one. Our aim in his book is to unite the scholars' and the enthusiasts' Trollope. We also wish, as Americans, to give a due sense of this writer's international and cosmopolitan aspects but, equally, to situate him in his uniquely English and Victorian contexts.

We have placed the emphasis on Trollope's works, but also included entries on key friends (and enemies) in his life, his major interests and affiliations, as well as important themes and techniques in his work. Every novel of Trollope's receives an individual entry. Most space is given to the Palliser and Barsetshire novels, and to such major stand-alone works as *Orley Farm* and *The Way We Live Now*. But there are full entries on the individual novels, travel books, and books of short fiction. Nearly everything Trollope ever published is mentioned, and the vast majority receive full consideration, from "Malachi's Cove" to *Sir Harry Hotspur of Humblethwaite*. We have tried to give an idea of the major movements of the plot in the entries on fiction without going into plot summary as such or naming every single character. Our stress is on the value the novels have in themselves as well as their place in Trollope's entire oeuvre.

We also wish to pay appropriate attention to the various phases of Trollope's career. Early Trollope might be defined as ending with the mature achievement of *Orley Farm*. Middle Trollope is defined as going from that novel to the return from his second trip to Australia. Late Trollope begins with the books too late to be mentioned in *An Autobiography*.

Abbreviations

Auto—*An Autobiography*

CYFH—*Can You Forgive Her?*

DC—*The Duke's Children*

ED—*Eustace Diamonds*

Ph F—*Phineas Finn*

Ph R—*Phineas Redux*

PM—*The Prime Minister*

Introduction

The general reader probably has three associations with Anthony Trollope: that he is prolific, heartily English, and indelibly Victorian. The prolificity is a fact. Combined with what most people took from *An Autobiography*—that Trollope wrote for money, and was unashamed of it—the aura of being a hack has hung over him. Whereas George Eliot completed seven novels, and Dickens fourteen, Trollope published more than forty. Although other nineteenth-century novelists—George Sand, Benito Pérez Galdós, James Fenimore Cooper—matched Trollope's level of production, none surpassed it, and certainly nobody in England. Trollope's prolific output means that each of his novels is not so different from the others as to constitute a significantly different imaginative world. With Dickens, *Little Dorrit* and *Dombey and Son* are two distinct realms of experience, even though depicted by the same hand, or with Shakespeare, where G. Wilson Knight could speak of the universe of *King Lear*, one shared by no other play. By contrast, Trollope's novels often occur in the same world; characters cross from their own books to scarcely related ones. Far from resulting from a lack of invention, these crossovers add to the depth of the imagined world, and sometimes allow the reader to see old friends in a different light.

One has to see the delight in Trollope as being largely one of theme and variation. His copiousness is an example of someone willing to adapt a core technique to a variety of forms and circumstances, as Haydn did in symphonic music and Rossini in opera. The reader understandably infers the prototype of what a Trollope novel is, but there are notable differences in the mood, concerns, and tonalities of individual novels. There is a sense where it is helpful to assume there is one "Trollope." At other times, however, it might be more useful to assume there are many "Trollopes." Trollope circulated widely, in serial and book form and also in such external contexts as the Tauchnitz editions of his novels, widely circulated in Europe and influential on, among others, Leo Tolstoy. This strengthens the sense of a bustling oeuvre at once coherent and diverse. But there is no case in which Trollope is simply repeating himself or doing hackwork. Every book of his attempts a situation, a perspective, or a plot development that the others have left unchronicled. Trollope had literary motivations over and above what he would defend as a legitimate pecuniary ambition for a professional writer.

That Trollope wrote so much does not mean most of it is not good, and that there is not a reason for each book within the sweep of the entire oeuvre. Trollope's body of work held together genre elements in the novel that later split apart. As Q.D. Leavis noted, after a certain point in the nineteenth century popular and elite taste split. Prolixity and seriality were mainly associated with more popular work such as genre fiction: romance, mystery, historical fiction, science fiction.

Two generations after Trollope, and after such prolific novelists such as Hugh Walpole had lost their reading public, one would have to look to genre writers in English such as Agatha Christie or Edgar Rice Burroughs to find the combination of the fecundity and relative quality of Trollope. Later writers like Simon Raven, who both adapted Trollope for television and emulated him in his fiction, were writing in a consciously Trollopian genre, as Angela Thirkell did earlier and with less irony. Trollope, in a sense, became his own genre. This made liking Trollope suspect in certain circles. The academic Henry Abelove has written that in the late 1970s his love of Trollope's fiction was "a secret and unaccountable pleasure" (483). In the past few decades, popular and elite taste have once again coalesced. Furthermore, the advent of seriality in mass media has made Trollope seem less of an outlier.

As for the hearty Englishness, this is a flawed conception from the start. Trollope at one point trained to be an Austrian army officer. He lived in Belgium when young. He found his vocation in Ireland. He travelled across the globe. Close to an eighth of his fiction is set outside England. Even in those set in England, Celtic, colonial, and Continental aspects make their appearance and contribution. This can be seen in two such obvious characters in the Palliser books as Isabel Boncassen and Madame Max Goesler. Trollope is a writer depicting a globalizing world whose components are more and more in dialogue with each other.

With regard to the Victorians, Trollope's career certainly fits neatly within Queen Victoria's long reign. Of the all major Victorian novelists he may be said to have most thoroughly captured the mid–Victorian era, which one might define as extending from the Great Exhibition held at the Crystal Palace in 1851 to the proclamation of Queen Victoria as Empress of India in 1876. Certain aspects of his work look back to the early Victorian, such as the role of the Oxford Movement in the Barsetshire series. But others—the rising tension in and about Ireland, the growing power of the United States, the rise of movements for women's and workers' rights—eddy into the late Victorian.

Yet Trollope has always held an anomalous place in Victorian studies. Although always prominent in academic studies of the field—and growing even more so from about 1995 onward—traditionally he had been rarely included in undergraduate level Victorian surveys. This is partially because his work tends to be long, and there is no set "shorter Trollope" that has become canonical, unlike George Eliot's *Silas Marner*. But part of this neglect has been that the traditional narrative of such a Victorian survey is the growth of the novel towards ever greater realism and ever greater representation of the middle class. Trollope certainly provides the realism. Only George Eliot in the Victorian era is more committed to realism as a mode than Trollope, although his garrulous authorial intervention might not seem realistic to us.

But Trollope's slew of aristocratic characters and great house settings militate against putting his work into the "rising middle class" paradigm. This is so even though Trollope himself was (though having some aristocrats in his lineage) middle class. He was neither an aristocrat nor married into the aristocracy. Much in the line of the "silver-fork" fiction of the previous generation, his portrait of the aristocracy involved a writer who was not of that ilk and readers who in the main were not either.

Especially in his early work, Trollope manifests conservative and anti-reform impulses. *La Vendée* is heartily opposed to the French Revolution (though advances no successful alternative) and *The Warden* joyously lampoons the cant and hypocrisy of reformers. But there is significant complexity here beneath the surface, and even more so as Trollope's career progressed. Trollope may not have written about the aristocracy being humbled by the middle class or the middle class replacing the aristocracy. But he did write about how intermarriage diversified the aristocracy and allowed the middle class a road to rise upward.

Deborah Denenholz Morse has discerned a more reformist impulse in later Trollope. *Is He Popenjoy?* shows the grandson of the dean of a cathedral being born a titled aristocrat. *Cousin Henry* displays a middle-class man marrying into a fortune he has helped his beloved gain, whereas *The Duke's Children* show brother and sister both marrying "beneath them" for love. *Lady Anna*, perhaps Trollope's most class-conscious novel, shows its heroine picking love, merit, and a new country over money and status. Sometimes in Trollope outsiders are not able to attain the standards of a gentleman, like Sir Roger Scatcherd in *Doctor Thorne*. Later in his career Trollope shows a world where the existence of the aristocracy does not preclude substantial social mobility. Yet those upper-class families who try to hold on to their privilege simply for their own sake, like the de Courcys in *Doctor Thorne*, are lampooned.

Trollope achieved these effects by painting on a wide canvas. A companion to Trollope must necessarily reflect this width. The reader will find here treatments of Trollope's most famous and beloved works, such as *Can You Forgive Her?* or *Barchester Towers*. But they will also find reference to obscure works rarely the subject of scholarship such as "How the Mastiffs Went to Iceland," his studies of Cicero and Thackeray, and "Miss Sarah Jack, of Spanish Town, Jamaica," Trollope is best known for his series novels and most acclaimed when, as Gordon Ray put it, he wrote at full length. Such a book as this inevitably brings the non-series and shorter novels more to the foreground of the reader's mind. The reader who enjoys Archdeacon Grantly scheming in the rectory at Plumstead Episcopi and is jolted by the murder of Mr. Bonteen on the way home from the Universe Club may also be moved by Cousin Henry's agonies over hiding his relative's will in a book, unsettled by the political murder of young Florian Jones, and amused by Trollope's feeling that the babies of North America are fed too many pickles by their mothers.

The Trollope that emerges from consideration of his full oeuvre is a haltingly yet unabashedly progressive Trollope. This Trollope, though hardly a Marxist and unlikely to favor any sort of radical revolution, insists that his society can and should be developing in a more inclusive direction. Trollope's famous phrase "advanced conservative-liberal" from *An Autobiography* encapsulates thus paradox with appropriate poise and complexity. Seeing Trollope's politics in a more dynamic light can also occasion a fuller appreciation of his literary power. We probably underrate Trollope's originality and the sheer force of his genius. He had an extraordinary talent that illuminated the novel as a genre in a particular way by anyone before or since. He painted society as he saw it, but this perspective could be as satiric as commendatory. His choice of character names, from the preposterous Mr. Popular Sentiment and Lord Boardotrade, to the flamboyant Plantagenet Palliser and Mountjoy Scarborough, to the verisimilar and totally apt Lily Dale and Harry Clavering, show the width of this palette of social representation. The Trollope we see in this book is also an international and cosmopolitan Trollope, who found his novelistic muse in Ireland, wrote more amply about Australia than any other English novelist, and set compelling stories in Prague, Nuremberg, Palestine, and the Suez. He also early on found an audience not just in Great Britain but outside it, in the United States and, via the Tauchnitz series of inexpensive editions, on the Continent.

If Trollope travelled the known world, he also illuminated an entire fictional world for his readers. Readers have felt that they can escape to the author's world. There seems a full set of characters and situations that could take them away from their current life and absorb them in a fully rendered universe. Trollope acquired a certain image as cozy and reassuring. During the Second World War, people began to read him as a consolation or distraction. Trollope-reading soldiers ranged from the American naval officer Gordon Ray, later to become an English professor famous for his praise of Trollope at full length, to the fictional General Liddament in the war trilogy of Anthony Powell. This popularity intensified the sense of Trollope as a comforting distraction, ballasted by the way the Victorian world, which was the present to Trollope, had by that point become the past. Trollope, who more than any other novelist depicted the Victorian world comprehensively and without mannerism, thus became more valued.

Whereas George Eliot actually wrote about this era only in *Felix Holt* and *Daniel Deronda*, Trollope devotes the vast majority of his work to the time in which he was living. He could be described as writing the contemporary. Yet, unlike Disraeli, he did not refer to real-life personalities in his novels. He was more intent on creating a fictional world. Mildmay in the Palliser books could easily have been named as, say, Lord Melbourne. But he was not. This is the aspect of Trollope that encourages readers to escape into his cozy and comfortable fictional world. It makes his work, for all its realism and contemporaneity, similar to science fiction or fantasy. The reading experience can be akin to playing games, or virtual reality, with their encouragement of the audience to situate themselves in the world very different from the one in which they actually live.

In the 1970s, Trollope's fortunes begin to rise. In 1974, the Simon Raven–scripted adaptation of the Palliser novels televised by BBC2 was aired. Its impact on academic work was immediate—the number of scholarly books on Trollope soared in the years immediately after 1974—and it brought a new generation of admirers to Trollope, especially in the United States, including people captivated by it as children, who grew up to be Trollope scholars. For this reason we include Simon Raven among our entries, as his adaptation of Trollope, and what might be called his continuation of Trollope in his *Alms for Oblivion* series, is key to how Trollope is highly regarded today.

Trollope has always had a large number of fans outside academia, among lawyers, politicians, and those who might not otherwise consider themselves literary readers. The Trollope for whom, according to Shirley Letwin, there is "no non-rational experience for a human being," is capable of appealing to many different constituencies. This was only accentuated by the successful television adaptation. In the 1970s, Trollope might well be said to have been understood and appreciated more outside academia than in it. Literary theorists—with the honorable, and extraordinary, exception of J.

Hillis Miller—tended to steer clear of Trollope or give him begrudging acknowledgment in general literary histories. Even Trollope enthusiasts might not have recognized that Trollope, through his Australian works, contributed substantially to delineating settler colonialism. Academic and general readers seemed far apart. Since the 1990s, though, academic criticism has begun to catch up, mingling new approaches like feminism, queer studies, and transnationalism with a willingness to read widely and comprehensively in Trollope's oeuvre and not simply focus on a few well-known works. Trollope is becoming more, and more deeply, understood, and this *Companion* seeks to facilitate that process of understanding.

Anthony Trollope:
A Brief Biography

Anthony Trollope was born at 16 Keppel Street, Bloomsbury, London, in 1815. The Trollopes came originally from Lincolnshire, where a distant cousin was a baronet. The novelist's father, Thomas Anthony Trollope, was a Chancery barrister who had graduated from New College, Oxford, but who had been inconspicuous in his career and was chronically in debt. His great hope in life was to inherit Julians, an estate held by his mother Penelope's family, the Meetkerkes, descended from the Dutch ambassador to England in the days of Queen Elizabeth I. The senior Trollope's uncle, Adolphus Meetkerke, was elderly and childless. Meetkerke remarried late, though, and, as Plantagenet Palliser feared in *Phineas Redux* would happen with the Duke of Omnium and Madame Max Goesler, a child was born who pre-empted the Trollope claim to the Meetkerke fortunes, particularly their Hertfordshire estate of Julians. (Trollope was later friendly with his distant cousin Cynthia Meetkerke, also a writer.) Thomas Anthony Trollope, shorn of his expectations, attempted to farm (an experience his son later fictionalized as Lucius Mason's agricultural efforts in *Orley Farm*). He continued to founder financially, tried and failed to earn money in the United States, and in 1834 fled with his family to Bruges in newly independent Belgium to escape his creditors. He died in that city on October 23, 1835, at the Chateau d'Hondt.

Trollope's mother, Frances Milton Trollope, was the daughter of a Bristol rector, William Milton (no known relation to the seventeenth-century poet), and his first wife, Mary Gresley (whose name Trollope later used as the title of one of his short stories). Through her mother, Frances was related to the Hellicars, a prominent Bristol merchant family. Her mother died when she was five and her father did not remarry until Frances was an adult. After his remarriage, Frances moved to London where she lived in Bloomsbury with her brother, Henry Milton, a Whitehall bureaucrat and, later, author of the novel *Rivalry* in 1840. There, Frances met Thomas Anthony Trollope, who also lived on Keppel Street. After the disappointment of her husband's financial aspirations, Frances tried to aid the family fortunes by cultivating the elderly Marquis de Lafayette, whom she visited at his estate in France, and, through his ward, Fanny Wright, engaging to travel to America. She was particularly interested in Nashoba Commune in Tennessee, where freed slaves were taught to work in order that they could one day be transported to Africa. The commune experienced controversy and failed, and Frances attempted various commercial ventures across the Ohio River in Cincinnati. These failed as well. But her frustration at the coarse side of American life inspired her to write *Domestic Manners of the Americans* (1832), which became a bestseller and established her writing career. This came too late, though, for the revenue gained to offset the husband's various defalcations, and most of Frances's literary success came after her husband's death.

Thomas Anthony and Frances had six children, one of whom, Emily, died in childbirth. Anthony was their fourth. He was born at 16 Keppel Street (a site now occupied by buildings of the University of London). He may have had some ancestral connections to the aristocracy, as his grandfather was the fifth son of the Trollope baronet of Casewick Hall in Lincolnshire, a degree of proximity to the title far less than that of the Meetkerke uncle—indeed, so distant that to inherit it would be to beg plausibility in a Trollope novel. The Trollope family was deeply established in Lincolnshire, and by ancestry Anthony was a member of the landed gentry, a class that produced other English novelists such as Jane Austen. But he grew up neither rich nor aristocratic, and indeed his early years were precarious both financially and socially. He attended the socially prestigious Harrow School from age seven to ten, but only because his father lived there and he went as a day pupil, a group looked down upon by the boarders. He left to go to a school run by Arthur Drury, the brother of his Harrow tutor Henry Drury, at Sunbury-on-Thames where for two unhappy years he was bullied by the other boys. Trollope's brothers had gone to the more prestigious Winchester School, and when a vacancy opened up for Anthony his father eagerly sent him there, hoping that his sons would follow his example by going to Oxford and redeeming his failed fortunes.

When Trollope's parents went to America, they took his three elder siblings, but not Anthony. Soon, money for Winchester ran out, and Anthony had to return ignominiously to Harrow as a day-pupil, this time a three-mile walk away from the school. Feeling abandoned by his family and looked down on by his schoolmates, he was deeply unhappy.

With the family having no prospects of affording him a university education, Anthony had to find a job. While he was residing in Bruges with his family, there was some prospect of his obtaining a cavalry commission in the army of the Austrian Empire. Anthony took this possibility seriously enough to learn German and French. This would have given him a very different life. The opportunity impressed him enough to be the imaginative spark for later works such as *Linda Tressel* and "Why Frau Frohmann Raised Her Prices."

In any event, the prospect of a commission was never realized, and Trollope was left floundering. Drury had opened a school in Brussels, and Trollope served as an usher there for a brief time. After his father's death, Trollope obtained a position in the post office by his mother's networking with a member of the Freeling family, a powerful family entrenched in the Civil Service much like the Tite-Barnacles in Dickens's *Little Dorrit*. His new position involved working at the General Post Office at St. Martin's Le Grand. Trollope's main supervisor, William Maberly, did not admire Trollope, and by his own assessment Trollope's early years as a postal employee were unsatisfactory both to him and to the organization.

Trollope's life turned around in September 1841 when he received an appointment as a postal surveyor's clerk in Ireland. First, his stamina, diligence, and social skills provided a better fit in this job, which involved traveling around Ireland and dealing with problems as they arose rather than just sitting in an office. Second, he was well paid in a country where most were poor, and no longer felt his life so precarious. Third, he developed an interest in what became his principal hobby, hunting. But most importantly, in Ireland Trollope found his wife and developed his true vocation. Rose Heseltine was the daughter of Edward Heseltine of the Sheffield and Rotherham Joint Stock Company. Trollope met her in 1842 when her family were on vacation in Ireland, south of Dublin. They married on June 11, 1844. The Trollopes had two sons, Henry Merivale, born in 1846, and Frederic James Anthony, born in 1847.

By the time Trollope married, he had begun to write fiction about Ireland. His first novel, *The Macdermots of Ballycloran* was published in 1847. Its reception was inauspicious, and its financial gleanings meager. But once Trollope got going as a writer, he did not stop. In all respects, Ireland provided a place for him to be autonomous and to develop and mature as his own person.

Trollope was transferred back to England as a postal surveyor in the southwest, a position he held for two years. He then returned to Ireland in 1855 as surveyor for Northern Ireland, living in Donnybrook near Dublin. He also travelled abroad for the post office to the Near East, which inspired a novel and two short stories, and to the Caribbean, which provided material for his first travel book. Trollope's travels on behalf of the post office both advanced his career and exposed him to scenes, characters, and situations that reverberated in his fiction. He transferred for good to England in 1859 as Surveyor for the Eastern District; by which time he had established a modest reputation as an author.

The Trollopes' sojourn in the southwest influenced such works as the Barsetshire series, *Rachel Ray*, and "Malachi's Cove," while the permanent appointment allowed him to become the definitive portrayer of what he called, in the opening to *Castle Richmond*, "daily English life." The Barsetshire series, starting as a quirky portrayal of a legal and ecclesiastical anomaly in *The Warden*, became a portrait of an entire fictional region; in these novels Trollope created a full-fledged reality unprecedented in English letters. When it ended with the *Last Chronicle of Barset*, readers still wished for more. The later Barsetshire books and the ambitious legal saga *Orley Farm* were successful. Trollope's first into English periodical publishing, contributions to William Makepeace Thackeray's *Cornhill* magazine, were equally so. All these ventures advanced Trollope's career as a popular writer. He suffered some reversals—his travel book about the United States was not the success his mother's was—but by his mid-forties, Trollope found his position in English literary life assured.

Trollope was able to achieve his extraordinary productivity while continuing to work in his postal position. *An Autobiography* relates his working methods; he rose early each morning so he would have time to write. But only Trollope's genius could account for both the extent and the high quality of what he produced.

In late 1859, Trollope, his wife, and his two sons settled at Waltham House in Waltham Cross, Hertfordshire, just outside London, where Trollope lived longer than at any other residence. Trollope continued to work for the post office until 1867, rising high in the organization—and was partially responsible for such milestones as introducing the pillar post box into England. But by the time he resigned he had developed other interests, and not just in his writing. He had seriously gotten involved in the world of publishing. He wrote for the *Cornhill* and the *Fortnightly*, and was one of the major forces behind the start of the *Pall Mall Gazette*. He eventually started his own periodical, *Saint Pauls*.

Trollope was an active supporter of the Royal Literary Fund, established in 1818 to support indigent or struggling writers, and frequently corresponded with the Fund's longtime secretary, Octavian Blewitt. Trollope befriended such literary figures as George Eliot, George Henry Lewes, and Richard Monckton Milnes. He bought a third-interest in the publishing firm of Chapman and Hall for his son Henry Merivale once he learned that Frederic Chapman, son of the firm's founder, wanted a partner. He travelled to America in 1868 for the second time, largely to promote his literary work. Moreover, in 1868 Trollope contested the Northern seat of Beverley as a Liberal. Though the seat was not a particularly winnable one, Trollope seriously desired to become an MP, and in his portrait of various elections in his later fiction there is a sense of his disappointment that he lost.

Even after he left the post office, Trollope continued his travels. The most significant of these were his two visits to Australia in 1871–2 and 1875, where his son Fred was attempting to be a farmer. Trollope admired the settler colonists of Australia and New Zealand and thought they had a great future. He befriended Australian writers such as G.W. Rusden and set several novels and short satires in the Antipodes and wrote a travel book about them. By then, Trollope had begun his second great series, the Palliser books, interweaving marital discord and concord and themes of the insider and outsider into a political chronicle.

Trollope had given up his house in Waltham Cross before he left for Australia, and when he returned to London he took up an abode at Montagu Square, resuming his residence in his childhood neighborhood of Bloomsbury, an area developing a reputation as a haven for intellectuals. The Palliser books were not the commercial and critical success the Barsetshire books had been, and public taste began to turn against Trollope. The final Palliser book, *The Duke's Children,* was truncated by its publisher's order and did not have the impact it should have. Perhaps his low point as a commercial author was with *Ayala's Angel*, which could only be serialized in Cincinnati, although too much should not be made of this, as at that time the *Cincinnati Commercial* had some prestige because of its prominent editor, Murat Halstead. Generally, though, Trollope's series novels always had an audience and sold well. His more experimental books and non-series novels were disappointments. *The Westminster Review*, in reviewing *Dr. Wortle's School* in 1881, said that Trollope and the now-unknown Scotsman William Black were roughly equivalents in both the merit and the prestige of their work.

As revealed in *An Autobiography*, Trollope had a professional approach to authorship that was both dedicated and ruthless. Though not indifferent to artistic achievement, his goal was to make a living with his work, and he did so. He was aware audiences wanted happy endings and likable protagonists, and in the main he provided these. This did not, however, mean he did not take risks or simply played into existing public taste. To write a dystopian novel set in a fictional future South Pacific country, or to write an explicit chronicle of contemporary political violence in Ireland—the subjects of two of

Trollope's posthumously published books, *The Fixed Period* and *The Landleaguers*—is hardly to play it safe.

Trollope was still vigorous in his early sixties. He travelled to South Africa and Iceland and continuing to write with even greater productivity. One of his greatest novels, *Mr. Scarborough's Family,* was the product of his last years and was published posthumously. In 1881, he travelled to Ireland to assess the changing political situation there and to do research for *The Landleaguers.* By then, he had moved to his final home, at West Harting near Petersfield in West Sussex close to the Hampshire border; at the time the area was rural but still within range of London. Trollope had felt ill for a year or so before he died—although clearly his juggling many ongoing projects in his last year of life suggests that he did not expect to die immediately. He passed away at a nursing home at 34 Welbeck Street, Marylebone, after suffering a stroke. In his last month, he was cared for by his son Henry. He was no longer mentally lucid, and his family was relieved when he died on Wednesday, December 6, 1882. He was buried at Kensal Green the following Saturday.

Rose Trollope lived until 1917. Henry lived until 1926, and was a custodian of his father's legacy. After publishing one novel, *My Own Love Story*, and spending much time on a life of Molière, Henry retired from the publishing firm and wrote no more. He died, leaving no heirs, in the Gloucestershire market town of Minchinhampton. Anthony Trollope's second son, Frederic, remained in Australia, his own son eventually inheriting the Trollope baronetcy whose attainment had once seemed so dim a prospect for his father.

Chronological List of Trollope's Major Publications

The Macdermots of Ballycloran (Newby, 1847)

The Kellys and the O'Kellys (Henry Colburn, 1848)

La Vendée: An Historical Romance (Henry Colburn, 1850)

The Warden (Longman, 1855)

Barchester Towers (Longman, 1857)

The Three Clerks (Richard Bentley, 1858)

Doctor Thorne (Chapman and Hall, 1858)

The Bertrams (Chapman and Hall, 1859)

The West Indies and the Spanish Main (Chapman and Hall, 1859)

Castle Richmond (Chapman and Hall, 1860)

Framley Parsonage (Smith, Elder, 1861)

Tales of All Countries (Chapman and Hall, 1861)

    "La Mère Bauche"

    "The O'Conors of Castle Conor"

    "John Bull on the Guadalquivir"

    "Miss Sarah Jack, of Spanish Town, Jamaica"

    "The Courtship of Susan Bell"

    "Relics of General Chassé"

    "An Unprotected Female at the Pyramids"

    "The Château of Prince Polignac"

Orley Farm (Chapman and Hall, 1862)

The Struggles of Brown Jones and Robinson (Harper, 1863; Smith, Elder, 1970)

North America (Chapman and Hall, 1862)

Tales of All Countries, second series (Chapman and Hall, 1863)

    "Aaron Trow"

    "Mrs. General Talboys"

    "The Parson's Daughter of Oxney Colne"

"George Walker at Suez"

"The Mistletoe Bough"

"Returning Home"

"A Ride Across Palestine"

"The House of Heine Brothers in Munich"

"The Man Who Kept His Money in a Box"

Rachel Ray (Chapman and Hall, 1863)

The Small House at Allington (Smith, Elder, 1864)

Can You Forgive Her? (Chapman and Hall, 1865)

Miss Mackenzie (Chapman and Hall, 1865)

Hunting Sketches (Chapman and Hall, 1865)

"Gentle Euphemia" (*The Fortnightly Review*, May 1866)

The Belton Estate (Chapman and Hall, 1866)

The Claverings (Smith, Elder, 1866)

Clergymen of the Church of England (Chapman and Hall, 1866)

Travelling Sketches (Chapman and Hall, 1867)

Lotta Schmidt & Other Stories (Strahan, 1867)

"Lotta Schmidt"

"The Adventures of Fred Pickering"

"The Two Generals"

"Father Giles of Ballymoy"

"Malachi's Cove"

"The Widow's Mite"

"The Last Austrian Who Left Venice"

"Miss Ophelia Gledd"

"The Journey to Panama"

Nina Balatka (Blackwood, 1867)

The Last Chronicle of Barset (Smith and Elder, 1867)

Linda Tressel (Blackwood, 1868)

Phineas Finn (Virtue, 1869)

He Knew He Was Right (Strahan, 1869)

"*Did He Steal It?*" (Virtue, 1869)

The Vicar of Bullhampton (Bradbury and Evans, 1870)

"Christmas Day at Kirkby Cottage" (*Routledge's Christmas Annual*, 1870)

The Commentaries of Caesar (Blackwood, 1870)

An Editor's Tales (Strahan, 1870)

"The Turkish Bath"

"Mary Gresley"

"Josephine De Montmorenci"

"The Panjandrum"

"The Spotted Dog"

"Mrs. Brumby"

On English Prose Fiction as a Rational Amusement (Virtue, 1870)

Sir Harry Hotspur of Humblethwaite (Hurst and Blackett, 1871)

Ralph the Heir (Strahan, 1871)

The Golden Lion of Granpere (Tinsley, 1872)

The Eustace Diamonds (Chapman and Hall, 1873)

Australia and New Zealand (Chapman and Hall, 1873)

Lady Anna (Chapman and Hall, 1874)

Phineas Redux (Chapman and Hall, 1874)

Harry Heathcote of Gangoil: A Tale of Australian Bush Life (Sampson Low, 1874)

The Way We Live Now (Chapman and Hall, 1875)

"Never, Never-Never, Never" (*Sheets for the Candle*, December 1875)

The Prime Minister (Chapman and Hall, 1876)

The American Senator (Chapman and Hall, 1877)

South Africa (Chapman and Hall, 1878)

Is He Popenjoy? (Chapman and Hall, 1878)

An Eye for an Eye (Chapman and Hall, 1879)

"Catherine Carmichael" (*Masonic Magazine*, 1878)

How the Mastiffs Went to Iceland (Virtue, 1878)

John Caldigate (Chapman and Hall, 1879)

"Henry Wadsworth Longfellow" (*The North American Review*, 1879)

"The Genius of Nathaniel Hawthorne" (*The North American Review,* 1879)

Thackeray (Macmillan, 1879)

Cousin Henry (Chapman and Hall, 1879)

The Duke's Children (Chapman and Hall, 1880)

The Life of Cicero (Chapman and Hall, 1880)

Dr. Wortle's School (Chapman and Hall, 1881)

Ayala's Angel (Chapman and Hall, 1881)

The Fixed Period (Blackwood, 1882)

Kept in the Dark (Chatto and Windus, 1882)

Marion Fay (Chapman and Hall, 1882)

Why Frau Frohmann Raised Her Prices, and Other Stories (Isbister, 1882)

    "Why Frau Frohmann Raised Her Prices"

    "The Lady of Launay"

    "Christmas at Thompson Hall"

    "The Telegraph Girl"

    "Alice Dugdale"

"The Two Heroines of Plumplington" (*Good Words*, 1882)

Lord Palmerston (Isbister, 1882)

"Not If I Know It" (*Life* Christmas Annual, 1882)

The Landleaguers (Chatto and Windus, 1883)

Mr. Scarborough's Family (Chatto & Windus, 1883)

An Autobiography (Blackwood, 1883)

An Old Man's Love (Blackwood, 1884)

The Noble Jilt (Constable, 1923)

London Tradesmen (Matthews & Marrot, 1927)

The Tireless Traveler: Twenty Letters to the Liverpool Mercury, 1875 (Berkeley: University of California Press, 1941)

The Letters of Anthony Trollope, ed. Bradford Booth (London: Oxford University Press, 1951)

The New Zealander, ed. N. John Hall (Clarendon, 1972)

Irish Famine: Six Letters to the Examiner, ed. Lance Tingay (Silverbridge, 1987)

Anthony Trollope: A Companion

All the Year Round

All the Year Round was founded in 1859 by Charles Dickens as the successor to his previous journal, *Household Words*. Dickens was forced to start his new journal when he left his publisher, Bradbury and Evans, who owned an interest *Household Words*. During his lifetime, Dickens made the magazine largely a vehicle for his extended friendship circle, which did not particularly include Trollope. Trollope's involvement with the journal occurred after Dickens's death, when the journal, now relaunched into its second series but still published on a weekly basis, was being edited by his son, Charles Dickens, Jr., with the assistance of his manager, George Holsworth. At the time, the journal still had considerable prestige as it basked in the posthumous fame of its creator. Trollope was pleased that the magazine wanted his final Palliser novel, *The Duke's Children*, particularly after the commercial failure of its predecessor in the series, *The Prime Minister*.

But he was less happy that the younger Dickens asked for the text of *The Duke's Children* to be cut by 25 percent. Trollope managed to do this without cutting whole chapters or significantly interfering with the arc of the book, although many reflective passages were cut from the serialized version, which diminished the psychological and dramatic impact of the last Palliser novel. The journal also serialized *Is He Popenjoy?*, and again asked for cuts, this time not for length but because the editors found references to pregnancy and to flirtation outside marriage too salacious for their readers. *Mr. Scarborough's Family* was the last Trollope book to be serialized in *All the Year Round* (from May 1882 to June 1883) and was not cut. The journal, even after another relaunch in 1889, rapidly lost its cultural centrality, and did not survive the nineteenth century, terminating in 1895.

See also: *The Duke's Children*; *Mr. Scarborough's Family*

Further Reading

Amarnick, Steven. "Trollope at Fuller Length: Lord Silverbridge and the Manuscript of the Duke's Children." *The Politics of Gender in the Novels of Anthony Trollope*, edited by Deborah Denenholz Morse, Margaret Markwick, and Regenia Gagnier (Burlington, VT: Ashgate, 2009), pp. 193–206.

Drew, John. "An Uncommercial Proposition: At Work on *Household Words* and *All the Year Round*." *Victorian Periodicals Review*, vol. 46, no. 3, Fall 2013, pp. 291–316.

Litvack, Leon. "Dickens and the Codebreakers: The Annotated Set of *All the Year Round*," *Dickens Quarterly,* vol. 32, no. 4, December 2015, pp. 313–337.

The American Senator

The American Senator was serialized in *Temple Bar: A London Magazine for Town and Country Readers* from May 1876 to July 1877 and published by Chapman and Hall in 1877. (The magazine was a successor of *Bentley's Miscellany.*) The political personage in the title, Senator Gotobed from the fictional western state of Mikewa, is not the central character of the book. Trollope said in *An Autobiography* that the publisher, indeed, objected to the title. Instead, Gotobed is what Henry James called a *ficelle*, a supplementary strand that enables the interaction of the main characters to take place. Much of the action takes place in the parochial English town of Dillsborough, a place the narrator assures us at the beginning is not just inconspicuous but distasteful. Dillsborough, on the border of the fictional counties of Rufford and Ufford, is a kind of rural non-place. This generality is curiously offset by having the name of Mary Masters's unsuccessful suitor, Lawrence Twentyman, be a name local to Cumbria and the Lake District.

In this book Trollope is interested in looking at England both closely and from a distance. Gotobed appropriately serves as an external lens on this small world. The presence of colonial reference in the form of John Morton's working in the colonial office and Arabella Trefoil and Monsour Green going off to Patagonia gives the feel of what James Buzard has termed "autoethnography." This mode of inquiry examines England though the sort of lens England would normally focus on foreign cultures. Gotobed is first encountered by John Morton in the context of Morton's status as a roving foreign policy expert, equally at home in Washington and Hong Kong. This sets up Trollope's fictional and cultural contrast between the cultural mores of Dillsborough and of Mikewa. Gotobed's observations in his letters and columns about the English fortify this impression. They give the book a resemblance to Trollope's incomplete and posthumously published *The New Zealander*. This is, similarly, an examination of England from a newcomer's perspective. Gotobed is a rare bird, a hybrid of the politician and man of letters. This is something in reality rarely instanced in American literature of the time with the partial exception of a figure such as John Hay.

The novel has a double love plot. Mary Masters is a deserving heroine who thinks Reginald Morton, owner of Hoppet Hall, too superior to her in wealth and breeding to marry her. This supposition is facilitated by Mary's stepmother, who does not want her stepdaughter to excel her own children's achievements. When Reginald suggests to Mrs. Masters that his aunt, Lady Ushant, would welcome her stepdaughter at her house in Cheltenham, Mrs. Masters responds with an almost feudal insistence that people must remain in the class into which they are born. Though not as fairytale-like an instance of the wicked stepmother trope as the character of Lady Kingsbury in *Marion Fay*, Mrs. Masters clearly does not have Mary's interests at heart. Reginald, in turn, is despised by another blocking figure, his aunt by marriage, who is the grandmother of the heir to Bragton, his first cousin once removed, John Morton.

Juxtaposed to Mary is the beautiful and fashionable Arabella Trefoil. Arabella strings John Morton along while keeping an eye on the wealthier and more prestigious

Lord Rufford. When John Morton dies, Arabella repents of her amorous scheming. The narrative gives her a second chance with marriage to the relatively benign Monsour Green. John's death makes Reginald the heir. Mary thinks this last development has made her totally ineligible but Reginald proposes to her nonetheless and they marry.

Trollope wrote *The American Senator* before *The Duke's Children*, which similarly has American themes in the figure of Isabel Boncassen. Mr. Boncassen, in his combination of political and cultural interests, is similar to Senator Gotobed. But a reference to Gotobed in *The Duke's Children* shows they are different characters. Gotobed seems more of a populist and self-conscious republican than the more urbane Boncassen. This is shown in the incident where Gotobed becomes the champion of a man named Goarly, who kills a fox belonging to Lord Rufford, as a gesture of egalitarianism, although he declines to give Goarly pecuniary support.

When Goarly is exposed as a rascal, Gotobed's theoretical premises about the constitutive inequality of English country life are somewhat refuted. Despite the comic potential of the name Gotobed, Canon Bardsley's *Dictionary of English and Welsh Surnames* (1871), available to Trollope at the time, reveals the name as Anglian from Cambridgeshire—"son of Godebert." The Senator's bearing the name may have been a desire to indicate his ancestry is essentially local and English despite his ability to cast a foreign eye on the doings of Dillsborough. Trollope goes deeply into aspects of English country life—for instance, hunting—in this novel. This is perhaps because he surveys an outsider's perspective. There is also a possibility of interoperable perspective here. Trollope began the novel while on his second trip to Australia, and the character of the American Gotobed has often been said to have something of Trollope's authorial perspective in it, as the external observer assesses a world in which he is "in" but not "of." *The American Senator*, while concentrating on a small English shire, portrays an English-speaking world diverse enough for someone from one part of it to have a very different perspective than the natives of another part.

See also: *Ayala's Angel*; Harry Hotspur in *Sir Harry Hotspur of Humblethwaite*

Further Reading

Buzard, James. *Disorienting Fiction: The Autoethnographic Work of Nineteenth-Century British Novels.* Princeton University Press, 2005.

Halperin, John. "Trollope, James, and the International Theme." *The Yearbook of English Studies*, vol. 7, 1977, pp. 141–147.

Harden, Edgar F. "The Alien Voice: Trollope's Western Senator." *Texas Studies in Literature and Language*, vol. 8, 1966, pp. 219–34.

Schelstraele, Jasper. *Incorporation, Authorship, and Anglo-American Literature, (1815–1918).* New York: Routledge, 2019.

Sullivan, Ceri. *Literature in The Public Service: Sublime Bureaucracy.* Basingtoke: Palgrave Macmillan, 2013.

Trotter, Jackson. "Foxhunting and the English Social Order in Anthony Trollope's *The American Senator*." *Studies in the Novel*, vol. 24, no. 3, Fall 1992, pp. 227–241.

Australia and New Zealand

Australia and New Zealand was published in two volumes by Chapman and Hall in 1873. Trollope visited the Antipodes twice, in 1871–2 and 1875. Both visits were ostensibly to assist his son Thomas, who had settled in northern New South Wales. But they also served as inspiration for not only a travel book (*Australia and New Zealand*, 1873) but a short novel (*Harry Heathcote of Gangoil*) and a full-length tale (*John Caldigate*). In addition, Trollope's "Catherine Carmichael" is set in pioneer New Zealand, and the futuristic, dystopian *The Fixed Period* is set in the fictional South Pacific former colony Britannula, which seems in many ways a fictionalization of New Zealand. There are also Australian elements in *Lady Anna,* as Daniel Thwaites and his new bride embark for Australia once England can no longer tolerate the way their relationship challenges class hierarchies. Henry James's assertion that Trollope did not write for posterity is not true of his work set in Australia and the South Pacific, because futurity—be it his own posterity, Australia's political destiny, or what life would be like in the area a century hence—was constantly on his mind when writing about the region.

This note was prevalent even when he mentioned the colonies in his work in the years before he visited there. In *The New Zealander*, an essay written in 1855 but rejected by Longman and not published until nearly a century after Trollope's death, he examined Britain as a future wasteland examined by a New Zealand tourist. In *The Bertrams*, his narrator states that the ability to offload personnel to Australia, Canada and New Zealand will prevent Britain from declining as did Rome and Byzantium.

Although Trollope was more than willing to set novels in Australia, his travel book about the region is the least narrative and most descriptive of all his travel writings. Australians, being aware of both British contempt for them and the scabrous nature of Frances Trollope's book about the Americans, still notorious after four decades, were apprehensive of a book that would upbraid and insult them. Not only, though, was Trollope nothing but complimentary about Australia and New Zealand and quietly confident about their future, but *Australia and New Zealand* is so sober and bureaucratic in mien as to make the entire question of opinion supererogatory. Trollope gave minute descriptions of the urban life of the areas he visited—in that order, Queensland, New South Wales, Victoria, Tasmania (which he wanted to be its own state, not federated with Victoria), Western Australia, South Australia, and New Zealand. At the time Trollope visited, it was not definite that all the Australian colonies would federate together or that New Zealand would be part of a distinct political configuration. So twentieth-century borders and polities should not be imposed on the Antipodes he observed. Trollope also speaks very practically about their economic basis, spending time on the wool and wheat industries in each area.

Trollope visited the Antipodes when their settler-colonial societies were, though not yet politically independent, already solidified. The basic framework of the society that still exists, though now much changed, was already there. Trollope achieves this effect partially by emphasizing the colonies' newness (in European terms). He stated that, unlike Canada or South Africa, British settlement was not preceded by anterior European colonists as was the case in these other lands. The empiricism of the book may well have been justified by Trollope on the grounds that few British readers knew much about Australia and New Zealand. By showing the complex and industrious reality of life Down Under, Trollope was upending his audience's expectations more productively than if he had lauded the wonders of Australian and New Zealand life. He was normalizing rather than exoticizing. This was the reverse of the usual strategy of travel writing about faraway lands.

In *Australia and New Zealand*, Trollope constructs the Antipodes as tantamount to an ideal liberal space, a laboratory for peaceful, gradualist, and humane change, and some critics such as Blythe have even seen him as favourably inclined towards indigenous people in Australia and New Zealand. Yet Blythe concedes that Trollope "rationalized the injustice" (187) of colonialism, and in internal settler terms some Australians saw Trollope as having been co-opted by the squattocracy-the closest thing to an aristocracy. In general, Australia was for Trollope a speculative space for evolutionary liberalism. This is seen in Trollope envisioning Queensland becoming so populous that part of it would have to become a new state with the city of Gladstone as its "future capital" (48)—something which turned out not to happen—and in Trollope naming his fictional capital of the future Antipodal nation of Britannula, the setting of *The Fixed Period*, Gladstonopolis. Trollope also assumed that the southwestern part of New South Wales, along the Murray-Darling watershed, would break away as a state, and that an Australian dominion on the lines of the recently constituted Canada would require more states than just the colonies which existed at the time of his writing. He proved to be wrong. But his diagnosis about the relative paucity of states did raise an organizational question that remained pertinent to Australia. The 1860s and the 1870s saw the emergence of responsible government in the Antipodean colonies that would by century's end evolve a defined shape for the polities of Australia and New Zealand and into Dominion status. Australia did not simply move from colony to nation in a linear way but remained closely involved with the mother country. As Helen Blythe points out, Trollope's travel accounts, while remaining on the surface, do fundamentally capture this complex weave.

Trollope did not require political obedience to Britain as the definition of what constituted a British colony. He referred to the independent and republican United States as the "colony, which of all others, Great Britain should feel the greatest glory" (*Australia and New Zealand* 8). An incipiently independent Australia and New Zealand, with their evolving parliamentary governance, are not only a continuance of Trollope's ideal England but a utopian laboratory for it. They afford the opportunity for smooth, functional, collaborative governance that Westminster may have augured but never seen. In *Australia and New Zealand*, Trollope, disregarding the withering tropical heat of north Queensland, saw the northern part of that Australian state as breaking off into a new state, with the city of Gladstone as its capital. Similarly, the capital of the New Zealand analogue of Britannula in *The Fixed Period* is Gladstonopolis. Whereas America was an alternate present, a variant course which, as is the marriage of Isabel Boncassen and Lord Silverbridge, could at times be coupled, the Antipodes could be Britain's seamless future. Even the re-annexation of Britannula after John Neverbend's inhumane policies are thwarted is temporary and custodial. This is in tune with Trollope's general opposition to annexation. This saw him (in the letters collected in *The Tireless Traveller*) stand up for King Cakobau in Fiji as much as he did in South Africa for the Zulu leader Cetewayo in Africa. Australia and New Zealand, with their early championship of women's suffrage and the secret ballot, were premonitory of a future liberal Britain for Trollope. This was a place where the political scene could potentially be all Gladstone and no Disraeli, where Britain could be dilated and renewed, but not through empire.

If with respect to Ireland Trollope hoped for a less strife-torn and religiously partisan future than proved to be the case, in the Antipodes he hoped for a slow emergence into autonomy. Here, the Antipodean nations could be at once separate from Britain but fundamentally still British in character. The robust nationalism of the Eureka Stockade of the 1850s and the republicanism of a Daniel Henry Deniehy was not in Trollope's line. Certainly he did not question the fundamental assumptions of white and Anglophone supremacy that underlay the Australian settler ideology. Jill Durey sees Trollope as fundamentally positive towards Australian indigenous people, and Helen Blythe praises the positive qualities of the portrait of the Māori servant in "Catherine Carmichael." But Blythe has elsewhere spoken of the elements of condescension and superiority in Trollope's treatment of indigenous people, elements shared, of course, by the vast majority of white Australians at the time.

Furthermore, many Australians suspected Trollope of sympathy with the squattocracy—as close to an aristocracy as Australia had. Although in *Harry Heathcote of Gangoil* Trollope characteristically tries to chronicle a social peace between the squatters and their more populist rivals, the free-selectors, for some Australian readers equivocation would not have been enough. Trollope tries to see a steady and seamless Australia and New Zealand wherever he can. If settler colonialism is inherently at once of a place and across places, Trollope's emphasis on seamlessness can be seen as a way both to acknowledge the transferability of this place while also acknowledging asymmetries of status and power. However, several Australian obituaries of Trollope still saw him as being too sympathetic to the squattocracy.

Trollope never stopped being a British writer. Yet in his fiction and nonfiction set in the Antipodes he wrote, to an extraordinary agree, almost as the native his son would become. In the section of the book on New Zealand, Trollope was willing to envision either the Antipodean colonies becoming part of a federated Britain or becoming independent. But he thought there would never be any organized hostility between colonies and the other country (unlike what happened with respect to the United States) and that the endemic British predisposition towards personal liberty would palliate the collective self-assertion seen in anti-colonial nationalism. Later Antipodean writers proved Trollope's hypothesis correct by both using his approaches to their lands and repurposing them for their far greater knowledge of, and stake in, their situation on the ground. They employ Trollopian approaches in ways that reveal them to be not just stock formulae imported from the mother country, but forms that could adequately contain the social, gender, and ethnic conjunctions transporting in Australia and New Zealand.

In literary terms, Trollope ended up being just as much a squatter as a free-selector, a propagator and not just an interloper. In Jeannie (Mrs. Aeneas) Gunn's *We of the Never-Never* (1908), the Chinese chef Cheon cooks a big Christmas dinner for the cattle station in the Northern Territory where the novel is set. Added to the original disjunction of a hot Christmas is a characteristic English Christmas meal being cooked to perfection by a Chinese migrant looked down upon by many at the station and perhaps even by the novelist herself. Here Gunn is clearly revising Trollope's derogatory portrait of Sing-Sing in *Harry Heathcote*. In the New Zealand writer William Satchell's *The Toll of the Bush* (1905), old Major Milward sees wizened sailor men "huge broad-chested sons already well past middle age" (255). They are reminiscent of the hard, fiftyish Peter Carmichael in "Catherine Carmichael," whose brutality is associated with an older, pioneer New Zealand that has now yielded to a more liberal era. Eve Milward's forced marriage to the Reverend Fletcher, who soon after bolts, leaving her technically married but sundered from her husband in heart and soul, is reminiscent of Lady Laura's marriage to Kennedy in *Phineas Finn*. Satchell's novel presents Fletcher's Puritanism, displayed in his dislike for a minister who distracts "our attention from the plain duty of doing our work," echoes Trollope for whom imaginative amplitude and a narrow religious dogma were always at loggerheads. Satchell built on Trollope's preference for tolerance and Broad Church latitudinarianism in depicting Antipodean life. Trollope, in other words, left part of himself in the Antipodes, and not just through his son Fred. He helped Australian and New Zealand writers glimpse their own lands.

Trollope hunted in Australia as he did in England and Ireland, quarrying the kangaroo in Queensland and New South Wales. The kangaroo hunt was a cultural form that embodied both settler colonialism and the attempted suzerainty of man over nature. But Trollope also lived his ordinary life while he was in Australia. Trollope first read of the dream of Scipio, which he addressed in his Cicero book, in a volume found in Australia. His writing career also unfolded in a routine way in Australian space. Trollope was serialized in Australia. The *Australasian* of Melbourne serialized *Phineas Finn* and *He Knew He Was Right*, whereas the *Illustrated Sydney News* serialized *Marion Fay*, praising him as a writer whose reputation extended wherever the English language was spoken. As important as was Trollope's setting of stories down under, his serialization there was just as crucial. His Australian serialization assisted in setting up institutions of reading and writing which extended beyond his own career into the future.

See also: *Lady Anna*; *North America*; travel

Further Reading

Blythe, Helen. *The Victorian Colonial Romance with the Antipodes*. New York: Palgrave, 2014.
Edwards, P.D. *Anthony Trollope's Son in Australia: The Life and Letters of F.J.A. Trollope*. St. Lucia: University of Queensland Press, 1982.
Elliott, Dorice Williams. *Transported to Botany Bay: Class, National Identity, and the Literary Identity of the Australian Convict*. Athens: Ohio University Press, 2016.
Moody, Ellen. "On Inventing a New Country: Trollope's Depiction of Settler Colonialism." *Antipodes*, vol. 31, no. 1, June 2017, pp. 89–101.
Starck, Nigel. "The First Celebrity: Anthony Trollope's Australasian Odyssey." *Antipodes*, vol. 31, no. 1, June 2017, pp. 83–88.
Steer, Phillip. "Gold and Greater Britain: Jevons, Trollope, and Settler Colonialism." *Victorian Studies*, vol. 58, no. 3, Spring 2016, pp. 436–463.

An Autobiography

An Autobiography was published posthumously in 1883 by Blackwood. Relatively few Victorian writers wrote autobiographies; of those, a nonfiction writer, John Stuart Mill, was the most famous, followed by Edmund Gosse. Dickens and Thackeray did not, as they were prevented from such work, if nothing else, by the difficulties of their married life—a situation that also applied to George Eliot. Mrs. Gaskell wrote the life of Charlotte Brontë, but did not write an autobiography. Conversely, Trollope never wrote a directly autobiographical novel as Dickens did in *David Copperfield* and Thackeray did in *Pendennis*, although the socially ambitious postal clerks and failed outsider political candidates who populate his fictions are opaque self-portraits. In the pages of *An Autobiography*, Trollope wrote his life story in ways later biographers emulated. He sketched his precarious childhood, his minimal initial promise, and his mother's leaving him behind when she journeyed to North America. The reader can see the analogies between Trollope's early years and the hobbledehoy heroes of books like *The Claverings* and *The Small House at Allington*. Trollope frankly relates his early years at the post office, the key role Ireland played in the growths of both his public and literary careers and his personal life, and his establishment as a writer. Much of the book is a recounting of his own writing, in which he gives assessments, in retrospect, of the relative strength and weakness of each of his books, and an accounting of its sales. This last is a very early instance of the use of statistics in assessing the public dissemination of literature, as the author gains the sort of distance from his work necessary to see it as a part of publishing history.

Trollope dispassionately described his own working methods. He rose early, wrote a given amount of words, and then turned in a full day of work at the post office, a routine he until his retirement. These working methods became controversial after the book appeared posthumously. Many saw Trollope as a hack writer who looked at his work in terms of output rather than artistic quality. But of greater moment for the latter-day student of his work is Trollope's sense of the relative strengths and weaknesses of his oeuvre, and his small revelations as to what he was trying to achieve in each of his fictions published before he undertook the writing of his own life.

Trollope broke with the tradition of autobiography both by placing the book aside to be published posthumously (thus it does not cover the last few years of his life) and by overtly renouncing the Rousseauistic aspiration to capture the inner life. He also made his autobiography more than a story of growing up by concentrating so much on his mature years and on his literary production, and of his accounts of and opinions upon his literary peers such as Dickens and Thackeray. There is an essential modesty to the book, and a capacity to see the world outside of his own lens. Trollope's representation of the world remained of more durable interest to readers than even he himself predicted. Trollope addressed the reader with disarming honesty and did not use his own life to put across either a flattering mage of himself—at one point he estimates his work unlikely to last beyond his own time—or to put across a particular ideology or doctrine of life. Yet *An Autobiography* is a narrative written at a certain point in time, and as such is not an unvarnished account of the author's soul but a literary document with its own tactical subtleties.

See also: Ireland; old age; Trollope, Frances

Further Reading

Aguirre, Robert. "Cold Print: Professing Authorship in Anthony Trollope's *An Autobiography*." *Biography*, vol. 25, no. 4, Fall 2002, pp. 569–592.

Allen, Peter. "Trollope to His Readers: The Unreliable Narrator of *An Autobiography*." *Biography*, vol. 19, no. 1, Winter 1996, pp. 1–18.

Kincaid, James R. "Trollope's Fictional Autobiography." *Nineteenth-Century Fiction*, vol. 37, no. 3, December 1982, pp. 340–349.

Ayala's Angel

Ayala's Angel was written in 1878 and published in 1881 by Chapman and Hall. Like *The Duke's Children*, the publication was delayed. This was less because Trollope was asked to make cuts than that publishers simply did not deem the book commercially viable. The novel was serialized in the US, in Cincinnati—site of Trollope's mother's most disparaging comments about Americans. It was scheduled to be serialized in Britain by the National Press Agency, which bought serialization rights but never used the story. Only the American serial edition had illustrations, which were left out of the Chapman and Hall edition, a striking omission for a novel about the offspring of an artist.

Ayala Dormer, the novel's protagonist, is a bit like Magdalen Vanstone in Wilkie Collins's *No Name* both in her flamboyant name, her contrast with her steadier sister, and her being the daughter of a bohemian and financially unstable father. Unlike Collins's character, though, she does not resort to underhanded means to redeem her fortunes. Ayala's father, Egbert, dies in middle age, leaving two daughters, Ayala and Lucy. They are taken in by their mother's two siblings. Their mother's brother, Reginald Dosett, an Admiralty clerk of only modest income who lives in unprepossessing circumstances in Kingsbury Crescent, takes in the staid Lucy. Their mother's sister, Emmeline, who had married the wealthy baronet Sir Thomas Tringle, takes in the flashier Ayala. Ayala, after making an impressive debut in what Deborah Denenholz Morse terms the *nouveau riche* atmosphere of the Tringle household, indeed proves too flashy for her own good. Lady Tringle's own daughters, Ayala's cousins Gertrude and Augusta (who are also rivalrous with each other), are distasteful to her. At the same time, the Tringle son, Thomas the younger, conceives a passion for his attractive cousin. Unlike in Jane Austen's *Mansfield Park*, where the foster-sister reciprocates the affection of her host's son, Ayala spurns Tom. After a family vacation in Rome with atmosphere Trollope must have gleaned during his visits to his brother Thomas Adolphus, the ménage's inclusion of Ayala is judged to have foundered. Soon, an exchange of wards is effected. Lucy goes to the Tringles and Ayala, no longer to walk in Kensington Gardens, assumes the genteel poverty of the Dosett household.

The combination of the fairytale or folktale structure (two sisters of different temperaments take different journeys and find appropriate destinies), as fitting in classical comedy as in modern fiction, is overlaid with details of mores. manners, and social life. These bring the narrative into a frame of contemporary realism. *Ayala's Angel* and *Lady Anna* are the only full-length Trollope novels named after their female protagonist. The three anonymous Continental novels were one volume only. *Marion Fay's* title character is not really its chief character. That Trollope chose the unusual name Ayala for his character must have been partially for the alliteration with the word "angel," and partially for the name's infrequent use as a forename and thus its exotic connotations.

Ayala has a dream of an Angel of Light who will come to rescue her. There is some moral chiaroscuro to that figure. Indeed, at first she thinks Tom Tringle may be that angel, even though her sister Lucy warns her that Tom is in fact a rather low form of the Devil. But, rather than choose between two men she knows as does Clara Amedroz in *The Belton Estate*, Ayala conceives in her mind a Platonic form of a male savior as yet unencountered. That the "angel" is a male reverses the Victorian ideal of the female

Angel in the House, enshrined in the poem of that name by Coventry Patmore of 1854. Paradoxically, Ayala has to scale down her expectations of an impossibly heroic male in order to find happiness with a real one. This emotional adjustment could equally apply to male idealizations of women, more common in literature in the Victorian era.

For this outcome to occur, though, Ayala must revise her expectations to an extent that the Angel emerges from unexpected contours. In Chapter XVI, attending Lady Putney's dance in the company of her friend of Nina Baldoni, Ayala meets Nina's cousin Colonel Jonathan Stubbs. Stubbs is physically unattractive. He is a military man who had done colonial service in India. He has an uncomely red beard and an enormous mouth. Stubbs seems the antithesis of the stylish, edgy Ayala. Having previously been turned down by an eligible young lady just for bearing the first name "Jonathan," Stubbs comes across as self-effacing to the point of ungainliness. Ayala immediately likes him, but thinks him too lacking in the sublime to be a lover. Trollope's point, though, is to underscore the appeal of the non-sublime in romantic love: that Stubbs ends up being Ayala's angel, even though his outward contours do not conform.

Indeed, it is straightlaced Lucy who comes to have the more Bohemian partner in Isadore Hamel, not only a sculptor himself but the son of an expatriate. Lucy, named after light, ends up with a sculptor, while the more overtly rebellious Ayala finds her Angel of Light is a less outwardly flamboyant figure. Ayala's anti-angel is Tom Tringle, variously called a lout, a Newfoundland dog, and a hobbledehoy, does not reform, unlike some of Trollope's hobbledehoys. Indeed, he represents the stagnant hobbledehoy, the hobbledehoy as lout. That the necklace which Tom Tringle offered to Ayala and she refused is re-gifted by his father as the Tringle family wedding present to Colonel and Mrs. Stubbs is a masterful piece of ironic detail that, for the narrator, closes the book on the Tringle family.

There is an overlap with *The American Senator* in the characters of Larry Twentyman (now happily married to the former Kate Masters) and Lord Rufford, and the way the Dillsborough rural setting in which Ayala's love for Jonathan Stubbs emerges complements the novel's portrait of sophisticated London and cosmopolitan Rome. Sir Harry Albury, master of foxhounds for the counties of Rufford and Ufford, and his half-brother Captain Benjamin Batsby represent the rural pole to the novel's London Traffics and Houstons. These characters make *Ayala's Angel* a kind of representational halfway-point between *Framley Parsonage* and *The Way We Live Now*. Indeed, in these two books one can perhaps see the ghost of a putative Dillsborough series that might have been Trollope's third sustained effort at world-building. This Dillsborough series would have braided the rural sphere of his first series with the cosmopolitan London of his second. It would have had a looser sense of unity more derived from the Palliser than the Barsetshire set. Given the protracted hunting scenes in both *Ayala's Angel* and *The American Senator*, it would have had more emphasis on riding to hounds. Some of the novel's traits such as intrusive narration and the third plot (of Frank Houston and Gertrude Docimer, where Frank decides to marry for love after being disappointed in his hopes of marrying for money) mirror the ample worlds of Trollope's series novels. In any event, Trollope's advancing years meant any putative Dillsborough series was a proposition that, if ever present in his mind, was never to be realized.

The elements and progression of the novel were by this time formulaic for Trollope.

But there are elements in *Ayala's Angel* that betoken the late-Victorian breaking through the mid–Victorian, much like the contemporaneous *Daniel Deronda* by George Eliot. These go beyond just the assertive female titular character. Sir Thomas Tringle objects to cousin-marriage as a concept, not because of the cousins involved, something very different from a similar situation in *The Bertrams*. The slight sense of the aesthete in Egbert Dormer and Isadore Hamel (and the more polemical Bohemianism of Hamel's father), and the way these Bohemian associations betoken what Frederik van Dam calls negative cultural capital that enhance the Dormer sisters' appeal, indicates the rise of a more art-for-art's sake attitude. There is also a background motion of capital (as even the aristocratic Tringle men must work in the City) replacing the hegemony of landed interest. Trollope subtly mediates between Ayala's managing, despite her wayward temperament to find social realization, and her fundamental eccentricity. He insists society must expand its rigid gender expectations to include young women of Ayala's level of unconventionality. Though *Ayala's Angel* does not equal *Mr. Scarborough's Family* as Trollope's late masterpiece, it is a capacious window on how the older Trollope viewed his changing world.

See also: *The American Senator*; hobbledehoy; *Marion Fay*

Further Reading

Cooper, Hyson. "The Hero of This Little History: Hobbledehoydom in Anthony Trollope's *Ayala's Angel*." *Themos: A Journal of Boyhood Studies*, vol. 4, no. 1, Spring 2010, pp. 3–23.

Kendrick, Walter. *The Novel Machine: The Theory and Fiction of Anthony Trollope*. Baltimore: Baltimore: Johns Hopkins University Press, 1980.

Morse, Deborah Denenholz, "'It went through and through me like an electric shock': Constructing Female Desire and the Realist Novel in Trollope's *Ayala's Angel*." *Victorian Vulgarity: Taste in Verbal and Visual Culture*, edited by Elsie Michie and Susan David Bernstein. New York: Ashgate, 2009, pp. 153–168.

Van Dam, Frederik, *Anthony Trollope's Late Style: Victorian Liberalism and Literary Form*. Edinburgh: Edinburgh University Press, 2016.

Barchester Towers

Barchester Towers was published by Longman in 1857. It is the linchpin of the Barsetshire series, the real first chronicle to which the *Last Chronicle* of *Barset* is the bookend. *Barchester Towers* is for many readers the quintessential Trollope. The publisher asked for revisions in the direction of propriety and inoffensiveness. This request is revealing. Even though the novel vigorously defended the established order in both church and society, its potential satire of ecclesiastical subjects was felt to be potentially risky. *Barchester Towers* was inspired by Trollope's visit in 1852 to the historic cathedral city of Salisbury, but Trollope created his entire fictional cathedral city and shire, with no resemblance to existing persons or places. Trollope deliberately eschewed spiritual or doctrinal content in his portrait of the life of the Church, focusing on social and interpersonal matters as he did elsewhere in his fiction. Trollope showed how clergymen and their families at once lived normal lives but on the other hand were put into particular positions and dilemmas by their profession. He was not overly idealistic about the clergy and saw them as human beings. But certainly he respected the Church and its mission, though theology and even belief are in the background of *Barchester Towers*.

Archdeacon Theophilus Grantly hopes to succeed his father as diocesan bishop of

Barchester. But any hope of this is dashed when a new Prime Minister comes in who, unlike his predecessor, has no personal connection with Grantly. The incumbent turns out to be Bishop Proudie, a Low Church clergymen far more evangelical and puritanical of mien than his predecessor. It soon transpires, though, that Bishop Proudie is little more than a figurehead, with the real power being exercised by Mrs. Proudie—a woman who has received no ecclesiastical training, but who is quite opinionated and knowledgeable on church matters—and the Bishop's domestic chaplain, Obadiah Slope, who manages to be simultaneously rigid and slack, dogmatic yet lacking conviction. Mrs. Proudie and Slope have a tactical alliance through which they essentially stage-manage the Bishop, making the new hierarch's opponents, such as Archdeacon Grantly, all the angrier. Mrs. Proudie uses the needs of others—such as Mr. Quiverful, who, with fourteen children, badly needs a subvention—to manipulate them into being pawns in her Machiavellian ecclesiastical games.

The narrator is highly intrusive, personalizing himself to the extent of saying he did not relish meeting Obadiah Slope. The anti-evangelical and pro-high church sympathies of the novel are undisguised, though Archdeacon Grantly is not lionized simply because he is High Church and the near-saintly Mr. Harding is described as lacking emphasis in his churchmanship.

The alliance of Slope and Mrs. Proudie is not personal or spiritual, but derives from ecclesiastical politics. Here, Trollope fully dramatizes the antagonism (often latently presented in his other novels, such as *Rachel Ray*) between High and Low Church, the Catholic-leaning Oxford Movement and Evangelical Christianity. Trollope mocks both Slope and Mrs. Proudie both because they do not entirely practice what they preach and because they try to live their religion too passionately, instead of seeing it with a sense of latitude and perspective. The saving grace of a this-worldly man of the cloth like the younger Grantly, is that at least his ideals do not lead him to overreach. Though the immediate cause of Mrs. Proudie's falling out with Slope is his interest in Signora Neroni, and his concomitant ambition for the Barchester deanery, this alliance is fostered by tactical convenience and overly impassioned religious enthusiasms inherently unstable. Slope overreaches himself in a comic way, as when he supposes that just because he has heard Eleanor Bold has defended him against some of his detractors, she is in love with him.

One of Bishop Proudie's first moves is to insist that Canon Vesey Stanhope, who had been holding a sinecure while residing abroad in Italy, return to residency at the Cathedral. Obeying his Bishop's demand, the Canon brings with him his indolent and raffish son Ethelbert, nicknamed "Bertie"; his daughter Charlotte, an old maid who handles all the practical affairs of the family and is herself not entirely benign; and his daughter, Madeline, known as Signora Neroni, because she had married an impecunious Italian man. Paulo Neroni, who had abused and abandoned her with a baby daughter. Disabled and largely confined to her sofa, Signora Neroni nonetheless exerts a powerful erotic allure, which is buttressed by a glamorous if insalubrious air of the foreign. She uses it to its full extent to manipulate men, even to the extent of engaging Slope's romantic attentions. Bishop Proudie's recall of the Stanhope family ends up precipitating far more trouble than he had envisioned or than their continued absence would have caused.

Obadiah Slope shows a keen interest in the widowed Eleanor Bold, as does Bertie Stanhope. The climax of the novel occurs as Ullathorne Court, whose architecture and estate is lovingly described by the narrator as the quintessential English stately home. The adjoining church, St. Ewold's, receives a new vicar, Francis Arabin. Arabin has studied at and ministered in Oxford and is inferentially identified with the high churchmanship of that university. In ecclesiastical terms, he is a foil to Proudie and Slope, without any of the younger Grantly's selfishness and ambition. Arabin is the ideal man for Eleanor. Like Eleanor's first husband, John Bold, he is intellectual, but unlike him, is free of reformist zeal and is more studious and contemplative, while certainly also a man of action and purpose (unlike Dr. Gwynne, the master of Lazarus College, who is a purely academic figure). His late avowal of interest in woman, however, not only seems to tug him in the direction of Rome and priestly celibacy (as High Church Anglicans were always accused of being, bolstered by the defection of John Henry Newman to Rome), but may represent a prolonged awakening to heterosexuality.

The outcome of this marriage plot, which is revealed to the reader long before the end, unfolds at the Ullathorne Sports, the lavish entertainment Miss Thorne of Ullathorne gives to the genteel people of the county. Here, Slope, seeing he is already beginning to lose the favor of Eleanor Bold, makes a desperate marriage proposal to her, even the launching of which she forestalls. When he does not take this with good grace and touches her physically, she strikes him on the ears, such is the force of her contempt and revulsion. Bertie Stanhope, who is narcissistic but not malicious, proposes to Eleanor as well, though he admits that he has largely been put up to it by his prudent sister Charlotte and her sense that his marriage to Eleanor would help financially stabilize the family.

Barchester Towers is full of contention and strife. But the book also has a cozy, pastoral feel to it which is not always true of Trollope's fiction. In the near-contemporaneous *The Bertrams*, for instance, religious skepticism is sounded. This is something, for all the varieties of ecclesiastical tendency in Barchester, unimaginable there. Barchester is sufficiently off the beaten track to be steadier in its beliefs. Once the Ullathorne Sports has concluded, it is clear Arabin will win out in his suit, and that the puritanical and bohemian extremes represented by Slope and Stanhope will be seen off. The ending of *Barchester Towers* thus represents a reaffirmation of a stable, conservative social order. This will not always be true for Trollope's later works.

See also: Doctor Thorne; intrusive narrator; Oxford Movement; *The Warden*

Further Reading

Franklin, J, Jeffrey. *Spirit Matters: Occult Beliefs, Alternative Religions, and the Crisis of Faith in Victorian Britain.* Ithaca, NY: Cornell University Press, 2018.

Kincaid, James L. "*Barchester Towers* and the Nature of Conservative Comedy," *ELH*, vol. 37, number 4, December 1970, pp. 595–612.

Lawson, Kate. "Abject and Defiled: Signora Neroni's Body," *Victorian Review*, vol. 11, no. 1, Summer 1995, pp. 53–68.

The Belton Estate

Trollope's 1865 comic novel was serialized in *The Fortnightly Review* and published in book form in London by Chapman and Hall in 1865 and in Philadelphia by

Lippincott in the following year. Trollope's only novel set in Somerset—as the novel calls it, "Somersetshire"—takes place at Belton Castle in the Quantock Hills twenty miles away from the county town of Taunton. *The Belton Estate* is one of Trollope's shorter and more paradigmatic works. It sits in a category that might be said to stretch from *Rachel Ray* at one end to *Lady Anna* at another in terms both of length and gravity of the situation—which lack the features of long novels such as *Framley Parsonage* and *Orley Farm* such as multiple plots and an overtly intrusive narrator, but are simpler and in some ways purer stories of English country life. Clara Amedroz, a Huguenot name—is daughter of Bernard Amedroz, the squire of Belton Castle. Her scapegrace brother Charles Amedroz having killed himself, Clara will not, under the laws of entail, inherit the estate. Belton Castle, like Humblethwaite in *Harry Hotspur of Humblethwaite*, will pass to a cousin, in this case Will Belton. Even though the Amedroz family has the money, the surname the estate is characterized by is the more English Belton, as it had passed into the Amedroz line when a Belton heiress married an Amedroz. This is something not lost on the family even when Captain Aylmer seems the more eligible suitor for Clara. Trollope, as somebody whose family had more money on the Meetkerke side but whose hope for a baronetcy pertained to the Trollope side, understood well this discontinuity between liquid assets and landed interest. Though the Amedroz/Belton situation is neither an encoding of his own family history or a biographical sport, it does indicate that he felt some personal stake in the plot of even one of his less intricately unfurled narratives. Will Belton recognizes the advantages of his name and genealogical position. Partially out of love, partially out of an ambition to unite the two claims (though only his is legally valid), Will proposes marriage to Clara. He does so even though she is, at twenty-five, what would have been considered an "old maid." She had first judged him as only a cousin, and therefore safe from love-making.

But by this time there is another contender for Clara's hand, a Captain Frederic Folliott Aylmer. Aylmer, who is the niece of Mrs. Winterfield, a dour, pious relation of Clara's mother who assumes a quasi-maternal role after Clara's own mother had died young. Captain Aylmer, MP for Perivale, assumes when campaigning the characteristics of evangelical Christianity, but when he is off-duty he is more latitudinarian. Mrs. Winterfield plans to leave her money to Captain Aylmer, which would be of considerable help to the cash-poor Amedrozes.

At Aylmer Park, Clara is scorned by Captain Aylmer's mother because she wants an heiress for her son. Even though it is not the Captain himself but his mother who has been hostile to her, Clara nonetheless sours on the relationship. Captain Aylmer tries to win her back, but is informed by Clara that she will not enter into a relationship where she is insufficiently esteemed, and that in addition she had decided she could not love him even before the incident with his mother.

A subsidiary strand is the story of Mrs. Askerton, Clara's older friend and confidante, who lives with her husband, a colonel, in Belton Cottage on the estate, and about whom there is, at the beginning, some unspecified mystery. It turns out that Mrs. Askerton was married to an alcoholic man and that she had taken up with Colonel Askerton before the death of her husband, thus (unlike Mrs. Peacocke in *Dr. Wortle's School*, who did not know her husband was alive) knowingly violating the mores of Victorian society. The Aylmer family asks Clara to drop the Askertons because of this perceived disrepute, which she refuses to do. The Askertons help mediate between Clara and Belton after the Aylmer possibility has blown up, using their own experience of life's vagaries to smooth the action of the novel toward a happy ending.

Henry James called the novel "stupid" because he saw it as bereft of ideas; he found Will Belton in particular, presented as a thinking man, but *sans* thoughts. (There is a certain irony in this judgment; years later T.S. Eliot described James as having a mind so fine no idea could violate it.) Critiquing the simplicity of the plot, James castigated Trollope for focusing only on the heroine (Clara Amedroz), hero (Will Belton), and villain (Captain Aylmer). But James did not acknowledge that Trollope had written many multiplot novels by this point. Trollope was giving the reader a simpler, purer, more "Dutch" alternative (as James put it, thinking of the simplicity of Dutch landscape painting). James even accused Trollope of not writing in a way that took into account the complex circumstances of adult life. The core of this point might be the rather stark contrast between Belton and Aylmer as suitors. On the other hand, this provides the animating drama of the novel. *The Belton Estate* is not major Trollope. But it has its charms.

See also: *Fortnightly Review*; *Ralph the Heir*; *The Vicar of Bullhampton*

Further Reading

Herbert, Christopher. *Trollope and Comic Pleasure*. Chicago: University of Chicago Press, 1987.
Turner, Mark *Trollope and The Magazines: Gendered Issues in Mid-Victorian Britain*. New York: Palgrave, 1989.

The Bertrams

The Bertrams, published by Chapman and Hall in 1859, was Trollope's second book with the firm that became his most frequent publisher. *The Bertrams* is still early Trollope, but it was composed after he had written four of the Barchester novels. Its air is more somber than the often comic ecclesiastical chronicles. Even Arthur Wilkinson's ecclesiastical vocation is differently portrayed. *The Bertrams* contains the suicide of a significant character, Sir Henry Harcourt. Suicide as a plot point recurs only rarely in Trollope's oeuvre as in the suicide of Ferdinand Lopez in *The Prime Minister*, Dobbs Broughton in *The Last Chronicle of Barset,* and Melmotte in *The Way We Live Now.*

The trip to Palestine (in the first part of the book) and Egypt (in the last) are fruits of Trollope's own travels in those regions. George Bertram's entrance into Jerusalem is anticlimactic and laden with the deflationary, disillusioned realism that nineteenth-century writers often used in approaching this subject. George Bertram, after being so reverential he insists on touring every Biblical site imaginable, writes two skeptical books, *The Romance of Scripture* and *The Fallacies of Early History*, and is frank with his clerical best friend Arthur that he cannot affirm the historicity of the Old Testament. Here there are echoes of the Higher Criticism of the Bible. These intensify a sense of spiritual anticlimax. They reflect Victorian intellectual crisis of faith in ways similar to the work of Arthur Hugh Clough and Matthew Arnold. It is no accident that this was the favorite Trollope book of John Henry Newman. This was not because Newman agreed with Trollope's tacit conclusion of muddle-through-it theism. It was likely because *The Bertrams* spoke vitally to Newman's own intellectual concerns and to the problems of what Trollope terms, in the novel's opening, the age of humanity.

The Bertrams is one of Trollope's few novels to contain lengthy scenes set at a university: Oxford. Trollope himself did not attend university. The undergraduate lives of George Bertram and Arthur Wilkinson are reminiscent of Cuthbert Bede's *The Adventures of Mr. Verdant Green*, published a few years before. They also reflect a very different Oxford than that of Francis Arabin in the Barchester books. George Bertram begins, at Oxford, an intellectual odyssey. This odyssey, while avoiding outright agnosticism, atheism, or secularism, reflects the impact of the Biblical Higher Criticism. It includes some skepticism towards the literal truth of the Bible, In other words, it is more the Oxford of Arthur Hugh Clough than of John Henry Newman or John Keble. Arthur Wilkinson has some of Arabin's intellectual aspirations. But early on he has to make a choice between academic life and providing for his mother via a living offered him by Lord Stapledean. Lord Stapledean, in turn, insists he make an explicit financial commitment to his mother that Arthur feels will forestall any potential of courtship of his beloved, Adela Gauntlet. But Mrs. Wilkinson misunderstands the nature of Stapledean's commitment, as is revealed towards the end in a highly farcical scene.

Trollope's narrator distinguishes between Adela Gauntlet, whom he leaves for the reader to describe because, however pleasant, she is not the main heroine, and Caroline Waddington, a far more complicated and tragic figure. Adela and Arthur are not related. Their relationship has the virtues of exogamy, which may also be what pulls Caroline in the middle of the novel towards Henry. Caroline's relationship with George, on the other hand, is complicated by her being his first cousin once removed. The problem is less here that this was considered too close a degree of kinship at the time but that they both have plausible expectations for the money of the elder George Bertram. There is a complicated skein of relationships, involving not just George, Caroline, and Henry being in a love triangle but George and Caroline being cousins. Such intricacy both gives the book unity and makes it involute. This latter trait is heightened by there being two George Bertrams in the novel, the protagonist and his monied uncle. This device, much like the two George Vavasors in *Can You Forgive Her?* or the two Peregrine Ormes in *Orley Farm*—each a grandfather and grandson pair—introduces a slightly sensation-novel element into the book. It draws the attention of the reader to the interplay of names and family relationships. Trollope's narrator calls Caroline Waddington his *donna primissima*, giving her the term for the lead woman character in an opera. Trollope is endowing Caroline with a certain tragic stature as well as a certain heaviness of tone. This is very different from the mock-epic of the Barchester books.

Caroline marries (Sir) Henry not for love but because she desires to situate herself in a worldly way. She finds her status as Lady Harcourt loveless and tedious rather than exalting. Her husband's suicide is thus a relief. Caroline makes the wrong choice of husband. But the plot allows her to recover and to have a second chance, without ever fully forgiving or exonerating her. There is not a sense of a fully happy ending. Caroline's marriage to George is understated and anticlimactic. Also the reader is told they will have no children.

George Bertram's friendship with Harcourt deteriorates both because of Harcourt's own personal flaws and because George makes the mistake of mixing in his friendship with Henry and his courtship with Caroline. Like Lord Chiltern and Phineas in *Phineas Finn*, two male friends become rivals over the same woman. Yet here George Bertram is somewhat the cause of this. George has Henry convey messages to Caroline and speaks to her of George's disappointment with her. This naturally leads to Harcourt and Caroline becoming intimate and eventually marrying. Their unhappy marriage in fashionable Belgravia incarnates the opposite side of Trollope's usual stress that a good income is necessary to domestic happiness. Here, money, also, cannot suffice if it is, as it is here, the only element binding two people together. The protagonist's father, Sir Lionel, also learns this lesson. His constant badgering of his elder brother for money has the effect of not just ending their relationship but causing the older George, despite his admiration of the younger George, to leave his nephew out of the will. That George the younger and Caroline at the end must do without the family money conversely emancipates them from a mere thirst for lucre.

The reductive nature of money-lust is illustrated by the folly of Sir Lionel. Sir Lionel is refused both by Miss Todd and his relative Miss Baker, because they are not so desperate for marriage as to marry him. Money also leads to the book's greatest tragedy. The rapid making and unmaking of Sir Henry Harcourt, his inability to combine public success with moral adequacy, and the way his seemingly glittering success is ephemeral, makes this novel resemble *The Way We Live Now*. This is so even though the two books have considerable differences in tone which in some ways incarnate the differences between the 1850s and 1870s. The novel's two foreign contemplative scenes, on the Mount of Olives and at the Pyramids, contrast Judeo-Christian and pagan living ideals and a dead past in ways that underscore the novel's oscillation between hope and despair, worldliness and disillusionment.

The combination of a certain dilettantism, a cultivated academic-aristocratic, and a visit to Palestine is reminiscent of a hero of Benjamin Disraeli's novels. *The Bertrams* is one of Trollope's most surprising works. It furnishes much entertainment as well as being informative about the intellectual background of the era. It may well be a book particularly apt for those who read and admire Victorian nonfiction prose.

See also: Oxford Movement; short stories; travel

Further Reading

Chappell, Lindsey N. "Anthony Trollope's Narrative Temporalities and the Emergence of the Middle East." *LIT: Literature, Interpretation, Theory*, vol. 27, 2016, pp. 29–49.

Dessner, Lawrence Jay. "The Autobiographical Matrix of Trollope's *The Bertrams*." *Nineteenth-Century Literature*, vol. 45, no. 8, June 1990, pp. 26–58.

Kelly, Kristine. "Aesthetic Desire and Imperialist Disappointment in Trollope's *The Bertrams* and the Murray Handbook for Travelers in Syria and Palestine." *Victorian Literature and Culture*, vol. 43, 9 September 2015: pp. 621–639.

Michie, Helena. "Rethinking Marriage: Trollope's Internal Revision." *The Routledge Research Companion to Anthony Trollope*, edited by Deborah Denenholz Morse, Margaret Markwick, and Mark W. Turner. New York: Routledge, 2017, pp. 54–65.

Can You Forgive Her?

Can You Forgive Her? was serialized in twenty monthly parts by Chapman & Hall and published in book form by that firm in 1865, the same method later followed by

Smith, Elder in the publication of *The Last Chronicle of Barset*. It was illustrated by Hablot Knight Browne, a.k.a. "Phiz," who drew for so many of the novels of Charles Dickens, after John Everett Millais, who was originally slated to illustrate the book, could not do it owing to the publisher's financial issues.

The first of what would be called the Parliamentary Novels or the Palliser Novels, *Can You Forgive Her?* is ostensibly centered on the romantic travails of Alice Vavasor. A young woman from a wealthy family, Alice "jilts" her cousin George Vavasor, and then her second fiancé, the decent but dull country squire John Grey, in favor of the more dashing and alluring—and even more exciting, politically ambitious—George.

The second plotline, and by far the most important, concerns the stormy early days of the marriage of Plantagenet Palliser, the heir to the Duke of Omnium to Lady Glencora M'Cluskie, who is as vivacious as Plantagenet is stolid, and as capricious as he is dutiful. Glencora is essentially bullied by "sagacious heads" in her family into marriage with Palliser (Ch. XVIII). She does so despite her passionate love for Burgo Fitzgerald, an aristocratic wastrel, whose impecuniousness, gambling, and raffish lifestyle threaten even her wealth. Palliser does not win her love, but his magnanimity toward both Glencora, and, in a remarkable scene, toward Burgo, win her loyalty.

Finally, a comic subplot involves Arabella Greenow, the widowed aunt of George Vavasor and his sister Kate, as well as of Alice herself. Generally referred to as "Aunt Greenow," Arabella, regarded as a flirt by her father, married a much older, but wealthy merchant, and, since his death, enjoys her inheritance (Ch. VII). An attractive woman in her 40s, she toys with the affections of two men: the prosperous if gauche Farmer Cheeseacre, and the down-at-heel but charming Captain Bellfield (Ch. LXIV). After choosing the Captain as a luxury item, she nonetheless and with typical brisk good nature, finds a bride for the disappointed farmer (Ch. LXXVIII).

The title suggests that Alice has transgressed in some way, and, by the standards of nineteenth century society, she has—a "jilt" was defined as "a woman who gives her lover hopes, and deceives him; one who capriciously casts off a lover after giving him encouragement" (Murray 4: 583; Figueroa-Dorrego 93). Earlier definitions are blunter, describing the jilt as a "Tricking Whore," and being "jilted" as "abused by such a one, also deceived or defeated in one's expectations, especially in Amours." Alice's three "jiltings"—first George, then Grey, then George a second time—weigh heavily upon her, and lead her to believe she is unworthy of Grey's (or any gentleman's) love. When she finally accepts Grey's renewed proposals, she does so ruefully, describing her conduct as "vile," but ultimately reflecting that he has "left her no alternative but to be happy," despite her "perverse" desire to be punished (Ch. LXXIV).

Alice's transgressive behavior parallels Glencora's desire to flout convention and to abandon the dull, dry Plantagenet in favor of the worthless, charming rakehell who has captured her heart. Despite Alice's strictures on Glencora's behavior throughout the novel, Alice is in fact on ground as shaky as is her friend and cousin Glencora. Indeed, in some ways she is worse situated. For all of his flaws, Burgo Fitzgerald loves Glencora more truly than George Vavasour can love Alice. While he desires Alice physically, as well as her money, George is, ultimately, a narcissist, and one so self-absorbed that he cannot feel true warmth for anyone other than himself. His charm, radical political ideas, and physical courage are only at a surface level. By the time he leaves England for America, George has been thrown downstairs by John Grey (whom he has contemplated killing), and has physically threatened both Alice and his sister Kate, going so far as to physically abuse Kate, breaking her arm.

By contrast, Burgo is the most attractive of Trollope's wastrels. Unlike Bertie Stanhope or Dolly Longestaffe, Burgo has a reserve of tenderness and, to use a favorite Trollopian word, manliness, that George lacks. Burgo's earnestness in describing to George the different kind of life he could share abroad with Glencora—"very different from this hideous way of living, with which I have become so sick that I loathe it"—meets only with cynical literary allusions from George, who mischievously urges Burgo to get the woman and the money (Ch XXIX). Leaving George, trying to persuade himself that running off with Glencora is the right thing to do, he is accosted by a very young woman, "no more than sixteen," the narrator tells us, who is a prostitute. Burgo is touched by the young woman's straits, and, perhaps, her response to his handsomeness, spends some of the little money he has buying her a meal, a bed for the night, and money for breakfast the next morning. He stays with her while she eats, comfortable despite the sordid milieu, and gently extracts a promise from her that she will not buy any gin.

It is virtually impossible to imagine George Vavasor matching Burgo's disinterested kindness under any circumstances; indeed, when, later in the novel, George is in a similar financial position to Burgo's and takes pity on the prostitute, his discarded mistress comes to him for financial and emotional support. At first he rejects her with the violence that is typical of him—"'Go,' he said repeating the word very angrily. 'Do as I bid you, or it will be the worse for you'" (Ch. LXXI). When she refuses, he threatens her with the police, and finally drives her out by discussing his own financial ruin (although he still has £500, five times what it cost him to set her up in a business when he abandoned her) and threatening suicide.

Alice's plotline and Glencora's echo each other. Each acts recklessly—Alice by spurning George, then Grey, then George again, Glencora declaring to Plantagenet that she does not love him—"not as women love their husbands when they do love them"—and seeking to ruin herself with Burgo, setting Plantagenet free to find a more suitable wife to give him the family he needs (Ch. LVIII). Glencora and Alice each feel self-hatred. Glencora, more conscious of her motivations, recurs to the original sin of having been forced to marry against her passions, but straightforwardly declares to Alice "I know what I am and what I am like to become. I loathe myself, and I loathe the thing I am thinking of," that is, the thought of abandoning Palliser for Burgo (Ch. XXVII). Alice's plot, after she breaks with George for the second time, is an extended exercise in self-punishment until Grey finally overcomes her "perverse" desire to suffer for her wrongs (Ch. LXXIV). Alice's self-hatred is less conscious than is Glencora's but far more persistent.

Burgo's earnestness reasserts itself in the extraordinary scene where the husband he would deprive of his wife comes to Burgo's aid, at Glencora's request (Ch. LXXVI). To Palliser, Burgo declares twice that he loves Glencora, that "It was not altogether her money," though that money would have saved him. Palliser, doing justice to his rival, says simply "I believe you." In the same chapter, Burgo repeatedly turns down Palliser's aid, declaring that the very circumstances that impel Palliser to aid him "make you the very man in the world,—indeed, for the matter of that, the only man in the world,—from whom I can't take aid." The only aid he will accept is Palliser's saying *adieu* to Glencora for him. Palliser does not judge Fitzgerald; the two men shake hands and part. The ease with which Palliser and Fitzgerald speak to each other, hindered only by Palliser's desire to induce Burgo to accept his financial assistance, shows both men at their best: the dry, emotionally repressed Palliser is kind and more spontaneous toward Burgo than we are used to seeing in him. Fitzgerald likewise rises to his best self, and openly shares his despair and hurt with his rival, without losing his grace.

But the emotional heart of the novel is in the relationships between Plantagenet and Glencora, between Alice and Glencora, and, to a lesser extent, between Alice and John Grey. Somewhat paradoxically, Alice presents herself as a moral authority to Glencora, repeatedly urging her to remain true to her wedding vows, and to Plantagenet. Both Alice and Glencora exhibit masochistic streaks, albeit of different kinds. Alice, after she comes to realize the grasping and selfish nature of George, and to reject him, seeks to punish herself for life by denying herself happiness with John Grey. Claire Jarvis persuasively argues that Alice's behavior is masochist, her "desire to suspend herself indefinitely in engagement" in reaction to her cousin's sadism and John Grey's overwhelming moral force (*Making Scenes* 101–102).

Glencora's masochism is of the "super-sensual" kind, a term taken from Gilles Deleuze, but applied to Trollope by Claire Jarvis. Glencora exhibits, as Jarvis notes, "the suspension of sexual satisfaction, the orchestration of scenes of humiliation with meticulously worded contracts and performances, and the use of an array of masochistic accoutrements" (*Making Scenes* 116–122). Glencora constructs a series of scenes, performative events, in which she quarrels with Plantagenet over her "duennas," forcing him to declare his unreciprocated love for her. At first bitterly resentful of Plantagenet, Glencora slowly comes to accept that he is an honest, well-intentioned man. He bores her, but she has a reluctant respect for his honesty. Glencora's offer to free Plantagenet from their marriage and to accept a life outside of Society as Burgo's lover is a scene in which she both hurts Plantagenet, and makes a genuine effort to salvage some happiness for each of them—Plantagenet will be better off with a more tractable woman who could love him, and she, even in ruin, would find some joy with Burgo.

Later, she waltzes with Burgo at Lady Monk's, signaling her dissatisfaction with her husband to his social circle, only to reject him in favor of Plantagenet. Subsequently, she refuses to speak with Burgo in her marital home. After thwarting Burgo's last advances, Glencora kisses him in front of Alice. Later still, in Europe, she sees Burgo in the casino, and pleads with Plantagenet to save him.

Plantagenet not only accepts her behavior, he brings her out of her suspended state by submitting to her needs. He compassionately leaves Burgo with Glencora at Lady Monk's. This shows his trust in his wife. He acknowledges the tragedy of her inability to love him, but declares his love for her. Most significantly, he rejects the political office he most yearns to fill, Chancellor of the Exchequer, in order to take Glencora on a tour of Europe. Glencora rewards him by mocking him, teasing him for his earnestness, and, he responds by bearing her taunts with his usual solemnity. When Glencora finds herself pregnant, and gives birth to a son and heir, their relationship takes on a more stable, though still barbed, tone. Yet in all of this, Plantagenet Palliser comes to realize his own fault—"his own wrong-doing," in that "he had married without love or requiring love" (Ch. LIX). Having learned to love Glencora, he bears her caprices and strictures as best he can, recognizing her need to perform, and for an audience.

Glencora's and Alice's efforts to prolong their suspension, as Jarvis puts it, also prolongs their own autonomy, and puts off the moment when they are at the mercy of their husbands. When that moment comes, however, the cousins find themselves in very different relationship to their husbands. Alice, having effectively surrendered unconditionally, fades from the narrative. Glencora, however, has found a different balance of power, one in which she is not a subject but rather, as Bernard Shaw describes Eliza Doolittle, "a consort battleship" (Shaw 751).

The third plotline, that of Aunt Greenow, reverses the dynamic. Where Glencora has only the power to destroy her marriage, and then to bait her long suffering husband, and where Alice is simply overwhelmed, by Grey's forgiveness, but also by his moral force, Aunt Greenow knows that her desire to dominate within her marriage will not find expression in marrying Farmer Cheesacre, despite his abjection in pursuing her. Instead, she chooses the financially dependent and weaker Bellfield, "whose poverty aligns with a submission that guarantees the widow leverage" (Jarvis, *Making Scenes* 125). Of the three transgressive women at the heart of *Can You Forgive Her?*, only Lady Glencora has not come to a place of rest in the narrative, and she alone remains integral to the rest of the Palliser series.

Trollope's perpetual interest in and sympathy for the less powerful overcomes his mid–Victorian biases in many, though not all, of his novels. As can be seen in his depiction of Irish and Jewish characters who spark his imagination, when a character becomes sufficiently three dimensional in his mind to absorb his attention, he transcends the stereotypes that mar some of his own writings and those of Dickens and Thackeray. *Can You Forgive Her?* demonstrates, despite Trollope's own conscious dislike of feminism, his strong empathy for his female characters, and his keen awareness of their relative powerlessness within their level of society.

See also: novel series; *Phineas Finn*; *The Prime Minister*

Further Reading

Figueroa-Dorrego, Jorge. "Miranda: Aphra Behn's Appropriation of the Literary Figure of the Jilt." *Aphra Benn and Her Female Successors*, edited by Margarete Rubik, LIT Verlag, 2011.

Jarvis, Claire. *Exquisite Masochism: Sex, Marriage, and the Novel Form*. Baltimore: Johns Hopkins University Press, 2016.

Moody, Ellen. "*Can You Forgive Her?*: Trollope's Roman Fleuve." *Trollope on the Net*. Hambledon, 1999.

Sutherland, John. "Power in *Can You Forgive Her?*" *British Library: Discovering Literature: Romantics and Victorians*. 15 May 2014. Archived at *https://www.bl.uk/romantics-and-victorians/articles/power-in-can-you-forgive-her*.

Castle Richmond

Castle Richmond was published in 1860 by Chapman and Hall. The plot concerns Clara Desmond, who at first prefers Owen Fitzgerald to his cousin Herbert, to whom she has become unwillingly engaged. But she then decides she is pledged to Herbert and will not even consider marrying Owen. The entire scenario is complicated by Clara's mother (somewhat confusingly, also named Clara) being in love with Owen. This is a relationship reminiscent of the role of Rachel Castlewood in Thackeray's *Henry Esmond*. In turn, Patrick, Clara's brother, is Owen's best friend. Owen and Herbert are also rivals for land, as Herbert was set to inherit the family property until he was accused of being illegitimate and must then go to London to try to eke out a life as a Chancery lawyer.

In the opening of *Castle Richmond*, Trollope announces his effective farewell to writing about Ireland, something which, even though punctuated by the returns of *An Eye for an Eye* and *The Landleaguers*, is largely true. Trollope's oeuvre from that point on is weighted towards representing aristocratic and upper-middle-class English life. Trollope says that Irish novels are now out of fashion. His reading public in general entertained a prejudice against the Irish. Trollope cites a figure in publishing as saying that the novel of Ireland is like the historical novel in not having a public and calls for novels of daily English life. Trollope here hints that his turn away from Ireland is commercial. Perhaps would have continued in the Irish vein if not for the philistinism of publishers and readers. Trollope made fun of the desire to represent, instead, daily English life, a desire which most of his oeuvre largely fulfilled. This showed that part of him was not just Ireland's chronicler but Ireland's advocate.

The portrait of the famine of the 1840s in *Castle Richmond* is disconcerting and, to contemporary tastes, upsetting. Trollope registers both the intensity and human loss of the famine. But there seems to be both a distance and an insensitivity to the full range of its horrors. Trollope underestimated the cost to Ireland in human capital. Karl Marx, in his 1867 *Outline of a Report on the Irish Question,* acknowledged a million dead and 1.6 million emigrated. This indicated that, some years after the publication of Trollope's novel, the population was still not near replenishment. Trollope endorses the consensus he describes. A rhetoric of self-reliance and the maintenance of laissez-faire capitalism meant that there should not have been, as there was not, any large-scale British government intervention to save starving Irish people.

Catherine Nealy Judd has argued that *Castle Richmond* recapitulates the features of traditional plague narratives. It shows both a threat to the social fabric and a subsequent recuperation, as well as a scapegoat figure in Owen Fitzgerald. Even though Owen has nothing to do with the famine, his expulsion serves to suture the revived community around Castle Richmond. The threat of the dispossession of an aristocrat, whether it is to be Herbert Fitzgerald or his cousin Owen, lingers over the entire novel. This dispossession traces the expulsion of the landless and the death of the starving, even if it does not come close to sounding the pathos of their condition.

The narrator of *Castle Richmond* is more like the narrator of *Orley Farm* than he is like Archibald Green of the early short stories. That there is a bit of Green in him is Trollope's concession that he knows Ireland well enough to pontificate about it, but not totally to judge it. Trollope saw Irishmen as more than able to assimilate in England. Also, Trollope may only incompletely portray the Irish working class, but he did depict working class Irish people as different from their English counterparts. For instance, he compared the proprietors of the pub near *Castle Richmond* somewhat favorably to the lowlife English duo, Mollett *père et fils.* This sociological analysis is not presented undiluted but leavened with psychological depth. This is seen in Lady Desmond's self-analysis of her love for Owen, occurring in chapter 16, "The Path Beneath the Elms." Castle Richmond is about Irish life, but England is always there as a lens through which Irishness is perceived.

See also: *An Eye for an Eye*; Ireland; *The Landleaguers*

Further Reading

Hennedy, Hugh L. "Love and Famine, Family and Country in Trollope's *Castle Richmond*." *Éire-Ireland: An Interdisciplinary Journal of Irish Studies*, vol. 7, no. 4, 1972, pp. 48–66.
Judd, Catherine Nealy. "Western Plague Literature, The Irish Famine, and Anthony Trollope's *Castle Richmond*." *Irish Studies Review*, vol. 25, 2017, pp. 215–240.
Matthews-Kane, Bridget. "Love's Labour's Lost: Romantic Allegory in Trollope's *Castle Richmond*." *Victorian Literature and Culture*, vol. 32, no. 1, 2004, pp. 117–131.

Chapman and Hall

Chapman and Hall was a publishing firm founded by Edward Chapman and William Hall in 1834; by the time Trollope published with them the business was headquartered in Piccadilly. The firm published quite a few (but not all) of his books. Trollope published *Can You Forgive Her?* With Chapman and Hall both in serial and book form in 1864–5. The firm also published the *Fortnightly Review*, to which Trollope was a frequent contributor. When Edward Chapman retired in 1866, Frederic Chapman, who had joined the firm when William Hall died and had become a partner in 1858, became the leading figure in the firm. To raise capital, he sold Trollope an interest in the firm; Trollope passed it on to his son, Henry Merivale Trollope; Henry held this interest for a few years. Paradoxically, though, Chapman and Hall was best known as the publisher of Dickens, and, as with Trollope's work for *All the Year Round*, the two writers were closer in a publishing context than they were as acquaintances or as kindred novelists. The Dickens connection did come into play peripherally when Chapman and Hall published *Can You Forgive Her?* and paid such a large advance to Trollope that they could not afford the services of John Everett Millais as illustrator. The firm had ready at hand Dickens's longtime illustrator, Hablot K. Browne, to fill in. Chapman and Hall published Dickens during his lifetime and purchased his copyrights after the author's death in 1870. Though Henry Merivale remained with the firm into the twentieth century he was not a major figure, and the firm was most often represented by another literary dynast, Arthur Waugh, the father of the novelists Alec and Evelyn.

See also: *The Fortnightly Review*

Further Reading

Waugh, Arthur, *A Hundred Years in Publishing*. Chapman and Hall, 1936.

The Claverings

The Claverings was serialized with the *Cornhill a*nd published, as Trollope's *Cornhill* serials were generally, with the allied firm of Smith, Elder. Though Trollope commanded a far greater stipend for this serial than for his breakthrough with *Framley Parsonage,* it did not do outstandingly well with the public, and has generally been lost in the riches of Trollope's fiction.

The Claverings, though, is one of Trollope's most satisfying full-length novels, with an exciting though at times melodramatic plot and a rich vein of humor. Harry Clavering is of the cadet branch of an aristocratic family. Given that this cousin, Sur Hugh, holds the title and resides at Clavering Park, Harry has to work for a living. A prototypical Trollope hobbledehoy, he thinks of going into the church, but desists and teaches at a boys' school while he thinks of a plan, Harry decides to become a civil engineer, leading to scenes resembling *The Three Clerks* or *The Struggles of Brown, Jones, and Robinson*. Though with a good education and background, Harry does not have the money to court his beloved, Julia Brabazon, sister-in-law of Sir Hugh, and so she marries the elderly and loathsome Lord Ongar. When Harry is down on his luck he lives in Bloomsbury (where Trollope himself was born) and his succession to the baronetcy was precisely what Trollope's father wished for, but of which he was robbed by fate. Harry's sister Fanny lives with his father at the rectory near Clavering Park. She is the object of the affection of the curate, The Rev. Samuel Saul. Saul at first upbraids Fanny for various lapses and then suddenly proposes marriage to her in the rain, after she has just stepped into a puddle. Fanny refuses him, but then comes around in the end.

Harry works in London, and falls in love with Florence Burton, daughter of his firm's head. He is put off, though, by her lack of upper-class associations. Indeed, her brother Theodore so upsets Harry by dusting his boots with his handkerchief that Harry does not dine with him even though he knows that doing so would aid his suit. He nonetheless becomes engaged to Florence. But before they are married Lady Ongar, now widowed, returns from the continent. Lady Ongar does not know of Harry's engagement to Florence, and seeks to resume their relationship. She brings in tow with her a leechlike best friend, Sophie Gordeloup (who some think is a Russian spy), and Sophie's conniving brother, Count Pateroff. Pateroff tries to blackmail Lady Ongar into marriage, and end Harry's dalliance with her. Lady Ongar responds by cutting off both Sophie and her brother. In turn, in defense of Lady Ongar's honor, Harry makes a defiant statement to his baronet cousin that causes Sir Hugh to end their friendship and rends the *amitié amoreuse* Harry had enjoyed with Sir Hugh's wife, Lady Hermione. But Harry has a rival for Lady Ongar: his cousin's younger brother, Archie. To further his suit, Archie Clavering has his friend, Captain Boodle, of the Warwickshire Boodles, ingratiate himself with Madame Gordeloup. This succeeds all too well, as Boodle becomes infatuated with her and places her above all other obligations.

Lady Ongar, much like Lady Laura in *Phineas Redux*, realizes that Harry has a new love that is greater than his for her. Unlike Phineas, Harry is not marrying a rich woman. Harry is resigned to live in poverty and toil in his chambers at the Adelphi as long as he follows the dictates of his heart. Providentially, though, there is news from the Baltic island of Heligoland, where Sir Hugh and his brother Archie were sailing. Both his cousins have died, which means Harry's father succeeds to the baronetcy as Sir Henry. Harry, his hobbledehoy stage now over, remains committed to Florence, but now they will have money. Indeed, Harry now stands to inherit a title, a rise in social status even higher than if he had risen to achieve a knighthood all on his own (a very unlikely prospect). This was probably influenced by the immediate Trollope family's yearning to inherit the Trollope baronetcy.

The utter lack of concern on the part of the new Sir Henry Clavering for his former ecclesiastical duties, and his frank gratification both at his cousins' no longer being in the way and of his no longer having to be a minister, are among the many amusing small turns Trollope enjoys with his readers. A mordant realism accompanies the otherwise half-fairytale, half-melodramatic overtones of the boat being sunk. *The Claverings* stands out from Trollope's many fictions of English life by such stylish. It perhaps represents the more comic side of Trollope's inheritance from Thackeray's *The Newcomes*, with *The Bertrams* as his more tragic side. The novel, though, did not always have the family as title; it was originally called *Harry Clavering* before Trollope decided to change it just before publication. References to Russia—not just Madame Gordeloup but the Russian railway from Moscow to Astrakhan that Florence's father is helping build—as well as the Heligoland that is so near to a unifying Germany, place the book's action within the long aftermath of the Crimean War and within the wider diplomatic and political history of the nineteenth century.

    See also: hobbledehoy; *The Struggles of Brown, Jones, and Robinson*; *The Three Clerks*

Further Reading

Christian, George Scott. "'Something Heroic Is Still Expected': Realism and Comic Heroism in *The Claverings*." *LIT: Literature Interpretation Theory*, vol. 14, no. 3, July–September 2003, pp. 205–22.
Swafford, Kevin R. "Performance Anxiety, or the Production of Class in Anthony Trollope's *The Claverings*." *Journal of the Midwest Modern Language Association*, vol. 38, no. 2, 2005, pp. 45–58.
Swingle, L.J. *Romanticism and Anthony Trollope: A Study in the Continuities of Nineteenth-Century Literary Thought*. University of Michigan Press, 1990.

clubs

    Trollope belonged to the Garrick, Athenaeum, and Cosmopolitan clubs, and attended occasions at the Arts, Civil Service, and Turf clubs. The Garrick, which he joined in April 1862, was his first convivial home, and, according to T.H.S. Escott, his favorite, although the Athenaeum was where he tended to be found in his later years. Both were newer clubs as compared to ones founded in earlier centuries such as White's and Boodle's, but both acquired a great deal of prestige and still exist and thrive in the twenty-first century. Trollope's third club, the Cosmopolitan, lasted only fifty years but is the source of perhaps the most vividly pictured club, the Universe in *Phineas Redux*.

    Gentlemen's clubs became institutions in the London society of the nineteenth century and provided a place where prominent men could engage in conversation free from the demands of work. They were also a way for people from different spheres of society to interact. Clubs served as a kind of enhanced civil society and in a less free society than Victorian England would have been a crucial node of unsupervised discussion between peers. Even in a society with substantial political liberty, clubs provided a more informal space where every utterance did not have the burden of public consequence. They also, inevitably, were a place for social climbing and what would later be called networking. Trollope's fellow club members included William Gladstone (Cosmopolitan), Edward Bulwer-Lytton (Athenaeum), William Makepeace Thackeray (Garrick), Charles Dickens (Athenaeum and Garrick), Matthew Arnold (Athenaeum). Trollope felt Thackeray, whose home life was difficult, ended up spending too much time in clubs.

Even as early as *The Struggles of Brown, Jones, and Robinson*, Trollope depicted gentleman's clubs as a place of real if limited refuge and harmony. Robinson, the young protagonist of the novel, is a member of the Goose and Gridiron Club, headed by "The Most Worthy Grand Goose." The Grand Goose is portrayed as a comical figure who in the end cannot do much for Robinson. But the compassion the club members show to Robinson when his firm goes bankrupt is genuine. The Acrobats Club in Pall Mall is where Louis Trevelyan in *He Knew He Was Right* finds acceptance, but also hears rumors disturbing to his social peace. In *The Prime Minister* Ferdinand Lopez is on the verge of being expelled from his club, but the presumption of innocence for a club member almost works in his favor, though in the end he is urged to resign or be quietly ostracized, a result that helps spur him to suicide. In *The Three Clerks*, not only is Alaric Tudor expelled from the Downing Club after his public disgrace, but so is Undy Scott, the man who recommended him. Clubs can be arenas of contention and even of violence. In *Phineas Redux* Mr. Bonteen is killed on his way home from the Universe Club.

There are few ladies' clubs in Trollope's world. Though in the 1880s several prominent places where women and members of both sexes could gather were established in London, female sociality was often domestic and quasi-sororal, whereas male sociality had to be conducted outside. In *The Last Chronicle of Barset* it is said "when I see women kiss I always think there is deep hatred." Similarly, in Trollope's description of men in clubs, sociality can often cover up dislike.

See also: Phineas Redux; The Struggles of Brown, Jones, and Robinson

Further Reading

Black, Barbara. *A Room of His Own: A Literary-Cultural Study of Victorian Clubland.* Ohio University Press, 2012.
Terry, R.C. *Trollope: Interviews and Recollections.* Palgrave Macmillan, 1987.

Cornhill

The *Cornhill* was a periodical started in 1859 by George Murray Smith, head of the already-successful and prominent publishing firm Smith, Elder, and Company. It was named after the location of the firm's offices, in the Cornhill ward and street in London's financial district The City. Trollope petitioned Thackeray to let him write for the magazine; Thackeray applauded the proposal and put Trollope into contact with Smith. The *Cornhill* was designed for what Smith viewed as a slightly more upscale and discerning audience. It featured leading Victorian artists such as Millais, Landseer, and Leighton, with more attention to design and the interrelation of word and image than was customary in nineteenth-century periodicals. It also contained nonfiction discussions of contemporary developments in politics, culture, and science, and was intended not just to appeal to the individual readers but to large circulating libraries.

Hoping to rival Charles Dickens's *All the Year Round*, Smith hired William Makepeace Thackeray, Dickens's closest rival among contemporary novelists, as editor. Thackeray solicited work from his novelistic peers such as Elizabeth Gaskell and George Eliot. Trollope's first novel to be serialized by the *Cornhill* was also his first to be serialized in any venue: *Framley Parsonage*, the fourth of the Barsetshire novels. Trollope hoped that the serial publication of this work would allow his family to move to England, where he could be more in view of and in touch with the literary potentates and taste-makers of the day. The serialization of *Framley Parsonage* in 1860 gave Trollope a new audience and brought him to worldly success more than any previous publishing venture. As Trollope temporarily put aside *Castle Richmond*, his Irish famine novel, to write *Framley Parsonage*, the serialization of the novel could be seen as representing, in a biographical sense, his full return to England. It could even be said that this serialization put Trollope in touch with his audience, which in turn reconfirmed his sense of mission as a chronicler of the lives of the English gentry clergy, and upper-middle-class.

If Trollope's relationship to his material and audience was at least in part conventional, the serialization of *Framley Parsonage* allowed Trollope to establish the conventions of the tacit contract between himself and his reader. The fifth Barsetshire novel, *The Small House at Allington*, was also serialized in the *Cornhill*, though the sixth book, *The Last Chronicle of Barset*, was published exclusively in book form by Smith, Elder. In 1865, Trollope co-founded *The Fortnightly Review*, which more or less replaced the role the *Cornhill* had played as an outlet for his work. The *Cornhill* inched slightly towards staid respectability, publishing Queen Victoria's Highland journals, though the presence of Leslie Stephen, father of Virginia Woolf, as editor indicates a certain through-line towards more experimental and modernist modes. In the twentieth century, though it ceased to be a major journal, it lasted three-quarters of the century until 1975, just as the Palliser series was being dramatized by the BBC.

Further Reading

Cooke, Simon. *Illustrated Periodicals of the 1860s*. Oak Knoll, 2010.
Delafield, Catherine. *Serialization and the Novel in Mid-Victorian Magazines*. Ashgate, 2015.
Glynn, Jennifer. *Prince of Publishers: A Biography of George Smith*. Allison & Busby, 1986.

Cousin Henry

Cousin Henry was published in 1879 by Chapman and Hall and serialized in two relatively minor weekly newspapers, *The Manchester Weekly Times* and the *North British Weekly Mail*. It is Trollope's only piece of fiction set in Wales. (Some Welshmen, such as Lord Llwddythiw in *Marion Fay*, appear in other novels.) Indefer Jones is the squire of Llanfeare in Carmarthenshire who is childless. Indefer much prefers his niece, Isabel Brodrick, who lives over the English border in Herefordshire, to his cousin Henry, a London clerk who had an ignominious undergraduate career at Oxford. Uncle Indefer, though, is a traditionalist—he reads only the most conservative newspapers possible—and is set in honoring the tradition of male inheritance. He urges Isabel to marry Henry so she can also enjoy the property, but she refuses, telling Henry that she is repelled by him.

In any event, Isabel's heart has already been won by William Owen, the socially inconspicuous grandson of an innkeeper. When Indefer dies, Henry inherits the property, but, unbeknownst to Henry, Indefer has made a last will leaving the property to Isabel. Nobody knows of this, but Henry finds the will in a book of sermons by the seventeenth-century divine Jeremy Taylor on Indefer's shelves. Henry then vacillates.

He neither reveals the will nor destroys it, reasoning that this inaction exempts him from having committed a crime. Meanwhile, the local newspaper, the *Carmarthen Herald,* suspects something is amiss, serving as a barometer for local sentiment which does not find Henry Jones an acceptable person to be Squire.

Goaded by Mr. Nicholas Apjohn, who is ostensibly his lawyer but who in reality acts as a detective-figure ferreting out the truth, eventually on behalf of Isabel, Henry sues the *Herald* and its proprietor, Gregory Evans, for libel. Apjohn, nominally representing Henry but in fact serving the truth, looks quietly forward to having Henry collapse on the cross-examination of the aggressive John Cheekey. But the cross-examination, much feared by Henry, never happens. Apjohn and Isabel's father, Mr. Brodrick, go over to Llanfeare. After resistance from Henry so great that Apjohn, his own lawyer, actually seizes him by the throat, they find the will in the book of sermons. Cousin Henry is persuaded to abdicate Llanfeare and return to London. Isabel inherits, but only after, on Apjohn's advice, assuming the name Miss Indefer Jones. Once she marries William Owen, he also changes his name to William Owen Indefer Jones. Trollope considered the alternate title *Uncle Indefer's Will* for the book. Even in its present state the transmutation of the name "Indefer Jones" across boundaries of gender, blood, and ancestry is an intriguing spectacle. So is the name of their son, William Apjohn Owen Indefer Jones. This name not only thanks the lawyer for his help but integrates his name into the landed gentry. In having a woman inherit the estate, having a figure of a lesser class background become her husband, and in insisting that dynastic inheritance rest on personal character and popular consent—so that the spirit of tradition should reign over the letter—*Cousin Henry* is a quietly provocative short novel.

See also: *Lady Anna*; *Rachel Ray*; short stories

Further Reading

Gray, Alexandra. "Gender, Inheritance and Sweat in Anthony Trollope's *Cousin Henry.*" *Journal of Victorian Culture*, vol. 24, no. 1, January 2019, pp. 106–119.
Polhemus, Robert. *The Changing World of Anthony Trollope*. Berkeley: University of California Press, 1968.

crime

Though Tolstoy is the Russian novelist to whom Trollope, with his representation of domestic life, is most compared, the roles of crime and madness in Trollope's work are more often reminiscent of Dostoyevsky. Though, unlike his contemporaries Charles Dickens and Wilkie Collins (and, as Lucy Sussex has argued, Frances Trollope in *Hargrave* and in *Jessie Phillips*), Trollope wrote no single book that can be seen as a precursor to the crime fiction genre. The criminal moments in Trollope are particularly shocking and affecting considering the society places so much stake on propriety and that an individual's social status correlates so much with his or her own ethical conduct. Indeed, upright behavior is so much the psychological norm in Trollope's world that criminality is cast as emotionally aberrant. Crime is often connected to madness or the suspicion of madness in Trollope. This is obvious in the case of Mr. Bonteen in *Phineas Redux* and more subtle in the case of Mr. Crawley in *The Last Chronicle of Barset*. Sometimes, though, crime is an aspect or symptom of weakness, as in the situation of Lady Mason in *Orley Farm*, where she does not tell the truth of the birth of her son Lucius in order to preserve his right to the estate he has so come to love.

Similarly, in *Cousin Henry* forgery and suppression are perpetrated in service to Henry Jones's claim to Llanfeare. The inverse of this is young men who actually are entitled to property in some way who squander their own fortune on gambling, such as George Hotspur in *Harry Hotspur of Humblethwaite* or Mountjoy Scarborough in *Mr. Scarborough's Family*. Here the Trollopian prototype of the black sheep is important. The black sheep is someone of bad character who can either slide into being a criminal, move forward into being a malleable hobbledehoy who can round out into somebody decent, or sink into depravity. The continuum between motives essentially of larceny and avarice, such as Lizzie Eustace, and deeper, more fundamentally amoral stirrings, such as that of Lizzie's husband Mr. Emilius, are also part of Trollopian criminal taxonomy.

A surprising amount of Trollope's criminals are clerics: The Reverend Mr. Emilius in *Phineas Redux,* who kills Bonteen; the Reverend Mr. Groschut in *Is He Popenjoy?* who seduces a farmer's daughter; and the Reverend Mr. Greenwood in *Marion Fay* who contemplates the murder of Lord Hampstead. This takes to an extreme a potentially gothic stress on external appearance masking a flawed inward character. The possibility of this psychological dichotomy lies behind criminality in much Trollope.

Another point on this map is personal cruelty so great that its manifestation amounts to criminality. Louis Trevelyan's suspicion of his wife Emily in *He Knew He Was Right* falls into this category, as does the tyranny of the men over their wives and daughters in *The Way We Live Now,* a book that, as Monika Smith has argued, is suffused with literal and metaphorical expressions of domestic abuse that are parallel to the financial skullduggery that is the book's manifest theme.

No matter who the criminal is in Trollope, the field of criminality is always the gap between appearance and reality. Sir Roger Scatcherd in *Doctor Thorne*'s apparent wealth and social status conceals not only his dissipated temperament but his having perpetrated more or less an honor killing to avenge the out-of-wedlock pregnancy of his sister. Mr. Emilius, the fashionable clergymen, is not only a fraud but a cold-blooded killer. Robert Kennedy in the *Phineas* books is a Calvinist teetotaler whose control of his wife Laura leads her to disgrace herself socially rather than live with him. In all these cases, crime in Trollope emerges when people reveal themselves as not what they seem. Conversely, the unjustly accused, such as Phineas Finn, Frank Crawley, or John Caldigate, may have their good character revealed by being tried for a crime. This may answer the question of why, if Trollope is typecast as a writer of Victorian respectability, is there so much crime in his work,

Trollope had no more occasion than any resident of greater London to see crime perpetrated in daily life. His early sojourn in Ireland, though, reveals not only the poachers and shebeen-brewers of *The Macdermots of Ballycloran* but the terrorists of *The Landleaguers* and the potential abuse of power by those in authority in all the Irish fiction. Criminal psychology and behavior do not truly predominant in any of Trollope's novels. Yet later writers such as Arthur Conan Doyle (who published in two of Trollope's major outlets, *The Pall Mall Gazette* and *The Fortnightly Review*), had studied

Trollope's rational orchestration of his plots and observations of the curiosities of urban London, just as Agatha Christie often structured her detective plots along Trollopian lines of bequest and inheritance and set her stories whose surface comity was disturbed by blood and mayhem. Trollope did not just depict crime in his fiction, he also has a place in the history of the crime novel.

    See also: *Doctor Thorne*; *The Eustace Diamonds*; law

Further Reading

Briefel, Aviva. "Tautological Crimes: Why Women Can't Steal Jewels." *Novel: A Forum on Fiction*, vol. 37, nos. 1 and 2, Fall, 2003–Spring, 2004, pp. 135–157.

Oberhelman, David D. "Trollope's Insanity Defense: Narrative Alienation in *He Knew He Was Right*." *Studies in English Literature, 1500–1900*, vol. 35, no. 4, Autumn, 1995, pp. 789–806.

Smith, Monika Rydygier. "Trollope's Dark Vision: Domestic Violence in *The Way We Live Now*." *Victorian Review*, vol. 22, no. 1, Summer 1996, pp. 13–31.

Sussex, Lucy. "Frances Trollope as Crime Writer." *Women's Writing*, vol. 18, no. 2, pp. 182–97.

Dickens, Charles

Dickens (1812–1870) and Trollope were peers and rivals as great Victorian novelists. Dickens admired Frances Trollope and was helpful in introducing her son to his friend, John Forster. Forster then sought writing opportunities for the younger Trollope. Dickens was far more popular in his day. But in the twenty-first century Trollope and Dickens probably are roughly comparable in their lay readership, though Dickens is still more prominent academically.

In Trollope's *Autobiography*, he places Dickens below George Eliot and Thackeray among contemporaries, denouncing Dickens's style. Trollope said Thackeray was a better model for younger writers than was Dickens. He also inferentially damned Dickens by discussing Edward Bulwer-Lytton immediately after commenting on Dickens. But Trollope admitted the vitality of Dickens's characterization and the wide popular appeal of his fiction. Though he denounced Dickens as "stagey and melodramatic," he admitted that his stories "touched the heart."

The modern reader of Victorian fiction does not need to choose between the two, as different as they are. The stereotypical contrast is Dickens as the plucky chronicler of the little man, Trollope as the serene historian of the rich and landed. This is untenable. Dickens decisively shifted his later work from an engaging picaresque pluckiness to serious artistic meditations like *Little Dorrit* and *Our Mutual Friend* which engage in a concerted critique of society. Trollope never focused on the trajectory of individual protagonists as Dickens did; perhaps he came closest in doing so in the books featuring Phineas Finn. Nor did he ever critique society in the sarcastic, fiery way Dickens did. Trollope came nearest to this mode in *The Way We Live Now*, where he reveals a different social vision. When Dickens wrote of his childhood, he was of necessity setting his novels in a different era, one before the railroad had replaced the stagecoach, before the Reform Bill, before the ascension of Queen Victoria. Trollope set the majority of his novels in contemporary times, something Dickens did less frequently. *Hard Times*, *Our Mutual Friend* and *Little Dorrit*, though, certainly touch aspects of Trollope's universe. Trollope published almost three times the fiction than Dickens did, which meant that

Dickens put a greater part of himself in each novel, but Trollope attained the more comprehensive social conspectus.

Though it can be accurately said that Dickens focused on the lower-middle to middle classes, Trollope on the upper-middle to upper classes, the writers converged in many aspects of their representation of English life and society. Trollope wrote more of cathedral towns than Dickens did, but Dickens's *The Mystery of Edwin Drood* is set in Rochester. Dickens wrote more of young men trying to make careers in London office life, but Trollope wrote *The Three Clerks, The Struggles of Brown, Jones, and Robinson*, and even *The Claverings*. Trollope wrote more about the aristocracy, but Dickens did so as well in *Bleak House*. Dickens wrote more of social protest and class inequity, but Trollope's *Lady Anna* and *The Landleaguers* address these issues. Dickens wrote of the Circumlocution Office, but Trollope actually had been a government bureaucrat and had seen government do good work. Dickens wrote up parliamentary profiles, but Trollope ran for office. Dickens sent his characters to Australia, but Trollope actually travelled there. Dickens excoriated American hypocrisy, while Trollope took of the United States what he would. Dickens satirized Mrs. Jellyby in *Bleak House* for caring about foreign suffering but not about people in England. Trollope, in his Irish and Australian fiction, shows a far greater awareness of colonialism than Dickens, and his stories and travelogues set on the Continent, in the Middle East, and in the Caribbean show more awareness of political and cultural change than Dickens, who defended the vicious Governor Eyre of Jamaica.

The Barchester novels, written when Dickens was still alive, reveal more traces of rivalry. The satire of Mr. Popular Sentiment in *The Warden* is a jab at Dickens, and Mrs. Proudie of the Barchester books was the one Trollope character who attained her own life among the reading public the way some of Dickens's early characters had. Steven Amarnick has argued that Trollope was writing back to Dickens's Christmas fiction in his Australian Christmas novel, *Harry Heathcote of Gangoil*. But the two novelists were not always pulling in opposite ways. Trollope assumed the reader knew Dickens. When Trollope refers to Bill Sikes of Dickens's *Oliver Twist* in *The Three Clerks*, he counts on the reader to get the reference. As Elizabeth Bridgham points out, both writers set key novels in cathedral towns. Both—Trollope in *The Macdermots of Ballycloran* and *The Kellys and the O'Kellys*, Dickens in *Barnaby Rudge*—called for an inclusion of Catholics and catholicity in British national space, without themselves being sympathetic to Roman Catholicism in religious terms.

After Dickens's death, two of Trollope's novels, *The Duke's Children* and *Is He Popenjoy?*, were serialized in *All the Year Round*, the journal founded by Dickens and edited, at that point, by Charles Dickens, Jr.

See also: Eliot, George; *Harry Heathcote of Gangoil*; Thackeray, William Makepeace

Further Reading

Amarnick, Steven. "A Christmas Cavil: Trollope Re-Writes Dickens in the Outback." *The Edinburgh Companion to Anthony Trollope*, edited by Frederik Van Dam, David Skilton, and Ortwin de Graef, Edinburgh: Edinburgh University Press, 2015, pp. 126–145.

Bridgham, Elizabeth. *Spaces of the Sacred and Profane: Dickens, Trollope, and the Victorian Cathedral Town.* Routledge, 2012.

Meckier, Jerome. "The Cant of Reform: Trollope Rewrites Dickens in *The Warden*." *Studies in the Novel* vol. 15, no. 3, Fall 1983, pp. 202–223.

Miller, J. Hillis. *The Form of Victorian Fiction*. University of Notre Dame Press, 1968.

Disraeli, Benjamin (Lord Beaconsfield)

Disraeli (1804–1881) was the Victorian figure who most thoroughly combined literature and politics. He was far more successful as a politician than Trollope, not only overcoming not just his Jewishness but his reputation as a farcical fop to become Queen Victoria's favorite Prime Minister and, in effect, the founder of the British Empire in a formal sense. Almost equally, though, Trollope's literary fame has eclipsed Disraeli's, though Disraeli started publishing earlier and as of 1850, even accounting for his being a decade older, would have appeared far more the success. (Curiously, Disraeli's major publisher, Henry Colburn, also published Trollope's second and third novels, *The Kellys and the O'Kellys* and *La Vendée*, which can be reckoned among Trollope's most ideologically conservative works.) But politics took Disraeli's time just as Trollope was beginning his unlikely ascent to literary fame. Disraeli's novels, such as *Coningsby* (1844) or *Sybil* (1845) were like Trollope's in in that they were painted on a broad social canvas and involved both political machinations and the manners and mores of the aristocracy and landed gentry. Disraeli, though, was even in his fiction launching the political program—the revival of conservatism as a modern electoral ideology, for which he became famous. Trollope's political vision, by contrast, even in the Palliser books tended in the direction of preference rather than prescription. This is evident in *The Bertrams*, Trollope's most Disraelian work not just in its pilgrimage to Palestine but its sense of, in Disraeli's phrase, "Young England" trying to define itself. Nonetheless, Trollope's novel lacks any sort of regenerative program for England.

It is difficult to understand why Trollope detested Disraeli so much. But he certainly did. In 1869, Trollope made a point of not just attacking Disraeli in *Saint Pauls* magazine but going beyond the equable posture of Disraeli's greater rival, William Gladstone, in doing so. In his *Autobiography*, Trollope called Disraeli a conjurer. Furthermore, Trollope lent Disraelian aspects to the two greatest villains of the Palliser series, Ferdinand Lopez and Joseph Emilius, as well as, more vaguely, Augustus Melmotte in *The Way We Live Now*. He also fiercely opposed Disraeli's policies of formally proclaiming a British Empire, allying with the Ottoman Empire against the Slavic states in southeastern Europe and Arabs in the Levant seeking self-determination (what was called "The Eastern Question"), and forging a new Toryism reliant on the mysticism of organic social bonds rather than merely deferring to hierarchies. Part of this might have been Trollope's Whig partisanship. Part of it might be attributable to anti–Semitism. (Disraeli's Jewish father, the literary curiosity-collector Isaac D'Israeli, had converted to Anglicanism, yet the family continued to bear the most Jewish of names.)

Sometimes, though, it seems that Trollope's dislike of Disraeli fueled his attitudes towards Jews rather than vice versa. Trollope was friendly with George Eliot even though Eliot's *Daniel Deronda* had a somewhat Disraelian hero who discovers his Jewish ancestry midway, and whose Zionism means the novel takes a Disraelian position on both the Eastern Question and social regeneration. Eliot's vision of society as a whole, rather than as just a set of practices and relations, is also closer to Disraeli's vision than to Trollope's. But there are times where Trollope is close to Disraeli, in his being an outsider to the British gentry but admiring it from afar. The house name of "Noningsby" in *Orley Farm* may, for instance, be an allusion to *Coningsby*. Did Disraeli make Trollope so angry because in the end they were so similar? Whatever the answer, it is clear that Trollope was more competitive with, and adversely emotional towards, Disraeli than to any purely literary rivals such as Dickens.

See also: Eliot, George; Gladstone, William Ewart

Further Reading

Flavin, Michael. *Benjamin Disraeli: The Novel as a Political Discourse.* Sussex Academic Press, 2005.
Hughes, Robert. "'Spontaneous Order' and the Politics of Anthony Trollope." *Nineteenth-Century Literature,* vol. 41, no. 1, June 1986, pp. 32–48.
Teal, Karen Kurt. "Against 'all that rowdy lot': Trollope's Grudge Against Disraeli." *Victorian Newsletter,* vol. 112, 2007, pp. 55–68.

Doctor Thorne

Doctor Thorne was published in 1858 by Chapman and Hall. It is the third novel of the Barchester series and its structural hinge in that it broadens the action out from the specifically ecclesiastical intrigues of the Shire. Its immediate predecessors in Trollope's work, *The Warden, Barchester Towers,* and *The Three Clerks* can all be described as social satires. *Doctor Thorne*, however, took a more pastoral and romantic turn which was consequential for Trollope. The novel opens by differentiating Barsetshire from the industrial Midlands, the territory written about by Elizabeth Gaskell, as a more quaint and out-of-the-way corner of England, at once stashing its fictional distinctiveness, apologizing for its seemingly lack of great social weight, and initiating the reader who has not read *Barchester Towers* to the peculiar and specific nature of the setting . The narrator, though, also makes clear that Barsetshire is in its own way modern. It has changed since the 1832 Reform Bill, for one thing now being divided into East Barsetshire and West Barsetshire, and states that it will concentrate on the more Conservative East, the Western portion having its rural steadfastness diluted by the latitudinarian Whiggery of such liberal magnates as lord de Courcy and the Duke of Omnium.

The Greshams are landed gentry in East Barsetshire. Francis Newbold Gresham more or less inherits his father's Parliamentary seat after his father passes away somewhat prematurely, But the younger Gresham has neither his father's experience or his political acumen, and in 1834, after the democratizing tendencies of the Reform Bill, family name alone will not be enough to keep him in office. Moreover, by marrying Arabella, daughter of the Whig Lord de Courcy, Gresham has made his Tory credentials suspect. He loses his seat, and, although Lady Arabella, aware that she has married a man without a title, insists he try to recapture it. He runs and loses several times, and, as a political figure, becomes ever more quixotic.

His son, the younger Frank Gresham, is, with Doctor Thorne himself, the co-hero of the story: Trollope's narrator offers a hero for admirers of each social class the aristocracy and the professional middle class. Frank Gresham goes to Harrow and Cambridge. But Greshamsbury is not well taken care of as an estate. Between his father's fecklessness and his mother's anxiety little is accomplished there. Frank is tempted by the money of the heiress Miss Dunstable. But she knows Frank does not love her, and refuses his proposal. Frank rededicates himself to the pursuit of his true love, Mary Thorne, although he sees in vain to win his family's approval for the financially unrewarding match. His most sympathetic auditor in his family is his sister Beatrice, who ends up, in the novel's most light-hearted strand, marrying highly eligible the Rev. Caleb Oriel. When the Gresham family, though, learns that Mary Thorne is the heir of the Scatcherd fortune, the situation is dramatically reversed. Mary's suddenly elevated status convinces Frank's family, particularly his mother lady Arabella, and her de Courcy relatives, that the marriage is desirable. Frank proposes to Mary while riding a donkey. This mock-allusion to Jesus's entry into Jerusalem on Palm Sunday does seriously conjure Frank's genuine humility and the true marital affection that will proceed from it.

Just as Frank is one of Trollope's most benign and winning portraits of a younger man, so is Doctor Thorne a paladin of late middle age. Not only in his avuncular attention and concern for Mary but in his care for his patients, the entire community, and even the rebarbative Sir Roger, Doctor Thorne is a facilitator, someone who tries to make others' lives better without credit or laurels for himself. Sir Roger, even though one of Trollope's worst knighted men (along with Sir Lionel in *The Bertrams*): a miscreant, a drunkard, and, as the revelations about his murder of Henry Thorne reveal, a killer, is yet portrayed with complexity. In the parliamentary election Sir Roger, as a Tory, defeats Moffat, favored by the de Courcy family because he is engaged to marry their niece. Sir Roger shows a brand of electorally successful populism that underscores the narrator's point, made at the beginning of chapter 17, that Britain is at this point the only major country in Europe that holds free elections. Despite all, Sir Roger's sheer ferocity of temperament and will to live, even as thinned by his dissolute, corrupt nature, is vividly if horrifically rendered. His son, the parodically named Louis Philippe Scatcherd (a parody made richer by the Trollope family's acquaintance with the Orléanist milieu of that French king) is as dissolute as his father. But Louis lacks Roger's will to live. Sir Roger Scatcherd, like Jude Fawley in Thomas Hardy's *Jude the Obscure*, starts out as a stonemason. But, unlike Jude, Sir Roger finds few initial obstacles to his worldly success. But Sir Roger's life reveals both the possibility of movement between classes in England and the consequences of innate moral temperaments. Lest Sir Roger's fall be viewed by the reader as aa a parable of what happens with the lower classes rise too much in society, the virtue and beauty of the illegitimate and Scatcherd-descended Mary is made manifest.

Mary Thorne's illegitimacy and her connection to the dissolute Scatcherd family, as discrete facts, may have been discreditable. Mary Thorne's illegitimacy combined with the penury makes her ineligible. But the revelation that she has money and property via the Scatcherds, despite their disrepute and her illegitimacy, serves as an equalizer that makes her quite eligible, much as does George Roden's Italian aristocratic ancestry in *Marion Fay*. Trollope did not express a sense of indicting or exposing the hypocrisy of this sudden shift in sentiment, as Dickens might have. He understood that the world will value people differently because of financial circumstances but does insist that we acknowledge, as in the case of Mary Thorne, that there is abiding personal worth underneath. Trollope does not condemn the de Courcy family for thinking Mary not worthy of Frank. He portrays them as superficial and psychologically limited by their wealth, in ways that will continue in the story of Lady Alexandrina's marriage to Adolphus Crosbie in the final two Barsetshire books.

Despite the fairytale ending, the book steadily records the intermittent and inconsistent rise of the middle class, epitomized anecdotally and in a humorous fashion by Dr. Thorne's professional rivalry with Dr. Fillgrave (underscored by the fact that both are competent, modern doctors) and Frank Gresham's thrashing of Mr. Moffat, a rising but not well-born local member of Parliament, for jilting his sister Augusta. Another incident involving Augusta—that she is courted by the lawyer Mortimer Gazebee, rejects him on the advice of her friend Lady Amelia de Courcy, only a few years later to see her friend marry Gazebee herself. This sour yet charming exemplary anecdote sets the tone for the novel's at times sentimental, at times acrid sense of a changing England.

Both the theme of illegitimacy, the emphasis on the medical vocation, and the setting just after the time of the Reform Bill prefigure aspects of the work of George Eliot. If there is a Trollope novel that had any influence on Eliot, particularly on *Middlemarch*, it was *Doctor Thorne*. There was a dramatization in 2015 televised on ITV written by (Lord) Julian Fellowes with Tom Hollander as Doctor Thorne, Stefanie Martini as Mary Thorne, Rebecca Front as Lady Arabella Gresham, and, in a bravura performance, Ian McShane as the drunken sir Roger Scatcherd. The series received good reviews and was well received by Trollope enthusiasts, but did not augur a Trollopian renaissance the way the 1970s Palliser series had.

See also: *Barchester Towers; Framley Parsonage*; novel series

Further Reading

Gurfinkel, Helena. *Outlaw Fathers in Victorian and Modern British Literature: Queering Patriarchy.* Madison, NJ: Fairleigh Dickinson University Press, 2013.
O'Toole, Tess. "Adoption and 'the Improvement of the Estate' in Trollope and Craik." *Nineteenth Century Literature*, vol. 52, no. 1, 1997, pp. 58–79.
Ziegenhagen, Timothy. "Trollope's Professional Gentleman: Medical Practice and Medical Training." *Studies in the Novel*, vol. 38, no. 2, Summer 2006, pp. 54–71.

Dr. Wortle's School

Dr. Wortle's School was serialized by *Blackwood's* in 1880 and published by Chapman and Hall in 1881. Dr. Jeffrey Wortle, Rector of The Bowick School, is a dedicated pedagogue who is yet not above seeking to advance himself socially through knowing the parents of his pupils. (This eventually pays off for him, as his daughter Mary marries Lord Carstairs.) Equally, he is attentive to his students, but very aware he is in a profit-making business. Wortle is assisted by his able younger lieutenant, the Rev. Henry Peacocke. Bowick educates young boy to prepare them to attend Eton. Thus the age of his charges is roughly between eight and fourteen. The plot revolves around Peacocke's wife Ella and whether her marriage to Mr. Peacocke is valid. As uncovered by the disappointed Wortle-school parent Juliana Stantiloup, there was a question of her still being married to her first husband, the loathsome drunkard Ferdinand Lefroy, at the time she married Peacocke. The unique angle on the profession of schoolmaster in the depiction of Wortle as a social climbing opportunist is quite different from Dickens's and Brontë's oppressive and absurd martinets. Particularly praised by Michael Sadleir, the novel is distinguished by the amusement Trollope finds in the facetiousness of Wortle and the genuine concern he evokes in the reader for the Peacockes' situation, which is morally impeccable even though legally dicey. Also of note is the role of California (which Trollope had visited in 1875) and the United States in general as, sensation-novel style, providing a faraway place where secrets can be hidden and unexpectedly resurface.

As Deborah Denenholz Morse has shown, Trollope's son Henry Merivale Trollope wrote Sadleir in 1923 that he felt Dr. Wortle was based on his father (Morse, *Reforming*). If so, this would be a complex self-satire given Wortle's tendentiousness and social ambition, although he also shows magnanimity and loyalty by refusing to fire Peacocke even at the risk of losing his socially prestigious clientele. As compared to the case of George Roden in *Marion Fay*, the postal clerk who ends up having aristocratic ancestry, Wortle is a man of letters who comes near to the aristocracy through his profession but is never of it. The two portraits approximate the ways in which Trollope did and did not rise in social class through his vocation as a novelist and his status as a public figure. Morse also mentions Mick Imlah's hypothesis that the character of Mrs. Peacocke—attractive, American, respectable despite some doubts as to that state, is reminiscent of Kate Field, the great chaste passion of Trollope's later years. This adds perhaps some impure motives to Dr. Wortle's belief in her virtue. One can also see some of Frances Trollope in Ella Peacocke's transatlantic journeying and self-reinvention after initial setbacks. Ella Peacocke's dark coloring might also imply she has some non-white ancestry. These conjectures, while not definite, do shed some light on what Trollope's personal stake might have been in the novel. They also illuminate the special quality of Mrs. Peacocke among Trollope's women as a figure who, whatever the truth of her marital history, has in her heart behaved respectably, and who only formal definitions of virtue, such as Mrs. Wortle's, would condemn. Trollope thus demonstrates that, though he expects men and women to observe social conventions and proprieties of manners, he does not measure them by a calcified code.

Lefroy's degeneracy and turpitude, and the blackmailing behavior of his surviving brother Robert, contrasts with the active, constructive role assumed by Ferdinand Lefroy's marital successor Peacocke. Peacocke undertakes research into the bureaucratic record of his wife's first husband without fear of what it might reveal. Like Bagwax in *John Caldigate*, though with far more personal a stake, or like Marie Goesler in *Phineas Redux*, Peacocke's detection finds truths that permit themselves and their loved ones to enjoy a broader and less fearful life. In smaller and more indirect ways, this may be the sort of effect Dr. Wortle, despite his vanity, might have on his young charges.

See also: Field, Kate; *Marion Fay*; *North America*

Further Reading

Markwick, Margaret. *New Men in Trollope's Novels: Rewriting the Victorian Male*. New York: Ashgate, 2013.
Morse, Deborah Denenholz. *Reforming Trollope, Race, Gender, and Englishness in the Fiction of Anthony Trollope*. Routledge, 2016.
Musgrave, P.W. *From Brown to Bunter: The Life and Death of the School Story*. New York: Routledge, 1985.

The Duke's Children

The Duke's Children was published weekly in serial form in *All the Year Round* (from October 1879 to July 1880) and in book form by Chapman and Hall in 1880. *The*

Duke's Children is in several ways a ghost story. Haunted from the very first chapter by the death of Glencora, Duchess of Omnium, the vivacious and often mercurial wife of the staid Duke, Plantagenet Palliser, her ghost overshadows the entire novel, and drives the widowed Duke into behavior that is both atypically passionate and violates his long held ethical standards.

The novel is haunted not just by the absence of Glencora, but also by her decisions, recent and those made long ago, hearkening all the way back to *Can You Forgive Her?*. In part, the Duke's behavior is in reaction to these decisions, in particular Glencora's encouragement, shortly before her death, of a match between their daughter Mary to Francis Tregear, the impecunious younger son of a Cornish family, a young man who can expect only a modest inheritance, and who Marie Finn describes as "quite likely to spend his money before it comes to him" (Ch. II). In the wake of Plantagenet's discovery of not just the romance, but Glencora's efforts to bring it to fruition, Trollope draws a portrait of the Duke as we have never seen him before: anxious, insecure, angry, and vindictive.

A third haunting in the novel is that, after the poor reception of *The Prime Minister*, *The Duke's Children* written as the preceding volume was published serially and was reduced in scope to fit securely in three volumes. At his publisher's behest, Trollope himself made the cuts, to preserve as much as possible of the texture of the novel (Amarnick 1). The manuscript, donated by Trollope's son Henry in 1918 to a Red Cross sale, ended up in the Chauncey Brewster Tinker Collection of the books and manuscripts of Anthony Trollope in Yale's Beinecke Rare Book and Manuscript Collection. More than thirty years after Bailey's urging the reconstitution of the original text, a team of researchers led by Steven Amarnick successfully published a new edition, restoring the excised material (Amarnick 1).

The publication of the full novel as Trollope had intended it creates a deeper, richer reading experience and answers some nagging questions the mutilated text poses. But the reception of the complete text 135 years after the publication of the 1880 edition requires a rethinking of the Trollope scholarship regarding the novel from the date of initial publication to the present. Long-held opinions of the 1880 version of the novel turn out to have been based on a much less nuanced, much more abbreviated text.

After so long a steeping of the critical consensus of the novel in the shortened text, not all critics and readers turn to the "new" edition—ironically, the original text—or are willing or able to compare the texts to comprehend the differences. After haunting the 1880 published version for so long, the original text, like a revenant, stalks the earlier publication, and seeks to replace it. (The textual changes are available on the Internet at *www.trollopesociety.org*.)

The first haunting is straightforward enough. Palliser's grief for Glencora is movingly, persuasively described in both versions of the novel. Indeed, he becomes in his last appearance "a nearly tragic figure" (Felber, "Advanced Conservative" 433). In the wake of Glencora's death, he discovers that it "was not only that his heart was torn to pieces, but that he did not know how to look out into the world." Having for so long thought of Glencora as a beloved burden, he discovers that in fact he is "helpless" without her, that "there was no one of whom he could ask a question." His grief is exacerbated by the fact that, throughout their life together, "there had been no other human soul to whom he could open himself." As Trollope writes, "He had so habituated himself to devote his mind and his heart to the service of his country, that he had almost risen above or sunk below humanity. But she, who had been essentially human, had been a link between him and the world" (Ch. I).

Palliser has, essentially, no relationship with any of his three children. Their relations were entirely mediated through Glencora, and with her death, he does not even know how to begin to create familial bonds, other than through appeals to duty and morality. It is not that Plantagenet wishes to dominate or tyrannize over Lady Mary, Lord Gerald, or his heir Lord Silverbridge; he simply does not know how to speak to them outside of the language of commands and rationality.

The Duke is aware of these failings on his part and at first tries to retain Marie Finn to help Lady Mary through her own grief. Marie, aware of Mary's love for Tregear, and Glencora's complicity in fostering that relationship, demurs to the Duke's request. Plantagenet, "almost with energy" despite his grief, calls upon the memory of Glencora, stating that "There was none other whom her mother loved as she loved you—none, none." Marie replies that, "There was no one lately, Duke, with whom circumstances caused her mother to be so closely intimate. But even that perhaps was unfortunate" (Ch. I).

Marie's demurral is motivated, at least in part, by the equivocal position Marie has always stood in with both Glencora and Plantagenet, and the sense that the happenstance of her friendship with Lady Glencora does not mean she has ascended to the social position of being a friend of the family. "'Genealogical uncertainty' is a feature of Trollope's presentation of 'Jewish identity,' a feature clearly evident in the series' major Jewish characters: Lopez, Marie Goesler, and Emilius" (Felber, "Advanced Conservative" 438). That genealogical uncertainty translates to social dubiousness. Marie's uncertain social standing has always been finessed by her benevolence toward the Palliser family—refusing to marry the Old Duke, saving Palliser's (and Silverbridge's) patrimony (*Ph F*); refusing the Duke's legacy to her of all his jewels, and assisting Lady Glencora in her efforts on behalf of the Coalition, and comforting her when it falls (*PM*). Marie's husband and fellow outsider (as an Irishman and a Roman Catholic), Phineas likewise has supported the Duke; when Glencora's rash support of Lopez is to be used in Parliament to damage Plantagenet, it is Phineas who skillfully defends both, and protects Glencora's name from being traduced in the House of Commons.

In *The Duke's Children*, Marie once more does her duty to the Palliser family; she forces Tregear to act, and to inform the Duke of his intention to marry Lady Mary. As the story comes out, Palliser's initial affront gives way to rage, in which he accuses her of "treachery." He sends Mary to be supervised by Lady Cantrip, the wife of an old political colleague.

Palliser becomes obsessed by Glencora's championing the romance between Tregear and Lady Mary. Although Francis Tregear is far superior to Burgo Fitzgerald, Lady Glencora's lover in *Can You Forgive Her?*, the echo in the situation wounds the Duke, and rankles in his heart. Acute enough to deduce that Glencora has confided in her closest friend, and unable to punish Glencora, Palliser turns on Marie Finn with an intemperate wrath we have never seen from him before. He dismisses Mrs. Finn as though she were an unfaithful servant, and in doing so, provokes her to write a letter in which she arraigns the Duke's honesty, and making the only demand she has ever made on him or his family—an acknowledgment of her honesty.

Despite these hauntings, the book finds a youthful vitality and enthusiasm in the younger generation. Each of Palliser's children disappoint him, albeit in different ways, and the resultant estrangement deepens, for a time, Palliser's unhappiness. Silverbridge, expelled from Oxford, abandons the Palliser allegiance to the Liberal Party and enters the House of Commons as a Conservative. The change of parties causes him acute pain, as does his rejection of the eminently suitable Lady Mabel Grex (who herself has a longtime romantic attachment to Tregear) in favor of Isabel Boncassen, daughter of the American Ambassador to the Court of St. James. Impressive as the Boncassens are, Palliser cannot but be displeased that his heir intends to marry an American girl "whose grandfather had been a porter" (Amarnick 14). Lord Gerald's expulsion and his heavy gambling likewise try his patience as well as bewildering him. Even Lady Mary, who is in every other way compliant, refuses to renounce her engagement to Tregear.

However, Silverbridge's expulsion from Oxford for painting the Dean's Lodge scarlet humorously prefigures the exploits of P.G. Wodehouse's Bertie Wooster novel, as does the return to the Beargarden, the club for dissolute young idlers from *The Way We Live Now* (1875), and loosely based on the Savage Club (Williamson 127–128). We also meet again some of the more engaging members of that club, which now more benignly resembles Wodehouse's Drones Club.

The scene in which Palliser dines with Silverbridge at the Beargarden is both humorous and touching, with the comedy stemming from the Duke's fish-out-of-water quality, as he politely exchanges pleasantries with Silverbridge's racecourse colleague, the dubious Major Tifto, and the Duke's simple pleasure in being his son's guest touching, as the last of their estrangement dissolves (Ch. XXVI–XXXVII).

Also both humorous and poignant is the plight of Lady Mabel Grex, who has both looks and status, but in courtship terms is leaving the first bloom of her youth, and is aware that, with her chance at being Countess of Silverbridge lost to Isabel and Tregear off the chessboard as well, her window of options, even though she is still beautiful and under twenty-five, is narrowing. Her elderly companion, Miss Casseway, is a figure of even greater pathos, a woman of some dignity but limited means whose only hope for comfort is for Lady Mabel to pull off an increasingly unlikely marital feat.

A more serious note is struck in this otherwise comical set piece is that the Duke, still unreconciled to Marie Finn, disparages his relationship with Phineas Finn (a speech of whose Silverbridge quotes), leading Silverbridge to conclude "'You don't care very much about him then.'" The Duke is compelled by his innate honesty to retract his dismissal of Phineas, and answers his son "Yes I do;—and in what I said just now perhaps I wronged him. I have been under obligations to Mr. Finn,—in a matter as to which he behaved very well. I have found him to be a gentleman. If you come across him in the House I would wish you to be courteous to him … if ever again I should entertain my friends at my table, Mr. Finn would be one who would always be welcome there" (Ch. XXVI). The Duke realizes he has wronged Marie, and has only acknowledged the fact with a very sparse apology, and tries to make vicarious amends by reaffirming his friendship with her husband.

In fact, once she has received the Duke's apology, Marie confides in Phineas, whose anger she manages to prevent him from expressing to the Duke. Despite the meager apology, Marie wishes to put the matter to rest. Phineas, however, throughout the entire Parliamentary session "was averse to meeting the Duke," and when they meet at Ischl, while Marie is making one of her trips to her business interests in Vienna, this time with her husband, Phineas's resentment is still strong. Though the Duke makes a much more full and sincere apology, Phineas avoids the opportunity to the travel with the Duke (Ch. LXI). The Duke, as usual obtuse to emotional currents, believes all is healed with the Finns, and even consults Marie as to Lady Mary's sickness, brought on by the emotional strain of being watched, and held apart from her lover. It is Marie who points out that eventually, if Mary holds her ground, her father will yield. The Duke comes to see this, and knows he must surrender.

Ironically, Plantagenet's yielding is what ends the long haunting. In accepting that he cannot control Lady Mary's choice of husband, nor Silverbridge's choice of Isabel Boncassen as his wife, the Duke begins to heal the estrangement between his children and himself. Likewise, in a process which began at Ischl, the ice between the Duke and Marie Finn, who returns to Matching to keep Mary company, continue to break, and when Marie warns the Duke of the harm that his obstinacy could do to his daughter, instead of responding with anger, he describes her loyalty to and advocacy on behalf of his daughter as "acts of friendship which no efforts on my part can repay" (Ch. LXVI).

Ironically, the Duke is fonder of Marie than he ever was before, having discovered her loyalty and honesty—two traits that he himself manifests throughout the novels. And Phineas and the Duke draw closer together, with the former finally crediting the sincerity of the reconciliation at Ischl, and the latter simply glad to be diverted with political chat at a high level, and the prospect of being of use again, in the House of Lords.

And so the role of Duke gives way to that of father, forgiving Silverbridge's political apostasy, only to rejoice when his son returns to the liberal fold, forgiving Gerald his thoughtless heavy gambling and welcoming Tregear. Palliser must go even further. He has to assure Mr. Boncassen that his daughter will be welcomed as Silverbridge's wife, and tells the American that, should Isabel become Silverbridge's wife, "she would also become my daughter," adding that her brightness and grace "will ensure her acceptance in all societies" (Ch. LXXI). The Duke also at least tolerates Tregear, even inquiring as to what he should call his new son-in-law, inquiring as to his first name, which he had not previously known.

In yielding, the Duke endeavors to do so gracefully. At the marriage of Mary to Tregear, his "hilarity" is noted, leading those who do not know him well to think of him as a "man with few cares, and who now took special joy in the happiness of his children,—who was thoroughly contented to see them marry after their own hearts." Beneath his jovial manner, however, he "was reminding himself of all that he had suffered" (Ch. LXXX).

And yet he is surrounded by his children, with whom he has forged genuine relationships, no longer mediated by a third party, whether Glencora, Marie, or Mary's first minder after her mother's death, Lady Cantrip. While those relationships are not perfect, they are direct, honest and real. Also, the Duke has friends—when Mary asks to have Marie Finn present, who is a friend to each of them, the Duke proposes that Phineas should join them. In surrendering the shadow of parental authority, the fastidious, high-minded Duke has waded into the confusing, sometimes discordant, sea of life from which he has so long abstained.

The book (more so in Trollope's full version) revolves around the growth of Silverbridge, from rebellion to adjustment, from hobbledehoydom to maturity, from the minor Falstaffian diversion of Major Tifto to assumption of the responsibilities of his rank and dignity, and from indecision to self-definition by choosing the right woman even though she is a nontraditional choice. The growth of Lord Silverbridge is the Palliser novels' portent for the future.

See also: hobbledehoy; novel series; *The Prime Minister*

Further Reading

Bailey, J.W. "*The Duke's Children*: Rediscovering a Trollope Manuscript." *Yale University Library Gazette*, vol. 57, no. 1/2, October 1982, pp. 34–38.

Commentary to the First Complete Edition of The Duke's Children *by Anthony Trollope*. London: Folio Society, 2015.

Felber, Lynette. "The Advanced Conservative Liberal: Victorian Liberalism and the Aesthetics of Anthony Trollope's Palliser Novels." *Modern Philology* , vol. 107, no. 3, February 2010, pp. 421–446.

Ragussis, Michael. *Figures of Conversion: The Jewish Question and English National Identity*. Durham, NC: Duke University Press, 1995.

Trollope, Anthony. *The Duke's Children*. Ed. Steven Amarnick, et al. London: Folio Society, 2015; New York: Penguin/Random House, 2017.

An Editor's Tales (1870)

An Editor's Tales was published in 1876 by Chapman and Hall. These stories revolve around an editor's life and derive from Trollope's own experiences at *The Fortnightly* and *Saint Pauls*. "The Turkish Bath" is a story dealing overtly with issues of insanity and just beneath the surface with those of homosexuality. The editor goes to a Turkish bath in London, where men being naked together imposes a certain informality and camaraderie. He meets an Irishman, Michael Molloy, who is trying unsuccessfully to succeed as a writer in London. Molloy breaches the anonymous camaraderie of the bathhouse by presenting the editor with a manuscript. This jolts him back from the reverie of naked male bodies into the world of work and publishing. Molloy burnishes his credentials, giving a false sense of accomplishment in New York and Constantinople, and then submits an unpublishable piece. The editor notices Molloy looking less and less respectable and coherent, and finally concludes he is mad. After Molloy ceases to show up at the baths, the editor finds out where he lives, meeting his long-suffering and patient wife, who tells the editor her husband is a good man fallen upon hard times. In fact Molloy had a decent education but simply could not make that amount to anything in the world in which he wanted to succeed. Like "Mary Gresley," the story, very unusually, is narrated in the first person plural, with the pronoun, "we," even though the reader understands that it is one editor telling the story.

In "Mary Gresley" Trollope uses the name of his maternal grandmother, implying some identification on his part with the young woman who strives so hard to get an editor to look at her work. Mary is beautiful and young, but the married editor feels no more than a fatherly sympathy with her. Mary explains that she is engaged to Arthur Donne, an impecunious man of the cloth, formerly her widowed mother's country lodger, and needs revenue from writing to support them both. The editor tries to encourage Mary, but she does not produce anything publishable. She is not writing just for money. She has genuine creative ambitions, but she realizes there is a market for her work. Though the editor feels her work is not good enough for his own journal, he gets two stories of hers published in a lesser outlet. By this point, though, Arthur Donne has been taken seriously ill. His dying wish, stemming from a combination of patriarchy and puritanism, is that his beloved give up writing, and so the literary career of Mary Gresley comes to a sudden and inglorious end.

"Josephine De Montmorenci" is also narrated by the editorial "we," but the narrator quickly steps back and basically tells the story through the third person point of view of a Mr. Brown, also an editor. Mr. Brown as approached by mail by a young woman calling herself Josephine de Montmerenci and offering a story "Not as Black as He's Painted." The editor is enthusiastic about the story but then is told by Josephine that he has to go through a literary representative of hers in order to pay for her work. When he refuses to do this, Brown is approached by a Mrs. Puffle who claims she is the sister in law of Josephine de Montmorenci. When the editor still balks, he is invited to visit the author at her home. Here, it is revealed that "Josephine de Montmorenci" is a pseudonym. The author is lame, and her real name is Maryanne Puffle, nicknamed Polly. The author when accused by the Editor, protests that Dickens and the Brontë sisters had used pseudonyms. But the Editor sees this as a different representation. Nonetheless, Mr. Brown believes in the power of the work and pities the author's circumstances so agrees to do as she wishes. As in so many of the *Editor's Tales,* the story has to do with a literary outsider and how the expanding authorial marketplace of the mid–Victorian era was an arena of possibility for them.

"The Panjandrum" is a satire of Trollope's own experience in editing and founding periodicals. It is set at the very beginning of his literary career (Lord Melbourne is still Prime Minister) before many of the periodicals to which he contributed existed. The narrator was nominally the editor of the journal, but in reality he was to be simply first among equals of a six-person collective, none of whom were to sign any of their articles. The group includes a woman, Mrs. St. Quinten, an Irishman, Patrick Regan, and four young Englishmen, including the narrator himself. The journal is slow to get off the ground, partly because Mrs. St. Quinten is more interested in socializing than in the process of actually setting up the periodical. But they persist and are on the verge of publishing when they find that in reviewing each other's work, there is no possibility of consensus. They also disagree on whether or not to publish fiction, though the story ends happily for the narrator as his tale is published by another periodical.

"The Spotted Dog" was published in *Saint Pauls*, March–April 1870. It concerns Julius Mackenzie, an educated but down-at-heel man who is forced to write for cheap illustrated papers in order to make a living. As many critics have speculated, Julius Mackenzie is a Trollope manqué, one who did not succeed, an alternate self-representation of the literary failure and drunkard. There is also something comic and grisly in Mr. Mackenzie doing his editorial work on the learned doctor's manuscript in the bedroom of Mr. Grimes, the proprietor of the Spotted Dog pub, which is Mackenzie's haunt. Mr. Mackenzie threatens to kill himself, his wife, and his children in order to spare them from for the degradation. Trollope said this was his favorite of the short stories. This statement underscores the risks he was willing to take in the form. Mrs. McKenzie in his drunkenness destroys the old doctor's manuscript which her husband is supposed to work on. The doctor's equanimity, in concluding that the manuscript was better lost than published and either ignored or ridiculed, is one of the saving graces of the story. The loss of the manuscript itself was no doubt as painful for Trollope to depict as was Mackenzie's suicide itself. The daughter of the doctor marries the army officer. This shows that there is a sense of meritocracy in the society.

"Mrs. Brumby," published in *Saint Pauls* in 1870, concerns a woman whose stories are rejected by the editor, but who makes herself so obstreperous that he soothes her ruffled feathers and even pays her off to leave him alone. It was the sort of story that, if the reader knows the author has been an editor in real life, seems derived from lived experience.

See also: *The Fortnightly*; *Saint Pauls Monthly Magazine*; short stories; *Tales of All Countries*; *Why Frau Frohmann Raised Her Prices*

Further Reading

Garcia-Fernández, Erin. "The Way 'We' Died in Trollope's *Editor's Tales*." *Victorian Periodicals Review*, vol. 59, no. 3, Fall 2017, pp. 467–87.
Liddle, Dallas. *The Dynamics of Genre: Journalism and the Practice of Literature in Mid-Victorian Britain.* Charlottesville: University of Virginia Press, 2009.
Ratcliffe, Sophie. "The Episodic Trollope and *An Editor's Tales*." *Victorian Studies* vol. 68, no. 1, Autumn 2015, pp. 57–83

Eliot, George

Anthony Trollope's friendship with George Eliot (1819–1880; pseudonym for Mary Ann Evans) and her partner George Henry Lewes, was launched when Lewes asked Trollope to help Lewes's son Charles get a job in the post office in August 1860. Trollope and Eliot—both late bloomers who did not start writing until past their first youth, and then took some time to find their true métier—were beginning to emerge as serious writers. Eliot became famous slightly earlier, with the publication of *Adam Bede* in 1859, while Trollope gained wide repute with *The Warden* in 1855. Trollope was intrigued by Eliot and recognized her as a major literary talent. Trollope did not object to Eliot and Lewes living together outside of marriage, and he shared their friendship circle, which included figures as disparate as Ivan Turgenev and Kate Field. Eliot's *Felix Holt* (1866)'s canvasses not just candidates running for office but the differences between authentic and demagogic radicalism and the consequences of a complicated inheritance structure involving entail. This is all quintessentially Trollopian. Eliot also was like Trollope in her venture into historical fiction, although *Romola* (1863) was a much stronger book, and one far more central to tis author's canon, than *La Vendée*.

Many aspects of *Middlemarch* (1871)—the provincial setting, the interlocking plots, and the presence of various strains of cleric (from the intellectual Casaubon to the self-doubting but ultimately benign Farebrother to the politically expedient and manipulative Tyke) are reminiscent of Trollope, especially *Orley Farm* and the Barchester novels. In turn, the fundamental plot of Middlemarch—that Dorothea's two husbands are the cold, demanding Casaubon and then the younger more vital cousin of

Casaubon, Will Ladislaw—may well have inspired Trollope's short story "Catherine Carmichael" (1878), set in New Zealand, where Catherine Baird first marries the old, hard-edged Peter and later his younger and more compassionate cousin John.

Nevertheless, the two writers have had almost totally distinct constituencies. George Saintsbury pronounced in 1894 that Eliot had "genius," Trollope only "fertility." Eliot's having written fewer novels actually added to her associations with artistic merit, as Trollope's productivity made him seem a hack by comparison. In the near century and a half after their deaths, George Eliot was taken up by the both the radical left and the sober center. Her maturity and moral vision were lauded by F.R. Leavis, and even as Victorian studies grew more radicalized and influenced by Marxism and feminism her fiction remained at the center of the Victorian academic canon. Trollope, on the other hand, was left to connoisseurs and aficionados, general readers who either abstained or were actively averse from academic theories, and people who came to his works via television adaptations. Trollope gained credence in the academic Victorianist canon only in the twenty-first century. Indeed, if one were to know of the writers only through their latter-day reputations, one would be surprised Trollope and Eliot were good friends, so different are their reputations. Part of the reason their kinship has not been acknowledged is due to Leavis's judgments. He belittled those aspects of Eliot's oeuvre such as her early *Scenes of Clerical Life* (1857), which have the greatest kinship with Trollope. But other aspects are indeed attributable to actual differences between the two authors. Eliot was more intellectually cosmopolitan than Trollope (though Trollope actually set more fiction abroad), and Trollope was a moderate Whig, whereas Eliot had some tendencies, shown in *Daniel Deronda* (1876), towards the socially minded Toryism represented by Trollope's great nemesis, Disraeli. *Daniel Deronda,* with its championship of an incipient Zionism, also tacitly took a different position on the "Eastern Question," that is, the dilemma of what to do about the decline of the Ottoman Empire, than did Trollope's great political lodestar, Gladstone.

Though neither was particularly committed to Christianity, Trollope tended to sympathize more with High-Church tendencies, whereas Eliot always had a soft spot in her heart for evangelical Protestants. Yet Deborah Denenholz Morse has seen Eliot and Lewes as reformist influences on Trollope. Fundamentally, Trollope and Eliot shared an identity, to use Trollope's phrase, as "advanced liberal-conservatives," although in each the emphasis was somewhat different. Trollope defended the propriety of Eliot's relationship with Lewes. He even noted that Princess Victoria, daughter of the Queen and wife of the heir to the throne of Germany, wished to see Eliot when the Princess visited England. Trollope's friendship with Eliot was one of his major literary alliances. Understanding that the two authors were in many ways like-minded is key to recognizing continuities in visions of the Victorian novel and Victorian liberalism.

See also: Disraeli, Benjamin; Lewes, George Henry

Further Reading

Leavis, F.R. *The Great Tradition*. London: Chatto and Windus, 1948.

Miller, J. Hillis. *The Form of Victorian Fiction: Thackeray, Dickens, Trollope, George Eliot, Meredith, and Hardy.* South Bend, IN: Notre Dame University Press, 1966.

Morse, Deborah Denenholz. *Reforming Trollope, Race, Gender, and Englishness in the Fiction of Anthony Trollope*. New York: Routledge, 2016.

The Eustace Diamonds

The Eustace Diamonds was serialized in *The Fortnightly Review* from 1871 to 1873 and published in book form by Chapman and Hall in 1872. The Eustace Diamonds of the title are a dazzling necklace, long in the noble Eustace family, and in the possession of Elizabeth, Lady Eustace, at the time of her husband's death. Lizzie Greystock, as she was prior to her marriage, claims that the late Sir Florian gave them to her as "her own peculiar property" (Ch. V), while the family lawyers battle to establish that they are heirlooms properly belonging to the family. The diamonds are stolen—three times, if counting Lizzie's initial claim to the Estate lawyers that they were a gift, once by her not revealing that the diamonds were in her hands at the time of the theft of the box, and then finally through the connivance of her maid. Lizzie's efforts to seduce her handsome cousin, Frank Greystock, come to nothing. Frank, repelled by Lizzie's pervasive dishonesty, resists her charms and remains true to his fiancée Lucy Morris.

Lizzie's house party at the Eustace family seat at Portray Castle gives her the opportunity to judge various suitors for her hand, including the tedious Lord Fawn and the engagingly "Corsair"-like Lord George de Bruce Carruthers. During the house party, one of the guests, Mrs. Carbuncle, coerces her strong-willed niece, Lucinda Roanoke, to become engaged to marry the loutish, much older Sir Griffin Tewett. As the day of the wedding approaches, Lucinda's atavistic aversion to her betrothed intensifies into outright hatred, and she goes mad as she is being physically dragged toward the wedding. With the diamonds gone forever, Lizzie marries a charismatic, enigmatic clergyman, who speaks her language of poetry and lies as glibly as she does.

Early in the novel, Trollope refers to Lizzie Eustace as "that opulent and aristocratic Becky Sharp," referring to the anti-heroine of Thackeray's *Vanity Fair* (1848) (Ch. III). The resonances between *The Eustace Diamonds* and *Vanity Fair* do not stop with their anti-heroines. Rather, just as *Vanity Fair* is subtitled "A Novel Without a Hero," so too Trollope's narrator denies the status of heroine or hero to all of the characters in *The Eustace Diamonds*—Lizzie, most obviously, but then Lucy Morris and Frank Greystock in turn. None of the other characters, of course, even qualifies for consideration as hero or heroine (Kendrick, "*Eustace Diamonds*" 151–152).

Another echo in *The Eustace Diamonds* of *Vanity Fair* is the presentation in both novels of the three women whose fortunes we follow—one villainous (Lizzie Eustace and Becky Sharp), one virtuous (Lucy Morris and, until her weakness is unmasked, Amelia Sedley), and one who cannot fit within the norms of the society of the novel (Lucinda Roanoke and Miss Swartz) (Cora 10).

Another parallel to *Vanity Fair* is that Lizzie the social climber (her father, although a retired Admiral, is most known as a demimondaine who is steeped in debt) finds that Society into which she is accepted is one of raffish titled scoundrels such as Lord George, brutes like Sir Griffin, and the rascally cleric, the Rev. Joseph Emilius, a charismatic but oily popular preacher. (The novel hints that Emilius is Jewish, and Trollope deploys a regrettable number of anti–Semitic tropes in him.) Just as the Steynes, Crawleys and Sedleys of Thackeray are hardly worth Becky's efforts—although Rawdon Crawley reveals hidden depths—so too, Lizzie finds herself in a wealthier, but no more exalted strata of society than that which her father occupied.

While Lizzie is less cruel than the openly unfaithful and ultimately murderous Becky Sharp, she is condescending (at best) to Lucy Morris, and far from kind to her dying husband, the debauched Sir Florian (Ch. I). Thereafter, Lizzie's cruelty is only occasionally and briefly alluded to, generally with respect to her harsh treatment of her much older paid companion Miss Macnulty, who thinks of her as a "young tyrant" (Ch. XXI; Ch. XXII). However, it is not for cruelty that Lizzie is most well-known, but for her falsehoods.

Lizzie concocts a series of falsehoods regarding her marriage to Sir Florian Eustace, her obtaining the diamonds from him, the extent of her knowledge of poetry, and effectively overwrites the prosaic (and sometimes even squalid) details of her life, to create herself as a figure of romance. In doing so, she steeps herself—or at least affects to do so—in the poetry of Shelley (whose "Queen Mab" she struggles with early on), Byron, and the Romantics. Although Lord George is much older than she is, Lizzie sees in him a man who might fulfill her Byronic fantasies of idealized ravishment by a "Corsair." Trollope's mildly disdainful view of Lizzie's favorite poets is more a condemnation of "Lizzie's hunting for her Corsair," in which she "makes the thoroughly characteristic mistake of letting literature precede life; she applies to poetry the same reversal of conveyance and conveyed which governs her own expressions" (Kendrick, "*Eustace Diamonds*" 155).

Another ground for the narrator's condemnation of Lizzie is that, beyond lying to others, she lives her life falsely—that is, she is almost entirely a creature of artifice, whose every gesture, word, and tone is part of a performance (Kendrick, "*Eustace Diamonds*" 139–140). What Trollope does not make explicit, though, is that every gesture, word, and tone, is also a gesture of control—Lizzie is seeking to create the life she wants to live, by playacting it. In so doing, she alienates the most worthy of those who are drawn to her, and even exhausts most of her hangers-on. In this one defect, Trollope occasionally shows some sympathy for the little girl who was urged by her father to pretend and entertain, and who was faced with poverty upon his death.

In this respect, the narrator must do double duty: delineating for the reader what statements within the fiction are meant to be truthful, and which are Lizzie's metafictions. Lizzie herself, by her perpetual recasting of her stories, makes the narrator's function more easily accepted, as we remember each successive version of the fibs she tells in her effort to lay claim to the diamonds, although she continually embroiders them (Kendrick, "*Eustace Diamonds*" 155).

Lizzie's most relevant lies—that the diamonds are hers, that they have been stolen, when in fact she still possesses them, and that the property and income left her are hers absolutely, are sparked both by greed and by ignorance. Her great weakness is that, despite her attainments, she simply does not have the financial education to fully understand just what it is she can and what she cannot plausibly lay claim to. As a result, despite her cleverness, her lies regarding the diamonds are easily caught. She simply lacks the knowledge to frame her fictions properly. Across the gulf of her dishonesty, she in this one facet of her character resembles Plantagenet Palliser, who, as heir to the Duke of Omnium, cannot grapple with the "physicality of his estate" to come, a trait that will inhibit his ability to deal with the landed aristocrats among whom he will preside (Maurer, "Nation's Wife" 58–65).

However, the legal complexities of Trollope's plot are legion. In an effort to ensure that he avoided the legal errors which drew critical condemnation of *Orley Farm* (1862), he engaged a barrister to draft the legal opinion upon which Mr. Camperdown stakes his claim. Ironically, modern legal scholarship suggests that Trollope's legal adviser, and his fictional "Turtle" Dove, to whom the opinion of counsel is attributed, may very well have been incorrect (Roth 883–886).

Palliser's honest ignorance only limits his efficacy. But Lizzie's lies spread throughout Society, and because of their frailty, begin to close doors to her. Thus, the impoverished Lord Fawn—he of the many sisters, each potentially in need of a dowry—backs out of his proposal of marriage to her, on the ground that the diamonds form an obstacle. Fawn is weak and vapid, but his biggest mistake is assuming that he and Lizzie share a sense of propriety. He assumes a certain standard of behavior on Lizzie's part. he supposes that she might renege on her consent when she realizes how poor he is (which he would consider proper behavior), but, at the same time, he could not anticipate that she would ever be accused of anything as improper as stealing her late husband's "family jewels." Lizzie, of course, "both steals the diamonds and wants to hold on to the engagement" (Ben-Yishai, "Fact," 126–127). Likewise, Lord George de Bruce Carruthers, who offers Lizzie good advice in how to handle her dealings with the police, and whom she sees as potentially incarnating her fantasy of the Corsair, comes to realize that she is too dangerous for a man like him, who lives hand to mouth, always looking for the next opportunity.

In a pleasing irony, it is the rascally clergyman Joseph Emilius who weds Lizzie. He wins her hand by speaking her language, leavened with some of the more purple prose from the Scriptures. Lizzie sees through his roguery. But her clerical Corsair wins her by both the whiff of brimstone he exudes, and by serving as an accomplice in her construction of a romantic idealized self very different from the scandal-plagued perjurer she has come to be seen as.

Ultimately, Lizzie's lies ripple out to the Pallisers. The old Duke, now ailing, is given an interest in life, besides his fruitless efforts to woo Madame Max Goesler, and is diverted by Lizzie's antics as retold to him by Lady Glencora and Madame Max. The Pallisers and their circle react entirely in character to the story. Lady Glencora eagerly takes up her cause, the elderly Duke bemoans the decline in the aristocracy, while being cynically amused by the scandal. Barrington Erle wants the most dramatically satisfying conclusion to the story. Plantagenet presumes Lizzie's innocence until reliable governmental judgment is to be had. Only the unlovable Mr. Bonteen, who is at Matching only on sufferance, sees through Lizzie immediately, and denounces her squarely—only to be rebuffed by Lady Glencora, whose dislike of him will only grow in later encounters.

Even the more putatively admirable characters dealing with Lizzie's claim to the Eustace Diamonds can find themselves drifting closer to her moral level. As Ayelet Ben-Yishai notes, where the executor "John Eustace is willing to forgo the diamonds for the sake of 'tranquillity,'" the family lawyer, Mr. Camperdown, defies his instructions. In a letter to Frank Greystock, he lies outright, saying that his firm has been instructed by the executor to sue Lizzie for the diamonds, even though John Eustace "has explicitly instructed him not to do so" (Ben Yishai, "Fact" 109–110). Lizzie's recourse to falsehood is contagious, and contaminates the hitherto dry but incorruptible Mr. Camperdown.

As in *Can You Forgive Her?*, in *The Eustace Diamonds*, we are once again placed among several transgressive women—the beautiful, but deceitful and selfish Lizzie Eustace; Lucinda Roanoke, with her strong resistance to marrying a man she despises; and Lizzie's perfidious maid, Patience Crabstick, through whose aid the Eustace Diamonds are finally stolen from Lizzie.

Lucy Morris, like Thackeray's Amelia Sedley, is not transgressive, except to the minor extent that she defends Frank Greystock against the condemnation of Lord Fawn and his family (whose governess she is), and so is exiled from Fawn Court. Lucy is instead an example of a figure often invoked by Trollope, but generally with some irony: Patient Griselda, whose loyal sufferings for the man she loves prove her loyalty and worthiness.

Lizzie, like Becky Sharp, survives her self-inflicted troubles, reputation a little blemished, but notoriety rather to her liking. She exists altogether on a higher plane than Becky, but like her, is a winner (by cheating) of the game, whose punishment is to be her own empty self, aching for better things, yet unable to leave off her artifice and lies to claim them.

Lucinda Roanoke begins the novel as a full participant in the unclean ways of her aunt, Mrs. Carbuncle. However, Trollope's view of Lucinda is more sympathetic to her as her revulsion for Sir Griffin breaks down her manners, her spirit, and, ultimately her sanity. The rough-riding American hoyden turns out to have a fractured fragility that cannot survive the game she sought to play.

Lizzie Eustace's methods of survival may not be admirable, but compared to Lucinda Roanoke's almost operatic fate, and Lucy Morris's withdrawal, there is a spiritedness to this anti-heroine that gives the novel its vitality. Not only are the Pallisers and their circle riveted by the scandalous risks Lizzie takes, but we the readers are as well.

See also: novel series; *Phineas Redux*; women

Further Reading

Ben-Yishai, Ayelet. "The Fact of a Rumor: Anthony Trollope's *The Eustace Diamonds*." *Nineteenth Century Literature*, vol. 68, no. 1, 2007, pp. 88–120.

Cora, Gina. "The Bad and the Good: How *The Eustace Diamonds* Changes Representations of Femininity in *Vanity Fair*." Trollope Prize, First Prize 2003. Archived at *https://sites.fas.harvard.edu/~trollope/2003.htm*.

Harden, Edgar F. "The American Girl in British Fiction." *Huntington Library Quarterly*, vol. 26, no. 3 May 1963, pp. 263–285.

Kendrick, Walter M. "*The Eustace Diamonds*: The Truth of Trollope's Fiction." *ELH*, vol. 46, no. 1, Spring 1979, 136–157.

Maurer, Sara. "The Nation's Wife: England's Vicarious Enjoyment in Anthony Trollope's Palliser Novels." *Troubled Legacies: Narrative and Inheritance*, edited by Allan Hepburn. Toronto: University of Toronto Press, 2007, 58–65.

Roth, Alan. "He Thought He Was Right (But Wasn't): Property Law in Anthony Trollope's *The Eustace Diamonds*." *Stanford Law Review*, vol. 44, no. 4, April 1992, pp. 879–897.

Sauttaur, Jen. "Commodities, Ownership, and *The Eustace Diamonds*: The Value of Femininity." *Victorian Literature and Culture*, vol. 38, no. 1, 2010, pp. 39–52.

Evangelical Christianity

A skeptical and satiric attitude towards evangelical Christianity is a major aspect of Anthony Trollope's novelistic vision. Indeed, it might be the part of his viewpoint on life most missed by twentieth and twenty-first century readers for whom the conflict between different strands of Christian belief is not as urgent as it was in Trollope's day.

It is important to understand that in the Victorian era "evangelical Christianity" existed within and outside the Anglican Church. In the late eighteenth century, the emphasis of the Anglican Church had been highly evangelical, and this was the consensus that the Oxford Movement and later Anglo-Catholic tendencies within the Church of England sought to challenge. Yet there were also evangelicals among dissenting groups as well as Methodists originally part of the Church of England but who had by the beginning of the nineteenth century attained a separate denominational identity. There were also Scots Calvinists, such as Mr. Kennedy in the Palliser novels. Trollope's focus, though, is on the evangelical elements in the established church. These, including Joseph Groschut in *Is He Popenjoy?*, Obadiah Slope in *Barchester Towers,* Samuel Prong in *Rachel Ray*, Jeremiah Maguire and the Stumfoldian milieu from which he hails in *Miss Mackenzie*, and Mr. O'Callaghan in *The Bertrams* who is a pleasure-hater from that same Littlebath milieu, are generally seen as hypocritical, dogmatic, and at times insincere. High Churchmen, in other words those more Anglo-Catholic or sympathetic to the Oxford Movement, such as Francis Arabin in *Barchester Towers,* are treated much more benignly. Trollope is never prescriptive. The young evangelical Samuel Saul in *The Claverings* is present as earnest and honest, even if not a particularly smooth suitor, and the Quakerism of Marion Fay in the late novel of that name is seen only positively. But in general, Trollope's denunciation of the harshness and hypocrisy of Christian fundamentalists are echoed by such contemporaries as the Brontë sisters, Dickens, and Thackeray.

Trollope upheld these principles abroad, in his tolerance of Catholicism in Ireland, in his skepticism of the reformed evangelism of the Dutch in South Africa when he visited there in the 1870s, and in his endorsement of the liberal, non-fundamentalist beliefs about the Bible of Bishop John William Colenso of Natal in South Africa. That Colenso was so roundly rebuked by Matthew Arnold for weakening the possibility of faith but praised by Trollope, when Trollope and Arnold's own religious positions—approving of historical Christianity, but not among its most fervent acolytes or practitioners—were roughly similar, shows how different Trollope's attitudes were than Arnold's. Trollope was skeptical of the reformist and purist energies of evangelical Christianity, and preferred the greater festivity (something shown in his Christmas stories) and ceremoniousness of the more Catholic tendencies in Anglicanism. But he admired reforming Churchman—such as Colenso or his character Mr. Peacocke in *Dr. Wortle's School*—when they embodied a combination of idealism and latitudinarianism. Trollope did appeal to evangelicals for his generally wholesome and moralistic approach, and he had a fitfully productive relationship with the evangelical periodical *Good Words*.

See also: *Barchester Towers*; Disraeli. Benjamin; *Good Words*; Oxford Movement; *Rachel Ray*

Further Reading

Durey, Jill Felicity. *Trollope and the Church of England*. New York: Palgrave Macmillan, 2002.

Herbert, Christopher. *Evangelical Gothic: The English Novel and the Religious War on Virtue from Wesley to Dracula*. Charlottesville: University of Virginia Press, 2019.

Leavis, Q.D. "Trollope and the Evangelicals." *Collected Essays of Q.D. Leavis,* edited by G. Singh. London: Cambridge University Press, 1987, pp. 182–92.

Pollard, Arthur. "Trollope and the Evangelicals." *Nineteenth-Century Fiction*, vol. 32, no. 3, December 1982, pp. 329–339.

An Eye for an Eye

An Eye for an Eye (1878), published by Chapman and Hall and serialized in *The Whitehall Review*, is a comparatively short psychological study, where the betrayal of an Irish girl by a rakish English aristocrat drives her mother insane. This novel is the one almost equally set in England (Scroope Manor in Dorsetshire, an Elizabethan house "with some pretensions") and in Ireland (The Cliffs of Moher) and the most elementally tragic in its assessment of the English-Irish interaction. The novel begins with the effects of its conclusion, that "an unfortunate lady" living "in a private asylum in the West of England," is ever justifying some past action of her life.

"An eye for an eye," she says, "and a tooth for a tooth. Is it not the law?" shows us that Trollope is less out to achieve suspense than give us concision, command, and stark emotional depth. Fred Neville promises his hand to Kate O'Hara, but reneges, when all is said and done, because she is Irish and not rich. Both the Nevilles and the O'Hara's experience tragedy that is, ironically, the one outcome they can truly share. Gender inflects the picture here. In *The Kellys and the O'Kellys*, when Barry Lynch threatens to commit his sister Anty to an asylum, the reader think that Barry himself should be the one committed. Male violence is grounds for condition to a lunatic asylum, but so is female self-assertion. This is another aspect of what happens to Mrs. O'Hara in *An Eye for an Eye,* that she is in effect punished for being Irish and a woman. The marriage allegory by which an Irish woman married an English gentleman was a paradigm for national unity. But *An Eye for an Eye* sees this marriage allegory decisively ended, as the English aristocrat rejects and abandons the rural Irish beauty, and that Trollope never represented the marriage allegory in a direct way shows that he was trying to achieve a more diffuse, complicated and ultimately untenable synthesis of enlightened Irishness within a British frame.

An Eye for an Eye is very unusual for Trollope in terms of narrative structure as it opens with what is chronologically the last scene in the book, with Mrs. O'Hara in an insane asylum. Whereas sometimes in Trollope the intrusive narrator foreshadows the end, here the final development in the plot is totally chronicled, and we are told the story will be of what led up to that. That the frame of the story is the aging Irish woman put in a lunatic asylum more or less for being Irish and in the wrong situation reshuffles the formal elements in ways that work in tandem with the novel's refusal of the marriage allegory. In other words it may seem on the surface that Trollope, in not having Kate and Fred marry, is shying away from Anglo-Irish miscegenation. But it might also be that he is revealing the sense in which Anglo-Irish acrimony cannot be healed by the marriage-plot. That Lady Scroope, in the novel's second chapter, feels that marrying an Irish Roman Catholic girl (whose appeal to Fred she has heard of from her Irish aristocratic friend Mary Quin) would be discreditable to Fred Neville inheriting her husband's title and rank reveals what, in a sense, is a foreordained plot. This was just Trollope's point in arranging the narrative material the way he did.

See also: *Castle Richmond*; Ireland; *The Landleaguers*

Further Reading

Durey, Jill Felicity. "*An Eye for an Eye*: Trollope's Warning for Future Relations between England and Ireland." *Victorian Review,* vol. 32, no. 2, 2006, pp. 26–39.
McCourt, John. "Writing on the Edge: Trollope's *An Eye for an Eye.*" *Variants: The Journal of the European Study of Textual Scholarship*, vol. 4, 2005, pp. 211–24.

Fawkes, Lionel Grimston

At the beginning of his long career, Fawkes (1849–1931) illustrated Trollope's 1875 novel *The Way We Live Now*. Originally, Luke Fildes, who had illustrated Dickens's *The Mystery of Edwin Drood,* was supposed to draw the Trollope book. But Fildes dropped out, and Fawkes stepped in to draw the half-satiric, half-elegiac, always clear and elegant illustrations for *The Way We Live Now*. Fawkes' penchant for the grand style might have been thought too sublime and transcendental for Trollope's sharp social satire. But Fawkes' illustrations, in their fine-grained and full-bodied vividness, captured the novel's various moods of aspiration, indignation, and liveliness. A few years on, Fawkes became, in a somewhat Trollopian sequel, an aide to the governor of Barbados, and painted several memorably realistic watercolors of the Caribbean. He rose in the military to the rank of Colonel of the Royal Artillery. In 1891, at the age of forty-two, he married Lady Constance Eleanor Kennedy, daughter of the second Marquess of Ailsa. They had two daughters, Monica and Lois. They moved to Canada in their later years. By then, the family had been struck by tragedy, with one of their daughters dying in childbirth, and the child that survived eventually dying young. Fawkes was the grandson of a patron of J.M.W. Turner's and had at least two Turner paintings in his possession.

See also: Holl, Frank Montague; Thomas, George Housman; *The Way We Live Now*

Further Reading

Hall. N. John, *Trollope and His Illustrators*. London: Macmillan, 1981.

Field, Kate

That Trollope describes, but does not name, Mary Katherine Keemle "Kate" Field (1838–1896) in *An Autobiography* speaks to the unique if at times tacit place she held in his life. Unusual for an American of her day, Field experienced in her youth both North and South Europe, first travelling to Italy and writing for American newspapers there while still a teenager. Trollope met Field in 1860 in Italy when he was visiting his brother, Thomas Adolphus Trollope, and made sure to see her on his trip to North America the following year.

Field occupies a major place in transatlantic Victorian literature, well above even her own substantial contribution as a journalist, publicist, and actor on the stage. She was, as described by her biographer, Gary Scharnhorst, at once charismatic, charming, and at times difficult in her interpersonal relations. She was one of the few people to not just meet but influence George Eliot, Henry James and Trollope. She also knew Dickens as well as Elizabeth Barrett and Robert Browning. Trollope may well have had romantic feelings for Field, though the affection never developed beyond the level of an *amitié amoreuse* which was a more or less accepted part of Victorian married life. Field was a lecturer, journalist and novelist during a forty-year career which took her across both America and Europe. It is likely that the two did not have sexual relations, although Trollope in his letters clearly indicates he desired her, and that he felt she would at least accept that disclosure in good part.

Field was more radical than Trollope on some issues. Neither favored women's suffrage, but Field supported home rule for Ireland, while Trollope opposed it. Field is often seen as influencing the young American women in *The Duke's Children* and *Dr. Wortle's School* and in the short story "The Courtship of Susan Bell," although these female characters conformed more to Victorian gender expectations than did Field herself. In addition, she well may have contributed to Trollope's depiction of women who wield cultural capital (as separate from that involving money) in his later novels such as *Ayala's Angel*. Field was also, in general, one of Trollope's passports to the mores and manners of the younger generation and thus the very distinct difference between the world of early Trollope and of later Trollope. Like Trollope, Field was a vigorous traveler and knew both Atlantic and Pacific, dying in still-independent Hawai'i in 1896.

See also: *The Duke's Children*; *North America*; short stories

Further Reading

Marcus, Sharon. *Between Women: Friendship, Desire, and Marriage in Victorian England.* Princeton, NJ: Princeton University Press, 2009.

Margolis, Stacey. "Trollope for Americanists." *J19: The Journal of Nineteenth-Century Americanists,* vol. 1, no. 2, Fall 2013, pp. 219–228.

Ratcliffe, Sophie. "The Way We Read Trollope Now." *Trollopiana*, no. 115, Winter 2019/2020, pp. 2–16.

Scharnhorst, Gary. *Kate Field: The Many Lives of a Nineteenth-Century American Journalist.* New York: Syracuse University Press, 2008.

The Fixed Period

The Fixed Period was serialized by *Blackwood's* in 1880 and published in book form by that same firm in 188, It is a work of speculative fiction set in the fictional Pacific Island nation of Britannula, a former British colony, in 1980 (just one hundred years later than its publication date). Britannula has become independent under the presidency of John Neverbend. Neverbend has implemented a series of progressive reforms, one of them that life, for both compassionate and economic reasons, should be terminated at sixty-seven. Neverbend narrates the novel in the first person, the only time other than the very different *The Struggles of Brown, Jones, and Robinson* where Trollope practiced this technique in his longer fiction. When the law was passed, it seemed a distant and faraway concern, as the founders of Britannula had all been young. But now President Neverbend is in his early sixties and his best friend, Gabriel Crasweller, is approaching the age where he will have to retire to "The College" and then be euthanized. Eva Crasweller, Gabriel's daughter, a young woman of particular beauty, tries to intervene, her case being especially strong as the President's son, Jack, is in love with her. Choosing Jack over Abraham Grundle, who is only interested in inheriting the money of her soon-to-be-dead father, Eva nonetheless cannot change the mind of Neverbend, who does not want to lose his friend but sees himself as a committed and just servant of the law. The situation is saved only by Britain, still in this timeline a dominant world power, reoccupying Britannula and reinstituting colonial status. Neverbend retires to England, and Jack and Eva marry.

This might seem a very unusual story for Trollope. It is a piece of speculative fiction, and can be analyzed alongside the efflorescence of utopian fiction in New Zealand of this period or the emergence of Anglo-American future history in the books of Edward Bellamy and H.G. Wells. But the future as depicted in *The Fixed Period* is not systematically different from the present. There is mechanical cricket, but the Cecil family is still socially prominent. Particularly, the roles of women are unchanged, which is necessary for the novel's marriage plot, but which begs the question of how the president's wife, Sarah, can argue the case against the law so strongly and yet herself not be in public life. Moreover, Trollope is more interested in the future than might seem apparent. His vision of settler colonialism is all about the future, and even in the Palliser novels such flourishes as Plantagenet Palliser favoring decimal coinage, only introduced a century later, and Phineas Finn favoring the disestablishment of the Church of England, yet to happen, the interest in futurity is there. At once comic, experimental, and terrifying, *The Fixed Period* is one of Trollope's most distinctive and adventurous fictions.

See also: *Australia and New Zealand*; *An Old Man's Love*

Further Reading

Birns, Nicholas. "The Empire Turned Upside Down: The Colonial Fictions of Anthony Trollope." *Ariel: A Review of English Literature*, vol. 27, no. 3, 1996, pp. 7–23.
Blythe, Helen. "*The Fixed Period* (1882): Euthanasia, Cannibalism, and Colonial Extinction in Anthony Trollope's Antipodes." *Nineteenth Century Contexts*, vol. 25, 2003, pp. 161–180.

Fortnightly Review

Trollope founded—as an initial investor—the *Fortnightly Review* in 1865, along with the positivist philosopher Frederic Harrison, the positivist (and, somewhat incongruously, pro–Catholic) essayist James Cotter Morison, and the positivist historian Edward Spencer Beesly. The first editor George Henry Lewes, was also sympathetic to Positivism and the movement's founder, the Frenchman Auguste Comte. Trollope himself cannot be considered a positivist. But he was a meliorist, in the sense that he believed society was, gradually, improving. The *Fortnightly* allowed him to work with men of similar convictions who were yet not rigidly affixed to the Liberal Party in a narrowly partisan or political way. Trollope yet ruefully remarked in his *Autobiography* that though the journal was willing to include contributors of non–Liberal persuasions, such writers did not want their work to appear in this context.

Though Trollope diminished his direct involvement in the *Fortnightly* after Lewes's resignation in 1866, three of his novels were serialized in the journal—*The Belton Estate, Lady Anna,* and *The Eustace Diamonds*. All three can be seen as among his edgier.

Belton features a portrayal of the rakish and insincere Captain Aylmer and a young woman who gave her heart to him. *Eustace* has its criminal heroine and frank portrayal of moral disrepute. *Lady Anna* depicts a working-class romance of a protagonist who affirmed a proletarian identity over an aristocratic one. Thus, the journal might be said to have accommodated a slightly more liberal version of Trollope. The other leading literary contributor to the *Fortnightly* was George Meredith, who had been a fellow contributor to the *Cornhill*. This shared affiliation reveals the two writers, for all their differences in mode, sharing a comic and liberal sensibility. The *Fortnightly* embodied the ideals of late Victorian liberalism. Its second editor, John Morley, was perhaps the quintessential representative of that idiom, being socially progressive, sympathetic as far as was within his vein to the subjects of British colonialism, and economically libertarian. This is not an exact match for Trollope's own ideological profile, but is indicative of his currents of thought. The crisis that eventually brought down Victorian liberalism, and the Liberal Party itself, were also those that reduced the journal to irrelevance after the first decades of the twentieth century,

The *Fortnightly* also served as a custodian of Trollope's reputation, as a later editor, T.H.S. Escott, was an admiring correspondent of Trollope's and later wrote a book on him, which helped carry Trollope's reputation over the inevitable decline after his death to its resuscitation in the twentieth century by Michael Sadlier. In 1905 Frederick George Bettany wrote an appreciation of Trollope for *The Fortnightly*, which termed Trollope "the old Liberal," an epithet which, in the context of the journal, was quite affectionate.

See also: *Pall Mall Gazette; Saint Pauls Monthly Magazine*

Further Reading

Campbell. Kate, *Journalism, Literature, and Modernity: From Hazlitt to Modernism*. Edinburgh: Edinburgh University Press, 2004.
Escott, Thomas Hay Sweet. *Anthony Trollope, His Work, Associates and Literary Originals*. Bodley Head, 1913.
Turner, Mark. *Trollope and the Magazines: Gendered Issues in Mid-Victorian Britain*. New York: Palgrave, 1989.

Framley Parsonage

Framley Parsonage was serialized in Thackeray's *Cornhill* magazine in 1860, then published by the allied firm of George Smith in 1861. In many ways, it marked Trollope's breakthrough to a larger reading public, especially, as the review of the book in *The Fortnightly Review* in April 1861 noted, as he clearly exceeded Thackeray's recent work in Thackeray's own journal. As Andrew Maunder points out, the mood of Trollope's fiction seemed to fit so seamlessly with the overall mode of the journal and was to their mutual benefit.

Framley Parsonage is the parish affiliated with Framley Court. Lady Lufton, of that establishment, has bestowed the living of the parsonage on young Mark Robarts, an Exeter physicians' son fresh from Oxford. Mark had been a classmate of her son, Ludovic, the current Lord Lufton, and Lady Lufton happily encourages the marriage between Mark and her good friend, Miss Monsell. But when Mark's sister Lucy attracts the attentions of the young Lord Lufton, his mother's enthusiasm for the Robarts connection pales.

Mr. Sowerby is a Member of Parliament, the squire of Chaldicotes and the brother-in-law of Harold Smith, the local MP. Smith cultivates the well-intentioned of the region by promoting missionary work in the South Pacific, a cause that becomes a fad among the local gentry. Sowerby, one of the first of Trollope's politically well-placed scoundrels, inveigles Mark Robarts into a loan, for which Mark soon finds himself responsible after Sowerby's default. Lady Lufton's scorn of the spearhead of radicalism—the Duke of Omnium—is amusing, as well as proceeding the first crossover into the eventual Palliser series. The Duke of Omnium's Gatherum Castle is not just a Whig social salon but a meeting-place for all and sundry to do business at large gatherings where they can make contact. The Duke is not thus just liberal in the letter but in the spirit of his hospitality, although he is also portrayed as indolent and hedonistic. In general in *Framley Parsonage*, as Stacey Margolis asserts, negative character traits can manifest themselves and distressing events happen, but the overall tone is of a sensibly optimistic stability.

Lady Lufton actually has to propose to Lucy because she has been so obstructive to her son's courtship of the young woman. This is a gesture of atonement, but also a manifestation of her son's passivity and her own agency. Trollope portrays in this character, if not necessarily an admirable woman, then certainly a strong one. Ludovic Lufton, his forename itself a bit parodic (Trollope was later to reuse it in *Linda Tressel*, set in Germany), has the courage to love and pursue Lucy Robarts. But Ludovic's passion, realistically, does not go outside the social forms and networks in which his life has been contained. His leaving for a six-week salmon-fishing expedition off the Norwegian coast is an index of his hopes that his problems will go away without him having actively to solve them. On the other hand, Lord Lufton not only insists on marrying Lucy but on giving Mark Robarts, Lucy's brother and his best friend, the loan he needs to stave off his creditors and retain his dignity. Furthermore, Lady Lufton is not at all opposed to the Robarts family as such. Mark Robarts' wife, Fanny, neé Monsell, has Lady Lufton as her great friend and mentor, and Lady Lufton very much admires Mark Robarts as a man and a clergyman. She simply does not think affection and esteem translate to a desirable marital connection. This is especially so when there are so many other greater fortunes potentially on the nuptial chessboard.

When Lady Lufton relents, it is a gesture of her own psychological integration. She allows her redoubtable will and her genuine compassion finally to relate to each other. Lucy shows her genuine worth by her nursing Mary Crawley during her time of illness. Whereas Mr. Sowerby, despite his high birth, ownership of Chaldicotes, and political influence shows himself to be a cad. This forces Lady Lufton to adjust her view of humankind more towards a posture that recognizes people's intrinsic worth along with their social rank. Trollope has already portrayed Lady Lufton as unostentatious in her display of her own wealth and status. He has aligned her temperamentally more with a middle-class woman like Lucy than with more complacent aristocrats like Lord Dumbello. Even more, her female self-assertiveness emerges as parallel to the overly unconventional femininity of Martha Dunstable. Trollope, in turn, makes clear that he at once admires the rural English gentry and does not have a radical critique of the existing social order. But, equally, this social order needs intermarriage and new ideas to sustain it. Trollope's social generosity does not extend to the Tozers, Jewish moneylenders who are portrayed in an ethnically stereotypical way. They are seen as being of a lower order even than the corrupt and reprehensible Sowerby.

Framley Parsonage continues some characters and situations from *Doctor Thorne*—the Doctor himself, the Gresham and Dunstable families, and even Lady Scatcherd, Sir Roger's widow, who at one point the Doctor is suspected or fancying as a future wife. The Arabins, the Grantlys, and Tom Towers reappear from his first two books. Equally, *Framley Parsonage* contains some situations that only pay off in the final two Barsetshire books. Griselda Grantly's marriage to Lord Dumbello seems only a minor and comic episode in this book—mainly for the affectionate somewhat barbed advice given to her by her grandfather's Mr. Harding—but it does set up Griselda's brother's far more transgressive courtship of Grace Crawley in *The Last Chronicle of Barset*.

The book contains cases of hypergamy, or marrying up (Griselda Grantly vis a vis Lord Dumbello), hypogamy, or marrying down (Lord Lufton and Lucy Robarts) and the more lateral, mature, and mutually respectful courtship of Doctor Thorne and Martha Dunstable. That courtship, in its open discussion of money as a motivation for marriage and also the guarantor of independence for people in a marriage, is brilliantly comic. This is exemplified in Chapter XXXIX, entitled "How to Write a Love Letter." Trollope fully accepts that Dr. Thorne and Miss Dunstable are conducting an honorable relationship in being explicit and transparent about each other's fortunes. Yet he does not elevate their courtship as an ideal form of love. Trollope, as Kucich suggests, might be embedding love in a milieu that, despite Barsetshire's aristocratic trappings, is thoroughly bourgeois.

John Everett Millais's illustrations for the novel, even though there were only six of them, helped achieve publicity and sales for the work. His portrait of Lucy Robarts wearing an impressive and dramatic dress helped bring across Trollope's plucky heroine and the small successes she achieves against entrenched social prejudices.

See also: *The Last Chronicle of Barset*; novel series; *The Small House at Allington*

Further Reading

Kucich, John. "Transgression in Trollope: Dishonesty and the Antibourgeois Elite," *ELH*, vol. 56, no. 3, Autumn, 1989, pp. 593–618.

Margolis, Stacey. "Trollope for Americanists." *J19: The Journal of Nineteenth-Century Americanists,* vol. 1, no. 2, Fall 2013, pp. 219–228.

Maunder, Andrew. "'Monitoring the Middle-Classes': Intertextuality and Ideology in Trollope's *Framley Parsonage* and the *Cornhill Magazine.*" *Victorian Periodicals Review*, vol. 33, no. 1, Spring 2000, pp. 44–64.

Gladstone, William Ewart

Gladstone (1809–1898) was a statesman admired without peer and almost without exception by Trollope. Gladstone was the leader of the Liberal Party for two generations and served as Prime Minister four separate times between 1868 and 1894. Gladstone read and appreciated Trollope; *The Eustace Diamonds* is one of the books he is recorded to have read.

Gladstone's political positions—principled, broadly Liberal, open to meaningful change, but by no means revolutionary or precedent breaking—were ones congenial to Trollope. Trollope, for instance, agreed with Gladstone on the Eastern Question—which combined the fate of the declining Ottoman Empire, the response to growing nationalism among the Slavs and Arabs of its domains, and the nature and character of British dominion in the Levant.

It is also clear that Gladstone on one level can be traced lightly in the person of the Whig leader. Gresham was far less a model for Plantagenet Palliser than was Lord Palmerston. Trollope, furthermore, did not write any novels urging specifically Gladstonian positions, especially on foreign policy. Although there is some of Gladstone's dedication and austerity in the character of Plantagenet Palliser, the later Palliser is a looser and freer man.

In 1876, Gladstone published a pamphlet, "The Bulgarian Horrors," about Ottoman Turkish atrocities against the Christian population of Bulgaria. The Turks had controlled Bulgaria for five centuries but were on the verge of relinquishing to growing movements for Slavic self-determination in Southeastern Europe. Trollope read aloud from this pamphlet to his family. He also, according to the *Pall Mall Gazette* (7 December 1876) spoke at St. James's Hall. Trollope noted that Britain had given Turkey a chance to reform by fighting on its side during the Crimean War. The Turks, for Trollope, had not risen to the opportunity. Supporting Gladstone here aligned Trollope with idealism, liberal internationalism, and what would later be called human rights. But it also, as Richard Dellamora points out, linked Trollope with a critique of Disraeli's philo-Ottomanism. Disraeli, of Jewish descent, was seen as placating the Turkish rulers of Palestine. This view, in turn, relied on a fear of the foreign and the other. There was a sense the Christian Bulgarians were more like the English "us" than were the Muslim Turks. Trollope's St. James's address openly lambasted the otherness of the Turks. Even the more idealistic Gladstone also played into this rhetoric.

Gladstone exploited this inevitable amalgam of hope and fear in the Midlothian campaign of 1879. In its eloquence and clear message, the Midlothian campaign was at once the antithesis of Trollope's own campaign for the seat of Beverley in 1868 and the ideal type of its fulfillment. Trollope was not overzealous or monolithic in his partisanship with respect to Gladstone. He remained friendly with George Eliot during the campaign, even though she was of a far more Disraelian cast of opinion. But Trollope did firmly put himself on one side in a conflict whose varying principles—Zionism and humanitarian intervention; cultural difference and self-determination—make it difficult for twenty-first century viewpoints to declare who was on the right side. Even more, the very sense that Britain was in the driver's seat to decide whether or not Bulgaria would be independent, whether or not the Ottoman Empire would endure, took even for that time an Anglocentric sense of the world as its norm.

Nonetheless, in temperamental terms Trollope was equable where Gladstone was militant, negotiable where Gladstone was unbending, and this difference was part of the politician's fascination for Trollope. In a letter to William Blackwood in 1880, Trollope defended Gladstone's sincerity and patriotism, but conceded that his bearing and attitude was not for everyone. Trollope in mien was simply more latitudinarian, higher in churchmanship, and had less exclusively political and ethical a view of life than did Gladstone. These divergent traits probably explain Trollope's own political failures.

Trollope wrote Gladstone in 1880 fearing he had been shunned by Gladstone and reassuring the politician that he sought no personal preferments for himself. Whatever larger anxieties this autumnal interaction represented were either paralleled or symptomatized in Trollope's disappointment that Gladstone was willing to bend towards the demands of Irish Nationalism—a subject on Trollope's mind in the last years of his life, as he was writing *The Landleaguers*. Trollope died somewhat disillusioned with Gladstone, although most likely this disillusion would have been temporary.

Like Trollope, Gladstone was both Whig and traditionally Anglican. Yet his temperament was measurably more puritanical than Trollope's own. Trollope admired Gladstone. But he did not model his own cultural temperament after him in any significant way. Trollope might well have been surprised to be of greater renown in the twenty-first century than Gladstone himself.

See also: Disraeli, Benjamin; *The Fixed Period*; *The Prime Minister*

Further Reading

Butte, George. "Trollope's Duke of Omnium and 'The Pain of History': A Study of the Novelist's Politics." *Victorian Studies*, vol. 24, no. 2, Winter, 1981, pp. 209–227.

Dellamora, Richard. *Friendship's Bonds: Democracy and the Novel in Modern England*. Philadelphia: University of Pennsylvania Press, 2004.

Felber, Lynette. "The Advanced Conservative Liberal: Victorian Liberalism and the Aesthetics of Anthony Trollope's Palliser Novels," *Modern Philology*, vol. 107, no. 3, February 2010, pp. 421–446.

Halperin, John. *Trollope and Politics: A Study of the Pallisers and Others*. London: Macmillan, 1977.

The Golden Lion of Granpere

The Golden Lion of Granpere, like *Nina Balatka* and *Linda Tressel,* is a short novel set in continental Europe. Like the previous two, it was intended to be published anonymously by Blackwood's, but because of financial disagreements Trollope published it under his own name and had it issued by two concerns that were for him reliable, if secondary, outlets. The novel was serialized in the evangelical publication *Good Words* and published by Tinsley, a firm usually associated with sensation fiction. *The Golden Lion of Granpere* is set in Lorraine, which, a year before the novel's publication in 1872, had been ceded by France to Germany. However, according to *An Autobiography*, Trollope actually wrote the story in 1867, and only slightly revised it for publication. Thus the story records that the Second Empire is over in France (which would not have been true in 1867), and that Napoleon III, carrying on previous efforts of the Protestant pastor Jean-Frédéric Oberlin, had improved the roads and social climate in the area. As with *Linda Tressel*, the story is set amidst the political changes in Europe in the 1860s and 1870s; yet Trollope shows considerable reticence in advertising any opinion of those changes.

Granpere is depicted as a rather remote place, where even gas lamps have not caught on yet. Marie Bromar lives with her aunt Josephine, second wife of George Voss, proprietor of the thriving local inn *Le Lion D'Or* at Granpere. Maire had been brought over from Epinal to Granpere at age fifteen to help her aunt run the inn. Soon, her aunt comes to regard her as a surrogate daughter. Voss has an adult son, George, from a previous marriage. George is twenty-five and living and working at an inn in nearby Colmar. It is revealed that Michel had sent George away because he feared his son's growing intimacy with Marie. There is no antagonism between father and son, but Michel makes clear he regards as improper the interest his son has taken in his wife's niece. When George decamps to Colmar to work at a larger inn run by Madame Faragon, who is impressed by George and seeks to engage him as her successor once she retires. Meanwhile, Adrian Urmand, an eligible young man, has made himself known at the inn in Granpere, and is put forward by Michel as a candidate for Marie's hand. Though Urmand abjures her guardian's help, he is determined to win her love on his own. He has everything about him that a promising young man should possess—except Marie does not love him.

As with the other two short continental novels, this story revolves around a young woman's determination that she will choose her own spouse. In isolation, this seems a particular quirk of the character, but, taking the three novels as a triptych, Trollope is emphasizing that with the modernization of Europe and political change will also come greater demands by women for autonomy and self-determination. Marie's self-assertion also sets off others to pursue their own insistent agendas, as when Michel Voss seems to prefer that his son George take over for Madame Faragon, and thus tacitly give up any chance of succeeding his own father at Granpere, rather than resume his dalliance with the forbidden Marie. Feeling pressured by circumstances, Marie agrees to marry Urmand.

Madame Faragon informs George of the intended marriage. George goes back to Granpere. After putting up a front of acquiescence to his father, George confronts Marie. The initial emphasis is less on declaring his persistent love for Marie than on upbraiding her for breaking her vow. Through this tactic, though, George elicits an admission from Marie that she still loves him. The problem for the young lovers is then how to break it to both Michel and Urmand that there is a new scenario.

The story ends with Michel Voss finally accepting of his son's preferences. Adrian Urmand, realizing that George Voss supersedes him in Marie's affections, also takes his displacement in good part by having a farewell party thrown for him at the inn. Although the reader is assured that George and Marie marry and the inn will prosper, the last dramatized scene is of the jilted lover observing the occasion as a gentleman befits. This show of good manners is a an omen that is momentary, if salutary, for a Europe in the slow process of major change. In Trollope's tacit trilogy of European young women, Lorraine yields happier outcomes than Nuremberg or Prague. Unlike in *Linda Tressel*, where the heroine dies shorn of love, or *Nina Balatka*, where to love the heroine has to give up her own family, Marie does not have to sacrifice anything, not even the good will of the affable Urmand, in order to have the man she wants.

The Golden Lion of Granpere, in book serial and book forms, was illustrated by Francis Arthur Fraser (1846–1924), who also illustrated books by Dinah Mulock Craik and Mark Twain. His vivid drawings gave a sense not just of the characters but of the rooms and furnishings amid which they lived.

See also: *Good Words*; *Linda Tressel*; *Nina Balatka*

Further Reading

Knelman, Judith. "Trollope's Experiments with Anonymity." *Victorian Periodicals Review*, vol. 14, no. 1, Spring 1981, pp. 21–24.
Wijesinha, Rajiva. *The Androgynous Trollope*. New York: University Press of America, 1982.

Good Words

Of all the periodicals in which Trollope had his fiction serially published, *Good Words* was perhaps the least likely to be a major forum for his work. *Good Words* targeted evangelical Christian readers and was published by a Scots Presbyterian, Alexander Strahan. It was edited by a Scotsman, Norman Macleod, later succeeded by his brother, Donald. *Good Words* emphasized or centered around positions that the novelist often satirized or exposed as hypocritical or despicable. In reality, though, the magazine seemed to be somewhat broad minded. It included art by John Everett Millais, whose work was much more aesthetic and associated with pleasure and abundance that is the stereotype of the evangelical aesthetic, as well as his fellow Pre-Raphaelite Edward Burne-Jones. Trollope ran into difficulty with the journal in the serialization of *Rachel Ray*. Even though this was a tender and even idyllic novel, the depiction of dancing (and possibly also the themes of beer-brewing and the hypocrisy of the evangelical minister Mr. Prong) caused the journal concern.

Some incongruity (though no manifest controversy) also emerged when *Good Words* serialized Trollope's novels *He Knew He Was Right* and *Kept in the Dark*. These books, one a study of monomania with respect to marital infidelity and the other a subtle psychological study of secrecy within marriage, were hardly Trollope's most reaffirming of conventional mores. They were both novels of what happened after marriage rather than courtship novels such as *Rachel Ray*. *Good Words* also published his novella of wayward affection, "Alice Dugdale," the short novel *The Golden Lion of Granpere*, set in Lorraine, and several of his most consequential short stories set on the Continent, such as "The Last Austrian Who Left Venice" and "Why Frau Frohmann Raised Her Prices." All these works were among Trollope's most cosmopolitan. They were highly inflected by contemporary politics and economic developments in Europe. By this time, *Good Words* had liberalized its taste slightly and become a more general-interest magazine. In general, *Good Words* clearly valued literary talent in a way but could not help the heterodox. Its contributors included sensation writers such as Mrs. Henry Wood, whose novel *Oswald Cray* was serialized in the journal, and fantasy and fairy tale writers like George MacDonald and Hans Christian Andersen, alongside more expected voices such as Dinah Mulock Craik. *Good Words* showed how an evangelical Christian journal of somewhat strict moral timbre could nonetheless both be imaginative and cosmopolitan in the Victorian era.

See also: Evangelical Christianity; Millais, John Everett; *Rachel Ray*

Further Reading

Delafield, Catherine. *Serialization and The Novel in Mid-Victorian Publishing*. New York: Routledge, 2016.
Ehnes, Cary. *Victorian Poetry and the Poetics of The Literary Periodical*. Edinburgh: Edinburgh University Press, 2017.
Srbernik, Patricia. *Alexander Strahan: Victorian Publisher*. Ann Arbor: University of Michigan Press, 1986.

Harry Heathcote of Gangoil

Harry Heathcote of Gangoil: A Tale of Australian Bush Life (1872, Sampson and Low, also published as the Christmas issue of *The Graphic*) does not announce its

Australian setting at the beginning. In its first two pages, it seems to be describing a man coming home to dinner. But when it is mentioned that, if the gum leaves crackle before Christmas, there will not be a blade of grass until February, the narrator reminds the reader this is not a European Christmas with snow and holly-boughs, but an Australian Christmas of heat and fire. Indeed, while it was serialized in the Melbourne *Age* as a story of Australian life, back in England, the *Graphic* ran the tale in its special Christmas number. Thus it was a tacit successor to Dickens' beloved Christmas stories, which Trollope believed had in later iterations lost sight of the spirit of Christmas.

Harry Heathcote shows Trollope's great elasticity of scope. He is as capable of telling an Australian story as an English or Irish one. It also displays a fundamental consonance of technique. The story is a recognizably Trollopian one of social rivalry, courtship, and a happy resolution. Australia did not inspire Trollope to a wholesale reframing of his style. But there are noticeable emphases. *Harry Heathcote* is the Trollope novel other than *Orley Farm* most concerned with farming and its problems. Australia is depicted as a land of economic opportunity. An orphan like Harry Heathcote can, at a young age, become a wealthy farmer. Harry owns land in a fertile area of Queensland; its size nearly matches that of an English county. Trollope uses words with distinct Australian associations,—"bush" "swagman," "paddock," "veranda," but he was always the tourist. He did not have roots in Australia sufficient to make sweeping generalizations about it. This is unlike his fellow Englishman, Henry Kingsley. In *The Recollections of Geoffrey Hamlyn*, Kingsley affronted nascent Australian nationalism. But to do this he had to know the country better than Trollope. Trollope nonetheless paid attention to Australia, and this attentiveness adds strength to *Harry Heathcote*. The hard work of shearing and selling wool, and trading it for other goods, is described in a more hands-on, materialist way than one finds in Trollope's description of English life.

The rather slight plot centers around the courtship of Giles Medlicot with Harry's sister-in-law Kate Daly. The obstacle to this courtship is that Medlicot is a free-selector, someone who has purchased a discrete plot of land from the government, and Harry Heathcote is a squatter, someone whom the government had granted the right to pasture sheep across a wide swath of territory. The squatters were seen as more aristocratic. Harry thus looks down on Giles as a newcomer and an interloper. But the narrative makes clear not just that Medlicot is a gentleman but that the social difference between the squatters and free-selectors is more or less arbitrary. As in his English books, Trollope seeks reconciliation across class boundaries; but here he took the further steps of showing those boundaries themselves as arbitrary. All Medlicot has to do to prove himself a gentleman is to disavow and denounce the actions of Bill Nokes. Nokes is a former employee of Medlicot who tries to burn down Harry's sheep farm. On the other hand, those Englishmen who saw Australia as a radically egalitarian society were shown that distinction of social status did actually exist there. Trollope nonetheless depicted Australia as a young country. The conflict is between potential brothers-in-law, and there is no senior generation present. Also, in Trollope's Australia a working-class man, the sheep shearer Jacko, behaves with considerably more assertiveness than he would in England. *Harry Heathcote of Gangoil* depicts the disputes between the squatters and the less well-off free-selectors as being amenable to resolution. Trollope's depiction of non–Europeans, though, is not so generous, as seen in his stereotypical and hostile portrait of the Chinese cook, Sing-Sing. The book is eloquent in showing the extremes of Australian weather and the vulnerability of the Australian landscape. It is a sterling example of how Trollope wrote well even when not unfurling himself, as Gordon Ray put it, at full length.

See also: *Australia and New Zealand*; *John Caldigate*

Further Reading

Durey, Jill Felicity. "Modern Issues: Anthony Trollope and Australia." *Antipodes: A North American Journal of Australian Literature*, vol. 21, no. 2, December 2007, pp. 17–76.
Moore, Grace. "Birds, Beasts, Fishes, and Reptiles: Anthony Trollope and the Australian Acclimatization Debate," *Animals in Victorian Literature and Culture: Contexts for Criticism*, edited by Laurence W. Mazzeno and Ronald D. Morrison, New York: Palgrave, 2017, pp. 65–82.

Harry Hotspur in *Sir Harry Hotspur of Humblethwaite*

Sir Harry Hotspur of Humblethwaite was serialized in *Macmillan's Magazine* in 1870 and published in 1871 by Hurst and Blackett, who had taken over the premises of Trollope's early publisher, Henry Colburn, at Great Marlborough Street. It was published in New York by Harper and Brothers. Like *Lady Anna*, this novel is set in the northwest of England, the "thwaite" suffix in itself telegraphing a Cumberland locale. Trollope braids in his own heritage by the use of his family name "Gresley" as Lord Alfred's surname.

Sir Harry Hotspur of Humblethwaite is a magnanimous but very private man entering old age. His son and heir had died unexpectedly, and the new heir, George Hotspur, is a first cousin once removed to whom he is not close. Though the baronetcy will unalterably pass to George, Sir Harry has a right to leave his two properties, Humblethwaite in Cumberland and Scarrowby in Durham, to his daughter Emily, and this is his planned course of action, even though he knows it means dividing the title and the estate. An obvious solution would be for Emily to marry George, But Sir Harry prefers another potential suitor, Lord Alfred Gresley, for his daughter. This is so even though (unlike in the similarly-circumstanced *Cousin Henry*) he has no personal dislike for George. Lord Alfred is ten years Emily's senior, and is amiable if not exactly passion-inspiring. Lord Alfred has the full support of Emily's father. But the young woman cannot bring herself to accept his suit, and spurns him. A further complication obtains, as for all that Sir Harry endorses Lord Alfred as a son-in-law, he also wishes his daughter's descendants to be surnamed "Hotspur." A man of higher rank than his daughter such as Lord Alfred would hardly desire to assume a new surname.

George Hotspur is an inveterate gambler who is heavily in debt. He has been observed by Mr. Stackpoole, intimate of the Hotspurs to have been present at, and lost money upon, a race meeting at Goodwood. He wishes to marry Emily not just for the semi-impure motive of uniting the title (which he will have in any event) and the land but for her money, both of which he needs to pay his racing debts to Captain Stubber. George, as he confesses to his mistress Lucy, also feels a sense of moral and even intellectual inadequacy to Emily. Emily, on the other hand, remains totally in love with George. She will not concede even after her family repeatedly confronts her with his character flaws. When George proposes to her by the waterfall of Airey Force near the lake of Ullswater, she tells him she will always be true to him, although she will need her father's consent to marry. This Sir Harry never gives. After George is proven irredeemably dishonest, Sir Harry has his lawyer, Mr. Boltby, draw up a statement by which George will agree to leave Sir Harry's family alone in return for his debts being paid off.

Like many of Trollope's young heroines, Emily realizes that her marital choice is her major opportunity to exercise autonomy in her life. She thus commits her entire soul to her illusion of George, even though in the end she knows he is worthless. But she finds she cannot do otherwise, and is unable to get over him. In other cases in Trollope, as with Clara Amedroz in *The Belton Estate* or Glencora McCluskie in *Can You Forgive Her?*, young women are able to reevaluate their decisions, or are able to convince others they made the right choice, as one sees with Clara Desmond in *Castle Richmond*. Emily is taken aboard by her family and dies in the July heat at the protestant cemetery of Lugano. Now left without both a son to inherit the land and a daughter to inherit the money, Sir Harry's final move is to make sure George gets nothing else but the title; Scarrowby and Humblethwaite itself will end up in the hands of his wife's nephew, a man of appropriate rank and conduct,

Despite its alliterative title having considerable comic potential, the novel has a sad ending. It avoids the marriage plot and centers on the plight of the aristocratic woman who is still a victim of the patriarchy. John Halperin has suggested that *Harry Hotspur*, in its poignant and melancholy conclusion coming out of a sense of the limits of women's agency, was an influence on Henry James's *Washington Square*. Additionally, Goodwood, the site of the race meeting central to George's reputation with Emily, may have inspired the name of Isabel Archer's suitor in James's *Portrait of a Lady*.

The natural comparison with *Harry Heathcote of Gangoil*, similarly a short novel with "Harry" in its title, yields a striking contrast. *Harry Heathcote* is named after a young man, ends optimistically, and is set in Australia. By contrast, *Harry Hotspur* is named after an older man, ends pessimistically, and is set in England—in the same Lake District as *Lady Anna*, where characters find happiness in Australia they cannot find in England. *Harry Hotspur of Humblethwaite* may be minor Trollope, but its unhappy ending presents an unusually tragic view, for him, of life in England.

See also: *Lady Anna*; *Ralph the Heir*

Further Reading

Halperin, John. "Trollope, James, and 'the Retribution of Time.'" *Southern Humanities Review*, vol. 19, 1985, pp. 301–308.

Pearson, David. "'The Letter Killeth': Epistolary Purposes and Techniques in *Sir Harry Hotspur of Humblethwaite*," *Nineteenth-Century Fiction*, vol. 37, no. 3, December 1982, pp. 396–418.

Hawthorne, Nathaniel

Hawthorne (1804–1864) was Trollope's most prominently placed and most ardent American advocate. The author of novels such as *The Scarlet Letter* (1850) and *The House of the Seven Gables* (1851), as well as many short stories, retellings of myths, and local-color sketches, Hawthorne was also US consul in Liverpool from 1853 to 1857, under the administration of his close friend Franklin Pierce. Just as Trollope knew and visited America, Hawthorne knew England very well. The two men met in Boston in 1861. Earlier, in 1860, Hawthorne at once noted the difference between their two aesthetics, saying that he liked "quite another class of works from those I am able to write" and praised Trollope's "solid and substantial" work. What is striking here is how early in Trollope's career this assessment came, and one is forced to assume that Hawthorne was largely talking about *Barchester Towers* and *Doctor Thorne*. But Hawthorne, who died before the balance of Trollope's oeuvre was published and did not live to see even the Barsetshire series finished, nonetheless discerned one of the key elements of Trollope's appeal, his ability to make the reader see a coherent and embodied vision of society. Yet Hawthornean elements can be seen in Trollope's work: the Irish novels and *La Vendée* pursue Hawthorne's interest in the provincial, colonial, historical, and Gothic. Although Hawthorne does not mention Englishness explicitly in his assessment of Trollope, he implies that Trollope's ability to be substantial has to do with his rootedness in English society, just as—according to Henry James who wrote on both Hawthorne and Trollope—Hawthorne's symbolic romances were a product of his lacking the institutional context that an English writer took for granted. David Heddendorf, though, has seen Hawthorne as influencing Trollope at least twice—Lady Mason's guilt in *Orley Farm* and Carry Brattle's disobeying society's sexual mores in *The Vicar of Bullhampton*.

Trollope wrote an essay on Hawthorne in 1879, "The Genius of Nathaniel Hawthorne," for the *North American Review*. In it he noted a temperamental difference between himself and Hawthorne. Trollope said that the American writer's mind "lost its fair proportions": and produced characters "barely within the limits of possibility." Trollope diligently gives plot summaries and character overviews of *The Scarlet Letter* and *The House of the Seven Gables*, disliking the figure of Pearl in the former, and finding the latter lacking in inspiration, but faithfully attending to both the details and the literary atmosphere of Hawthorne's work. He then treats the 1860 romance *The Marble Faun*—in which he found the beauty of the language able to compensate for the lack of an "arranged plot," and many of the short stories, including "Rappacini's Daughter." Trollope praises two points which might lead to some deeper sense of affinity between him and Hawthorne. He makes clear Hawthorne is an heir to the Puritans of the seventeenth century, while writing in a much more imaginative way. Given Trollope's repeated denunciations of repressive Evangelical Protestantism in England, the same could be said of Trollope. Secondly, Trollope notes the shift between Hawthorne's American and Italian settings. Yet he praises the consistency of style between them, that Hawthorne does not feel compelled to inject local color, as it were, from the outside. By the late point at which Trollope wrote his essay on Hawthorne, a new generation of American writers (including Mark Twain) had emerged, permitting Trollope to make broader generalizations about English and American literature while eulogizing Hawthorne. Because Henry James's book on Hawthorne appeared in the same year as Trollope's essay (1879), modern-day readers have the opportunity to compare two very different writers assessing another writer whom both admired, despite their stylistic differences.

See also: Field, Kate; James, Henry; *North America*

Further Reading

Giles, Paul. *Transatlantic Insurrections: British Culture and the Formation of American Literature, 1730–1860*. Philadelphia: University of Pennsylvania Press, 2001.

Heddendorf, David. "Anthony Trollope's *Scarlet Letter*." *Sewanee Review*, vol. 121, no. 3, Fall 2013, pp. 368–375.

Margolis, Stacey. "Trollope for Americanists." *J19: The Journal of Nineteenth-Century Americanists*, vol. 1, no. 2, Fall 2013, pp. 219–228.

He Knew He Was Right

He Knew He Was Right was serialized from October 1868 to May 1869 and published by Alexander Strahan in May 1869. It contained sixty-four illustrations by Marcus Stone, a young man at the time who later became a prominent member of the Royal Academy. The novel takes the feminist concerns Trollope had raised in earlier novels (*Can You Forgive Her?*, *Phineas Finn*, *The Bertrams*), and centers the compelling main plot around the core question, not of mere marital incompatibility or unhappiness, but of the scope of women's autonomy. While Lady Laura Kennedy chafes at the restrictions her husband Robert places on her, the principal source of her discontent is that she married the wrong man, without love, knowing that she loved another. *He Knew He Was Right*, however, goes further. The novel was written in 1867–1868, "during which a bill to grant property rights to married women under common law was being fiercely debated in both Parliament and the press" (Jones 401). In it, Trollope presents two very distinct and opposed views of marriage. The first, rigidly held by the eponymous Louis Trevelyan, is best captured by the dictum attributed to Sir William Blackstone's *Commentaries on the Law of England*: "in law a husband and wife are one person, and the husband is that person," a notion based on the complete suspension of the "very being or legal existence of woman ... during the marriage" (Jones 402–403; Blackstone 1: 442).

The contrary view, that derived from the writings of John Locke, posits that the decision to enter into a contractual relationship must be voluntary, that "a self-destructive contract is not valid"; and that "breach of the contract by violation of its terms makes it dissoluble" (Jones 406). Applied to marriage contracts, Locke's "theory thus posits a 'self' who possesses certain inborn and inalienable rights"; thus, the nascent understanding of marriage as a contractual relationship leads to the conclusion that "if women were to marry on contractual grounds, then presumably they too had such a 'self,'" despite the common law tradition (Jones 406).

Thus, for all the flaws of Locke's contractarianism applied to marriage, "contract theory was nevertheless an important stepping-stone for feminism. By granting the premise of an independent female subject, it opened a Utopian space for feminists to argue against oppressive law." As Wendy Jones notes, "[i]f *He Knew He Was Right* is not unambiguously valuable *as* feminist polemic, it is nevertheless valuable *to* feminist polemic" (Jones 406). Jones contends that this is "because [the novel] espouses an ideal of married love that ... has already been articulated within the discourse of Lockean contract." Trollope's endorsement of marriage for love, and his "following through on the contractual implications for women of that endorsement," expressly supports "the connections between married love, the domestic ideal, progress, and liberty that Victorian feminists invoked" (Jones 406).

The newly wed Emily Trevelyan (*née* Rowley, one of eight daughters of an impecunious diplomat) clashes with her husband Louis over a seemingly trivial issue, whether to receive a friend of her father's to visit her in her new home in London. Colonel Osborne, the old family friend, is described as an "ancient Lothario" who is "fond of intimacies with married ladies, and perhaps was not averse to the excitement of marital hostility" (Ch. I). Osborne's mischievous delight in flirtation and provoking hostility between husband and wife are reminiscent of the profligacy and liaisons of the similarly named Captain George Osborne from Thackeray's *Vanity Fair*.

Aware, as his wife is not, of Osborne's reputation, Louis would prefer Emily to refuse to see Osborne. He imperiously orders her to do so, offending her by his implied distrust, but even more by his treatment of her as subordinate to him. Louis even acknowledges to himself that "wives are bound to obey their husbands, but obedience cannot be extracted from wives, as it may be from servants, by law and with penalties, or from a horse, by punishment and manger curtailments" (Ch. V). Over time, as the estrangement deepens, Louis half-convinces himself that Emily has been unfaithful, uses their son as a bargaining chip, and, as he rehearses his grievances, goes increasingly mad. Finally, he dies, but as he is expiring, Emily gives him her hand to kiss if he believes in her fidelity to him. Louis kisses her hand; "the verdict of the dying man had been given in her favor" (Ch. XCVIII). After he dies, Trollope simply writes that "at last the maniac was dead, and in his last moments he had made such reparation as was in his power of the evil that he had done" (Ch. XCVIX).

Trollope's sympathy extends to both parties, but less convincingly toward Louis. Trevelyan's "putative madness" is not unlike the criteria used in the controversial *M'Naghten* test for criminal responsibility for a defendant's proven actions. Under that test, a defendant was legally insane, and thus not responsible for his actions, if he did not know right from wrong (Oberhelman 791). The very title of the novel hints at the test, by pointing to its elements, while Trollope's narration shows us that "the character knows he is right, and that ethical stance divides him into two legal persons, two characters" (Oberhelman 791).

And yet, the nature of Trevelyan's madness is not so global as to render him wholly unable to plan, or to take action—his seizure of his son from Emily and escape to the Continent show that he retains such abilities (Ch. LXII). Rather, his partial insanities—here, monomania—raised "for the Victorians the perplexing possibility that a man like Trevelyan might be deemed neither mad nor sane" (Wiesenthal 228). The novel's "scrutiny of social, legal, and ethical implications of such a newly-recognized medical condition imparts a distinctively contemporary accent to an otherwise familiar main plot." In sum, Trollope's "self-conscious use of the *Othello* story in *He Knew He Was Right* goes further than association or allusion to 'examine the relevance of Shakespeare's play to mid–Victorian society'" (Wiesenthal 228).

Ultimately, Trevelyan may not be mad at all; as Christine Wiesenthal suggests, his symptoms sound more in Burton's *Anatomy of Melancholy* than the diagnosis of monomania, long since repudiated. Rather than clinical or legal insanity, the too-stubborn, would-be "masterful" man knows that he is not right. Trevelyan's pride and hubris impels him to cling to his ever-less-trustworthy belief in his own rectitude; melancholy—depression, in modern parlance—deepens from his self-inflicted isolation, from both his true self and from his wife and child. In the moments before his death, by kissing Emily's hand, Trevelyan, that turbulent, self-hating monster, makes the only reparation he can, and seals it with a kiss.

See also: marriage plot; *Phineas Finn*; *The Way We Live Now*; women

Further Reading

Jones, Wendy. "Feminism, Fiction and Contract Theory: Trollope's *He Knew He Was Right*." *Criticism*, vol. 36, no. 3, Summer, 1994, pp. 401–414.

Oberhelman, David D. "Trollope's Insanity Defense: Narrative Alienation in *He Knew He Was Right*." *Studies in English Literature, 1500–1900*, vol. 35, no. 4, Autumn, 1995, pp. 789–806.

Wiesenthal, Christine S. "The Body Melancholy: Trollope's *He Knew He Was Right*." *Dickens Studies Annual*, 1994, vol. 23, 1994, pp. 227–258.

hobbledehoy

The hobbledehoy is a character type found in unique concentration in Anthony Trollope's fiction. He is a young man, usually in his twenties, who has not succeeded in terms of either marriage or career. He has not fit into the conventional modes of male success. He seems adrift and rudderless. Trollope himself was a late-blooming son of a large family who secured a job in the post office only in his mid-twenties, began writing only in his thirties, and became successful as a novelist only in his forties. He thus based his portraits of hobbledehoys somewhat on his own experiences. But he was also calling attention to larger patterns of development among Victorian men. Victorian men were expected to ascend quickly from the immaturities of boyhood to the responsibilities of manhood, to assume jobs or positions of authority and distinction, and to marry and sire children. That many young men found themselves adrift was a social phenomenon that threw a wrench into Victorian ideas of male development and privilege.

Trollope gives his most thorough definition of hobbledehoy in *The Small House at Allington,* where he describes hobbledehoys as an awkward subcategory of young men who are undeveloped, insecure, and unsituated. Johnny Eames and his fellow clerks in London are key examples in this book. Although the chief signs of the hobbledehoy are often thought to be lack of fulfillment in marriage or a vocation—and Trollope often emphasizes these deficiencies—the descriptions in *The Small House at Allingham* emphasize social and even physical unease. There is also a sense that these young men lack sexual development, as they appear unintegrated into the heterosexual economy in ways that make them appear in today's terms either queer or involuntarily celibate. Above all, they abstain or are indifferent to the sociality, the clubbability expected of British men of the period. While they are expected to mingle easily with their peers, they find socializing difficult. Yet Trollope, in introducing the reader to Johnny Eames, the hobbledehoy figure in *The Small House at Allington*, warns us not to rule him out prematurely. Indeed, not only does Trollope find unfulfilled potential in hobbledehoys, he sees them as valuable precisely because their potential, unfulfilled, has had more time to sift and become enriched, like fine wine. Indeed, even though Trollope is often perceived as critical of Romanticism, his description of the hobbledehoy is reminiscent of the Wordsworthian romantic solitary. Some of Trollope's hobbledehoys are idealists, like George Bertram in *The Bertrams* who will not take his uncle's money because he does not want to seem desperate for it. The hobbledehoy is prone to solitude, long walks, and aimless, idle dreamings. These reveries make the hobbledehoy a deeper and more reflective person once he succeeds. In the case of Johnny Eames and his fellow clerks, the immaturity of the hobbledehoy can also make them fail as suitors to women who are more mature than they are.

Can there be female hobbledehoys? The hobbledehoy's problems are those of a young man ill-equipped to operate in public space. Public space in Victorian times was only inhabited by women if they were outcasts (as Lady Laura Kennedy in the Palliser books becomes after her separation from her husband) or had achieved a singular and extraordinary fame. Yet there are young women in Trollope who fundamentally redefine themselves and their identity. These include Lady Anna in Trollope's novel of that title or Ayala Dormer in *Ayala's Angel*. Still, women's roles in Trollope's society are so constricted as not to allow them to occupy the indefinite space of the hobbledehoy. Katherine Mullen points out that women telegraphers and typists began to occupy their sort of public office space towards the end of the nineteenth century. The phenomenon of the working woman only emerged when Trollope was nearing the end of his career. But it is seen in the late short story "The Telegraph Girl." "Hoyden" is used in *Barchester Towers* and *The Eustace Diamonds* (in the former as Eleanor Bold and in the latter not of Lizzie Eustace herself but of a hypothetical woman realistically represented) but "hoyden" is an indelible trait more than a developmental stage.

The trajectories of Trollope's characters seem to argue that development can be haphazard or unpredictable. Harry Clavering only really fulfills himself when his cousins' boating accident in Norway mean his father becomes the baronet, and he the heir. Charley Tudor in *The Three Clerks* only achieves his destiny when he redirects his amorous attentions from the woman he thought he loved to her sister. The hobbledehoy is a paramount example of Trollope's overall sense that life is never as predictable as people think it will be.

See also: *The Claverings; The Small House at Allington; The Three Clerks*

Further Reading

Cooper, Hyson. "The Hero of This Little History: Hobbledehoydom in Anthony Trollope's *Ayala's Angel*." *Themos: A Journal of Boyhood Studies*, vol. 4, no. 1, Spring 2010, pp. 3–23.
Langbauer, Laurie. "The Hobbledehoy in Trollope." *The Cambridge Companion to Anthony Trollope*, edited by Carolyn Dever and Lisa Niles. London: Cambridge University Press, 2010, pp. 113–27.
Mullen, Katharine. *Working Girls: Fiction, Sexuality, and Modernity*. London: Oxford University Press, 2016.

Holl, Frank Montague

Frank Montague Holl (1845–1888) was the illustrator of *Phineas Redux*. He drew exciting scenes of murder and imprisonment, electioneering and romantic tragedy. He was particularly deft at capturing Phineas's changing state of mind as he careened from grief to determination, peril to exoneration. Of all of Trollope's illustrators other than Millais (whose portrait he painted), Holl was the most successful as a visual artist. He also had the most thorough immersion in the arts, as his father, uncle, and grandfather were all engravers. Trollope says in *An Old Man's Love* that he knows how Thackeray's Beatrix looks as she was drawn by an artist under the novelist's own eyes. The same might have been said of Holl's Lady Laura. Like many of Trollope's illustrators, he attained membership in the Royal Academy, but was never outstanding as an academic painter. His paintings were narratives committed to telling stories of people as much as renderings of scenes, and this made him the ideal illustrator for one of Trollope's most suspenseful entertainments. Holl took on more work than was good for him, but, unlike Trollope and more like Sir Walter Scott, his did not have the stamina to handle such a massive workload.

See also: Millais, John Everett; Small, William; Thomas, George Housman

Further Reading

Gilmartin, Sophie. "Frank Holl and *The Graphic*: Sketching London's Labour in Light and Dark." *Frank Holl: Emerging from the Shadows*, edited by Mark Bills, Philip Wilson, 2013, pp. 90–107.
Hall, John N. *Trollope and His Illustrators*. London: Macmillan, 1981.

homosexuality

The heavy emphasis on homosocial space, and the way men and women express affection to each other in intimate same-sex friendships, have given rise to curiosity about the extent of queer reverberation in Trollope's corpus. Eve Kosofsky Sedgwick's argument that men achieve intimacy by proxy through trafficking in women is highly pertinent to many Trollopian plots, particularly ones, as in *The Duke's Children*, in which a friend marries his friend's sister, or, as in *Castle Richmond*, when a man, Owen Fitzgerald, jilted by a young woman, Clara Desmond, finds solace in the containing affections of her brother, Patrick, or, as in *Phineas Redux,* where a rejected suitor for the hand of a young woman, Violet Effingham, becomes friends with the man who had successfully courted that woman. Kathy Psomiades has made a similar argument with respect to *The Eustace Diamonds* and the way the marriage-plot buttresses the heterosexual exchange of women at a time when the acceleration of capitalism might problematize it. Sedgwick also argues that Trollope's relationship with his mother feminized him and that his following her line of work as author intensified this anxiety about having a feminine inner self. Trollope's experience in single-sex schools such as Harrow and Winchester also undoubtedly led to his witnessing gay crushes among the boys in school. In her poem "The Warm Decembers" Sedgwick portrays a Trollope voyeuristically obsessed with the victimized female in an observed love affair and feeling some sort of unarticulated constraint in his stereotypical masculine gender role. Leonard Sheingold has seen Trollope's prolific literary output as an index of sexual repression, as illicit desires are sublimated into literary production.

In the *Phineas* novels, Phineas's irresistibility to women mingles with his awareness that to succeed in politics he will have to be nearly as popular as other men. This insight brings him close to being—as was said of Trollope's another subject, Julius Caesar—that he was every woman's man, every man's woman. In *The Bertrams*, Sir Lionel Bertram urges his son George to court Caroline Waddington on the grounds that Lionel's brother, George, had loved Caroline's deceased father when they were both young. Not only is this a heterosexual recuperation of a thwarted gay love (and incestuous, as Waddington was George's son-in-law), it is uttered as routinely as if the elder Bertram had loved Caroline's mother. The partial setting of *The Bertrams*, the Middle East, is also the scene for homoerotic valences in the story "A Ride Across Palestine." Here, an older man feels affection for a young woman who disguises herself to him as a young man, but who he eventually realizes is in fact a young woman. Similarly, in

Linda Tressel Ludovic Valcarm explains away, to his intended, Linda, his dalliance with a young woman in a blue frock by explaining that the figure was in fact a transvestite young man seeking to escape the authorities. "The Turkish Bath" is set in London and its portrayal of men seeing each other's nakedness and constructing hierarchies different from the world in which they are dressed brings up nearly overt questions of male-male sexuality and power.

In *Barchester Towers*, Francis Arabin's late avowal of heterosexual interest speaks to certain anxieties raised in England about priestly celibacy among High Church Anglicans. The unusually fleshly nature of the scuffle in *Cousin Henry* by which Indefer Jones's will is wrested from Henry Jones also has potential queer overtones. Sharon Marcus, in her analysis of *Can You Forgive Her?*, argues that Trollope was aware of a contemporary category of "female marriage" and that the friendship between Alice Vavasor and her cousin Kate as well as between Alice and Lady Glencora not only exemplifies this state but underscores the hierarchal and non-companionate nature of the initial state of Glencora's marriage to Plantagenet Palliser. Marcus's reading exemplifies the way that same-sex desire is not just able to be read between the lines in Trollope, but is actively articulated on the surface. Locutions such as George Bertram in *The Bertrams* "picking up" various Englishmen on his way home from the Middle East, in this light, are not just given contemporary queer interpretation, but are something Trollope put on the surface to be read there.

See also: *The Bertrams; Cousin Henry*

Further Reading

Flint, Kate. "Queer Trollope." *The Cambridge Companion to Anthony Trollope*, edited by Carolyn Dever and Lisa Niles. London: Cambridge University Press, pp. 99–112.

Marcus, Sharon. "Contracting Female Marriage in Anthony Trollope's *Can You Forgive Her?*" *Nineteenth-Century Literature*, vol. 60, no. 3, December 2005, pp. 291–325.

Markwick, Margaret. *New Men in Trollope's Novels*. New York: Ashgate, 2007.

Psomaides, Kathy Alexis. "Heterosexual Exchange and Other Victorian Fictions: *The Eustace Diamonds* and Victorian Anthropology." *Novel: A Forum on Fiction*, vol. 33, no. 1, Autumn 1999, pp. 93–118.

Sedgwick, Eve Kosofsky. "The Warm Decembers." *Raritan*, vol. 6, no. 2, Fall 1986, pp. 51–62.

Sheingold, Leonard. *Is There Life Without Mother? Psychoanalysis, Biography, Creativity*. Hillsdale, NJ: Analytic Press, 2000.

"How the 'Mastiffs' Went to Iceland"

"How the 'Mastiffs' Went to Iceland," was privately printed by J.S. Virtue in 1878 and also published in the *Fortnightly Review*. Unlike Trollope's other travel narratives, it is not a full-length book, and places the author as one of a group, not a solitary traveler with his own agenda. The narrative starts out with observations on the west of Scotland and the Faeroe Islands, only then getting to Iceland, where the travelers stayed in the south, visited only Reykjavik and areas within fifty miles of the capital such as Thingvellir. Later English travelers such as Ethel Tweedie, who visited the northern city of Akureyri in 1888, saw much more of the island. So did William Morris, who began travelling to Iceland, for specifically medievalist purposes, in the 1870s. The fact that Trollope was travelling in a group limits the sense of authoritative assessments typical in his travel narratives and makes it more of a collective enterprise.

The trip was organized by John Burns and the ship was commanded by Captain Kerr, aided by Captain Ritchie. The company also included two admirals and an Australian, Campbell Finlay, who perhaps occasioned the comparison of the trip to Captain Cook's voyages, as well as a painter and a natural philosopher. That there were women in the company (and Mrs. Burns was given equal billing with her husband as the host) also changed his perspective and made it both less solitary and less bureaucratic.

Trollope regarded his journey as part of semiprivate conviviality and not public fact finding. This difference is all the more notable because Iceland, like Australia and New Zealand, was a settler colony, even though its settlement by the Vikings, as Trollope notes, goes back to the tenth century and the founding of the Althing, the first parliament, whose site near Thingvellir Trollope visited. Trollope, though, was not as interested in Iceland's Viking origins as were earlier chroniclers such as Sir John Barrow or as William Morris would be. Trollope noted that most people in Iceland could speak English—interestingly in today's perspective, as otherwise one might see this as a result of mass media and American military presence. He admired the high literacy rate in Iceland, closely associated with the island's Protestantism. And though Trollope noted the presence of the Danish colonial governor in Reykjavik, he did not see the colonial status of Iceland as a political problem his writing needed to address. This was very different from all his Anglophone settler-colony travelogues, where the political future was a key element of his descriptive diagnosis. That the "mastiffs" as a group were named after the ship makes their joint identity, as extant on sea as on land, as important as the target-land of their journey.

See also: Ireland; Scotland; travel

Further Reading

Kassis, Dimitrios. *Icelandic Utopia in Victorian Travel Literature*. London: Cambridge Scholars Press, 2016.

hunting

Trollope discovered fox-hunting as a pleasurable activity during his time in Ireland. Though often seen as primarily an upper-class, landed pursuit, field sports included men of all classes and of varying degrees of virtue and vice, as indicated in the hunting novels of R.S. Surtees (alluded to by Trollope in the surname of the curate in *The American Senator)* and the semi-parody of them in Dickens's *Pickwick Papers*. Hunting provides the basis for the friendship between Phineas Finn and Lord Chiltern, transcending both ethnic and religious differences between English Protestant and Irish Catholic. Hunting was a largely masculine sphere. Trollope himself probably associated his hunting hours in Ireland with other attainments of normative masculinity such as his marriage to Rose Heseltine and his increasing career stability and success. Trollope found hunting both captivating and amusing. He wrote copiously on the pastime not just in his novels but in the *Hunting Sketches* published by the *Pall Mall Gazette* and later in book form by Chapman and Hall.

Women occasionally participated in the hunt both in real life and in Trollope's fiction. This is witnessed by the sporting proclivities of Lizzie Eustace in *The Eustace Diamonds*, although in moral terms she is not a particularly favorable example. Yet

Trollope's published hunting sketches presumed a largely male audience and operated to push the public sphere of Victorian print culture in a more male-gendered direction. Indeed, as extraneous as a modern audience generally finds the hunting scenes, the predominantly female audience of Trollope's initial publication probably found them (as Trollope conceded in his *Autobiography*) supernumerary. Trollope, though, was determined to indulge his delight in hunting. In "The Lady Who Rides to Hounds," included in *Hunting Sketches*, Trollope classes hunting ladies and hunting parsons as unlikely Nimrods (a colloquial terms inspired by the great hunter mentioned in Genesis) who make up for this unlikeliness by participating in the hunt with unusual gusto and attentiveness. Trollope further divides lay hunters into those who demand assistance while hunting and those who demand none, a contrast that can be seen in the interaction between Lucinda Roanoke and Lizzie Eustace in Chapters 38 and 39 of *The Eustace Diamonds*. In *The American Senator* Arabella Trefoil robustly participates in fox-hunting as a prelude to fortune-hunting. However, the scene in *Ayala's Angel* where Nina Baldoni is encouraged to view the chase, but not participate in it, is more representative.

Only rarely does hunting actually affect the plot of a Trollope novel. An instance of this is *Ralph the Heir,* where Squire Gregory Newton is killed in a hunting accident, meaning that his nephew inherits his estate instead of his son. *The American Senator* has the greatest proportion of hunting scenes in any of Trollope's novels, perhaps because hunting as a community activity might have struck Senator Gotobed as one of the key divergences between English and American social life. The character of Captain Glomax—a major figure in the hunt, but of no particular financial or social status outside of it—is puzzling to the American. Glomax is, however, accepted as a matter of fact by the English. The Senator's deluded championship of the scoundrel Goarly because he mistakenly sees him as a misunderstood individualist illustrates by contrast the community feel of the hunt, where the humble man like Laurence Twentyman can be at some sort of par with the great and the good. Similarly (and in a bit of self-satire by Trollope), in *Marion Fay* the post office clerk Samuel Crocker avails himself of the right to hunt in Cumberland even though such an activity might be thought to be (by George Roden, at least, and, revealingly, not by Lord Hampstead) above his social station. The narrator of *Marion Fay* nonetheless complains, in giving an account of the Braeside Harriers, about the excessive fashion associated with hunting.

Heather Miner has determined that the hunting scenes in Trollope's novel possess an essentially conservative valence. The rural, landed verities are perpetually codified by riding to hounds. This is true in many respects. But it is counterweighted by the Irish reverberation of the sport in Trollope and the Surtees-esque raffishness associated with its presence as a theme of fiction. Certainly, as Rob Boddice points out, contemporaries such as Edward Augustus Freeman denounced the sanguinary nature of hunting. Trollope and Freeman had a spirited, amicable debate about the cruelty involved in hunting, with Freeman making many pleas for avoiding cruelty to animals in ways that anticipated later animal rights movements. Trollope did not at all see cruelty to animals as a problem with hunting. Yet on the other hand hunting brings into focus most of the depiction of animality in Trollope's oeuvre. There are times, such as the Hampshire beaver-hunting described in *The Three Clerks,* when Trollope finds the pastime farcical and preposterous when pursued without a due sense of sport. Hunting was transnational for Trollope, as he participated in the kangaroo hunt in Australia and endorsed all the settler prerogative this entailed.

In the generations following Trollope, animal rights became more of a concern and hunting began to seem an upper-class anachronism. Even twentieth-century novelists not unsympathetic to hunting such as Nancy Mitford, Evelyn Waugh, and Anthony Powell began to depict the hunt more satirically. This left Trollope as one of the last novelists to truly capture the pastime at its peak.

See also: *The American Senator*; *The Eustace Diamonds*; Ireland

Further Reading

Bigelow, Gordon. "Trollope and Ireland." *The Cambridge Companion to Anthony Trollope*, edited by Carolyn Dever and Lisa Niles. London: Cambridge University Press, 2010, pp. 96–109.

Boddice, Rob. "Madness and the 'Morality of Field Sports': E.A. Freeman and Anthony Trollope, 1869–1871." *The Historian*, vol. 70, 2008, pp. 1–29.

Miner, Heather. "Trollope and the Hunt for West Country Identity." *Victoriographies*, vol. 1, no. 2, 2011, pp. 221–242.

intrusive narrator

The intrusive narrator in the English novel may be said to be the invention of Henry Fielding. In *Tom Jones* (1749), Fielding introduced a narrator who both makes generalizations about human nature and addresses the audience on what to think about particular characters and situations. The intrusive narrative mode is often identified with the eighteenth century. Jane Austen's narrators, though they make generalizations, are less obvious in their intrusions into the text. When Trollope's elder contemporary William Makepeace Thackeray used intrusive narration, to at least some extent he was knowingly alluding to the fictions of the century whose lifestyle and modes he so loved. Trollope, however, was not operating out of nostalgic pastiche. Neither was the intrusive narrator a simple endorsement of Fielding's jaunty picaresque over Samuel Richardson's psychological interiority; Trollope sampled both.

Trollope does not make as forthright a defense of his literary technique as George Eliot does in Chapter 17 of *Adam Bede*. Eliot's philosophical generalizations in *Middlemarch* are both of greater depth and of more strenuous aspiration than Trollope's narrative observations. Eliot writes at such a level of abstraction—even didacticism—that the reader knows her moral observations are meant to be taken pretty much as verities. But with Trollope it is less certain whether these are just his own opinions or those of the day; their charm and pertinence stems in part from the sense that they emanate from the middle of an actual social situation.

But certainly Eliot and Thackeray would be the most comparable to Trollope's use of the intrusive narrator among his contemporaries. In Europe, the most comparable figures would be Benito Pérez Galdós, particularly in *That Bringas Woman* (1884), and Leo Tolstoy, who learned from and amended Trollope's technique. It is important to note that Trollope did not use the intrusive narrator all the time, and that many nineteenth century novelists both in England (Emily Brontë) and on the Continent (Gustave Flaubert, Theodor Fontane) did not commonly use the intrusive narrator either.

Dickens was a special case; as Mikhail Bakhtin notes, Dickens put his intrusiveness into the double-voicing of his own description, particularly through the use of sarcasm.

In his *Autobiography*, Trollope says the author should "make himself pleasant" and for him pleasant apparently also meant present. Sometimes this presence involves simply voicing opinions the reader will probably feel. When the narrator exclaims "Oh, Johnny Eames!" after Johnny has violated his love for Lily Dale by kissing Amelia Roper, he is simply stating what another writer might imply to the reader by chronicling it. James thought that novelists who admitted their stories were made up were robbing themselves of the chief relevance of their work. The reader many know the novel is an illusion and the action is not really happening, but suspends disbelief in the course of the act of reading. Trollope's Victorian contemporary, Eneas Sweetland Dallas, defended Trollope's telling the reader how the plot would go as it made his books more moral and philosophical in orientation. At other times, the intrusive narrator sets the scene for the reader, providing us access and intimacy to the setting. When, at the beginning of *The American Senator,* the narrator says that they never could comprehend why people would live at Dillsborough, he is showing us that the place is inconspicuous but the people in the novel can nonetheless be interesting. At times the intrusive narrator speeds up the time of the book. In *The Bertrams* "all the necessary records" of the ensuing three of four months are pressed into a few pages. But the most notorious example of the intrusive narrator in Trollope is when the reader is advised what to think about a given character or situation. The narrator tells the reader of *Barchester Towers* in chapter 12 that Eleanor Bold will marry neither Obadiah Slope nor Bertie Stanhope, but that she will be saved from the priggishness of the one and the lassitude of the other. The goal here is to reassure us that Eleanor will be happy. But the intrusive narration also tells us we can assume a relationship of trust with the author. Trollope accuses writers who keep such things a mystery of manipulating their readers.

It is this sort of confidentiality that Trollope seeks in his intrusive narration, not a laying bare of the device or an estrangement later championed by the Russian formalist critics. Yet the reaches of literary history and the suppleness of language itself have meant that it is not illegitimate for critics to bring in such aspects. Trollope's younger contemporary Henry James loathed the intrusive narrator. James defined the artistry of his fiction by reacting against it. James filtered the actions of his novels through a limited point of view. This point of view was presented to the reader sans overt authorial contrivance. Indeed, James laments that Trollope took a particular satisfaction in rending a literary curtain which James thought had good reason to stand. Wayne Booth defended Trollope against poor artistry. But Booth did not center *The Rhetoric of Fiction* (which defended obtrusive narration) around Trollope. Thus Booth did not fully absolve Trollope of the charge of a lack of narrative skill. Some of Trollope's books, such as the short novels *Kept in the Dark* or *Cousin Henry*, do not have intrusive narrators. It may be there is a correlation between intrusive narration and Trollope at full length. (The Victorian critic Geraldine Jewsbury had reservations about just these aspects of Trollope's work.) In *The Warden*, the narrator even remarks that he is in the first volume of the novel, overtly letting the reader know it is a novel. This gesture violates the suspension of disbelief, but it also correlates intrusiveness and expansiveness.

The Trollopian narrator is not necessarily the same thing as "Trollope" himself, however much they might resemble each other. The intrusive narrator in Trollope is rarely seen as a deliberate and justifiable artistic strategy. It is often pictured as a narrative defect, a narrative aspect that has to be defended (as Booth does), or an eccentricity that can be enjoyed. Michael Riffaterre, though, analyzed Trollope's technique as one of stylistic self-awareness. The descriptive details in his character sketches, Riffaterre argued, seemed clichéd and obligatory in their thoroughness, but in their detail foregrounded Trollope's ever-present technique. Intrusive narration is thus a conscious choice that Trollope made to exemplify his own particular strengths as a novelist.

   See also; *An Autobiography*; James, Henry; *The Warden*

Further Reading

Allen, Peter. "Trollope to His Readers: The Unreliable Narrator of *An Autobiography*," *Biography*, vol. 19, no. 1, Winter 1996, pp. 1–18.
Booth, Wayne. *The Rhetoric of Fiction*. Chicago: University of Chicago, 1961.
Kahn, John E. "The Protean Narrator, and the Case of Trollope's Barsetshire Novels." *The Journal of Narrative Technique*, vol. 10, no. 2, Spring, 1980, pp. 77–98.
Lewis, Monica C. "Anthony Trollope and the Voicing of Victorian Fiction." *Nineteenth-Century Literature*, vol. 65, no. 2, September 2010, pp. 141–65.
Markwick, Margaret. *New Men in Trollope's Fiction: Rewriting the Victorian Male*. New York: Routledge, 2016.
Miller, J. Hillis. "Trollope's Thackeray." *Nineteenth-Century Fiction*, vo. 37, no. 3, December 1982, pp. 350–57.
Pickering, Samuel R. Jr. "Trollope's Poetics and Authorial Intrusion in *The Warden* and *Barchester Towers*." *Journal of Narrative Technique*, vol. 3, no. 2, May 1973, pp. 131–40.
Riffaterre, Michael. "Trollope's Metonymies." *Nineteenth-Century Fiction*, vol. 37, no. 3, December 1982, pp. 272–292.

Ireland

Trollope's adult life truly began in Ireland. It was there, in present-day County Offaly, that he had his first job in the post office, as a surveyor's clerk, which began his career of many years in that service. It was there that he met his wife, Rose Heseltine (though she was not herself Irish). And it was there that he discovered his vocation as a novelist.

Trollope chronicled Ireland from the Repealer movement—mentioned in *The Kellys and the O'Kelly's* as embodying "the hopes of Ireland"—to the Phoenix Park murders, from the famine of the Hungry Forties through to the rise of Charles Stewart Parnell. He found an Ireland still wounded by the reabsorption of its short-lived Parliament (a side effect of the American revolution) into Westminster in 1801, and he left an Ireland that would erupt into revolution, independence, and civil war while the sisters in *The Landleaguers*, Ada and Edith Jones, would still be only in middle age. In this—even though Trollope was not Irish, and his novels cannot be considered Irish fiction—he filled a gap in the representation of Ireland that otherwise would have been left vacant. Maria Edgeworth and Sydney Owenson, Lady Morgan were writers in the early nineteenth century who literarily traversed Trollope's Irish terrain in the era previous to him. The collaborative female team of Somerville and Ross may be said to have taken up representing Irish Ascendancy life where Trollope left off. But they did not begin publishing until the 1880s. Without Trollope, there would have been few writers to delineate the Ireland of the 1840s. Whereas William Carleton (1794–1858), formerly a Catholic, converted to Protestantism and began to produce stereotypical renditions of Irish Catholics in his sketches, Trollope, while remaining Protestant and sometimes sketching unsparing portraits of Catholics, never stooped to caricature or stereotype. John Banim (1798–1842) wrote more empathetically about Irish Catholics, but more in the vein of the historical novel than was Trollope's wont. Trollope's friend Charles Lever, though he wrote much of Ireland, stayed within the purview of the Irish military tale established by C.H. Maxwell and satirized by Thackeray in *Barry Lyndon*, and he tended more to anecdote than the serious social representation, that Trollope, whatever his persistent British prejudices, nevertheless soberly undertook. Indeed, he was countering the usual image of the Irish as comic buffoons prevalent in English fiction.

In his remarks on the history of the novel in his 1879 essay on Dickens and Thackeray, Trollope states that the English novel was galvanized by what Walter Scott decided to do for Scotland and what Maria Edgeworth did for Ireland. Thus Ireland can arguably be seen as the start of the novel form in which Trollope wrote. His career could be said to recapitulate his sense of the overall tradition in Irish origins, something perhaps glossed by the name of Thady Macdermot in *The Macdermots of Ballycloran* recalling Edgeworth's Thady Quirk in *Castle Rackrent*. At the beginning of *Castle Richmond*—a novel whose very title might be seen as alluding to Edgeworth's—Trollope states that Irish novels are as out of fashion as historical novels, that publishers want stories of current English life, and thus that this will be his farewell to Ireland. Though in fact this proved not to be true, these remarks cast a different light on Trollope's migration to the lives of the English upper and upper-middle classes as subject. There is a sense that this might have been prompted by career imperatives as much as active predilection. But Trollope was also hinting that his particularly rich and robust portrait of "daily English life" (to use his own sarcastic phrase from *Castle Richmond)* had been inspired by his attempt to render life in the at least half-alien culture of Ireland. Trollope brought his outsider's gaze back among his own people.

Herbert Fitzgerald in *Castle Richmond* thinks he will have to make his own way in life by apprenticing to a London Chancery lawyer (the profession of Trollope's father). This foreshadows Phineas Finn's later career as an Irish MP in London. In this career, Phineas is accused of adultery, fights a duel, and finds himself on trial for murder. But none of this seems to come his way simply because of his Irish background. His wide acceptance into London society and his political career are truncated far more by his own conscience than by a disqualification related to his Hibernian heritage. In fact, Phineas is able almost to drop his Irish identity once he has proven himself in London. But his Irish origins are crucial to such moments as his voting for Church disestablishment, where some hint of his Catholic faith motivates his actions. He does this in a northern English constituency where such a move would be controversial. Phineas became successful as an Irishman. But he does not do so in Ireland itself.

If the half-Catholic, half-Protestant Phineas becomes a clubbable gentleman, at other moments Trollope inserts racialized space into his portrayal of Ireland. In the remark in *Castle Richmond* by Herbert's aunt that she would prefer Islam to Catholicism, there is a presence of an eastern "Other" alongside the Irish one. This sense of difference also applies to Irish space. The differing logistics in Ireland matter in Trollope. There are greater distances between town and country in different counties. Furthermore, there is greater diversity between counties. Trollope said, in the opening to *Castle Richmond*, that Essex is no better a setting than Leicestershire, and thus neither is better than Cork. In fiction, setting should be accidental, not subtend the novel at its core. Yet Kerry in *Castle Richmond*, Roscommon in *The Kellys and the O'Kellys*, Clare in *An Eye for an Eye*, and Galway in *The Landleaguers* are different in Trollope's depiction of them.

Part of Trollope's interest in Ireland was to testify to his admiration for the land and the people, so often ignored or derogated by his peers. In addition, some Irish predilections, such as hunting, are used by Trollope to show an essential commonality between the Irish middle class and the English aristocracy. This is shown in the friendship of Phineas Finn and Lord Chiltern in the two *Phineas* novels. But Trollope is also hoping that integrating Irishness into a truly United Kingdom will broaden the English temperament and maneuver it away from an evangelical Protestantism that he finds overly restrictive. The great commonality between his Irish fiction and the rest of his corpus is a steady antagonism towards evangelical Protestants. Trollope's Protestant Irish clerics, such as the Reverend O'Joscelyn in *The Kellys and the O'Kellys*, come off no better than his Catholic clerics such as the rabble-rousing Father Brosnan in *The Landleaguers*. Though not a Roman Catholic or even sympathetic to Roman Catholicism, Trollope wanted a more plural society that would be catholic, with a small c, in the sense of inclusivity. Though by the time of *The Landleaguers* he had grown pessimistic, and although unlike his idol Gladstone he opposed Irish home rule, Trollope never gave up hope of conciliation between England and Ireland.

See also: *Castle Richmond*; *The Landleaguers*; *The Macdermots of Ballycloran*; *La Vendée*

Further Reading

Corbett, Mary Jean. *Allegories of Union in Irish and English Writing: 1790–1850: Politics, History, and the Family from Edgeworth to Arnold*. London: Cambridge University Press, 2000.

Edwards, Owen Dudley. "Anthony Trollope: The Irish Writer." *Nineteenth-Century Fiction*, vol. 38, no. 1, June 1983, pp. 1–42.

McCourt, John. *Writing the Frontier: Anthony Trollope Between Britain and Ireland*. London: London: Oxford University Press, 2015.

Tracy, Robert. "The Unnatural Ruin: Trollope and Nineteenth-Century Irish Fiction." *Nineteenth-Century Studies*, vol. 37, no. 3, 1982, pp, 358–82.

Is He Popenjoy?

Is He Popenjoy? was serialized in *All the Year Round* from October 1877 to July 1878. As with *The Duke's Children*, the editor Charles Dickens, Jr., asked for cuts, but this time because of potentially controversial themes of illegitimacy. The novel was published in book form by Chapman and Hall in 1878. Just as Trollope wrote *Lady Anna* during his first voyage to Australia, he wrote *Is He Popenjoy?* on his second voyage to Australia, beginning it in Brindisi and ending it in the middle of the Indian Ocean. But, unlike the earlier novel, *Is He Popenjoy*? evinces no Australian thematic connections.

At the beginning of the story, Lord George Germain is heir to his brother, the Marquis (*sic*; not the usual English spelling of "Marquess") of Brotherton. But Lord Brotherton comes home from Italy with an Italian woman, Caterina Luigi, who he claims is his wife. He expels his mother and his siblings from the estate of Manor Cross so that the purported new Marchioness and her son, Lord Popenjoy, can settle in. Popenjoy is a courtesy title, a title given by courtesy to the son of an Earl (or higher). It is called a courtesy title because the earldom ultimately belongs to the father who holds the main title, but allows his son, by courtesy, to use a title as well to give him due honor as heir. The courtesy title is the only truly unique name in English society, one not shared with other family members or with a rank that has public stature. The holder of the courtesy title is the only person in his family with that name, which is why the potential of two possible Popenjoys in the Germain family means matters have run amok. This is different from the similarly-plotted *Ralph the Heir*, where there are two potential claimants named Ralph, but one of them cannot be the heir and still be Ralph. *Marion Fay* (Lord Hampstead) and *The Duke's Children* (Lord Silverbridge) also have courtesy titles. The holder of a courtesy title is always known by the last name and not the first name, unlike everybody else in the family. Even Popenjoy himself, when he succeeds to the marquessate, will be known to his family by his first name. This is seen at the end of *The Duke's Children* where the married Isabel Boncassen struggles to call her husband Plantagenet rather than Silverbridge.

The conceit, or even central joke, of the novel is that both possible Popenjoys, the Marquis' son and his brother Lord George's son, are babies. The tale is thus not of a Tichborne-style claimant who arrives alleging his right to the title as an adult. It is one of a disputed marriage which, if it is not legitimate, will lead to an alternative heir. The Venerable Henry Lovelace, the Dean of Brotherton Cathedral, becomes concerned for the rights of the potential offspring of his daughter Mary. Mary is married to George Germain, the Marquis' brother and heir. The Dean wants to disprove the legitimacy of the alleged current Popenjoy in the hope those rights might pass to a future Popenjoy borne by his daughter. His son-in-law is, in turn, tempted by his flirtation with Adelaide Houghton. Yet George Germain stays sufficiently true to his wife for the scenario to play out in his favor without scandal. Adelaide's cousin, Jack de Baron (in perhaps a slight reflection of the Crawfords in Jane Austen's *Mansfield Park*) appeals to Mary Germain. But she grows in her marriage and ends up being both Marchioness of Brotherton and mother of the genuine Popenjoy. There is suggestion of at least potential adultery in Mary's relationship with Jack de Baron, especially in the scene in the fifth chapter of the second volume, where Mary prepares for the ball at which the Kappa-Kappa is danced. This comes very near to breaking out of the then-pregnant prosperities of how a married woman's life was represented.

Despite dealing with the aristocracy, *Is He Popenjoy?* is not a silver fork novel because it is not out to titillate the audience with the lives of rich, socially elite people even though most of its readership will be out of that group. As Frederik Van Dam observes, the materialism of the aristocracy is criticized in the book. With this conjunction of current aristocratic lifestyles and the implied materialism of the book's own middle-class audience, *Is He Popenjoy?* recognizes the social importance of the aristocracy to English life. But the novel also show aristocrats as normal people with normal human desires and plights, and, effectually, projects aristocracy out towards the middle class. Trollope indeed gives his middle-class audience a sense of what the lives of English ladies and gentlemen in the extended sense might be.

The novel is also set in a changing London where social roles and identities are simply far less clear-cut than they were in the world of the Barchester novels. Scumberg's Hotel in Albemarle Street is foreign-owned and indirectly managed. The Rev. Joseph Groschut, the converted Jew, whose sexual and ecclesiastical impudence are the despair of Henry Lovelace, the rival feminists Baroness Banmann—who promotes women's rights while styling herself still a baroness of the Holy Roman Empire—and the American physician Olivia Q. Fleabody, bespeak a more plural and multiracial social tableau. So does the oft-mentioned dark complexion of the half-Italian baby initially alleged to be Popenjoy. A leitmotif in *Is He Popenjoy?* is the Kappa-Kappa. This is a dance of allegedly Moldavian origins that becomes the fad of the day. Mary Germain dances the Kappa-Kappa at the gracious Mrs. Montacute Jones's festive late-spring party. Trollope uses the Kappa-Kappa dance as a humorous thread. But he also uses it to point out the accelerating social life of late–Victorian London and the increasing curiosity about the foreign and modern in high English society. Even the foreign nature of the Marquis' Italian wife, at one time compared to a woman from the Russian peninsula of Kamchatka, is, however set aside by the plot, also part of its cosmopolitan aspects. The son of the foreigner loses out in this novel. But in *Marion Fay* Trollope has the son of an Italian aristocrat pronounced eligible to marry the daughter of a peer. Though of high ecclesiastical rank, Henry Lovelace is the grandson of a stable keeper who, partially through his own social ambitions, becomes not just Dean of Brotherton but grandfather of a future Marquis. The title of the Marquis and the deanery of the clergyman have the same name. This calls attention to their difference as much as their similarity. That the delegitimizing of the first Popenjoy means that the grandson of the Dean of Brotherton will, as Popenjoy, someday be the marquess of Brotherton smooths out this difference. But the understanding that, to perpetuate itself, the aristocracy must in marital terms branch out a bit is endorsed here as elsewhere in Trollope's oeuvre. In the background, London as such is growing more mercantile. The marketplace of products, as portrayed in *The Struggles of Brown, Jones, and Robinson*, is extending to that of ideas. Olivia Fleabody's feminist campaign is portrayed as not just polemical but money-making in nature.

As Robert Tracy points out, the surname Germain—though well attested in the annals of the British aristocracy—is also a pun on "germane." Popenjoy is a name both deliberately comic and memorable. *Is He Popenjoy?* combines this sort of jaunty humor with the seriousness of the underlying stakes to produce one of Trollope's darkest and yet most scintillating comedies.

See also: *The American Senator*; *Dr. Wortle's School*; *Marion Fay*

Further Reading

Hagan, John. "The Divided Mind of Anthony Trollope." *Nineteenth-Century Fiction*, vol. 14, no. 1, June 1959, pp. 1–26.
Tracy, Robert. *Trollope's Later Novels*. Berkeley: University of California Press, 1978.
Van Dam, Frederik. *Anthony Trollope's Late Style: Victorian Liberalism and Literary Form*. Edinburgh: Edinburgh University Press, 2016.

James, Henry

As a novelist, Henry James (1843–1916) had many interests in common with Trollope: transatlantic high society, youth and maturation, and individual psychology. Yet his attitude toward Trollope was always laced with criticism. In the same 1883 essay he praised Trollope for being "strong, genial, and abundant" but said Trollope's work was "of a quality less fine" than Dickens, Thackeray, or Eliot, and that he "published too much" to the point of "gross fecundity." James makes Trollope's productivity seem almost a vice. He recollects that on the one occasion when he came into contact with Trollope, on an 1986 transatlantic voyage, all Trollope did was stay in his room and write, an assiduity judged almost to be *gauche.*

Trollope was frankly commercial in his approach. James, though at times yearning for financial success, dedicated himself, in the way of Flaubert, to making the novel into an art form. James accordingly turned away from the obtrusive narration and gestures to the reader of Trollope. He preferred to set his characters in a sort of proscenium where they would be presented as not being the products of artifice and given, as fictions, their own cognitive independence. James's use of point-of-view and free indirect style posited a more artistically deliberate alternative to Trollope's freewheeling, editorializing rambles. James also allowed for irony, surprise, and upending the reader's expectations. This marked him as divergent from Trollope's ardor to observe the author-reader contract to the letter. Yet James's early reviews of Trollope are strangely emotional. They reveal a sense of envy and emulation was well as artistic disapproval.

But James also learned from Trollope. Both novelists center their stories on the wealthy and on those adjacent to them, without ever being snobbish or admiring wealth for its own sake. Both present a gallery of characters in a common milieu but with distinct relationships between and among individuals; this technique has made both novelists' works amenable to later representation in movie and television adaptations. Trollope reveled in the depth and variety of English cultural institutions—Parliament, the Church of England, horse-racing, the hunt—whose absence in American culture James found contributing to the morbidity and inwardness of Nathaniel Hawthorne. Both chronicle a world in which the steamship and the telegraph are bringing the people closer, and in which American power is rising. James is often judged to have borrowed from Trollope at one very specific point. Isabel Boncassen, the young, fresh, physically robust, wealthy American girl who wins the heart of Lord Silverbridge in *The Duke's Children*, is quite similar to James's Isabel Archer in *Portrait of a Lady* (1881), who is also a high-spirited, venturesome, and suddenly rich American girl who wins the heart of the reformist peer, Lord Warburton. Isabel Boncassen gladly accepts Silverbridge's proposal, and they become "Darby and Joan," whereas Isabel Archer rejects Warburton and marries the impecunious, scheming, and sadistic Gilbert Osmond, for whom there could be no worse spouse. This underscores the way in which James would not let his characters have the happy endings that Trollope seemed to cherish. The roles of Lady Mabel Grex and Frank Tregear in *The Duke's Children*, as a man and a woman romantically interested in each other, but too poor to marry, leading the man to marry a wealthy woman, limn the contours of the plot of James's *The Wings of The Dove* (1902). In this novel, Kate Croy and Merton Densher plot to have Merton marry the rich and terminally ill Milly Theale. Though we have no record that Trollope read *Portrait of A Lady*, it was published in 1881, as Trollope was writing *The Landleaguers*, and we do know Trollope kept up with reading his younger contemporaries, as his fatal stroke occurred while reading T. Anstey's *Vice Versa*. Thus it is reasonable to speculate that the way the impresario Mahomet M. Moss and Madame Socani seem romantically involved even as Moss tries to seduce the young singer Rachel O'Mahony mirror the way Gilbert Osmond and Madame Merle have some sort of connection while Osmond courts Isabel Archer. Perhaps Trollope was recognizing how James had borrowed from him, in the manner of the two Isabels, and was stylishly returning the favor.

Whatever the fate of this conjecture, James and Trollope had different approaches to writing fiction. But they spoke to the same issues. James rebuked Trollope so vigorously precisely because he felt they were on common terrain. Importantly, James's doubts about Trollope did not blind him to the British author's virtues. He even noticed Trollope's practical cosmopolitanism, the way his postal work and travel writing took him to so many corners of the world, something stereotypes of Trollope tend to mask. James's assessment could curiously be said to have helped Trollope long term. That Trollope was not seen as part of the canon of high literature—that he was not a writer one had to read, or that reading would help one ascend into more rarefied cultural climes—meant that he could resurface in the twentieth century as a guilty pleasure, to be read in the same way detective stories or thrillers were read, with the same lack of inhibition by cultural pretense. If James had seen Trollope as Dickens' equal, later critics like Michael Sadleir might not have taken Trollope up with the same verve and gusto. Thus, as James said, "Trollope did not write for posterity; he wrote for the day, the moment; but these are just the writers whom posterity is apt to put into its pocket" (qtd. Smalley 545).

See also: Hawthorne, Nathaniel; intrusive narrator; *North America*

Further Reading

Michie, Elsie. "The Odd Couple: Anthony Trollope and Henry James." *Henry James Review*, vol. 27, no. 1, Winter 2006, pp. 10–23.
Polhemus, Robert. *The Changing World of Anthony Trollope*. Berkeley: University of California Press, 1968.

Jews

Trollope wrote in a mid–Victorian atmosphere where a man of Jewish descent, Benjamin Disraeli, could become Prime Minister; where Protestantism, especially evangelical Protestantism, had a natural empathy for the people of Israel; and where the fellow novelist he most respected, George Eliot, could devote an entire novel, *Daniel Deronda*, to extolling the Zionist cause. Yet, as Trollope's novels reveal, Victorian England was also a world where there was routine and casual anti–Semitism. Jews entering public life are subject to calumny and vitriol. This is seen in Trollope in the references to Jewish moneylenders in *Mr. Scarborough's Family* and in several of Trollope's characters.

The Rev. Joseph Emilius in *The Eustace Diamonds* and *Phineas Redux* is revealed to be a Central European Jew, forger, and murderer. The Rev. Joseph Groschut in *Is He Popenjoy?*, similarly a converted Jew turned Anglican cleric, is not as bad as Emilius. But he is no paladin, either. Ferdinand Lopez—remembering that Spanish surnames in England were often associated with Sephardic Jewry—in *The Prime Minister* is a cad, swindler, and opportunist who beguiles a respectable English girl, Emily Wharton, to marry him, leading to despair and disaster. In *Framley Parsonage*, Ludovic Lufton speaks to his mother about possibly testing the market for some acreage on his estate, but avers that he does not want "a Jew tailor" (*Framley Parsonage* p. 168) investing his savings at Lufton. Solomon Aram in *Orley Farm* is singled out precisely because he does not conform to the stereotype of a Jew, which is more frequently shown in Trollope's fiction by figures such as M. Mahomet Moss in *The Landleaguers* and, inferentially, Melmotte in *The Way We Live Now*, who fits the Jewish stereotype of the heedless speculator and whose wife is described as having Jewish features. This is true even though Melmotte himself is never identified as a Jew. All these characters and situations underlie the accusations by scholars such as Bryan Cheyette, Christopher Herbert, and Michael Ragussis that Trollope is deeply invested in an anti–Semitism that is in turn constitutive of a certain vision of English landed gentility. In *Doctor Thorne*, as Cheyette points out, Trollope opens by saying that not only is England not a commercial society, but that hopefully she will never become one. Jews, when successful in English society, were associated with trade, capitalism, and mobility.

Yet this process of commercialization is one that was incurably occurring in Trollope's own time. This is demonstrated by works of his such as "Why Frau Frohmann Raised Her Prices," *The Three Clerks*, and *The Struggles of Brown, Jones, and Robinson*. Trollope himself had Jewish connections by marriage. Trollope's sister in-law, Theodosia Garrow Trollope, was half–Jewish, her mother having been one of the performing trio of Abrams sisters.

And there are several moments in Trollope where he seems more sanguine about the possibility of a convergence of Jew and Gentile. In *Rachel Ray*, Mr. Hart is sponsored as a Liberal candidate for a rural Devon constituency backed by middle-class and Evangelical Christian elements. He is foiled by landed and High Church interests. There is no sense that Mr. Hart's defeat is one for all time. In the next election, he might have a chance, and he is not described so adversely by the book's narrator as to preclude him from that chance. This is especially true, as Steven Amarnick has argued, because the thrust of the novel as a whole is towards greater pluralism and less narrow intolerance. In *Nina Balatka*, Anton Trendellsohn, a Jew, wishes to marry the gentile Nina Balatka. Not only does the narrative permit them to marry, but it is not just Nina who makes a sacrifice for love. Anton has been proven steadfast by not believing false rumors of Nina's infidelity. Intermarriage will cost him as much of his standing among Jews. In addition, as Amarnick shows, Anton as a name is a version of Anthony. In turn, Trendellsohn, not a naturally occurring Central European Jewish surname, but rather "Mendelssohn" with a T put on it, has the same initial letter as Trollope. The Jew, Trollope might be implying, *c'est moi*. Cheyette, though, has argued that Trollope's story is only superficially philo–Semitic. According to Cheyette, Trollope Orientalizes the milieu by seeing deep anti–Semitism as a Central European phenomenon. Thereby, he excuses the more indirect and "tasteful" mechanisms of British anti–Semitism.

There are conflicting signals about whether Madame Max Goesler in the Palliser books is a Jew herself or simply the widow of a Jew. But she is certainly portrayed as a benign character, both in her refusal to take advantage of the generosity of the aging Duke of Omnium and her marriage to the tested but in the end virtuous Phineas Finn. Finn, an Irish Catholic, and the presumed Jewess Goesler are among Trollope's most multi-ethnic marriage-couples, and Phineas' closeness to Jewishness is heightened by his having a Hebrew name meaning a dark-skinned person in the language of the Old Testament, as well as the traditional legendary links between the Semitic Phoenicians and aboriginal Irishmen. In Phineas and Madame Max's relationship, Trollope does not enforce a mandatory High Anglican gentility.

The unresolved question is whether Trollope believed the character of the Jew was eternally fixed, or whether he believed Jews could change by intermarriage adaptation, and modernization. This is the difference between an actively racialist anti–Semitism and one that was merely unexamined or habitual. In *South Africa* Trollope said that, contrary to stereotypes about Jews as hoarding and avaricious, he found them as fiscally liberal as other people. Yet conversion to Christianity and entry into the priesthood do not improve the moral character of Emilius or Joseph Groschut in *Is He Popenjoy?*, though they both enjoy temporary intimacy with the aristocracy. If we do assume Madame Max is Jewish, we must note that her marriage to Phineas does not produce children, so Trollope does not let us see genealogically what hybridity might bring. The status of the Jew in Trollope remains contingent and unresolved.

See also: Disraeli, Benjamin; *Doctor Thorne*; *The Eustace Diamonds*; *Nina Balatka*

Further Reading

Amarnick, Steven. "Can You Forgive Him? Trollope, Jews, and Prejudice." *The Routledge Research Companion to Anthony Trollope*, edited by Deborah Denenholz Morse, Margaret Markwick, and Mark W. Turner, New York: Routledge, 2017, pp. 336–46.

Cheyette, Bryan. *Between "Race" and "Culture" Representations of "The Jew" in English and American Literature.* Stanford, CA: Stanford University Press, 1996.

Herbert, Christopher. *Culture and Anomie: Ethnographic Imagination in the Nineteenth Century.* Chicago: University of Chicago, 1991.

Park, Clara Claiborne. "Grease, Balance, and Point of View in the Work of Anthony Trollope." *Hudson Review*, vol. 60, no. 3, Autumn 2007, pp. 435–44.

John Caldigate

John Caldigate was serialized in *Blackwood's* (which Trollope misunderstood as wanting cuts, which he was prepared to make, but which were not made) and published by Chapman and Hall in 1879. It is Trollope's longest and most ambitious novel involving Australia, although not all the action is set there. John Caldigate comes from a well-to-do family but gets into bad habits and falls into debt. His debts are paid off and he goes to Australia to seek a new fortune, having fallen in love with Hester Bolton before he leaves. In the goldfields of New South Wales, he and his friend, Dick Shand, make a profit. Though Caldigate reforms, Shand falls further into dissolution, and drops off the canvas. Caldigate takes up with a local woman, Euphemia Smith. Although he states his intention of marrying her, he neither marries her nor gives a legally enforceable promise of marriage. Caldigate returns to England a redeemed man, marries Hester, and they have a child. Hearing of Caldigate's newfound wealth, Euphemia, with an unscrupulous male associate, tracks him to England and files a lawsuit against Caldigate, in which he is defended by John Jorum. He is convicted and sentenced to prison. Shand's reappearance exonerates Caldigate. But, even before that his case against him had been basically disproven by the exertion of Samuel Bagwax, a postal clerk who demonstrates that Euphemia had forged a postmark in her effort to blackmail Caldigate. Bagwax, perhaps the book's most memorable figure, is not only a heroic self-portrait of Trollope, but of the modern bureaucrat who uses the meticulous procedures of his trade in favor of justice and the happiness of others. Trollope here welded his moralizing as a novelist, his professional expertise and sense of ethics as a former postal worker, and his optimism that colonial stories can, and should, have happy endings. The novel is clairvoyant both in its sense of Australia as an open society and one economically dependent on natural resources. As Kate Thomas points out, the traditional marriage plot has to vie for visibility with a more novel postal plot. This dislodges the centrality of traditional narrative momentum, and therefore, potentially, of the Eurocentric gaze itself.

The extreme sensationalism and melodrama of this plot is noticeable, and links *John Caldigate* with the sensation novels of Wilkie Collins and Mary Elizabeth Braddon. There is a relation between the sensation novel as a genre and distance. This is seen in the presence of Australia in Mary Elizabeth Braddon's *Lady Audley's Secret* or for that matter in Frances Trollope's *The Widow Barnaby*. Australia is so far away that one can lead another life there, and this is ideal for the sensation novel's emphasis on secrets and duplicity. Equally, Australia is reachable by post and has an interoperable postal system with that of Britain. Thus Bagwax's researches, though involving vast amounts of space, can bear fruit.

An interesting counterpoint in *John Caldigate* is that, Sydney aside, the major Australian places in the book, Ahalala and Nobble, are, though vividly described, completely fictional. Yet Cambridgeshire, and Cambridge itself, are described with exacting realism. This indicates how, despite his Australasian travels, colonial space for Trollope was also conjectural space, something reaffirmed in a very different genre in Trollope's *The Fixed Period*.

Though *John Caldigate* has traditionally been one of Trollope's most neglected novels, in the early twenty-first century it attracted a striking upsurge of interest centered around its colonial themes. In 2015 Simon Grennan's graphic novel, *Dispossessions: A Novel of Few Words*, adapted the book, playing up the analogy between the novel's themes of greed, risk, and loss and those attendant on the process of colonialism itself. *John Caldigate* is coming to be classed as one of Trollope's major long fictions.

See also: Australia and New Zealand; The Fixed Period

Further Reading

Grennan, Simon. *Transforming Anthony Trollope: "Dispossession," Victorianism and Nineteenth-Century Word and Image.* Leuven: Leuven University Press, 2015.

Setecka, Agnieszka. "'Gold…. Was Certainly Very Attractive; But He Did Not Like New South Wales as a Country in Which to Live': The Representation of Australian Society in Trollope's *John Caldigate*." *Studia Anglia Posnaniensia*, vol. 52, no. 4, 2017, pp. 395–408.

Thomas, Kate. *Postal Pleasures: Sex, Scandal, and Victorian Letters.* London: Oxford University Press, 2012.

Van Dam, Frederik. *Anthony Trollope's Late Style: Victorian Liberalism and Literary Form.* Edinburgh: Edinburgh University Press, 2016.

The Kellys and the O'Kellys

The Kellys and the O'Kellys, published in 1848 by Henry Colborn, was much more optimistic in tone than Trollope's debut novel, *The Macdermots of Ballycloran*. Unfortunately, Trollope soon found that Irish novels of any sort were not in demand, as his second novel sold only 140 copies.

In *The Macdermots of Ballycloran* Trollope depicts Mohill as "an impoverished town—the property of a non-resident landlord—destitute of anything to give it interest or prosperity—without business, without trade, and without society." Similarly, in *The Kellys and the O'Kellys* he writes that the village of Dunmore

> has nothing about it which can especially recommend it to the reader. It has none of those beauties which have taught Irishmen to consider their country as "the first flower of the earth, the first gem of the sea." It is a dirty, ragged little town, standing in a very poor part of the country, with nothing in it to induce the traveler to go out of his beaten rack.

Trollope quotes from Thomas Moore's lyrical eulogy of Ireland to show he is doing something very different from Moore's poetry or local-color novels such as those by Maria Edgeworth or Lady Morgan. Far from saying that the reader should value Ireland more because there is quaint or peculiar interest there, he casts Ireland as a reflection of the universal. It is distinctive only in its poverty and anonymity, drawing his Irish fictions towards a critical social realism.

All of Trollope's Irish novels have common aspects. But they are inflected by the time in which they were written and Trollope's sense of himself as a novelist. While *The Kellys and the O'Kellys* is as Irish as *The Macdermots*, it is much more typically Trollopian, with its excursus on hunting—a pastime Trollope became an aficionado of while in Ireland—and horse racing, its parallel plots, and its happy ending in an affirmation of nuptial bliss and the exclusion of malefactors. Barry Lynch's attempt, verging on violence and insanity, to defraud his sister Anty (Anastasia) of her share of their father's inheritance is remedied by how Anty's suitor, Martin Kelly, begins to feel real love for her after at first passively being comfortable with her as a source of wealth. Francis O'Kelly, Lord Ballandine, also ends up marrying for love and rescuing Fanny Wyndham from the similarly avaricious plans of Lord Cashel. Though separated by class and religion, Martin Kelly and Francis O'Kelly enjoy an easy male camaraderie. They are linked by structural analogies (both are plagued by malignant young wastrels, Lord Kilcullen and Barry Lynch), and though the plot does not end with the two families intertwining by blood, the outcome clearly exudes hope not only that both can get along but that there could be an Ireland which has room for the humanity and happiness of both kinds of people. That Francis O'Kelly (Lord Ballandine) feels himself Irish despite being able to go to England and function there, that he does not want to make his way in London and have to name his son Ernest, is an affective forerunner of the much more politically radical identification with Ireland of Florian Jones in *The Landleaguers*.

There is a lack of miscegenation in *The Kellys and the O'Kellys*. At the end, they remain separate families, with no hint or potential of intermarriage. But this does not preclude the realization that Lord Ballandine, in remaining Irish, is slowly and, admittedly, slightly relinquishing his Anglo privilege, if not his aristocratic status.

The Kellys and the O'Kellys has some early Trollopian quirks. Salient among those are the Disraeli-like references to Sir Robert Peel and Daniel O'Connell as real political figures. (The novel was published by the same publisher as Disraeli's 1840s novels, Henry Colburn.) But the horse-racing intrigues surrounding Brien Boru (the horse, not the medieval Irish warrior), and the double plot that enables not only narrative variety but an insight into diverse social strands are convincing. Trollope neither talks up nor talks down the Irish too much—instead, he employs a clear-eyed lens he was to apply to the English in his major fiction.

See also: Ireland; *The Macdermots of Ballycloran*

Further Reading

Berol, Laura. "The Anglo-Irish Threat in Thackeray and Trollope's Writing of the 1840s." *Victorian Literature and Culture*, vol. 32, no. 1, 2004, pp. 103–116.

Faulkner, Karen. "Anthony Trollope's Apprenticeship." *Nineteenth-Century Fiction*, vol. 38, no. 2, September 1983, pp. 161–188.

Kept in the Dark

Kept in the Dark is Trollope's most psychologically intricate short novel. It was published in 1882, the year of Trollope's death, in *Good Words*, where twenty years earlier Trollope had serialized *Rachel Ray* and a decade earlier had published *The Golden Lion of Granpere*. That same year, Chatto and Windus published the novel in book form. Set in Devon, *Kept in the Dark* concerns the inner feelings of a couple in whose marriage trust has been broken. George Western decides his marriage to the former Cecilia Holt is lacking in moral grounds after he finds out she was once engaged to the rakish Sir Francis Geraldine. Having not told him this at first, she finds it a secret too big to disclose. When Cecelia's Italian friend Miss Altifiorla finds out the power of this secret, she uses it as a psychological hold over Cecilia. Miss Altifiorla revenges herself on Western, who had expressed his dislike for her openly, and makes her own play for the hand of Sir Francis. She gets her comeuppance, however, and George and Cecilia are reconciled. George learns to be less rigid and understands that for a marriage to be successful he has to be emotionally open, and Cecilia learns to discard the rhetoric of the secret after learning how it can be exploited by bad actors such as Miss Altifiorla.

The theme of the secret brings the book close to the genre of the sensation novel, but the emphasis is on the psychological status of the characters. The title phrase "kept in the dark" comes from George Western's musings about how Cecilia has burst the illusion of a Victorian married man that he is the first to capture his wife's heart, and moreover had gone to a point of keeping it a secret from him. Helen Blythe has commented that the novel is a drama of men learning to realize they have imposed their own image of women over reality. Cecilia's non-disclosure has thus ruptured the assumptions of the patriarchy and of the differential treatment of men and women. This causes George and Cecilia to have to renegotiate their marriage on a more psychologically egalitarian basis.

Kept in the Dark is one of Trollope's most satisfying shorter novels. It is written with an intensity, austerity, and psychological acuity of the sort for which Trollope does not often receive credit. It is an example of the same sort of marital difficulties examined in *He Knew He Was Right*, with the fortunate difference that George Western is a man able to listen to reason. Like *Is He Popenjoy?*, *Marion Fay*, and even *Ayala's Angel*, there is an Italian element to the *dramatis personae*, here, in the person of Miss Altifiorla, which may well be due to the influence of Trollope's brother Thomas Adolphus, and certainly is a hallmark of the later work.

See also: *He Knew He Was Right*; *Lady Anna*

Further Reading

Blythe, Helen Lucy. "Forms of Storytelling;, Repetition, and Voices in Anthony Trollope's *Kept in the Dark*." *The Routledge Research Companion to Anthony Trollope*, edited by Deborah Denenholz Morse, Margaret Markwick, and Mark W. Turner, New York: Routledge, 2017, pp. 177–90.
Cockshut, A.O.J. *Anthony Trollope: A Critical Study*. New York: New York University Press, 1968.

Lady Anna

Lady Anna was serialized in the *Fortnightly Review* between April 1873 and 1874. It was published by Chapman and Hall in 1874. Trollope wrote the novel aboard ship during his journey in 1871 to visit his son Fred in Australia. Both in terms of the maritime scene of its composition and the role Australia plays in the novel's ending, the novel could be included among Trollope's Australian fiction, although for most of its course it is thoroughly ensconced in the Lake Country to the northwest of England. The novel is one of the few Trollope set in a "past," even though it is the 1830s of Trollope's youth and not the previous century, as is the case with *La Vendée*. The novel is also, with *Harry Hotspur of Humblethwaite*, one of Trollope's two Cumberland novels. The novel's local landmarks like Applethwaite and Lovel Tarn, though made up, are very redolent of actual Cumberland and Westmoreland names. Real landmarks like Derwentwater are prominently mentioned. With the prominent role played by Daniel Thwaite and his tailor father, the local suffix "—thwaite" is present in this novel, in *Marion Fay* where there is a character called Mr. Amblethwaite, and in *Harry Hotspur*. Chapter 26 of the novel is entitled "The Keswick Poet," and this sage figure who gives Daniel Thwaite advice about love and money is clearly based on the Lake District's most famous literary personage, William Wordsworth. The figure of Daniel's father, Thomas Thwaite, a radical working-class activist, described as being friends with the leading poets of the day, reflects the considerable social unrest and cultural energy in northwest England during that period.

As background to the present time of the novel, in the 1810s Lord Lovel marries a young woman of modest background named Josephine Murray. Six months into their marriage, though, he informs her that she is already married. Thus, Josephine is neither his wife nor Lady Lovel. Lovel tells Josephine she can live with him in his yacht off Sicily as his mistress, but not in any other role. Josephine, who considers herself the rightful Lady Lovel, not only spurns the Earl's offer but believes there is no other marriage and sues for her right to be the legitimate countess. She is evicted from Lovel Grange, though, and, with her young daughter, Lady Anna, she seeks refuge with a kindly and politically radical tailor, Thomas Thwaite. Lady Lovel takes action in court to prove there was no bigamy, and her suit is successful. But Lady Lovel is not given the right to occupy Lovel Grange, nor does she receive the respect of the aristocracy in the two lake counties. Unlike in *Orley Farm*, where Lady Mason tries to keep an estate not legally her own, Lady Lovel is entitled to the estate and is trying to occupy a home and land that is legally hers.

By the time Lady Anna is nearing adulthood, her father, in his sixties, returns from Italy to Lovel Grange. He acknowledges Anna as his daughter. Yet he makes no move to see her and continues to deny her legitimacy. When the old Earl dies, he leaves his money to an Italian woman living with him, Camilla Spondi (not, it is implied, the same Italian woman to whom he had alleged a previous marriage). The title and land, though, are entailed in the male line. They thus pass to his distant cousin, Frederic Lovel. It occurs to the lawyers representing both Josephine Murray and the new young earl that the perfect way to resolve the situation would be for Frederic Lovel to marry Lady Anna.

The Countess recognizes the appeal of this solution. She seeks to damp down the growing sense of affinity between Anna and Thwaite's son, Daniel. Daniel and his father have accompanied the countess and Anna to London. Anna agrees to meet Frederic Lovel. She grows to like and respect him. But Anna's heart is given to Daniel. Anna urges a compromise whereby her title would be acknowledged but Frederic would keep the remainder of the estate. Frederic persists in courting Anna, and the two branches of the Lovel family take a trip to the ruins of Bolton Abbey together. Here, Anna sprains her ankle. This injury leads Frederic to proclaim his love, which Anna graciously spurns.

There are several speculations possible as to why the novel is set in the near past. One of those may be the aforementioned opportunity to allude to Wordsworth and other luminaries of the age. Another might be because the class difference between Anna and Daniel might have seemed less drastic later in the nineteenth century. But a tempting angle would be to note that the novel is set in the period of Trollope's own boyhood. Further, the Countess's scrambling for money and status, although done in a very different mien, is not dissimilar to that of Trollope's own mother, Frances Milton Trollope, as she struggled with a brood of children and an impecunious husband. Indeed, when Lady Lovel despairs of her daughter's obstinacy, she repairs to London and takes rooms in Keppel Street, near Russell Square. This was where Anthony Trollope himself was born.

The story at its core is a struggle between mother and daughter. Lady Lovel wants the title not out of greed or out of ambition but to vindicate the validity of her marriage. Lady Anna, like other Trollope heroines such as Nina Balatka, Linda Tressel, and Clara Desmond of *Castle Richmond*, wants to make the choice of her heart. Lady Lovel's increasing bitterness at Anna's insistence on marrying out of her class turns her violent, in a manner reminiscent of Robert Kennedy in *Phineas Redux*.

There is also the larger question of Lady Anna's title. If it is indeed legitimate, would be unseemly for her to marry a tailor's son? The solution to this social quandary is a kind of double win. The right of Lady Anna and her mother to their titles is vindicated, but Lady Anna and her husband go off to Sydney and lead a new life in the Antipodes.

Though in legal terms he is entitled only to the earldom and estate, Frederic Lovel also gets money. Both Lady Anna and, on the authorial level, Trollope himself, do not want to see the status of an English earl become meaningless. There is individual disinvestment in the class system, but this is combined with a total lack of any institutional critique of it. In a cameo portrait of the rector of Yoxham in Yorkshire, who marries Daniel and Lady Anna, Trollope makes clear that he recognizes the contamination of English society by preoccupations with class and power. But Trollope nonetheless stresses that there could be considerable value to it.

The novel ends by promising a sequel in which the travel of the happy couple is chronicled and Daniel will be portrayed as older and wiser. Trollope never wrote such a sequel, although Australian narrative material that might have been used in furthering the chronicle of the Thwaites was employed to advance the very different plot of *John Caldigate*. The narrative leaves open the question of whether Anna Thwaite will use the title of "Lady." Is it "Daniel and Lady Anna Thwaite" in Australia? Whatever the intention or demeanor of the bearers, this appellation would inevitably come across as snobbish in Australian terms. The issues of downward mobility, upward mobility, and the new landscape of the colonies are left off the canvas in *Lady Anna*. But they would be factors in Australian colonial life, as Trollope's travel book *Australia and New Zealand* demonstrates. Trollope is usually seen as confirming the entrenched power of the British aristocracy and landed gentry by hypergamy (the worthy young man or woman marrying up into the upper classes). But Lady Anna's hypogamy, and her adaptation to the more modest and geographically distant circumstances of her husband, give a revised picture of Trollope's sense of social mobility. Lady Lovel, though, is vindicated against the defamation offered by her late husband, and, with the young Earl graciously offering her a home for life, she enters old age satisfied.

In 2015 Craig Baxter adapted the novel, along with the story of Trollope writing it while bound for Australia, into a play, *Lady Anna, All at Sea*.

See also: Harry Hotspur in *Sir Harry Hotspur of Humblethwaite*; *John Caldigate*

Further Reading

Morse, Deborah Denenholz. *Reforming Trollope: Race, Gender, and Englishness in the Fiction of Anthony Trollope*. New York: Routledge, 2016.
Tracy. Robert. *Trollope's Later Novels*. Berkeley: University of California Press, 1978.

The Landleaguers

For *The Landleaguers* (1883, published by Chatto and Windus) Trollope made two trips to Ireland when he was already in ill health in order to conduct research and make sure of the novel's contemporary relevance. He completed about three-fourths of the novel, and his publisher issued the book in its unfinished state. That Trollope chose to spend his final strength writing about contemporary Ireland shows how closely he followed issues there and how bitter his disappointment was that the Irish population was tending more towards revolution and opposition to the English presence there rather than the sort of negotiated, plural settlement he might have wished for. Emily Lawless's *Hurrish* (1886) is a novel by a younger Anglo-Irish writer which, though different from Trollope's work in tone and torque, similarly expresses hope for a peaceful and pluralistic solution to the Irish question. This hope for peace was dashed by the Civil War and partition of the country in the early twentieth century. *The Landleaguers* mentions the Phoenix Park murders which effectively paralyzed any kind of Irish reform for the next thirty years, and so Trollope is able to register the near-term future of our world.

In *The Landleaguers*, Gerard O'Mahony, sometime member for Cavan, is in fact an American elected by Irish Catholics because he would advocate their cause eloquently in Britain. That he is universally judged to make a fool of himself illustrates the risks of this sort of representation: that extending the franchise to the Irish will produce demagogues and opportunists using the Irish cause as an excuse to advance their own interests. But Trollope also instructs the reader that integrating Ireland into the British polity means allowing the people of Ireland full access to democracy as that obtained in Britain itself.

Trollope clearly did not want Irish reform to be the back door to socialism and collectivism. Where it is the disruption of food during the famine of *Castle Richmond*, or the price-control of rents in *The Landleaguers*, he sees any infringement of laissez-faire economics as ruinous to Ireland, and does not want the Irish peasantry sustained by government handouts. His excursus on the state of Ireland in the third volume of *The Landleaguers* is apologetic advocacy, being the sort of overview that should have been better placed at the beginning of the novel. This chapter is so polemical and vitriolic that, if placed any earlier in the book, would have repelled too many readers to be worth the author's while. Yet Trollope never seemed dead-set against the Irish.

In the novel ten-year-old Florian Jones, scion of an ascendancy family, converts to Catholicism. He makes common cause with the rebels, but then tattles on them when pressed by his father and the Protestant social order. Florian consequently is killed by the rebels in retaliation. This shocking death illustrates how, in the long run, the landlords and their tenants had to have more in common in order to build a sustainable society together. Trollope's son, in his postscript to the incomplete novel, says Lax, the alleged murderer of young Florian, was going to be hanged. But Trollope had prompted enough doubts about the excessive, Javert-like zeal of Yorke Clayton, the suitor of Florian's sister Edith, in his pursuit of Lax, that the reader can easily surmise that the case against the brigand was not totally proven. In Trollope's Irish fiction, there can be happy events, but no happy endings.

An Irish Landleaguer in the novel is described as a Brawny Miletian. Trollope meant by this a black Irishman, since the Miletians were alleged to be the aboriginal migrants from the eastern Mediterranean to Ireland. The constant presence of Jews alongside Trollope's Irish—visible from Madame Max and Phineas to the courtship of Rachel O'Mahony by the Jewish music impresario Mahomet M. Moss in *The Landleaguers*—alludes both to the fantasized Phoenician ancestry of the Celts and to the common status of Jews and Irishmen as religious and social outsiders in Britain.

Though Trollope wrote travel books about the West Indies, North America, and the Antipodes, and even wrote about his late-in-life voyage to Iceland, he wrote no travel books about the non–English place dearest to his heart, Ireland. Indeed, a model of this might have been Samuel Johnson's *Journey to the Western Isles of Scotland* (1775) in which he at once promoted and naturalized Scotland to the English people. Perhaps Trollope could not do this because, despite his harmonizing and peace-loving tendencies, he could not be sure of a steady future for Ireland. Indeed, he was keenly aware—as *The Landleaguers* shows—that the tensions so brilliantly depicted in his Irish fiction would be hard to quell.

See also: *Castle Richmond*; Ireland; *Phineas Finn*

Further Reading

Bigelow, Gordon. "Trollope and Ireland." *The Cambridge Companion to Anthony Trollope*, edited by Carolyn Dever and Lisa Niles. London: Cambridge University Press, 2010, pp. 96–109.

Wagner, Tamara S. "Speculating on American Markets: Foreign Money Matters and the New British Businessman in the Victorian Novel." *Symbiosis: A Journal of Anglo-American Literary Relations*, vol. 14, no. 2, October 2010, pp. 195–217.

The Last Chronicle of Barset

Last Chronicle of Barset was published by Smith, Elder in 1867. Unusually for Trollope, it was never serialized in a current periodical. It was at first serialized by the publisher in sixpenny parts and then eventually serialized as a complete book. *The Last Chronicle* was a huge publishing success. The death of Mrs. Proudie occasioned a greater response than any character in an English novel since that of Dickens's Little Nell a generation before. Its illustrations, by the underestimated George Housman Thomas, were memorable adjuncts to the book's compelling story.

Trollope was determined to bring the Barset series to an end, and, unlike the Palliser books, where some potential loose ends remain, everything is wrapped up in this final novel. An entire generation had come to maturity since the beginning of the Barsetshire saga. John Bold the younger, Eleanor Arabin's son by her first marriage, is now fully grown. Susan "Posy" Arabin, Francis's own daughter, is in the prime of her girlhood. John Bold the younger, firstborn son of Eleanor Arabin, is now nearly grown to manhood. Other characters from *The Warden* and *Barchester Towers* include Mr. Harding—still hale, playing his cello, and offering sage advice to his grandchildren until his death near the end of the book—and Archdeacon Grantly, still ensconced at Plumstead Episcopi and still as conventional as ever. The Grantlys provide the main connection between the first two books and the plot of this one. Their daughter Griselda has married more than well by becoming Lady Dumbello. Yet their son, Major Henry Grantly, after service in India, the birth of an infant daughter, and the death of his previous wife, has become engaged to Grace Crawley, the daughter of the impecunious perpetual curate of Hogglestock, Josiah Crawley. There are also connections to *Framley Parsonage* (the senior and junior Lady Lufton—the latter the former Lucy Robarts—play a role), and *Doctor Thorne* (the doctor's niece by marriage, Emily Dunstable, ends up marrying Bernard Dale). The connections to *The Small House at Allington* are more significant. *The Last Chronicle* not only provides the sequel to the stories of such characters as Bernard Dale and Joseph Cradell; it places the seal on the tragic abandonment of Lily Dale, the futility of Johnny Eames's courtship of her, and the gratifying ruin of Adolphus Crosbie, the man who had jilted her. Of all the characters in the previous book, the one who is not brought back, and who receives only an incidental mention, is Obadiah Slope. Slope's absence inevitably makes the book less comic and satiric, and more moving and tragic.

The plot involving Lily Dale bolsters this tragic element. So does the suicide of the financier Dobbs Broughton and the bittersweet renunciation of the painter Conway Dalrymple by Dobbs Broughton's wife, Maria. Upon Maria's husband's suicide in at his offices in Hook Court, she drifts over to the unadmirable and not particularly principled financier Augustus Musselboro, for whom she had earlier expressed loathing. Indeed, Musselboro does not even have the courage to convey to her the news of her husband's death. Yet for Maria, Musselboro nonetheless becomes the only viable option as a life partner. But the darkest strand of *The Last Chronicle of Barset* is its major plot, the accusation against Josiah Crawley of signing his name to a cheque of Lord Lufton's agent, Mr. Soames. This accusation is seized upon by Mrs. Proudie in another of her ecclesiastical causes. This sudden tarnishing of the character a clergyman whose previous reputation has been morally impeccable, even if he has not flourished financially, raises the prospect of not just disgrace but prison. It threatens to undo the love of his daughter Grace and Major Grantly, whose family already considers the Crawleys beneath them. The Crawley cheque plot gives the novel and element of mystery or crime novel. Crawley is a character is close to a Dostoyevskyan holy fool. He has some of both the purity and the rebarbative qualities of a Dostoyevsky character such as Father Zossima. Francis Arabin's observation that he likes Crawley more after Crawley has been through the ordeal of accusation and exoneration also brings up a Dostoyevskian sense of sin, catharsis, and redemption. Crawley's singularity of character emerges in apposition to Mortimer Tempest, the chairman of the ecclesiastical commission examining his case who is fair and compassionate. But Tempest lacks Crawley's radically individual spirituality. Crawley, like Lily Dale, represents attitudes of unworldliness and sacrifice out of kilter not just with the psychology but with the very anthropology of the realistic novel. Crawley is also an intellectual who reads Greek tragedy as a way to understand his own trauma and suffering. Another novelist who found he could create such a character might have gone in a more speculative or even metaphysical direction. But Trollope, while delighting in the subtlety and distinction of his creation, firmly puts the lid back on. He goes on as a chronicler of English daily life, having sounded the alternatives.

Barset as portrayed in this book is not as pastoral nor walled-off from the rest of the world as it might have seemed previously. The machinations not just of Dobbs Broughton and Musselboro in the financial world but those of the pathetic Crosbie give a glimpse into the world of *The Way We Live Now*, and the Major's determination to marry Grace has an element of real transgression across class lines more convulsive than the courtship of Lucy Robarts and Lord Lufton in *Framley Parsonage*. On the other hand, however, the now-reformed Lady Lufton urges the Archdeacon to be more generous towards his son's intended precisely on the basis of her own previous experience.

Emily Dunstable is united to Bernard Dale in ways that also resolve loose ends from the fourth and fifth book, and also make the Dale family a fulcrum of social mobility and integration. Lily, however, is left out; known familiarly as "L. D." by Johnny Eames when he had hopes of courting her, her initials are now, as she scribbles in her notebook, "O. M." for old maid. Yet Lily's exclusion from the marriage plot is also a form of transcendence, at least as much of one as a Trollope character ever experiences. Trollope recognizes the nobility of her suffering even though he also recognizes it as abnormal. He also depicts her not wanting to be re-absorbed into the patriarchal model of marriage, as part of her rejection of Eames even after Crosbie is dead occurs because she finds she likes her independence. She may be alone, but she is free.

The novel portrays a large and heterogeneous canvas. Toogood is a cousin of both Eames and Crawley. This ties together the plot strands without making the relationships too homey and organic, since Eames and Crawley do not know each other except through Toogood. Similarly, the suicide of Dobbs Broughton and the death of Mrs. Proudie follow closely on each other in the narrative. But they are causally unconnected and only slightly complementary structurally. The reintroduced plot strands from *Framley Parsonage* and *Doctor Thorne* reveal aspects of Barset life that do not revolve around the moral dilemmas of either Josiah Crawley or Lily Dale.

The Crawley and Eames plots dominate the book. But an unusual aspect of *The Last Chronicle* is that the third plot, the Conway Dalrymple-Clara Van Siever courtship, is significantly part of the design of the book. It indeed one of its most interesting facets. This distinguishes *The Last Chronicle* from other Trollope novels like *The Eustace Diamonds* where the Lucinda Roanoke plot seems more improvised. Dalrymple is painting Clara as a model for Jael, the woman who kills the Canaanite general Sisera in his tent in the Biblical book of Judges. He advances himself both amorously and socially through his painting, but the violent and decidedly ungenteel subject of Jael and Sisera questions the socially constructed givens of the male/female relationship. Clara as a model is the subject of the male gaze. But as an actress—which she is, even though in a stationary mode—she is playing a woman who not only prevails over a man but deceives him. Clara Van Siever, the daughter of a Dutch merchant, achieves what Lily Dale did not with respect to Lady Alexandrina de Courcy, outmaneuvering her more socially privileged rival for her beloved's hand. Dalrymple himself is the model for Sisera comically, but effectively communicates the reversal of gender hierarchies. This is bolstered by the fact that marrying Dalrymple will save Clara from the unwelcome embraces of her other suitor, Augustus Musselboro. Dalrymple, despite his self-interest, shows considerable valor not only in how he treats Clara but also how he behaves toward the bereaved Maria. Dalrymple has succeeded in marrying up. But Clara will not be without power in the relationship. However satisfied Bishop Proudie might be that his interfering wife will, because dead, no longer boss him around, the novel does not portray a tidy reaffirmation of male will.

Crawley is ultimately exonerated. It is discovered that the cheque from Soames was something Eleanor Arabin had sent on to Crawley in hope of alleviating his chronic penury. This brings the action full circle. The presence of Arabin threads the narrative back into the series' second book. In that book, Crawley had been the unnamed man who keeps Arabin from sliding over totally in the direction of John Henry Newman and Rome. That his exculpation (and Mrs. Proudie's passing from the scene) means Grace can marry Henry integrates Crawley's uncanny and at times uncomfortable holiness back into a domestic plot, as may befit Anglican sainthood. But the reader does not forget either the gravity of Crawley's plight or the intensity of his character.

Traditionally, *The Last Chronicle* was considered Trollope's greatest work. With the production and airing of the Palliser series on television in the 1970s, and the attention paid to *The Way We Live Now* during the 1980s and after, though, its status has somewhat faded. But *The Last Chronicle* is far more than a satisfying conclusion to the series that made Trollope's name. The anti-reformist agenda of the early books is gone. It is replaced by a sense of society as a curious mechanism held together by idiosyncratic and infinitesimal building blocks. In Mr. Harding's deathbed scene, Bishop Proudie, himself now a widower, opposed in ecclesiastical terms to the deceased's kith and kin, nonetheless comes to mourn. This is Trollope's greatest scene of reconciliation, made even more masterful by a slight comic touch. *The Last Chronicle of Barset* lacks a manifest social agenda. But that does not mean it is not a compelling social novel. Just as the short story "Why Frau Frohmann Raised Her Prices" shows the very moment where a precapitalistic world yielded to one centered on market forces, *The Last Chronicle* shows the Victorian world passing from provinciality and complacency to urbanity and critical awareness.

See also: novel series; *The Small House at Allington*; Thomas, George Housman; *The Way We Live Now*

Further Reading

Hirsch, Gordon, and Louella Hirsch. "Trollope's *The Last Chronicle of Barset*: Memory, Depression, and Cognitive Science." *Mosaic: An Interdisciplinary Critical Journal*, vol. 39, no. 1, March 2006, pp. 165–179.
Merchant, Peter. "Inhabiting the Interspace: De Tabley, Judges, 'Jael.'" *Victorian* Poetry, vol. 36, no. 2 Summer, 1998, pp. 187–204.
Miller, J. Hillis. *Communities in Fiction*. New York: Fordham University Press, 2016.

law

From the vantage point of the twenty-first century, interrogating Trollope's relationship with the law makes perfect sense. His novels engage with legal and political changes affecting the rights of women (*He Knew He Was Right*), real property (*Mr. Scarborough's Family*), heirlooms (*The Eustace Diamonds*), and criminal procedure (*The Three Clerks, Orley Farm, Phineas Redux*). These novels reveal not only Trollope's willingness to question the law and conventions of his day, but also a strong attraction to the law and legal thinking itself.

Trollope's critics, in his own lifetime and to the present, frequently blame him for inaccuracies, that is, misstating and misapplying legal principles. Catching Trollope out in arcane errors of procedure or substance is a leitmotif in Trollope criticism. By contrast, Charles Dickens largely escapes, because his depictions of the law are highly impressionistic and obscure the legal issues in cases arising in his novels to the point that they are often unidentifiable.

While Dickens's legal framework was more eighteenth century than nineteenth, the legal issues in *Bleak House* are lost in the mists of the Court of Chancery and viewed only dimly through that mist (Gest 409–410). Unlike Trollope, Dickens's "aim was to ridicule, satirize, and caricature all that he disliked and despised, and he saw much in the law and lawyers of England to dislike and despise" (Gest 405). Dickens evokes an expressionistic vision of a callous system that damages lives without thought—Mr. Vholes removing his gloves as if he is skinning his hands, the menace in Mr. Tulkinghorn's hard-grained, close, dry voice.

Trollope's depiction of the law rarely employs the stagecraft so typical of Dickens. This is so even though his recurring character, the defending barrister Mr. Chaffanbrass, has a theatrical presence and method. Rather, Trollope situates his lawyers and the law as it was at the time the novels take place. He thus gives his contemporary critics and modern legal historians much to assess, and thus much to fault the author.

Trollope ruefully admits as much in *Phineas Finn* (Ch. XXIX), deploring "those terrible meshes of the Law! How is a fictionist, in these excited days, to create the needed biting interest without legal difficulties; and how again is he to steer his little bark clear of so many rocks," without a pilot. Trollope admits to having on occasion obtained the help of "a benevolent pilot," that is, a qualified lawyer to "vet" his legal assumptions, such as Charles George Meriwether, who wrote the legal opinion given by the fictional barrister Mr. Dove in *The Eustace Diamonds*, in order that Trollope might evade the scornful criticism poured on the legal framework in *Orley Farm* by lawyers (Pionke 129).

Trollope's fascination with the criminal law reflects at first a pronounced dislike and later a deep ambivalence to the reforms of the nineteenth century, especially cross-examination. Trollope "implicitly asserts the authority of his overt critique of the law through his meticulous reproduction of this broader system; according to this logic, his accurate representation of professional distinctions, codes of conduct, courtroom rituals and other legal details makes true his account of legal untruthfulness" (Pionke 133).

For Trollope "in no way is the fundamental injustice of lawyers' misplaced loyalties more apparent … than in the relatively recent procedural innovation of the cross-examination of witnesses" (Pionke 132). He famously compared "tolerance of the abuses of cross-examination to the widespread practice of skinning eels while they were alive to guarantee their freshness: both were tortures 'allowed even humane people'" (Schneider 48). Cross-examination was well established by the late 1850s, but was nonetheless controversial (Pionke 132; Schneider 48, 50). Indeed, "while Trollope was not alone among Victorian novelists in deploring cross-examinations, he was probably the Victorian era's most prominent critic of their abuse" (Schneider 56). Trollope's disdain for what the narrator alternatively labels "browbeating of witnesses" and "breaking down and crushing a witness" is grounded in "his fundamental aversion to lawyers serving the interests of their clients, and not the larger claims of truth" (Pionke 132; Schneider 57). However, Trollope's vision of the legal system is not entirely even-handed. He accepts as a given the tilt in favor of the prosecution inherent in the fact that, until after Trollope's death, "the law denied [the accused] to give evidence in his own defense, or to call upon his wife to do so," under the theory that they were incompetent to testify, having a vested interest in the case (Bentley 147). While the accused could give an unsworn statement—one that was not evidence as it was unsworn—the prosecution could call witnesses in rebuttal and the judge could comment on their statement in summation, suggesting how much weight, if any, the jury should give it (Bentley 148–152).

Trollope's animus toward cross-examination makes for some effective (and sometimes quite amusing) courtroom scenes—Mr. Chaffanbrass alone accounts for three of them, in *The Three Clerks*, *Orley Farm*, and *Phineas Redux*. When we first meet Mr. Chaffanbrass, the "dirty" and "unkempt" Old Bailey barrister is quite a nasty piece of work. Trollope's description of him "includes both an indictment of Chaffanbrass's delight in inflicting pain—'it may be said of him that the labor he delighted in physick'd pain'—and lack of civility" (Schneider 59, 58). He does not appear materially changed in *Orley Farm*. But in *Phineas Redux*, we get a glimpse that there is more to the man. After declaring that meeting Phineas will in no way assist his defense, and may even mar it, Chaffanbrass leaves the meeting telling his instructing solicitor that "I have sometimes felt as though I would give the blood out of my veins to save a man. I never felt in that way more strongly than I do now" (*PR*, Ch. LX). A modern-day reader of

Trollope's legal fiction can see commonalities between Chaffanbrass and the late John Mortimer's wily, lovable Old Bailey Hack, Horace Rumpole.

Much of Trollope's interest in the law has to do with his narrative needs and his interest in the portrayal of character. In *Orley Farm,* the penurious provincial lawyer Samuel Dockwrath is contrasted with the urbane Matthew Round, and the established barrister Thomas Furnival with his ambitious young colleague, Felix Graham. In *Cousin Henry,* the machinations of Nicholas Apjohn against his own nominal client, Henry Jones, are crucial to the happy ending of the plot. But nonetheless there is strong reason to see Trollope's repeated r to the law and the theater of the courtroom as indicative of an interest in the law and its practice. Himself the son of an unsuccessful barrister, and a former civil servant, a certain amount of legal training appears to have been a part of his youth. Coral Lansbury contends that the publication of John Frederick Archbold's *Digest of the Law,* which recommended a plain, factual, straightforward manner of statement in declarations pleading facts and conclusions of law impressed Sir Francis Freeling, Secretary of the Post Office from 1798 to 1836, under whom Trollope was hired as a clerk. Lansbury asserts that Freeling revamped post office written reports to conform to Archbold's advice about plain, clear, concise pleading. Trollope's training in writing post office reports thus influenced his novels by leading him to write comprehensible, clear prose unadorned with unnecessary flourishes or effects. T.H.S. Escott proposed that another legal mind also inculcating these stylistic virtues: Anthony's father, Thomas Adolphus Trollope, the failed barrister who taught Antony how to write a letter, emphasizing "clearness, conciseness, abstinence from the repetition of words or ideas, and the non-introduction of any unnecessary or irrelevant matter," and "at the same time he instructed him by example in the theory and practice of *précis* writing" (Escott 19–20).

Richard Mullen also remarks that the post office "placed great emphasis on well-composed documents," adding that "Freeling, in particular, was noted for the lucidity of his reports, and his example permeated to the most junior of clerks" (87). In particular, Mullen quotes Trollope's contemporary, the poet Henry Taylor, a clerk at the Colonial Office, as describing a clear writing style as "a pillar of good government," with "the leading rule is to be content to be common-place," a description, Mullen notes, often attached to Trollope's writing (87–88).

As Susan Humphreys notes, Trollope "brought to the composition of fiction asset of habits that should have produced the dreary jargon of official reports and letters" (264). However, the insistence on clarity, concision, and specificity insisted upon by Archbold (and Sir William Blackstone as well [*Commentaries* 3: 311]), brought lucid matter-of-factness to the inspiration on which he depended.

See also: *Cousin Henry*; *Orley Farm*; *Phineas Redux*; post office

Further Reading

Bentley, David. *English Criminal Justice in the Nineteenth Century*. London: Hambledon, 1998.

Escott, T.H.S. *Anthony Trollope: His Work, Associates, and Literary Originals*. London: John Lane, Bodley Head, 1913, pp. 19–20.

Humphreys, Susan L. "Order—Method: Trollope Learns to Write." *Dickens Studies Annual*, vol. 8, 1980, pp. 251–271.

Lansbury, Coral. *The Reasonable Man: Trollope's Legal Fiction*. Princeton, NJ: Princeton University Press, 1981.

McMaster, R.D. *Trollope and the Law*. London: Palgrave Macmillan, 1986.

Mullen, Richard. *Anthony Trollope: A Victorian in His World*. Savannah: Beil, 1992.

Pionke, Albert D. "Navigating 'Those Terrible Meshes of the Law': Legal Realism in Anthony Trollope's *Orley Farm* and *The Eustace Diamonds*." *ELH*, vol. 77, no. 1, Spring 2010, pp. 129–157.

Schneider, Wendie Ellen. *Engines of Truth: Producing Veracity in the Victorian Courtroom*. New Haven, CT: Yale University Press, 2015, pp. 48–100.

Lewes, George Henry

Lewes (1817–1876) was a man of letters who wrote on many topics ranging from science to literature. He knew and wrote about most of the major Victorian novelists. He was a major figure in keeping philosophical issues before the public, researching and keeping the public abreast of developments in science, and later psychology. He was not just a popularizer, though. He was a serious speculative thinker in his own right. He was the partner of George Eliot, though they never formally married. Trollope's willingness to be part of the circle that would not object to their relationship (and to Lewes's not objecting to his wife Agnes Jervis's relationship with another man) shows Trollope's ability to embrace, or at least tolerate, unconventionalities.

Trollope first met Lewes at a dinner for the *Cornhill* sponsored by his friend George Smith. He immediately respected Lewes's erudition and acumen. Trollope helped choose Lewes for the editorship of the *Fortnightly Review*, in which capacity Lewes served for just over a year. Trollope appreciated the hard work Lewes put into writing for sundry periodicals over many years. He respected Lewes as a fellow citizen of the republic of letters. In his eulogy for Lewes, published in the *Fortnightly Review* in January 1878, Trollope refuted the positivist Frederic Harrison's observation that Lewes began as a journalist and ended as a scientific and philosophical thinker, by saying when Lewes "was working as journalist, critic, and novelist he was becoming the mathematician, the physicist, and the chemist he was." In Trollope's mind, Lewes taught himself in these fields not just by reading in them but by writing about them. Trollope thus defended journalism as a field, and thus the larger world of commercial authorship as a whole. He believed journalism served as a vehicle for self-improvement that in turn could benefit the general public. Lewes, in turn, understood the classicist aspects of Trollope more than most. Lewes was someone with whom Trollope could discuss his interest in Cicero and Caesar. He had a mind more abstract than Trollope's. Yet Lewes was immersed enough in the practices of daily life to solicit Trollope's own latent capacity for abstract thought. Trollope's friendship with Lewes shows Trollope as a figure engaged at the vital center of Victorian intellectual life.

See also: Eliot, George; *Fortnightly Review*

Further Reading

Hardwick, Elizabeth. "George Eliot's Husband." *The Collected Essays of Elizabeth Hardwick*. New York: New York Review Books, 2017, pp. 38–43.

Tjoa, Hock Guan. *George Henry Lewes: A Victorian Mind*. Cambridge, MA: Harvard University Press, 1977.

Linda Tressel

Linda Tressel, like Trollope's other two short continental novels, was published anonymously by Blackwood. The firm issued the novel in 1868 after it was serialized in

Blackwood's Magazine from October 1867 to May 1868. The story is set in Nuremberg, described by Trollope as a picturesque small city dominated by Lutheran Protestants though situated in largely Catholic Bavaria, and in the household of the widow Staubach in a red house on the Schütt island in the Pegnitz river. The widow is a pious Protestant—an Anabaptist, not a Lutheran—who has responsibility for her deceased brother's daughter, Linda Tressel. At the time of the story, Linda is twenty. She is beginning to feel torn between her aunt's puritanical piety and the dancing and merriment pursued by her female contemporaries. They live with a maid, Tetchen, and a lodger, Peter Steinmarc. By the time Linda is near to maturity, the feeling between Frau Staubach and Herr Steinmarc has grown so friendly that Tetchen believes a marriage is imminent. As Linda suspects, though, the widow turns Steinmarc down—only to suggest that he propose to the niece instead. After some adjustment, Steinmarc gladly turns to the pursuit of the younger, more alluring Linda.

Linda, though, finds Steinmarc both too old and inherently repulsive. She vastly prefers his young relative, Ludovic Valcarm, who loves her and who braves the river on a Sunday morning in order to declare his passion. But she also refuses him at least outwardly, although secretly she returns his feelings. She is willing, though, to come to an arrangement with her aunt that she will continue to spurn Valcarm if Frau Staubach ceases to encourage Steinmarc. Steinmarc, increasingly frustrated by Linda's refusal, is torn between wanting to bring her to heel and trying to conciliate her not only to secure her hand in marriage but to obtain the house itself. Increasingly feeling trapped, Linda decides to appeal for advice to Herr Molk, a friend of her deceased father, who lives in the fashionable Egidien Platz. Herr Molk shocks her not just because he expresses his belief that Steinmarc, a contemporary of his and Linda's father's, is trustworthy if advanced in years, but that Ludovic Valcarm is a scapegrace who is at that very moment in prison. Furthermore, Ludovic has been seen cavorting with a young woman in a blue frock.

While Linda agrees to marry Steinmarc in January in order to buy time, Ludovic convinces her to escape before that. He confesses that he had been in prison because of his political liberalism and, in an odd cross-gender moment, that the young woman in a blue frock was in fact a young man wearing women's clothing in order to escape the city. Ludovic and Steinmarc escape to Augsburg together but Linda falls ill, does not follow Ludovic's instructions, and is apprehended by old connections from Nuremberg who return her to her aunt's fold.

The point of the failed escape is less that Ludovic was better than Peter (even though the story never presents him as anything but an unjustly incarcerated political prisoner) but that Linda Tressel, as an autonomous person, has the right to choose her mate. In this instance she will not bend (in this respect much like Clara Desmond in *Castle Richmond*), and not having control over her own fate drives her to thoughts of suicide. When Linda, her heart and body broken by the ordeal, dies in 1863, her aunt finally realizes that, even if she was right about Valcarm, she was wrong to force her niece to marry Steinmarc, who in any event had soured on Linda.

By depicting Nuremberg as a place of slower-paced life and more traditional customs than England, but limiting its exoticism by stressing how its populace is more Protestant than Catholic, Trollope gives his English reader both an entertaining sense

of difference and a reassuring familiarity. The audience for *Linda Tressel* did not necessarily know much about Germany, which was not a traditional stop on the Grand
Tour for young English gentleman, nor the German language and culture, which was
not taught as often to young ladies as French and Italian, despite German preemi-
nence in music. Much as Trollope's novels circulated on the Continent through the
Leipzig-based Tauchnitz editions of his work, so in this book and its two companions
did the subject of the Trollopian oeuvre itself dilate out towards continental Europe.
On the other hand, elements of the story, such as the hard old man versus the charming
young man as suitor, are comparable to other Trollope stories such as "Catherine Carmichael," and the story's critique of dour, restrictive Protestantism could apply as much
in Nottinghamshire as in Nuremberg. Written in 1867 and set from 1860 to 1863, the
story has some relation to the process of German unification, which was unfolding in
those years, though Trollope renders any point in this respect very oblique.

Despite its being published anonymously, critics such as Henry James, who reviewed it for *The Nation* in June 1868, figured out the authorship fairly easily, and generally praised it.

See also: *The Golden Lion of Granpere*; *Nina Balatka*

Further Reading

Knelman, Judith. "Trollope's Experiments with Anonymity." *Victorian Periodicals Review*, vol. 14, no. 1, Spring
    1981, pp. 21–24.
Overton, Bill. *The Unofficial Trollope*. London: Harvester, 1982.

Lotta Schmidt and Other Tales

Lotta Schmidt and Other Tales was published by Alexander Strahan in 1867. It contains some of Trollope's most ingenious and entertaining shorter fictions.

"Lotta Schmidt," published in the *Argosy* (July 1866), is set in Vienna, before the
seven-week Austro-Prussian war transpiring as the story appeared, although the narrator refers to the war in telling the story. The story begins with the erection of a statue
of Prince Eugene of Savoy, an Austrian military figure of the eighteenth century well
known in England for his collaboration with the Duke of Marlborough in the War of
the Spanish Succession. Lotta and her friend Marie work for a high-class clothing store
in Vienna during the day but make merry in the city at night. The narrator is careful to
explain that, unlike in London, this is a pastime for respectable young ladies and also
that Lotta, although with features that might be read as Jewish, is not a Jew. Herr Crippel is in love with Lotta. But at forty-five he thinks he is too old for her, and that she
will end up with her suitor Fritz Planken, an eligible young man much like Marie's fiancé, Stobel. But Planken is almost as interested in another girl, Adela Bruhl, and Lotta,
charmed by Herr Crippel's playing on the zither, marries the older man, in an inversion
of how a similar scenario will play out in *An Old Man's Love*. The setting of Viennese
dancers and exuberant youth is, for Trollope, an atypical and winning one.

In "The Adventures of Fred Pickering" the title character marries Mary Crofts
when he is twenty-five, and she nineteen. Fred Pickering had given up the potential of
lucrative career as a lawyer in order to practice journalism in Manchester. After mar-

rying, the couple move to London where they live in Museum Street and, Fred tries, without success, to get a job in London journalism. Finally, he is hired as the London correspondent for the *Salford Reporter*. He meets various literary figures, and obtains small patronage from them, but is simultaneously discouraged about pursuing the literary profession as a career. He submits a strongly argued and deeply felt piece on Milton's *Samson Agonistes*, only to be told by an editor that his paper does not review old books. This humiliation culminates in Mr. Burnaby, a man for whose book he had done an unacceptably opinionated index, giving him a £10 note. Fred becomes reconciled to his fate. He returns to Manchester for an attorney's clerk job subsidized by his father. But he does not totally give up his literary dreams.

"The Two Generals" is an American story, set in Kentucky during the Civil War. The Reckenthorpe brothers are divided in their allegiances. Frank is for the North while his older brother Tom does what is expected of him and supports the South. Despite being a Northerner herself, Ada Forster, a young woman whom both brothers love, chooses Tom. Frank and Tom oppose each other on the battlefield. Frank sees Tom wounded by gunfire (not his own). Frank then urges Tom to give up Ada in return for his liberty. But Tom refuses. Frank then proves too honorable not to let him go. Tom returns home to marry Ada. But the end of the story makes clear, despite the Southern man getting the girl, the narrator's own anti-slavery convictions.

"Father Giles of Ballymoy" is narrated by Trollope's alternate persona, Archibald Green. It is set in an Irish town affected by the potato famine. Green does not understand that he and Father Giles are supposed to share a room at an inn (which Father Giles has generously agreed to do). He ejects the priest, shoving him downstairs and hurting him. Green is lambasted by the crowd at the inn for doing so, realizes his mistake, and is chagrined. Green and Giles reconcile, in a way that is a patent allegory of possible reconciliation between Catholics and Protestants in Ireland.

"Malachi's Cove" is the only Trollope work set in Cornwall, and one of the few set truly among the laboring classes. Malachi Tringlos is an old man who, somewhat like Wordsworth's leech-gatherer, gathers seaweed along the shores to sell as manure. Mahala "Mally" Tringlos, his granddaughter, helps him, until she is warned to desist by the neighboring farmer, Gunliffe. When she does not back down from plying her trade, Gunliffe sends his son, Barty, to intimidate and rival her. Mally loathes Barty until he falls into a whirlpool. Moved by his vulnerability, she realizes that she loves him.

"The Widow's Mite" first appeared in the evangelical magazine *Good Words* in 1863. It concerns a young woman, Norah Field, who wore an ordinary coat to her wedding and donated the money saved to relief for the poor. The story, in retelling the New Testament parable of the widow who gives her mite to the temple, can be read in different ways as Christian, sentimental, and feminist, because the point is not just Norah's altruism in giving up a beautiful wedding dress but the way that this is one of the few things a married woman, not in control of her own property, can do to help the poor. Like *Rachel Ray*, published later in the same magazine, the story tacitly argues for a provision like the first Married Women's Property Act, passed by Parliament in 1870.

"The Last Austrian Who Left Venice," is, like "Lotta Schmidt," about the Seven

Weeks' War of 1866 and nearly contemporaneous with it. The Austrian forces have evacuated Italy, and Venice rejoices as it was wholly Italian in population and sentiment and loathes the Austrians as foreigners. But love still transpires across enemy lines. Nina Pepé is in love with Hubert von Vincke, an Austrian officer of artillery. Hauptmann (Captain) von Vincke, while doing his duty, had been attentive to and compassionate toward the Italian population. But when he speaks to Carlo Pepé of his wish to have the hand of Carlo's sister Nina, Carlo objects, not on personal but nationalistic grounds. War breaks out, and Carlo fights for the Italian cause. But Italy does not do well militarily, and gains Venice only because Prussia (as chronicled at the beginning of "Lotta Schmidt") has defeated Germany in the war's other front. Once Italy wins, Nina feels freed from her nationalistic vow to abjure Hubert, and finds him, wounded, in Verona. She leaves with him for Trieste, then still Austrian. The story, set in the Italian terrain more closely associated with Trollope's writer brother, Thomas Adolphus, once again displays both Trollope's interest in politics and his sense that love and domestic happiness is more important than anything political.

"Miss Ophelia Gledd" is set in the United States. Ophelia Gledd is a tall woman from Boston who to the narrator's eyes is not conventionally beautiful, although in Boston society, by a certain sort of convention, she is treated as if she were beautiful. Ophelia is courted by two men, the Englishman John Pryor and the American Hannibal Hoskins (a clear play on the name of Abraham Lincoln's first Vice-President, Hannibal Hamlin of Maine). Ophelia, in the end, decides she wants to marry Pryor, provided he makes as much of an effort to fit in with her world as she does in his. The narrator, the same Archibald Green who narrates some of Trollope's Irish stories, observes that American women are more independent than English women and think nothing of taking the initiative in relationships with men. The story depicts the sights and sounds of Boston, being particularly evocative in its description of sleighing; but Trollope cannot help criticizing the Boston scene for a certain provinciality. Ophelia is often said to be modeled on Kate Field; she is also a precursor of the later character, Isabel Boncassen, in *The Duke's Children*.

"A Journey to Panama" relates the story of a young women sailing out to Peru unwillingly to marry an older man to whom she has become betrothed. The woman confides in our narrator, a middle-aged man, about her plight as the ship nears the Isthmus of Panama and they transfer across (the canal will not be built for decades). When they reach the Pacific, the ship receives mail, and the young woman finds out her betrothed has died. She goes to San Francisco, refusing to take up the proffered hand of the narrator because he has heard her be derogatory to the man she now mourns. Though this drama of sacrifice and renunciation, the reader learns about Panama and South America in general, as well as sea travel. Part of the story's appeal is that of travelogue and vicarious journey.

See also: *An Editor's Tales; Tales of All Countries; Uncollected Stories*

Further Reading

Kohn, Denise. "'The Journey to Panama': One of Trollope's Best 'Tarts'—Or, Why You Should Read 'The Journey to Panama' to Develop Your Taste for Trollope." *Studies in Short Fiction*, vol. 30, no. 1, 1993, pp. 15–22.

Tintner, Adeline. "James's 'The Patagonia': A Critique of Trollope's 'The Journey to Panama.'" *Studies in Short Fiction*, vol. 32, 1995, pp. 59–66.

The Macdermots of Ballycloran

The first, rather Gothic pages of *The Macdermots of Ballycloran* might have intrigued their first readers. The novel was published by Thomas Cautley Newby in 1847. The story focuses on a run-down demesne in central Ireland and a killing that leads to a politically inflected trial and execution. But those readers would have little inkling that they were reading the beginning of the oeuvre of perhaps the preeminent Victorian realist. Ireland was to tinge not only those books Trollope explicitly set there but the very modes and methods of his novelistic approach.

The Macdermots at once inaugurates Trollope's narrative voice and also is somewhat uncharacteristic of it. Rather than the assertive, omniscient generalizations of the English novels, Trollope's narrator is something of an outsider. In two of Trollope's short stories set in Ireland—including the first narrative fiction he ever composed, the story "The O'Conors of Castle O'Conor, County Mayo" (1841), he uses the persona of Archibald Green, a callow, perpetually inadequate Englishman. He is Trollope's semi-satire of himself as an outsider.

What is notable about *The Macdermots of Ballycloran* is not just its Irish setting but its tragic and pessimistic tone. Few of Trollope's works end so tragically. Certainly, none are so raw in temper or so bitter at the hypocrisies of the establishment. This is seen in Trollope's castigation of the Birmingham philanthropist who gives to noble causes all over the world but is able to do so by his expropriation of his poor Irish tenants. The Macdermots are a family with a proud background but penniless in the present and held at bay by vulgar, rising interests. The mature Trollope would have ended this opposition in either reconciliation or the evil side getting its comeuppance. Yet in this early novel there is nothing that the main character, young Thady Macdermot, can do to avert his family's grim destiny, and epitomizing it in his own death.

In *The Macdermots* Trollope avoids a Catholic-Protestant opposition. The Macdermots are Catholic but of patrician ancestry. But plebeian characters are given power and made "plausible" by the Macdermots' improvidence. The villain of the novel, the policeman Captain Myles Ussher, bears the ultimate Protestant Ascendancy name, recalling the seventeenth-century Anglo-Irish bishop famous for attempting to supply the exact date of the Creation. The Catholic cleric Father John McGrath, cosmopolitan and French-educated, is depicted very positively. His dilemma, torn between being a man of the world yet deeply sympathetic in moral and pastoral terms to his rural Catholic congregation, is capaciously rendered. Trollope is sympathetic to the Irish peasants who are illegally brewing whiskey. He finds the police persecution of them to be excessive. The author's feeling for the executed Thady (who is close to being the novel's point-of-view character), for his mad father Larry, and for his beguiled and devastated sister Feemy (Euphemia) shows a sympathy for the socially ostracized, marginalized, and sidelined. This shows a real inclination for the underdog that defies not just prejudice against the Irish but Victorian mores about emphasizing the exemplary and uplifting in fiction. Indeed, Trollope comes very near to acting as advocate even as he makes clear his intent is neither sectarian nor polemic. At the end of his career, though, Trollope came to feel very differently about the ideologically prompted revolutionaries in *The Landleaguers*.

In that novel he is much less favorable to the Catholic priests whom he accuses of abetting rebellious fervor.

Trollope thought highly of *The Macdermots*. In *An Autobiography* he spoke of the "pathos" of its plot. Yet it was a failure with the reading public. In turn, Trollope shied away from some of its features, such as its bittersweet-to-sad ending and its frank portrayals of poverty and lunacy, as well as its slightly historical setting (it is marked as being before the ascent of Queen Victoria by the reference to "Our Lord and Sovereign the King" [312]). Newby, the publisher of the book, also published Emily Brontë's *Wuthering Heights*, and the melancholy, pessimistic tone of *The Macdermots* is comparable to that with which Brontë's Yorkshire moors are laden.

See also: *Castle Richmond*; Ireland; *The Kellys and the O'Kellys*

Further Reading

Bigelow, Gordon. "Form and Violence in *The Macdermots of Ballycloran*." *Novel: A Forum on Fiction*, vol. 46, no. 3, Fall 2013, pp. 386–405.
Johnson, Conor. "*The Macdermots of Ballycloran*: Trollope as Conservative-Liberal." *Éire-Ireland: An Interdisciplinary Journal of Irish Studies*, vol. 16, no. 2, 1981, pp. 71–92.
Tingay, Lance O. "The Reception of Trollope's First Novel." *Nineteenth-Century Fiction*, vol. 6, no. 3, December 1951, pp. 195–200.

Marion Fay

Marion Fay was serialized in England in *The Graphic* from December 1881 to June 1882 and in Australia in *The Illustrated Sydney News*; it was published by Chapman and Hall in 1882. William Small illustrated the serial version. Trollope wrote the first part of the novel in the mid–1870s before turning to *Dr. Wortle's School*. He then completed *Marion Fay* during his sojourn in the Swiss Alps in August and September 1879.

Lionel Trafford succeeds his uncle, Lord Kingsbury, in the peerage and the occupation of the great house of Trafford Park in Shropshire. But the nephew's radicalism diverges sharply from the hyper-Toryism of his uncle. The radical Lord Kingsbury's son, Lord Hampstead, goes even further than his father, declaring openly atheist and republican views (something very unusual for an aristocrat in Trollope). Lord Kingsbury's daughter, Lady Frances Trafford, is in love with George Roden, an undistinguished, middle-class postal clerk who is friends with her brother. When the novel begins, Lady Kingsbury has died (one of the reasons her children are so headstrong) but Lord Kingsbury has remarried Clara Mountressor, who bears children of her own; because of the presence of Lord Hampstead, they can never inherit the title. The new Marchioness thus conceives a hatred for Lord Hampstead. She wishes to have him put out of the way. Meanwhile, Lord Hampstead is concealing that he also loves someone from a different class. This is the virtuous young Quaker woman, Marion Fay.

The theme Trollope develops in the story of the liberal Lord Kingsbury is reminiscent of Lord Warburton in Henry James's *Portrait of a Lady*. It shows the rise of political radicalism as a viable option for all classes in late Victorian society. Equally, though, the radical Marquess's refusal to permit his daughter to marry a man of lower rank shows there are limits in applying radicalism to one's own life. But, as Frederik van Dam asserts, the novel as a whole reveals that Trollope's sense that social class in England is not rigid. Intermarriage is an expression of this relative mobility.

The novel turns around the potential marriage of Lady Frances Trafford to George Roden. Both Lady Frances's father, Lord Kingsbury, and his son and heir, Lord Hampstead, object to the marriage on grounds of the disparity of the couple's social standing. Yet Lord Hampstead falls in love with Marion Fay, of little social standing and of Quaker background. In one of Trollope's most affirmative portrayals of a low-church Protestant figure, Marion's father, Zachary Fay, lives with his only surviving child at 17 Paradise Row. Zachary Fay is considered a wealthy man locally. But in the broad scheme of things he is only moderately well off. Zachary urges his daughter to marry for love, even if her beloved is a man of high social standing, because someone who stands truly before God will follow his or her heart. Lord Hampstead is drawn to Marion precisely because she scorns typical feminine frippery and is not concerned with wealth. However, Marion does not intend to marry Lord Hampstead. This is not because she believes she is socially inferior or that she is too modest, but because she suspects, rightly, that she will die of consumption like several of her family.

Lord Hampstead's stepmother, the Marchioness, wishes both her stepson and stepdaughter to be alienated from their father. In her darkest moments, she even wishes them dead. She employs the family chaplain, Mr. Greenwood to try to achieve one or even both ends. Greenwood is one of Trollope's darkest depictions of a priest, almost a scheming prelate out of Jacobean drama, someone who indeed explicitly compares himself to Macbeth. Frustrated in his desire to achieve ecclesiastical benefices such as the living at Appleslocombe at the second Trafford estate in Somerset, Greenwood is so irreligious that he can even contemplate himself as a murderer. His only doubts about doing so would be that, like Macbeth and Banquo's descendants, he would kill only for the good fortune of the Marchioness's offspring, who would have no will or reason to thank him. Mr. Greenwood's plans for an accident to happen to Lord Hampstead at Appleslocombe finally become too sordid even for the Marchioness. She tries to walk back her desire for a chance accident to happen to Lord Hampstead or Lady Frances, stating that her desire was only to see them beneficially married. Mr. Greenwood is bought off by the Trafford family and agrees to retire out of their midst.

The Illustrated Sydney News, in its prefatory note to the serialization of *Marion Fay*, particularly praised Trollope's portrayal of the alliance across classes of the postal clerk Roden and Lady Frances—and does not mention that the revelation of George's Italian aristocratic ancestry (that he is in fact the son of the Duca di Crinola) makes that division far less severe. But the end of the book does not simply restore the status quo ante. In the novel Trollope clearly takes a position that aristocrats should not exclusively marry each other, and that the snobbery of people like Lady Amaldina Hauteville for Frances' choice is severely misplaced. On the one hand, the death of Marion is convenient for keeping the blood of the Trafford family undiluted by those of lower rank. On the other hand, Lord Hampstead is last seen preparing to wander the world, free to marry someone else. The children of the Marchioness (a figure at some points reminiscent of the evil queen in Shakespeare's *Cymbeline*) will not necessarily inherit as she had schemed. Lord Hampstead insists on punishing only Mr. Greenwood, both for propriety's sake and as a warning to his stepmother. The same Italian aristocratic ancestry that makes the putative heir in *Is He Popenjoy?* disreputable serves to give Roden repute in the eyes of the aristocracy.

The novel may seem to mix a fairytale ending (particularly if one sees Trollope, a former postal clerk, himself identifying with Roden) with a slight critique and partial reaffirmation of class prejudices. But the novel is at its core about gender. The third plot—Clara Demijohn's vacillation between the virtuous Daniel Tribbledale and the odious Samuel Crocker—is about a woman's capacity for making her marital choice meaningful, and this pertains to Lady Frances as well. Mrs. Roden extracts from Lord Hampstead an admission that there is a double standard, that men can fall in love below themselves and not outrage society but if a woman does so, her reputation is ruined. There can be fallen women, like Carry Brattle in *The Vicar of Bullhampton*, but not in the same sense a fallen man. The fact that the novel is named after Marion shows the importance its narrative places on nobility of character. Indeed, Marion is almost a woman out of later Dickens, a self-sacrificing ascetic like Esther Summerson in *Bleak House*, or like Mariana (the probable origin of her name) in Shakespeare's *Measure for Measure*. Lord Hampstead's passionate declaration of posthumous love for Marion in Chapter 52, calling her his wife even when he visits her tomb after she has died, is a scene of striking emotional depth and power.

J. Hillis Miller (*Others*) has seen the impact of the early death of Trollope's sister Cecilia in the novel's depiction of the death of Marion Fay when still young. The title of the book is either deceptive or oracular, as Marion Fay is not a major character. But her altruism, self-sacrifice, and honor might be said to serve as an example for the more socially ensconced people who remain. Her Quaker dress, as she herself notes, renders her exotic, but also humble and plain. Though, as Robert Tracy (*Later Fiction*) points out, there is no tear-moving portrayal of Marion's death. We are left in no doubt that the world is a worse place without her, but made more noble by her memory. The preposterousness of the bureaucrat Roden turning out to be an Italian aristocrat suggests—rarely for Trollope—a class-conscious sentimentalism, which Marion Fay's virtue and humble origins counterpoint. Yet the strong comic element in the book—several of its initial reviewers called it a burlesque—tugs against any pathos, and makes the book a curious, though quite engrossing, hybrid.

See also: *Ayala's Angel*; *Is He Popenjoy?*

Further Reading

Kaftan, Robert. "*Marion Fay*: Trollope's Satiric Fairy Tale." *Victorian Institutes Journal*, vol. 16 1988, pp. 191–93.
Miller, J. Hillis. *Others*. Princeton, NJ: Princeton University Press, 2001.
Tracy, Robert. *Trollope's Later Fiction*. Berkeley: University of California Press, 1978.
Van Dam, Frederik. *Anthony Trollope's Late Style: Victorian Liberalism and Literary Form*. Edinburgh: Edinburgh University Press, 2016.

marriage plot

Though the marriage plot, the orientation of the action of a novel centered upon the courtship of a young man and woman resolving in marriage, is a staple of nineteenth-century British fiction. Nonetheless, Trollope wrote marriage plots in his own way and arguably for his own purposes. Pertinent here is the fact that Trollope began as a writer of fiction focused on Irish subjects, and the marriage allegory—the expression of Irish and British unity, or alternatively Irish reconciliation to British domination—was central to British imaginings of how the predicament of British colonialism in Ireland could be happily resolved. Even though Trollope deploys the Irish marriage allegory in his fiction only when it is broken—as in *An Eye for an Eye*—or when the non–Irish partner is as multicultural (or more so) as the Irish partner, as in the marriage of Madame Max Goesler and Phineas Finn in *Phineas Redux*—it is important to think of the marriage plot in Trollope as being not only about individual relationships but also about collective identities. In *The Duke's Children*, Lord Silverbridge's marriage to the American girl Isabel Boncassen represents the rise of American power and the revitalization of the British aristocracy with new blood. Lady Mary Palliser's marriage to Frank Tregear, an impecunious if aristocratic Cornishman, has a slight whiff of the Celtic outsider represented more graphically in the Palliser series by Phineas Finn. At other times, the marriage plot represents Trollope's ecclesiastical preferences, as when Eleanor Bold remarries the High-Church Francis Arabin rather than the low-church Obadiah Slope or the raffish Bertie Stanhope, or his sense of the widening of British class circles, as in *Cousin Henry* when Isabel Broderick marries the middle-class William Owen rather than her cousin, the heir to Llanfeare, Henry Jones. In *Lady Anna,* the title character and the tailor Daniel Thwaites defy the English class system entirely by living in Australia. This shows how nuptial happiness can subvert the idea of Britishness or ramify it beyond its usual bounds. Exogamy rather than endogamy is a major theme for Trollope. Marriage often represents a broadening, whether of class, nation, or temperament. In *The Duke's Children*, the cousins Tregear and Lady Mabel Grex, who are themselves romantically involved, nonetheless turn their erotic gaze outward. This is not only because that is where the money is. The lovers sense—even before the revelations of Mendelian genetics—that cousin-marriage will be a confining path for them. This is so even though in this case Lady Mabel fails while Tregear succeeds. Trollope can approve of endogamy if it is not literal, for instance in *The Golden Lion of Granpère* when George Voss marries Marie Bromar, the niece of his stepmother—a match at first objected to by Voss's father not because of any closeness of degree but because neither is rich.

Sometimes, though, Trollopian marriage plots focus on individual psychology, or are even morally prescriptive. Glencora M'Cluskie finds a measure of happiness with the repressed and dutiful Plantagenet Palliser in *Can You Forgive Her?,* having to reject the more exciting and, implicitly, equally alluring Burgo Fitzgerald; in the same book, Alice Vavasor rejects the high drama of her scapegrace cousin George for the unobtrusive responsibility of John Grey. There is a double lesson here. Marriage is about durability, not passion. Additionally, the magnetic, charismatic male will not necessarily make the best husband for a young lady.

Inevitably, the marriage plot has to do with money. In *Framley Parsonage,* Doctor Thorne's marriage to Martha Dunstable occurs only after the two have reassured each other they are financially secure. In *Phineas Redux*, Madame Max wins Phineas's heart after undertaking to travel to Europe to prove his innocence of the murder of Mr. Bonteen. But she also has the ability to offer him financial security without the burden and disrepute attached to her rival, Lady Laura Kennedy. Trollope does not disrespect financial motives in courtship. But he insists they be accompanied by, or grow into, real love. The more altruistic the suitor, the better, as in *Miss Mackenzie,* when the protagonist rejects the offers of the self-interested curate Mr. Maguire and the slightly more complexly self-interested businessman Samuel Rubb for John Ball. Ball retains his interest in her even after he, not she, is proven the legal heir of her brother Walter Mackenzie. In *The Bertrams,* Caroline Waddington gives up money her grandfather might have left her in her second marriage to George Bertram, but this is palatable because she has become disillusioned with the worldliness of her first marriage to Sir Henry Harcourt.

Courtship also tests the force of promises that are bound by the law of the heart if not by external law. In *John Caldigate,* John Caldigate tells Euphemia Smith that he would marry her, which the lady takes for an ironbound commitment, and which the man tries his best to evade. In *Castle Richmond,* Lady Clara Desmond keeps her pledge to Herbert Fitzgerald even after his cousin, Owen Fitzgerald, who she loved at first, seemingly comes into the possession of the property and title that had been expected to go to Herbert. Trollope recognizes that marriage, and the courtship that leads to it, are social forms. They are influenced by factors such as money, prestige, and worldly power. Yet for Trollope there is an inward and even spiritual element of marriage that can call upon the very best aspects of those who participate in it. In *Kept in the Dark,* the fact that Cecilia Holt was once engaged to Sir Francis Geraldine leads her eventual husband, George Western, to doubt the moral legitimacy of their marriage. In the short story "Alice Dugdale," the simple and good-hearted Alice wins the heart of the dashing Major John Rossiter over the haughty Georgiana Wanless through her high moral character. Although Trollope recognizes that the way of the world is that financial advantage might play a persuasive role in who people decide to marry; yet financial security for him is only one ingredient in a complex relation of purpose, temperament, and above all physical attraction. He grants its importance. For instance, Gerald Maule's marriage to Adelaide Palliser in *Phineas Redux* would not happen if the old roué Mr. Maule senior had not given up his claim on Maule Abbey. But he does not allow it to rule.

Trollope's men are generally wise to think that the rejection of a marriage proposal is not the final word. In *The Claverings*, Fanny Clavering rejects Samuel Saul, the Evangelical curate, in the most direct way possible, yet he still wins her hand. On the other hand, Henry Jones in *Cousin Henry* never quite realizes how much Isabel Brodrick detests him. This revulsion is not just moral and temperamental but physical.

Suspense and the marriage plot play a variable role in Trollope. In "Alice Dugdale," the reader knows virtually from the beginning that Alice will become the wife of John Rossiter. There would be no possible poetic justice if events were to transpire otherwise. But few would pick Madame Max Goesler, of the three women Phineas Finn encounters in the novel of that name, to end up being his wife at the end of *Phineas Redux*, and it is only Lady Clara Desmond's obstinacy, not any inherent marriage plot logic, that urges her to keep faith with Herbert over Owen in *Castle Richmond*. Even if the reader knows that there will be a marriage at the end, it is not always clear either who will be the parties to that marriage or what the moral, psychological, and logistical grounds for it will be.

The marriage-plot can work as a device to bring peace between the squatters and free-selectors of Australia in *Harry Heathcote of Gangoil*; in *The Golden Lion of Granpere,*

George Voss and Marie Bromar's courtship occurs amid differences between Catholics and Protestants and the impeding German repossession of Lorraine. This shows that the marriage plot can contain global energies and connect geographical disparities. For some writers, the marriage plot was an obligatory part of the Victorian novel. For Trollope it was an ingenious effect of which he was the greatest and most subtle tactician.

See also: *Can You Forgive Her?*; *John Caldigate*; *Phineas Redux*

Further Reading

Ablow, Rachel. *The Marriage of Minds: Reading Sympathy in the Victorian Marriage Plot.* Stanford, CA: Stanford University Press, 2007.
Marcus, Sharon. "Contracting Female Marriage in Anthony Trollope's *Can You Forgive Her?*" *Nineteenth-Century Literature*, vol. 60, no. 3, December 2005, pp. 291–325.
Michie, Elsie. *The Vulgar Question of Money: Heiresses, Materialism, and the Novel of Manners form Jane Austen to Henry James.* Baltimore: Johns Hopkins University Press, 2011.

medicine and doctors

Though medicine as a profession is depicted far less frequently in Trollope than law or politics, doctors appear in a significant portion of his oeuvre. (Dr. Wortle in *Dr. Wortle's School* is a Doctor of Divinity, not a medical doctor.) In his second novel, *The Kellys and the O'Kellys* the heroic Doctor Colligan, even though he is in financial need and looking for an opportunity to be a wealthy aunt's tenant, refuses to cooperate with Barry Lynch in his attempt to murder his sister. This admittedly rather primal instance of medical ethics shows the physician to be both a human being, with human needs and temptations, and a professional whose internalized code of practice is as stringent as that of the Anglican and Roman Catholic clergymen in the books.

Another Irish doctor, Malachi Finn, is the father of the politician Phineas Finn, and his medical practice establishes a solid middle-class identity that provides a foothold for his son to enter public life. Though in general medicine was associated with the middle class more frequently in Britain than in the United States, where the absence of a titled aristocracy meant well-off professional men were in effect the social elite, some of Trollope's physicians rise high in society. Omicron Pie is one of the characters that suture the Barsetshire and Palliser books together. Like Henry James's Sir Luke Strett or Virginia Woolf's Sir William Bradshaw, Sir Omicron Pie has gained a knighthood through his profession. Another doctor to rise in social position in the course of a Trollope narrative is Dr. Crofts in *The Small House at Allington*. When Lord De Guest prefers the counsel of Dr. Crofts to his elder colleague Dr. Gruffen, it is a testimony to the merits of skill over experience, which augur a field ready for a career open to talents, and hints that Crofts will be successful in his courtship of Isabella Dale,

John Bold in *The Warden* is a young surgeon with progressive ideals to match. His early death makes perhaps a similar comment on the limits of scientific advance in Victorian England as does the failure of the idealistic doctor Tertius Lydgate in Eliot's *Middlemarch*. Doctor Thorne in the Barsetshire novels (*Doctor Thorne* and *Framley Parsonage*) is a rural family doctor who becomes a well-off gentleman and whose family becomes entangled, overtly and covertly, with the traditional aristocratic families of the region. When the doctor finally marries, though, it is to Martha Dunstable, herself the daughter of a man who has made money in medicine (selling it, not practicing it) and a woman of wealth more than of good breeding. This indicates that perhaps there are still certain invisible barriers between the medical man and high society. More unobtrusively, Dr. Fillgrave in the Barsetshire series, notwithstanding his allegorical name, is diligent in attending to the births, deaths, and illnesses of the people in the county, while Dr. Rerechild, even as he does his best, cannot replace the long-dead Dr. Bumpwell in the hearts of the elderly people of Barchester.

Dr. Olivia Q. Fleabody, the American feminist (from Vermont) briefly mentioned in *Is He Popenjoy?*, is a physician and as such is threatening to the novel's sense of masculine privilege, and her domiciling at the end of the novel represents the curtailment of female professional ambition. As opposed to some other nineteenth century writers, Trollope is scant in his representation of the medical woman. There are few nurses, midwives, or any persons that could be called medical women in Trollope's novels, but he does represent childbirth and old age as occasions where women perform the acts of caring for the sick that are formalized scientifically in medical practice. Furthermore, Lucy Robarts's nursing of Mary Crawley in *Framley Parsonage* has a healing effect even though Lucy is not acting in a professional capacity. Lady Sarah Germain in *Is He Popenjoy?* is described as being informally "doctor and surgeon to the poor people—never sparing herself." Mrs. Draper in *The Last Chronicle of Barset* is a kind of nurse in that she knows of and understands Mrs. Proudie's heart condition in a way that Bishop Proudie does not.

Trollope's lone treatment of infectious disease is in *Marion Fay,* which concerns the blight that tuberculosis brings upon a young and virtuous life. A Trollope novel that may be said to deal with medical ethics is *The Fixed Period*, where a fictional future society euthanizes people who exceed the age of 67. This influenced the famed surgeon Sir William Osler's thinking about old age and death. Though lawyers can help decide the fate of a life, doctors routinely confront issues of life and death, and clergymen at least in theory the fate of a soul, which makes Trollope's representing them slightly different than those of other skilled professions.

See also: *The Fixed Period*; law

Further Reading

Berk, Steven L. "Sir William Osler, Ageism, and *The Fixed Period*: A Secret Revealed." *Journal of the American Geriatric Society*, vol. 37, no. 3, March 1989, pp. 263–66.
De Lyon, Hilary. "On re-reading Trollope." *British Journal of General Practice*, June 2005, vol. 55, no. 215, June 2005, p. 486.
Ziegenhagen, Timothy. "Trollope's professional gentleman: medical training and medical practice in *Doctor Thorne* and *The Warden*." *Studies in the Novel, vol.* 38, no. 2, Summer 2006, pp. 154–171.

Merivale, John Lewis

Merivale (1815–1886) was a lifelong friend of Trollope's. He went to school with him at Sunbury (a prep school) and Harrow. As a child Merivale, Trollope, and another friend formed a "Tramp Society" where they would walk on foot around the counties near London. They also walked together in Ireland. His father was a prominent barrister and his elder brothers Herman and Charles, who Trollope also knew, became, respectively, a secretary in the colonial office and an ecclesiastic who was a historian of Rome and whose work helped inspire Trollope to write on classical subjects. John Merivale worked, in a job more Dickensian than Trollopian, as a registrar in the Court of Chancery. Trollope named his eldest son, Henry Merivale Trollope, after him. Though not an intellectual, Merivale was somebody around whom Trollope could relax and be on terms of easy intimacy before and after he became famous, a condition which Merivale assisted by introducing Trollope to the firm of Longman, which eventual published *The Warden*. The work of the registrar in the Court of Chancery (the position Merivale held) is mentioned in the *Eustace Diamonds* and is for a brief time the unwanted destiny of Herbert Fitzgerald in *Castle Richmond*; of course Chancery is far more central to Dickens's *Bleak House*. Merivale's son George, like Trollope's son, emigrated to Australia in the 1870s.

See also: law; the past

Millais, John Everett

Millais (1829–1895), the famed pre–Raphaelite painter, was a close friend of Trollope. Throughout his working life, Trollope consulted with Millais about matters of art and illustration (for his own works, but also about such issues as Bohem's bust of Thackeray). Millais's illustrations of *Framley Parsonage*, particularly that of Lucy Robarts looking downward appareled in her highly expansive dress, became iconic despite there only being six of them. Millais' illustrated three of Trollope's greatest novels, *Orley Farm*, *Phineas Finn*, and *The Small House of Allington*; his images helped make Lily Dale Trollope's best-loved female character. Millais' portrait of the then-minor character Plantagenet Palliser, engaging in dolorous dalliance with Lady Dumbello, not only showed foresight in understanding that character's potential in Trollope's universe but framed the way future illustrators depicted him—and also influenced the casting of his character in the 1974 television adaptation of the Palliser novels. The Millais illustrations for *The Small House at Allington* garnered such accolades that George Housman Thomas, in illustrating what was in many ways a sequel to that novel, *The Last Chronicle of Barset*, was inevitably compared somewhat negatively to Millais. Millais would have illustrated *Can You Forgive Her?*, except the publisher, Chapman and Hall, had paid Trollope so large an advance that the firm could not afford Millais, a situation about which Millais was characteristically obliging. Millais also contributed the frontispiece to *Rachel Ray* (after it was rejected by *Good Words*) and *Kept in the Dark*.

In his illustrations for *Orley Farm*, Millais used imagery of light and dark to portray the knowing ambiguity of Lady Mason's moral and social status and the unknowing peril of her son. The illustration of the farm itself, in its pastoral abundance and settled, robust domesticity, give the reader of a sense of why Lady Mason has such a heavy psychological investment in the property. For *Orley Farm*, one of Trollope's most intricately plotted novels, Millais supplied more than 35 illustrations which responded with suppleness to the novel's rapid changes of mood. The two Millais illustrations in Chapter XXII of the first volume of *Orley Farm*, "Christmas at Noningsby," are suggestive in their contrasts. One depicts the sedate decorum of the morning religiously attentive Christmas in the country. The other portrays the evening at Nonigsby, where during the riotous game of blind man's bluff Felix Graham notices the beauty of Madeline Staveley. They are masterpieces of tone and are filled with nuance corresponding to that of the prose. The illustration of Monkton Grange as the men prepare for the hunt brings Trollope's particular interest in the sport alive. Millais was skilled in depicting both the differing dress and demeanor of men and women in Victorian societies, but the subtleties of their interaction, even when love was not at issue, as one sees in his illustration of Lady Mason with her lawyer, Mr. Furnival, and his wife. With both *Orley Farm* and *The Small House at Allington,* Millais's name appeared prominently on the cover, in type only to a degree smaller than that accorded the author.

Trollope's friendship with Millais was the closest thing in his career to his mother's close collegiality with the illustrator Auguste Hervieu while in the United States in the late 1820s. Trollope and Millais's friendship, though, was at once less stormy and more distant, and did not involve going into business together. Most importantly, Trollope's friendship with Millais illustrates the porousness of any distinction between romanticism and realism, nature and society, in Victorian English culture. The pre–Raphaelite aesthetic pleasures of Millais and the robust embrace of the public social arena in Trollope had, in their literary/visual dialogue, a happy meeting.

See also: Fawkes, Lionel Grimston; Holl, Frank Montague; Thomas, George Housman

Further Reading

Barlow, Paul. *Time Present and Time Past: The Art of John Everett Millais.* London: Ashgate, 2004.
Cooke, Simon. *Illustrated Periodicals of the 1860s.* New Castle, DE: Oak Knoll Press, 2010.
Mason, Michael. "The Way We Look Now: Millais' Illustrations to Trollope." *Art History*, vol. 1, no. 3, September 1978, pp. 309–40.
Moody, Ellen. *Trollope on the Net.* London: Hambledon, 1999.

Miss Mackenzie

Miss Mackenzie was published in 1865 by Chapman and Hall. As revealed in Trollope's *Autobiography, Miss Mackenzie* was the one novel in which Trollope intended not to insert a love plot, but in the end he could not resist it. Some critics have alleged that Trollope centered his novels around love plots because he knew readers would approve. But that he was unable to pull off even this one experiment in restraint suggests that the marriage plot was central to who he was as a writer. But what the novel does retain is a protagonist who is a conspicuously middle-aged woman—not old, perhaps, but certainly not young, not even as young as the age-anxious Lady Mabel Grex in *The Duke's Children*. Miss Mackenzie has financial expectations but ends up being deprived of her elder brother's money, which goes to his relation by marriage, John Ball, as the money had originally come from the Ball family. With limited means, she repairs to the spa community of Littlebath (also seen in *The Bertrams*). Littlebath and its evangelical community, "the Stumfoldians," repressive in its routine hominess, is amusingly rendered. The way these Christian communities could absorb women is bought home in a comic way that still leaves the reader in no doubt as to the grim fate Miss Mackenzie avoided by leaving Littlebath.

Her late brother's business associate, Samuel Rubb holds himself out as her last chance, and thinks she is available to him just because she is down on her luck. Rubb could indeed have a chance if he were just a bit more subtle. But Mr. Maguire, the curate of the Reverend Mr. Stumfold at Littlebath, is totally after Miss Mackenzie's money. Rubb, of a lower social standing, ends whatever chance he has when he begins to intrigue financially with the Mackenzie family. Both fatuous lovers are depicted with great comic effect. Strange crossings exist between the Ball and Mackenzie families— both have baronetcies, the sister of the Ball baronet marries the cousin of the Mackenzie baronet, and the Ball baronet's brother leaves his money to his Mackenzie nephews, not to his own family. When the eldest Mackenzie brother passes away, the money ends up going not to Miss Mackenzie but to the Ball heir, John. This creates a paradoxical situation where the beneficiary of her disinheritance in fact loves her. This dilemma is resolved in the novel's happy ending. Sir John Ball, a widowed father of seven, ends up finding love again and successfully courting Miss Mackenzie, thus reuniting her with her fortune. Thus, in *Miss Mackenzie* Trollope did not end up evading the marriage plot. Indeed, the novel extended the genre to include middle-aged men and women often excluded from such narratives.

Two other points worthy of note: Chapter XXVII, "The Negro Soldiers' Orphan Bazaar," is one of the few representations of blackness in Trollope, and depicts London society raising money for children whose freed fathers had taken up the Northern cause in the American Civil War. It is also a scene in which Trollope introduces such Palliser series characters as Lady Glencora and the Duke of St. Bungay.

See also: evangelical Christianity; *Rachel Ray*

Further Reading

Heath, Kay. "In the eye of the beholder: Victorian age construction and the specular self." *Victorian Literature and Culture*, vol. 35, no. 1, March 2006, pp. 27–45.

Maunder, Andrew. "'Alone into the wide, wide world': Trollope's *Miss Mackenzie* and the Mid-Victorian Etiquette Manual." *Victorian Review*, vol. 20, no. 2, 2000, pp. 48–74.

Mr. Scarborough's Family

Mr. Scarborough's Family was serialized, posthumously, in *All the Year Round* (May 1882–June 1883) and was published in book form in 1883 by Chatto & Windus. In the hands of any other author, *Mr. Scarborough's Family* would read like a thought exercise in legal reasoning similar to the satirical fictitious law reports by A.P. Herbert in his *Misleading Cases in the Common Law* and its sequels (1927–1935), or in the often mechanistic formulaic plots of the so-called "Golden Age" mystery novels. Indeed, "nowhere else in Trollope's work is a complete novel so susceptible of an allegorical interpretation" (Booth 131).

And the plot would have fit in either context: John Scarborough, the Squire of Tretton in Hertfordshire, decides as a young man to evade the entail that constrains him to leave his estate to his eldest son. He does so by marrying his wife twice, in separate churches, first before the birth of his older son Mountjoy, and then later, before the birth of his second son, Augustus. After Mountjoy has landed himself so deeply in debt that the entire estate would go to his creditors, Scarborough, who is slowly dying of an unnamed ailment that does not impair his intellect, reveals the second marriage license and records it as the *only* one. The disinherited Mountjoy receives financial support from Scarborough's honest lawyer Mr. Grey of Grey and Barry, and from Augustus himself. Only when Augustus, too full of himself and angry that his father should have tried to cheat him, suggests that his father should die sooner rather than later, does Scarborough reveal the earlier records, and reinstate Mountjoy as the legitimate heir and "elder son" under law.

This unlikely and somewhat meretricious plot works because Trollope invests heavily in the emotions of his characters. Thus, Mountjoy Scarborough—who is well aware that his gambling addiction (as we would today recognize it) has doomed the estate to foreclosure—aches not as much for his own loss as he does at the slur on his dead mother's chastity implicit in his father's scheme. At first, Augustus Scarborough plays his hand intelligently, by financially supporting his brother, acting unshocked at the revelation that he, who has trained as a barrister, is in fact the rightful squire-in-waiting. Over time, however, the cool-blooded Augustus's anger grows over his nearly being cheated of his inheritance, and his references to his father's plots become increasingly bitter, until "his second son only desired his [father's] death and almost told him so to his face" (Ch. XXI; XIX–XX). This last insult from Augustus incites the dying father's rage, and Scarborough begins to envision Augustus's downfall and Mountjoy's reinstatement.

Scarborough himself is "Trollope's closest approach to a plot-spinning villain" (Kendrick 78). However, although he has acted "like a sensation novelist who plots his fictions in advance," Scarborough's hesitation to implement the scheme until it is clear that Mountjoy cannot be saved as heir "has something Trollopian about it" (Ch. LIV; Kendrick 78). Trollope "elicits considerable sympathy for the helpless and dying man, whose body is 'one mass of cuts and bruises'" (Kendrick 78). Scarborough is even more sympathetic, in that his courage in the face of grisly operations and death is understated, with a touch of the debonair. Also, the ailing Scarborough is "affectionate to his children, and anxious above all things for their welfare, or rather happiness" (Ch. I). He has curtailed his own spending to save up an inheritance for Augustus, and we discover later that he has been a bounteous landlord to the agricultural tenants, whose cottages he has rebuilt and improved. He has also built a school for the local children, both those raised in the Church of England and those outside of it (Ch. I, XXI). His humor may be perverse, but it is merry, even as he confounds the lawyers.

Trollope's own "values—truth, honesty, duty—find their spokesman in Scarborough's attorney Mr. Grey, who was an honest man, and had taken up the matter of the Scarborough inheritance simply with a view of learning the truth" (McMaster 146). Grey, who acknowledges that what "has guided me through my professional life has been a love of the law," is animated by a conviction that "the law and justice may be made to run on all-fours" (Ch. LV). Trollope here captures the lawyer's jargon perfectly. Even in the modern practice of law, it is not uncommon to hear cases that reach the same result described as being "on all fours" with each other. Grey's feeling that his connection with Scarborough's machinations leads him to "feel[] that his own probity has been contaminated by them, even though he has been as much a victim of his client's duplicity as anyone else" (Wall 330). Scarborough's "success in making the law an ass positively drives Mr. Grey into premature retirement" (Wall 330). Grey's understandable bitterness ultimately leads him to an overly harsh view of Scarborough's character.

Unlike either of his sons, Scarborough is moderate, well-intentioned, and generally kind. However, he is vengeful when hurt, and surprisingly pertinacious in his vengeance, even as he is dying. Despite Augustus's training and practice at the Bar, his father falls in with Augustus's plan to pay off Mountjoy's debts at a much lower figure with estate funds that would have gone to Augustus; then, after redeeming Mountjoy's and the estate's credit, he makes a frontal assault on Augustus. He decides that if Augustus must inherit the acres, "he shall have them bare," and orders Mr. Grey to strip both Tretton and his London home, "to sell everything which it would be in the squire's legal power to bequeath. The books, the gems, the furniture, both at Tretton and in London, the plate, the stock, the farm-produce, the pictures on the walls, and the wine in the cellars" (McMaster 146).

Mountjoy's response to the despoiling of the library at Tretton is quite funny and a little sad. Reflecting that he is not yet thirty years old, he tries to read several of the ten thousand volumes; "He took out book after book, and told himself with something of sadness in his heart that they were all 'caviar' to him." He is particularly daunted when he is confronted by a sentence of sixteen lines in a volume of *Clarendon's Rebellion* in which he gets hopelessly entangled, and then utterly loses his nerve with modern poetry. Gloomily, he concludes that "three or four days at the club might see an end of" the entire library so carefully assembled and maintained by his father (Ch. LIII).

Scarborough toys with the notion of stripping the estate of its trees, but Grey prevents it, to avoid a potential claim of "waste" of the estate under the entail. Grey's (and Trollope's) legal reasoning is sound here. As Sir William Blackstone wrote in his magisterial *Commentaries*, waste is "a spoil and destruction of the estate either in houses, woods, or lands; by demolishing not the temporary profits only, but the very substance of the thing, thereby rendering it wild and desolate" (III.2: 223). Blackstone further states that "if the particular tenant, I say, commits or suffers any waste, it is a manifest injury to him that has the inheritance, as it tends to mangle and dismember it of its most desirable incidents and ornaments, among which timber and houses may justly be reckoned the principal" (III.2: 225).

Indeed, in a passage omitted from later editions of his text, Blackstone cites a case quite like that of the Scarboroughs in which "Lord Barnard, who was tenant for life without impeachment of waste, with remainder to his eldest son in tail; and having conceived a displeasure against his son, from motives of spleen, began to pull down the family mansion, Raby Castle; but he was restrained by the chancellor, and ordered to repair it." As Blackstone explains, "Since that case, such a tenant has been restrained from cutting down avenues and ornamental timber in pleasure grounds, and also young trees not fit for timber; and also trees upon a common two miles distant from the mansion house, which had been planted as an ornament to the estate" (I.2: 283–284).

The resemblance between the cases, in terms of the extremities to which the angry fathers were prepared to go, is more clear in the original case report, which states that the "the Defendant the Lord Barnard having taken some Displeasure against his Son, got two Hundred Workmen together, and of a sudden, in a few Days, stript the Castle of the Lead, Iron, Glass Doors, and Boards, etc. to the Value of £3000" (McMaster 146, n25).

The novel's subplot involves Harry Annesley, the heir of Peter Prosper, the squire of Buston, who antagonizes his uncle by "unwisely show[ing] a cavalier distaste for his uncle's pleasure in reading lugubrious sermons to the family." In retaliation, Prosper proposes marriage to the strong-willed and domineering Miss Thoroughbung in order "to disinherit Harry by spitefully getting a son to displace him" (McMaster 136). Prosper gives way when he realizes that Miss Thoroughbung's conditions and domineering nature will make his life a misery. He is punished by having to endure her reproaches, and accedes to Harry's status as heir.

The law of inheritance and real property and the obsessive desire to control not just the property itself but its future use (and thus the lives and fortune of the heirs) is a key theme in *Mr. Scarborough's Family*. The novel contrasts the traditional natural legal view of an underlying moral order which the law administers serves, and enforces—Mr. Grey's perspective—while Scarborough himself, Grey's junior partner Mr. Barry, and to a lesser extent, Augustus, represent the newer agnostic approach of Jeremy Bentham, in which determinations of right and wrong are reduced to a mere personal preference (McMaster 136–138).

Scarborough's vindictiveness is held in check by the law of waste. Indeed, this is the only time Mr. Grey successfully reins in the old man. But in fact Scarborough successfully induces Augustus to assist in his own ruin by paying off Mountjoy's creditors. This allows Scarborough to divest Augustus and reinstate Mountjoy. The old man, now on his deathbed, reveals to Augustus how he has been manipulated. He dismisses Augustus with vindictive satisfaction. Atypically, the unrepentant Scarborough dies satisfied that he has saved the estate for Mountjoy and that he has avenged himself on Augustus. All of Mr. Scarborough's plots, however, have only delayed the inevitable. His eldest son returns to Monte Carlo, gambling away all his father bent and twisted the law to save (Ch. LXI). The Dostoyevsky of *The Brothers Karamazov* might have written the novel more luridly and passionately. But he would have recognized the themes of inheritance, gambling, and fatal character flaws.

Further Reading

Edwards. P.D. *Anthony Trollope: His Art & Scope*. London: St. Martin's, 1978.

Kendrick, Walter M. *The Novel-Machine: The Theory and Fiction of Anthony Trollope*, Baltimore: Johns Hopkins University Press, 1980.

McMaster, R.D. "Trollope and the Terrible Meshes of the Law: Mr. Scarborough's Family." *Nineteenth-Century Fiction*, vol. 36, no. 2, September 1981, pp. 135–156.

Wall, Stephen. *Trollope and Character*. London: Faber & Faber, 1988, pp. 324–333.

Nina Balatka

Nina Balatka was published anonymously by Blackwood's in 1867, and serialized in *Blackwood's Magazine* from October 1866 to May 1867. It was the first of Trollope's three short Continental novels. Trollope knew French and German, and he lived in Belgium (where his father died), and when young had at one point hoped to be appointed to an Austrian cavalry regiment. Though his brother Thomas Adolphus Trollope frequently set his work in France or Italy or wrote about the French and Italians, he did not set much work in Germany or Central Europe in general. The Continent features prominently in Anthony Trollope's fiction as a place to go when one is disgraced, when one has little money, or, as occurs when Lord Chiltern and Phineas Finn fight on Blankenberg sands, to duel. The settings of the three short novels Trollope situated in continental Europe were all in or adjacent to the German-speaking world: *Nina Balatka* in Prague, *The Golden Lion of Granpere* in Lorraine, and *Linda Tressel* in Nuremberg. Their authorship was discovered by R.H. Hutton, then editor of the *Spectator*, and in general the literary critic of his day that Trollope most respected.

Nina Balatka is a Christian maiden in Prague (described as just that, not as specifically Czech or Slavic, although the name suggests that ethnicity). Nina's father, the merchant Josef Balatka, had drifted into a business collaboration with a Jewish father and son named Trendellsohn, angering his former partners, the Christian Zamenoy families, to which Balatka is related by marriage. The Zamenoys are even more upset when Nina begins to show interest in the Trendellsohn son, Anton, and it becomes clear that marriage between them is likely despite their religious differences. The Balatkas live in a house whose deed is held by the senior Trendellsohn, Stephen. When Josef Balatka dies, Anton Trendellsohn asks for the deed, which in fact was held by Nina's Zamenoy uncle. But Souchey, the indispensable servant of the Balatkas, is manipulated by a servant overtly sympathetic to the Zamenoys, Lotta Luxa, to put the deed in Nina's desk. When Anton finds it, he suspects her of fraud, and a strain is put on their friendship.

As in *Linda Tressel*, this is not just a story about a young woman pursuing love outside of accustomed social norms, but of female despair as Nina, like Linda, contemplates suicide by jumping into the Moldau from a bridge. However, even though the sociological divide between Nina and Anton is even greater than that between Linda Tressel and Ludovic Valcarm, Nina's story has a happier ending. Although marrying a Christian is, for Anton's family, as big a step as marrying a Jew is for Nina, especially since the Jewish community looks to Anton to be its leader and hope for the future, the two young people end up together, even though Nina knows that she will not see her gentile relatives again and that her new social circle will center around Jewish women such as Anton's niece Ruth Jacobi. Although the Jewish girl Rebecca Loth is also in love with Anton, and make an eloquent speech about why marrying within one's group is better, like her namesake in Sir Walter Scott's *Ivanhoe* she stands aside and lets the Gentile girl, Nina, claim Anton.

Despite the happy ending, there is a sinister undertone to the story, epitomized by Souchey, the mysterious, androgynous servant of Josef Balatka, who is the moral hinge of the story, but until the very end seems likely to swing either way. There is a sense that market forces—as those that lie behind the Balatka-Trendellsohn business collaboration—are erasing ethnic traditions. But there is also that a mixed marriage entails drastic renunciations in order for it to take place. Hence, the novel takes place at once within and outside a modernizing world.

Trollope visited Prague in 1865. *Nina Balatka* is full of the atmosphere of that city as he sensed it, including an expansive description of the great Moldau (Vltava) River. Although the 1848 revolt by Bohemian nationalists against their Austrian overlords was of recent memory, there is little sense of that event or of any specifically Czech content in *Nina Balatka*. The novel's intent is philo-Semitic and in favor of Christian-Jewish intermarriage. Indeed, it stands as Trollope's most positive fictional depiction of Jews.

It must be noted, though, that by setting the story abroad he limited any potential applicability to English life, and in a sense the Slavic Balatkas, by becoming "Christians" when seen in apposition to Jews, were in anything as enfranchised in European terms by Trollope's depiction of them as were the Trendellsohns.

Nina Balatka was adapted by Henry Ong for the stage in 2016.

See also: *The Golden Lion of Granpere*; Jews; *Linda Tressel*

Further Reading

Cheyette, Bryan. *Between "Race" and "Culture" Representations of "The Jew" in English and American Literature.* Stanford, CA: Stanford University Press, 1996.

Cohen, Monica. "The Paradox of Literary Commercialism in Trollope's *Nina Balatka.*" *Novel: A Forum on Fiction*, vol. 47, no. 3, Fall 2014, pp. 383–402.

North America

Trollope did not accompany his mother, Frances Trollope, to the United States in 1827; her rather unpleasant stay led her to write her famously controversial *Domestic Manners of the Americans.* Trollope briefly visited New York City, Saratoga Springs, and Montréal on his way back from the Caribbean in 1858. He made his second visit to the country in 1860, on the verge of the Civil War, on a special postal mission. He took two further trips to the United States, to read from and publicize his work in 1868 and to pass through the country from west to east on the way back from his second trip to Australia in 1875.

North America was published in late 1862 by Chapman and Hall in two volumes. The first chronicles Trollope's journey through most of New England, the Upper Midwest (Minneapolis, Wisconsin, Chicago), New York, Boston, Philadelphia, and Baltimore, with a detour to Canada along the way. The second volume starts in Washington, D.C., then describes Trollope's treks as far west as St. Louis, though no further. The book does not venture west of the Mississippi; it was not until 1875, upon his return from Australia, that Trollope transited through San Francisco and visited Utah. In the second volume Trollope describes his return to Washington via the Ohio River. His description of Cincinnati, the city upon which his mother had founded her critique of America, is more equable; for example, he observes the American quirk for naming streets after numbers and trees, and says nothing about the way that in the United States aristocrats tended to live in cities, whereas in England by definition they lived in the country.

This condition, though, was different just across the South, across the Ohio River in Kentucky, in the Border South, and Trollope's account reflects his keen observations on conditions there. Trollope visited a bluegrass farm run by its gentleman proprietor, and admired the unostentatious ease of the life there, though he minimized the cruelties of slavery in Kentucky by generalizing that a gentleman seldom sold his slaves there. Trollope closely observed Kentucky, and saw how the way the state did not lately fall into the category of either North or South made the job of its native son, Abraham Lincoln, in both suturing the Union and maintaining its constitutional principles all the harder. Trollope met and admired John J. Crittenden, the Kentucky politician who proposed a last-ditch compromise to save the Union without war. Trollope witnessed the failure of Crittenden's proposal in his few tumultuous months in a nation on the verge of dividing itself. Unlike other British writers, such as the London *Times* correspondent William Howard Russell who reported from New Orleans and other Southern hot spots during the Civil War, Trollope never visited the Deep South.

Trollope ends his narrative with reflecting on the general state of American life, examining cultural forms as distinct as hotels—generally perceived, in their grand form, to be an American innovation—law and lawyers, the post office, and literature. On this last topic, Trollope observes that Americans still read English books more than their own authors, though James Fenimore Cooper and Washington Irving were esteemed. He also laments that American publishers pirated books without heed to English copyright, a circumstance ameliorated legally only after Trollope had died, in the 1890s. Trollope gained a consistent American publisher in magazine and book form, *Harper's*. But he probably never realized the revenue from American consumption of books that he would legally have deserved under the new regimen.

In *North America* Trollope states that he approved of republican government in general. Indeed, he saw England as basically a republic. But Trollope was skeptical of universal suffrage because it associated democracy with corruption. Despite the Civil War, Trollope did not see America as a failed experiment, neither does he rhapsodize about the country in his account. Although he was optimistic about Union success in the war, his partisanship for that cause was perhaps midway between Lincoln and Crittenden. He did not think the United States would ever return to its pre–1861 size, and that even if the South returned to the fold the West would split off. This might be an index of Trollope's discerning the external forms more than the internal pulse of America. It was also reflective of the nuanced British attitude towards the American conflict, which Trollope explains by noting how noncommittal the United States had been in the Crimean War, although this was to confuse two wars with very different stakes attached to them. References to the American Civil War in *Miss Mackenzie* and *He Knew He Was Right* show that Trollope paid detailed attention to the conflict. Despite writing at a far more critical time than his mother had, Trollope's book was found unexciting by the general public, and, though it went into several editions and was republished even after the end of the Civil War, it did not come near to matching his mother's success.

If Trollope did not match his mother's vitriol towards America, nor that of Charles Dickens in *Martin Chuzzlewit*, neither did he rhapsodize about America so much either to excite the transatlantic public or to titillate the British. The book, indicatively, contained at the end the full texts of the Declaration of Independence and the U.S. Constitution, showing both that Trollope was laying evidence of American life and principles before the British reader (who, this implies, did not necessarily know these documents in any detail). It was not until the publication of James Bryce's *The American Commonwealth* (1888) that Frances Trollope's view of America was replaced by a more sober, practical, and contemporary commentator, one who recognized both America's political maturation and its loss of the spark of frontier innovation that the Trollopes, mother and son had, though their differing lenses, observed. The shady investor Hamilton K. Fisker in *The Way We Live Now* (his name a play on the then–US Secretary of State, Hamilton Fish) was a somber indicator of this.

Trollope had good relationships with both Nathaniel Hawthorne and his son

Julian. He praised the former while keeping up relations with the latter, who became one of his first important critics. Through Kate Field, Trollope met Mark Twain and Joaquin Miller when they were touring England. Trollope was foiled, though, in his attempt to have interview with Brigham Young, patriarch of the Mormons in Utah, in 1875. When Trollope came to Young's door, Young asked him if he was a miner. Thinking Young meant the term metaphorically, Trollope responded that he was a writer and journalist. Young then asked Trollope if he worked for his bread. Upon Trollope's affirmative response, Young insisted that he was, indeed, a miner. With this conclusion, the interview was at an end.

Yet, if the somewhat idealized portraits of Boncassen in *The Duke's Children* and Senator Gotobed in *The American Senator* are to be believed, Trollope had high opinions of Americans as both statesmen and gentlemen of letters. In both his portrayal of Isabel Boncassen in fiction and the impact on him of Kate Field in real life, his high opinion of American young women was featured in two short stories of his, "Miss Ophelia Gledd" and "The Courtship of Susan Bell." (Trollope never set a full-length novel in North America.) In turn, he was popular in America, though never a success on the lecture circuit like Dickens, Thackeray, or, later, Oscar Wilde, and Joseph Conrad. American readers tended (as they have continued to do) to see Trollope's work as quintessentially English, and to esteem or denigrate him based on their valuation of that quality.

As optimistic a "last word" as Isabel Boncassen might have been with respect to Trollope's treatment of North America, she was in fact not his final American character. Ella Beaufort Peacocke in *Dr. Wortle's School* is the American wife of a scapegrace husband who weathers aspersions on her morality with grace and integrity. In *The Landleaguers,* his last novel set in Ireland, Trollope is particularly vitriolic against American-fostered support of Irish radicalism. The relative comity with the transatlantic Republic on display in *The American Senator* and *The Duke's Children* is far less steady in *The Landleaguers.* Trollope also plays with his foremost American literary detractor, Henry James, as Mahomet M. Moss's shady sexual past with Madame Socani parallels Gilbert Osmond's dubious liaison with Madame Merle in *Portrait of a Lady* (1881), even as James himself had partially modeled his heroine, Isabel Archer, on the young spirited American girl Isabel Boncassen in *The Duke's Children.* Trollope hoped British sympathy about the assassination of President James A. Garfield would tamp down American advocacy of Irish nationalism. This awareness of US politics and his reading of younger American novelists such as James show that even late in his life, Trollope had a transatlantic eye that helped elucidate his last vision of what the future might be. "Never, Never—Never, Never" was a "condensed novel" and "after the manner of Bret Harte" and was serialized in *Sheets for the Candle,* a Massachusetts magazine. If an American writer had written this story, it would have been seen as an anti–English parody of *The Small House of Allington.* But Trollope was ribbing himself and ventriloquizing America.

Trollope was a supporter of the United States, but never envisioned it becoming a greater world power than Britain. The United States was a place where fortunes could be increased. In *The Way We Live Now* Augustus Melmotte lures investors to a scheme to build an American railroad that ends up being fictitious. But Trollope did not see the United States as ever being wealthier than Britain. Nor was there a sense that, if

Lord Silverbridge and Isabel Boncassen had a son, that he would be a Churchillian figure who would at times consider himself half-American. That Isabel calls her husband "Abraham" at one point just after they are married may be a mock-allusion to Abraham Lincoln. Trollope saw the United States as a British colony that had happened to become independent; though larger in scale than the mother country, he felt it would never really attain more political or cultural consequence. Frances Trollope disliked the Americans, but did not underestimate the country as a whole. Her son liked the people much better, but simply failed to comprehend the future scale or nature of American power, both political and cultural. Unlike his writing on Australia and New Zealand, Trollope's prophetic sense failed him when writing about the United States.

Part of the reason for this is that Trollope, though lacking his mother's animus or vitriol, found parts of American social life hard to take. Unlike Mark Twain, he did not relish life on the Mississippi, nor traversing that river by boat. Trollope's account of his voyage down river from St. Paul, Minnesota, to La Crosse, Wisconsin, is harrowing. It is replete with episodes of American mothers fattening their babies with thrice-daily diets of roast beef and pickles, and in general making too much of their children and advertising this presence too overtly in public. Trollope found the American adults on the boat insufficiently gregarious and outgoing. He judged the frenetic pace of American life likely to lead its pursuers to an early grave.

Considering his interest in British settler colonies, Canada plays a surprisingly small role in Trollope's oeuvre. Two chapters, "Lower Canada" (Québec) and "Upper Canada" (Ontario), are folded into Trollope's record of his itinerary from New Hampshire to New York via Niagara Falls and Chicago. Trollope did not visit New Brunswick or Nova Scotia, though he stated that, if Canada were ever to become self-governing, those areas must be included in the new state. Though the success of the Canadian confederation is alluded to in *Phineas Finn*, just a few years earlier in the book on North America Trollope had been dubious, lamenting that Montréal and Toronto were underpopulated; he does not see Canada as viable politically on its own. Trollope observed that Canada was poorer than the United States. He saw that this condition actually made it easier for the newcomer to thrive in Canada than in an American polity where prosperity was beginning to lock out the working man. He argues that if Canada did become a nation it would need its own monarch, to be selected from among the princes of the British royal family. Montréal might have been a good setting for a Trollopian story of cultural contrast and marital reconciliation. But Trollope never wrote fiction on such a subject.

See also: *The American Senator*; Australia and New Zealand; *The Duke's Children*; Trollope, Frances Milton

Further Reading

Claybaugh, Amanda. "Trollope and America." *The Cambridge Companion to Anthony Trollope*, edited by Carolyn Dever and Lisa Niles. London: Cambridge University Press, 2011, pp. 210–223.

Kissel, Susan S. "'What Shall become Of Us All': Frances Trollope's Sense of the Future." *Studies in the Novel*, vol. 20, no. 2, Summer 1988, pp. 151–166.

Margolis, Stacey. "Trollope for Americanists." *J19: The Journal of Nineteenth-Century Americanists*, vol. 1, no. 2, Fall 2013, pp. 219–228.

Montgomery, Maureen. *Gilded Prostitution: Status, Money, and Transatlantic Marriages, 1879–1914.* New York: Routledge, 1989.

Smith, Walter E. "Anthony Trollope in America: A Brief Survey of His Publishing History." *The Princeton University Library Chronicle*, vol. 62, no. 3, Spring 2001, pp. 479–500.

novel series

There were few precedents for the sort of novel series Trollope wrote twice, in the Barchester novels (1855–67) and the Palliser novels (1864–1879). In France, Honoré de Balzac had written *La Comédie Humaine*, a huge novel-cycle that was tantamount to the writer's entire oeuvre. In Balzac, major characters from one book reappear in others as minor figures, while the total action takes place in a common world. Still, there is no continuity of a major character being carried over from book to book other than in the three books of *Lost Illusions* (1837–1843), which is in effect one long novel. Trollope was unquestionably influenced by Balzac. This was true both directly—*La Vendée* is virtually a "prequel" to Balzac's *Les Chouans* (1829)—and indirectly in his portraits of social, clerical and political life in a cosmopolitan society. However, Trollope's novel series, unlike Balzac's *Comédie*, are only a subset of his entire oeuvre, and he knew when his imagination was done with them.

But Trollope's two series take characters such as Mrs. Proudie, Obadiah Slope, Plantagenet Palliser, and Phineas Finn across life-trajectories in unprecedented ways. Sir Walter Scott wrote series of novels such as *Tales of My Landlord* (1816–32). They were unified by narrative perspective, theme, and approach but did not have characters continue across books. Thackeray wrote *The Virginians* (1857) as a sequel to *Henry Esmond* (1852), but he took the story no further than the two books. Trollope's mother, Frances Milton Trollope, wrote the *Widow Barnaby* trilogy (1839–55), in which the same character continued across three books.

James Fenimore Cooper's *Leatherstocking* quintet (1823–1841) came closest to Trollope. Though written out of chronological order, the books tell the tale of Natty Bumppo from the young woodsman of the Upstate New York forests of *The Deerslayer* to the old trapper of the middle-American grasslands of *The Prairie*. Cooper, who in different measure shared Trollope's mix of interest in urbane society and of outdoor life, came closest to Trollope in investing so much of an authorial fate in a character that went across novels. But Trollope far more thoroughly evoked an entire world. In Trollope's oeuvre, reoccurrence of minor figures such as Archdeacon Grantly or the Duke of St. Bungay mattered nearly as much as the larger arc created by focusing of a major protagonist.

Trollope decided to resurrect the characters of Septimus Harding, Eleanor Bold, and Archdeacon Grantly from *The Warden*, a shorter, more intimate novel, in the much broader and more ambitious *Barchester Towers*. Here, he was making a very different move than Dickens did when he created an entire world in each novel and then inaugurated an entirely new one in the next. Trollope invented a shire, Barsetshire, and a cathedral city, Barchester, for his characters. His aim was to develop an entire world. (Though the topography and culture of Lincolnshire is very different, Jill Durey has suggested that Trollope's knowledge of the Trollope baronets in that shire, and their ecclesiastical entanglements and ramifications, may have given him some detail for his fictional Barsetshire.) At the beginning of *Doctor Thorne*, Trollope states that modern reform of the shires has divided Barsetshire into East Barsetshire and West Barsetshire. He indicates that that Dr. Thorne's story takes place in East Barsetshire. The overview he gives here broadens the Barsetshire series beyond the story of the Harding-Grantly family into the limning of an entire fictional world.

The next three Barchester books, *Doctor Thorne, Framley Parsonage,* and *The Small House at Allington*, feature the central characters in *Barchester Towers* only in minor roles. *Framley Parsonage* is the one in which they matter most, as the marriage of Mr. Harding's granddaughter, Griselda Grantly, is featured. The emphasis is on other great families of the Barsetshire aristocracy and their nemeses, suitors, and hangers-on. But in the final book of the series, *The Last Chronicle of Barset*, the plotline of the Grantly family is taken on to the next generation. Lady Lufton and Martha Dunstable Thorne from the third and fourth books appear in the final book in roles of some prominence. Furthermore, the fates of Mrs. Proudie and Obadiah Slope are resolved. Trollope also concludes the Johnny Eames-Lily Dale plot, and brings the trajectories of as many characters as possible to full closure. Trollope was clearly wearying of this world. (One late short story of Trollope's, "The Two Heroines of Plumplington," was clearly set in Barset.)

More unusual than most novel series by other authors, Trollope's Palliser and Barsetshire novels are set in the same world. Plantagenet Palliser is a minor character in *The Small House of Allington*. Silverbridge—the parliamentary constituency represented by Plantagenet Palliser and then his son—is in Barsetshire. A portrait of Lady Glencora Palliser is mentioned in *The Last Chronicle of Barset*. Dr. Mortimer Tempest, Crawley's examiner in that novel, introduces Lord Silverbridge as parliamentary candidate in *The Duke's Children*. *Miss Mackenzie* (1865) has Palliser characters such as the Duchess of St. Bungay crop up, and Dolly Longestaffe (as the name is spelled in *The Way We Live Now*) reappears in *The Duke's Children*. If Trollope does not go as far as Balzac in giving his characters free rein to drop into any of his novels, he does envision overlap among them.

Other Trollope books have shared settings. *The American Senator* and *Ayala's Angel* both take place in another, more northern fictional shire, Dillsborough, and the Twentyman family is present in both. Both *The Bertrams* and *Miss Mackenzie* fictionalize Bath as the evangelical spa community Littlebath. Several of Trollope's short stories feature the same semi–Trollopian narrator, Archibald Green. Seriality is widely afoot in Trollope's world.

Twice, Trollope folded the conclusion of a story previously the center of an entire book into a successor book not mainly about that subject. In *Phineas Redux* we see the conclusion of the disastrous entanglement of Lizzie Eustace with Mr. Emilius, most of which is related in the earlier *The Eustace Diamonds*, and *The Last Chronicle of Barset* contains the final episodes of Johnny Eames's quixotic love for Lily Dale. The major plot in one book becomes a subplot of the next.

The Barsetshire series, with the consistent thread of Mr. Harding and the Grantlys, is a degree more unified than the Palliser books, where the Pallisers disappear for long stretches of the action. Neither the Barsetshire or Palliser novels are as systematized as later series such as John Galsworthy's *The Forsyte Saga*, Marcel Proust's *Remembrance of Things Past,* Anthony Powell's *A Dance to the Music of Time*, C.P. Snow's *Strangers and Brothers,* or Simon Raven's *Alms for Oblivion*. Trollope, though, takes care to always have the "stitching" family in the Barsetshire novels, the Grantlys, present. In *Framley Parsonage*, Griselda Grantly marries Lord Dumbello; in *The Last Chronicle,* her brother Henry marries Grace Crawley, even though neither relationship is the major plot of their respective books. The Grantly/Harding family is only dominant in the first, second, and sixth of the Barsetshire books. Similarly, the Pallisers really dominate the first, fifth, and sixth books of the series named after them. In *The Eustace Diamonds*, the Palliser characters only appear in the final chapter, "What Was Said About It All at Matching?," to provide a kind of Greek chorus on the follies and travails of the novel's wayward lead character, Lizzie Eustace. The Palliser novels contain an internal diptych concerning Phineas Finn, an Irish Member of Parliament, and his social and political progresses and reversals in London. Here, Plantagenet Palliser and his wife, Lady Glencora, are part of the general background. But they feature most when the threatened remarriage of the Duke of Omnium, Plantagenet's uncle, threaten the inheritance of Lady Glencora's husband and son. The Duke dies and Madame Max ends up marrying Phineas, giving the Irish outsider a small role in suturing an English duke's inheritance. The second Phineas novel, *Phineas Redux*, also continues and resolves the stormy marriage of Lizzie and the loathsome and, it transpires, murderous Mr. Emilius. The Palliser books are not totally integrated. The lead couple of the first Palliser novel, *Can You Forgive Her?,* Alice Vavasor and John Grey, barely reappear in the rest of the series. But Trollope stitches the six books together more systematically than he did with the Barsetshire books.

If the focus of the Barsetshire novels is the Church of England, that of the Palliser books is politics. This does not mean every event in either series has to do with these themes. Much in both series has to do with love, courtship, and marriage. But just as in the Barchester novels new bishops come and high and low church war over doctrine and liturgical practice, so in the Palliser books do Liberals and Conservatives go in and out of office and politicians struggle between principle and pragmatic need. The last two books of the Palliser series, *The Prime Minister* and *The Duke's Children*, show the growth of Plantagenet Palliser into an exemplary statesman. In the final book, Palliser, now out of office and having succeeded to the dukedom, learns to live with his children's unconventional marital choices. As with the Barsetshire series, Trollope signals the close of the sequence by exploring the lives of a younger generation of the main family and by making sure to mention as many characters from the previous books as possible. *The Duke's Children* (in Trollope's original version, later cut at the insistence of his serial publishers) ends with the younger member of the next generation, Lord Gerald Palliser, saying that, with what the Duke had let his elder siblings get away with, he himself would have much to attend to in restoring a high moral code to guide his actions. This might promise a seventh Palliser novel. But it is clear that Trollope, as with the Barsetshire books, was wrapping up the sequence in six.

The mention of the serialization of *The Duke's Children* calls to mind the fact that almost all of Trollope's novels from *Framley Parsonage* onward were series, in that they were serialized in magazines before or concurrent with their book publications. The two novel series can be seen as providing six installments of a single long novel, just as every installment of a serialized novel was one iteration of a longer book. Trollope's novel series, though, were not all bound into one narrative. Still, Trollope's tendency to pursue novel series runs parallel with the almost soap opera–like fascinations of the domestic drama ongoing incidents in his character's lives.

Surprisingly few British novelists writing immediately after Trollope followed his example in composing novel series. Thomas Hardy's Wessex novels were set in a common fictional place (as with Barsetshire) but did not have overlapping characters between books. The same was true of Hugh Walpole's novels set in the fictional Glebeshire. Margaret Oliphant's *Chronicles of Carlingford*, whose composition overlapped with Trollope's series, is the closest parallel, but Oliphant also did not influence later writers. These tended to avoid wanting to commit to reusing characters and scenes that might alienate readers who did not want to come read later installments of a series without prior knowledge of events depicted in earlier ones and who might lack time and scope to go back to read the earlier books. Only with Galsworthy's *Forsyte Saga*, which was influenced by Zola's Rougon-Macquart series and by Trollope, did the novel series assume once again a major place in British fiction.

See also: *Barchester Towers*; *Doctor Thorne*; *Phineas Finn*; *Phineas Redux*

Further Reading

Dever, Carolyn. "Trollope, Seriality, and the 'Dullness' of Form." *Literature Compass,* vol. 7, no. 9, September 2010, pp. 861–866.

Durey, Jill Felicity. *Trollope and the Church of England.* Basingstoke: Palgrave Macmillan, 2002.

Felber, Lynette. *Gender and Genre in Novels Without End: The British Roman-Fleuve.* Gainesville: University of Florida Press, 1995.

Goodlad, Lauren M.E. "The *Mad Men* in the Attic: Seriality and Identity in the Narrative of Capitalist Globalization." *Modern Language Quarterly,* vol. 73, no. 2, June 2012, pp. 201–235.

Langbauer, Laurie. *Novels of Everyday Life: The Series in English Fiction, 1850–1930.* Ithaca, NY: Cornell University Press, 1999.

old age

Trollope, who died at sixty-seven, lived longer than many other major Victorian novelists (Thackeray, Dickens, Eliot, the Brontë sisters, and Wilkie Collins were all younger when they died). He was the last of the major mid–Victorian novelists to die, and was able to respond in his fiction to the full range of events of the 1870s, including the beginning of Anglo-German rivalry, the rise in financial power of the United States, the new configuration of Continental Europe, and rising tensions in Ireland. Yet he also lived fewer years than Queen Victoria, than his political idol William Ewart Gladstone, and younger contemporaries such as George Meredith and Margaret Oliphant. Had Trollope lived just a few years longer, he would have seen Gordon's humiliation at Khartoum, the rise of Charles Stewart Parnell in Ireland, and the beginnings of serious movement towards Australian federation. These events would have surely found their way into his fiction. Trollope's death in 1882 made his oeuvre securely a part of the mid–Victorian era. In *The Last Chronicle of Barset,* Mrs. Grantly distinguishes between the extreme old age of her late father-in-law, the Bishop, and the relative advanced years of her own father, Mr. Harding. At his death, Trollope fell far more into the latter category.

It is questionable, though, whether Trollope had wanted to live longer. Though he died at the height of his powers—*Mr. Scarborough's Family*, published posthumously in 1883, is considered one of his greatest works—he seems to have prepared for the end, finishing *An Autobiography* in 1876 with the expectation that he would fail to include only the few remaining years of his life. In a letter of June 8, 1876, he told his Australian friend G.W. Rusden that, as of "that leisure evening of life, I must say that do not want it. I can conceive of no contentment of which toil is not to be the immediate parent. As the item of passing comes near me I have no fear as to the future—I am ready to go." Trollope lived into old age, but not extreme old age, and, though Gladstone for one did not necessarily slow down even into his eighties, Trollope might not have wanted to be physically restricted to producing works in a smaller compass.

In Trollope's novels, "old age" begins early. *An Old Man's Love* sees William Whittlestaff deeply in love with Mary Lawrie, but willing to relinquish her to his younger rival, John Gordon, because he feels he is too old. Yet Whittlestaff is only a vigorous fifty. The title, though, has a second valence. An old man's love is that which is willing to go beyond possessiveness, to relinquish Mary because he can see the larger picture. Old age thus brings wisdom.

Other elderly suitors in Trollope are seen less heroically. In *Phineas Redux*, the old Duke of Omnium has affections for Madame Max Goesler that go beyond an *amitié amoreuse*. But she refuses his advances because she knows it will lead to the imputation that she seduced him only for his money. In *Orley Farm*, Sir Peregrine Orme falls in love with Lady Mason, but she refrains from marrying him when she realizes the seriousness of the legal troubles in which she is involved. In both cases, the old men are seen as willing, and the women who have to forebear, in a way, to bring the old men to their senses.

Therefore, Trollope's treatment of old age in men has much to do with virility, both with the male's biological ability to sire children long after women who are generational peers are unable to bear them. Those men who do well in old age are those, such as Plantagenet Palliser, who were hardly epitomes of masculine sexuality in their youth; as an old man Palliser is "never very old" because he had "never been very young." In the Barsetshire novels, Septimus Harding uses old age as a platform to exhibit his virtues of humility and humanity, and the bedesmen of Hiram's Hospital who he tries to protect are themselves even older men. Josiah Crawley in *The Last Chronicle of Barset* is resentful because he is trapped in the position of perpetual curate of Hogglestock while younger men rise higher, but he manages to conjure a kind of saintliness out of a life of victimization and being bypassed for advancement.

The Bertrams depicts the category of the elderly man, like Sir Lionel Bertram in that novel, whose only remaining life-mission is to scavenge and live off others. Otherwise old men in Trollope's fiction, from John Scarborough in *Mr. Scarborough's Family* to Indefer Jones in *Cousin Henry*, are largely there to die and leave money to their sons or heirs, launching a contest that provides fuel for the plot. In both of these novels, the old men influence the future and the lives of the heirs through altering the terms their will. This may have paralleled Trollope's own sense that the only sure way a writer can be immortal is through the bequest of their work. Trollope did this literally by writing at least one work intended to be published posthumously. By the time he died, he produced several more. His late futuristic novel, *The Fixed Period*, depicts the world—or a small south Pacific component of it—in 1980, exactly a hundred years after he wrote it. This illustrates the idea of a mind able to penetrate and affect a future it will never know.

Its theme, the endorsement of euthanasia for people over sixty-seven and a half (the age at which Trollope died), illustrates Trollope's awareness that greater longevity, enabled by medical and public health advances, could be a social problem in modern times.

The older woman in Trollope is in a different position. Only rarely able to dispose of her own finances, she can exert her power through intrigue—as in the case of Lady Lufton in *Framley Parsonage*—or through remaining attractive—as Lady Mason is in *Orley Farm*; she is able to attract men even though she has an adult son. Conversely, Lady Glencora in the Palliser series is never allowed to get old, being killed off by her author before she has to deal with her husband's retirement and the maturation and marriages of her children. For some Trollope characters, old age is a blessing. For others, being denied old age is a gift.

See also: Harry Hotspur in *Sir Harry Hotspur of Humblethwaite*; *Mr. Scarborough's Family*; *An Old Man's Love*

Further Reading

Heath, Kay. "Trollope and Aging," *The Routledge Research Companion to Anthony Trollope*, edited by Deborah Denenholz Morse, Margaret Markwick, and Mark W. Turner, New York: Routledge, 2017, pp. 295–305.

An Old Man's Love

An Old Man's Love was published posthumously by Blackwood's in 1884. The story centers on William Whittlestaff, who is fifty years old but has little to show for his life's work. Whittlestaff has had no public career, little money, and only the rudiments of gentility; he has not even been able to afford a manservant. His chief aide in life is Mrs. Baggett, his housekeeper; she is a benign version of Mrs. Jewkes in Samuel Richardson's *Pamela*. Mrs. Baggett serves as an intermediary between Whittlestaff and the young woman who comes to capture his affections. Whittlestaff had an inclination towards an academic career (he loves reading classical Latin authors), but his family did not encourage those tendencies. Living in Hampshire, a shire which Trollope lived near at the time he wrote the book, and from which his mother hailed, Whittlestaff is something of a Trollope manqué, a Trollope if he had never married nor achieved anything in either his career in the post office or as a writer. He has lived an unfulfilled and incomplete life, and comes to see Mary Lawrie as the beacon of light that might, astonishingly, complete it. Mary accepts Whittlestaff's proposal, only to reconsider it when a younger suitor, John Gordon, comes along. The novel's vivid description of Mary Lawrie is one of Trollope's most fetching characterizations of an attractive young woman. If readers are so inclined, they can see in it echoes, perhaps, of his passion for Kate Field, which was neither acted upon or realized.

Inevitably, this is not the first time Whittlestaff has loved. Indeed, it is the shadow of the past that gives the novel both its drama and its ultimate moral insight. Earlier in his life (readers know because Mrs. Baggett has told Mary Lawrie), he courted Catherine Bailey. But he had lost her to an Old Bailey lawyer, Mr. Compas. Whittlestaff's real moral triumph is not to see John Gordon as Mr. Compas. This is an index of his own maturation. But it also stems from differences in his feelings for the two women, and his discernment of genuine merit in Gordon's character. Even if Whittlestaff thinks he would still be a better husband for Mary, he realizes that it is the chivalrous thing to do to yield to the younger man. Like *The Fixed Period*, *An Old Man's Love* is a meditation on age and on Trollope's own mortality. This novel is less optimistic about the potentialities of old age than the more speculative *Fixed Period*. Old age's greatest gift is its ability to understand the larger picture and yield to the younger when they have merited concession.

The pastoral description of Gar Wood, with its roving deer and picturesque appearance, is one of Trollope's most pictorially rendered landscapes. It provides a very English counterpoint to the Kimberley diamond mines in which John Gordon does business with the questionable Fitzwalker Tookey (one of Trollope's most ingenious character names) and for which Trollope obviously uses the research that went into his South Africa travel book. Readers at first might think John Gordon will be disqualified, and Whittlestaff's suit accepted, because Gordon has been involved in some potentially shaky dealings in Africa. But, true to Trollope's belief that settler colonies provided a way for Britain to expand beyond itself both territorially and cognitively, Gordon's African associations actually help him in his suit and assist in Whittlestaff's conceding. As Kay Heath also points out, Whittlestaff seems to resign himself to a perpetual bachelor existence under the domestic sway of Mrs. Baggett, thus evincing not only renunciation but a kind of asceticism.

The lasting import of *An Old Man's Love*, Trollope's last completed novel, lies in its acknowledgment of the horizons of youth, itself stretched through time. John and Mary could conceivably still have been alive at the start of the Second World War.

See also: *Australia and New Zealand*; *The Landleaguers*; old age

Further Reading

Heath, Kay. "Trollope and Aging." *The Routledge Research Companion to Anthony Trollope*, edited by Deborah Denenholz Morse, Margaret Markwick, and Mark W. Turner, New York: Routledge, 2017, pp. 295–305.
Herbert, Christopher. "Trollope and the Fixity of the Self." *PMLA*, vol. 93, no. 2, March 1978, pp. 228–239.
Tracy, Robert. *Trollope's Later Novels*. Berkeley: University of California Press, 1978.

Orley Farm

Orley Farm was published as a serial (March 1861 to October 1862) and in book form (1861–1862) by Chapman and Hall. The novel has a more mature and darker tone than the four Barsetshire novels that precede it, hearkening back to Trollope's most recent Irish novel *Castle Richmond* (1860). Like *Castle Richmond*, *Orley Farm* involves the upper classes in the sordid circumstances of criminal acts and financial pitfalls more typical of Trollope's foolish young male protagonists. Mary, Lady Mason, the second wife of the much older Sir Joseph Mason, produces a will with a codicil amending the original will presided over by Sir Joseph's attorney Jonathan Usbech. This new will still leaves Sir Joseph the younger the main property of Groby Hall. But Lucius, the son of Sir Joseph's second marriage, inherits Orley Farm.

Sir Joseph challenges the will, asserting the codicil is forged, and loses. Twenty years later, a second case is brought at the instigation of the vindictive solicitor Samuel Dockwrath, who has a grudge against Lady Mason and will lose some of the acres he farms if Lucius comes into possession. Lady Mason is now not only accused of forgery, but additionally of perjury. She is acquitted, although readers have come to know her guilt.

Lady Mason, unlike Lizzie Eustace, does not commit a particularly lavish crime. The main bulk of her husband's estate goes to her stepson, with only a competency diverted to young Lucius. The plan is modest, credible, and practical. Lady Mason, in her late forties, is "still an attractive woman, despite the studied sobriety of her dress, and it is not altogether clear whether her appeal is something she knowingly exploits" (Wall 290). Certainly, that appeal is "clearly powerful enough to secure the professional devotion of her lawyer Mr. Furnival, despite his growing private conviction of her guilt." Mr. Furnival may have "become susceptible in his successful middle age," but Lady Mason's "subtle attractions are not only felt by lawyers with a penchant for pretty women" (Wall 290–91). The upright and scrupulous Sir Peregrine Orme and his daughter-in-law show a strong loyalty, and in Sir Peregine's case, outright devotion, to Lady Mason and her cause.

The tragedy in *Orley Farm* is that Lady Mason's deceit cuts her off from happiness because she cannot herself live with it. Acquitted in not one but two trials, at the end of the day she confesses her guilt to her son Lucius and to Sir Peregrine and Mrs. Orme. The Ormes remain loyal to her, even though Lady Mason cannot accept Mrs. Orme's "attempt to administer spiritual consolation" (an admirable way to describe a conversation that ends with Lady Mason "almost shrieking in despair") (Wall 298).

The "chivalric devotion of Sir Peregrine" remains steady, and "it is only increased by Lady Mason's refusal to exploit it in the interests of her self-preservation." The "tragic irony is that the old man's love has been so selfless that it has aroused in her an answering affection which ensures it cannot be reciprocated; she cares for him too much to marry him, since to do so must be to injure him" (Wall 299). Despite this mutual tenderness, after her trial and as Lady Mason is readying herself to depart to the Continent, Sir Peregrine still desires to marry her. Although he accedes to the notion that no marriage will take place, readers are informed that his heart is broken, and warned: "It is seldom that a young man may die from a broken heart; but if an old man have a heart still left to him, it is more fragile" (Ch. LXXVI).

The two romantic subplots involving young lovers does not match the passion and the genuine love of the elderly Sir Peregrine and Lady Mason. Felix Graham's successful courtship of Judge Staveley's daughter Madeline is never in much doubt, and "Lucius's suit to Mr. Furnival's daughter Sophia is at first countenanced and then rejected by a girl who knows how to look after her own interests all too chillingly" (Wall 299–300). The romance and high-society milieu here resemble the silver-fork fiction of the 1820s and 1830s—except that the participants here not denizens of urbane London, they are landed gentry. Conversely, there is a strand of gritty everyday life as represented by the commercial traveler Kantwise.

But the main action in *Orley Farm* is in the legal arena. In addition to the well-drawn trial scenes (despite the hostile reaction of legal critics, these scenes sparkle), Trollope's own passion in this novel is in his evisceration of a system that, as he sees it, exalts mendacity and verbal tricks over truth. The issue is personal to Trollope, who had himself been called as a witness and subjected to cross-examination. But even more, the creation of a structure of falsehoods taken as true through words meant to deceive is a weaponization of Trollope's own innocent joy in building "Castles in the Air," which led him to writing novels (*Autobiography*, Ch. III) Where Trollope himself seeks to use his fictions to inculcate truths, "in *Orley Farm* the characters constantly cross-examine themselves and others in an attempt to reduce and refine meaning" (Fisichelli 643). The outcome of the case hinges on the "contending lawyer's inability to ask the right question at the proper time…. At the conclusion, Lady Mason, although guilty, is acquitted because the prosecuting lawyers have failed to ask one specific question of Bridget Bolster" (Lansbury 83; Fisichelli 643).

That "such a question should go unasked is precisely Trollope's point"; the tactics and techniques of "the courtroom have so far separated themselves from the impartial pursuit of the truth that oversight becomes almost inevitable." So Mr. Furnival "speaks of Lady Mason in such a way as to convince the jury that a guilty woman charged only with the 'small and petty' charge of perjury, a mere verbal malfeasance, is innocent" (Fisichelli 643–44).

Furnival "closes his case fully aware of the dichotomy between the truth and his lies. For Trollope, Lady Mason's trial is the inevitable rhetorical result of a system which fosters speech for speeches' sake despite the Babellike distortion it produces. Through a skillful combination of peroration and verbal intimidation Mr. Furnival persuades the jury against the truth" (Fisichelli, 644).

Neither Mr. Furnival, who over the course of the novel "had privately become convinced of his client's guilt and is regarded with contempt by Mr. Chaffanbrass, who has never doubted it," nor Chaffanbrass himself are very perturbed by persuading the jury of the innocence of a guilty forger. In fact, Chaffanbrass, amusingly, prefers to represent the guilty, as we see in his defense of Phineas Finn (the one innocent client he represents in his three appearances).

Trollope himself, of course, holds the exact opposite view of matters than his fictional barristers do; as he reminds us, of the "five lawyers concerned, not one of whom gave to the course of justice credit that it would ascertain the truth, and not one of whom wished that the truth should be ascertained" (Ch. LVI). Trollope vents his frustration with the comment that he "cannot understand how any gentleman can be willing to use his intellect for the propagation of untruth, and to be paid for so using it" (Ch. LVI). Here, of course, Trollope's straightforward Victorian exaltation of truth as the product of the trial process does not take into account the respective roles the various players participating in that process, and, in particular, the special obligation of the defense counsel.

That role and its obligations were crystallized in a way defense lawyers still admire by Henry, Lord Brougham in his 1821 defense of Queen Caroline on charges of adultery:

> An advocate, in the discharge of his duty, knows but one person in all the world, and that person is his client. To save that client by all means and expedients, and at all hazards and costs to other persons, and, amongst them, to himself, is his first and only duty; and in performing this duty he must not regard the alarm, the torments, the destruction which he may bring upon others. Separating the duty of a patriot from that of an advocate, he must go on reckless of the consequences, though it should be his unhappy fate to involve his country in confusion [Freedman 1322].

Trollope's moral qualms aside, he "clearly relishes the forensic technique of 'his old friend' [Chaffanbrass] as it is displayed in *Orley Farm*" (Wall 302–3). Even in the novel, the authorial condemnation (and that of the young idealistic lawyer Felix Graham) is balanced by "the moderate Judge Staveley, who defends Chaffanbrass and his like; 'Believe me that as you grow older and also see more of them, your opinion will be more lenient—and more just'" (Wall 301). In fact, Chaffanbrass's forensic firepower is not as effective here as in his earlier and last appearances; "Bridget Bolter is a dogged reiterator, and even Mr. Chaffanbrass cannot do much to shake her." Mr. Furnival, cross-examining the timid and uncertain John Kennedy, "has little difficulty in demoralizing him and demolishing his evidence" (Wall 301).

With all else being equal, one "of the reasons Lady Mason wins her case is that in the court-room itself, she, like Phineas Finn, simply does not look guilty—although of course she is and he is not" (Wall 301). While Trollope makes his unhappy heroine pay: her son's attitude toward her is less than affectionate after her confession, Sir Peregrine's loss of her is likely to lead to the end of his life, and she moves into the world of the Burgo Fitzgeralds, the Mrs. Carbuncles, and other twilight people of Trollope's novels.

Unusually for Trollope, this moral ending feels forced. It is as if, unable to deny the practical victory of Furnival and Chaffanbrass, Trollope still felt a need to bring about a kind of justice, and, at least in the world of his own creation use his creator's license to, in the words of Wallace Stevens, "let be be finale of seem" (Stevens 62).

Further Reading

Fisichelli, Glyn-Ellen. "The Language of Law and Love: Anthony Trollope's *Orley Farm*." *ELH*, vol. 61, no. 3, Autumn, 1994, pp. 635–653.
Lansbury, Coral. *The Reasonable Man: Trollope's Legal Fiction*. Princeton, NJ: Princeton University Press, 1981.
Wall, Stephen. *Trollope and Character*. London: Faber and Faber, 1988, pp. 288–305.

The Oxford Movement

The Oxford Movement (sometimes called the First Oxford Movement to distinguish it from the more liberal revival that began in 1889, with the publication of *Lux Mundi*), was inaugurated by John Keble in a sermon entitled "National Apostasy" in July 1833, and led by John Henry Newman until Newman's conversion to Roman Catholicism in 1845. The leaders of the Movement—including Keble, Newman, Richard Hurrell Froude, and Edward Bouverie Pusey—were co-authors of a series of pamphlets, published under the title *Tracts for The Times*, that set forth their vision.

The goal of the Tractarians was to promote a renewed vision of the Church of England as a fully "catholic" church—that is, a church fully in the apostolic tradition, and to reclaim its traditional order and sacramental heritage. Hence the term "Anglo-Catholic," denoting loyalty to the Established Church of England, while embracing sacramental religion (Wirenius, "Not Charity" 284–85; Williams 130, 133).

In accordance with this view, John Keble, in his seminal sermon "National Apostasy," preached the independence of the Church from the State, and the first Tract declared the "Apostolic Succession, and not political or social convention, to be the basis for her ministry" (Williams 135). In his magisterial study of the Church of England, Robert Rodes, Jr., points out that this embrace of the Apostolic Succession, while sincerely held, was also a means to "counter the loss or feared loss of temporal advantage," and upon which to re-establish independence from government interference (Rodes 246).

As champions of the sacraments, Keble and Pusey "revived the almost forgotten doctrines of the Real Presence and of the Eucharistic sacrifice" (Williams 135). The Tractarians argued for the freedom of the Church from political interference based on its sacred character and function, and Newman began to formulate a distinctly Anglican theology of the Church's proper scope of authority and to sketch out the "Via Media," the Church of England's famous middle way of reconciling its Catholic prayer book with the Protestant ecclesiology established in the Thirty-Nine Articles (Wirenius, "Not Charity" 285).

The Liberal Government of the time set out to find and eliminate ecclesiastical abuses and unjustifiable privileges, which had led to priests being appointed to multiple parishes, some of whom did not perform their duties in either, as well as the gross disparity between parishes and dioceses with regard to funding, affecting their ability to obtain incumbents (Wirenius, "Not Charity" 286 and 286n25). While agreeing that the Tractarians and other High Church leaders saw the Government as infringing on ecclesiastical control over matters both spiritual and temporal, Rodes points out in addition that the spread of the franchise to Dissenters, Roman Catholics, and the poor (who were more likely to identify with the Evangelical school of churchmanship) undermined the traditional assumption that the civil government constituted the voice of the Anglican laity (Rodes 244–46).

Trollope addresses the first two of these issues in *The Warden* (Hiram's Hospital) and in *Barchester Towers* (the absent prebendary Dr. Vesey Stanhope). Even more masterfully, he depicts the inequitably low stipends awarded less influential clergy in *Framley Parsonage* and *The Last Chronicle of Barset* through his portrayal of the financially struggling "perpetual curate" Josiah Crawley. Trollope engages more specifically with the churchmanship and the perceived disloyalty of the Oxford Movement's members as well. In *Barchester Towers*, we are introduced to the Rev. Francis Arabin, who, we are told, "took up the cudgels on the side of the Tractarians, and at Oxford he sat for a while at the feet of the great Newman" (*BT* Ch. XX). We are further told that "Mr. Newman left the Church of England and with him carried many a waverer. He did not carry off Mr. Arabin, but the escape which that gentleman had was a very narrow one" (*BT* Ch. XX). Trollope's depiction of Arabin captures both the rise of the Anglo-Catholic revival called the Oxford Movement, and its fall. Arabin is emblematic of the eager young scholar-priests who followed the Movement and then were faced with the stark choice of following Newman in his "swimming the Tiber" (that is, converting to Roman Catholicism) or remaining loyal to the Established Church (Baker 137–38, 140).

The Tractarians' reaction to the ecclesiastical reforms of the Liberal Party, which was in power at the time, was painfully defensive, not unlike Archdeacon Grantly's stubborn defense of his father-in-law's sinecure in *The Warden*. Unlike the Anglo-Catholics of the Oxford Movement, the traditionalist ("High and Dry") Grantly is a firm defender of the Church's temporalities, but fully accepts the power of Parliament and the Government of the day to alter their arrangements. By contrast, the Tractarians felt the need to theologize their opposition to change, explaining to some extent their frankly unimpressive record on the social issues of the day.

This reaction had two dimensions. First, like the so-called "High Church" party, allied to the Conservative Party, the Tractarians were also implacably opposed to the Liberal Government's ecclesiastical reform bills. While the Tractarians themselves did not support the abuses targeted by the Government, they thought that the proposed measures impermissibly infringed upon the Church's control over its temporalities—property, benefices, and the very establishment of the Church of England (and of Ireland, Scotland, and Wales) (Clarke 1: 12–13). Their commitment to Church autonomy as a corollary of Church authority often led Newman and his colleagues to defend ecclesiastical privileges that were, simply, indefensible. Moreover, "there were no martyrs, unless this name could be applied to the non-resident clergy, the pluralists [i.e., holders of multiple livings] and highly paid bishops and canons whose emoluments were threatened" (Wirenius, "Not Charity" 286).

Second, even regarding those reforms with respect to laborers and the poor that were plainly salutary, Newman and the First Oxford Movement leaders were distrustful of the non-theistic approach which, in their view, guided the Liberal Party's prescriptions (Wirenius, "Not Charity" 286–87; Kenyon 368–69). The Liberals' efforts to create the most inclusive state Church in terms of doctrine was seen by the Tractarians as fatally watering down creedal Christianity, let alone the sacramental view of it held by the Tractarians themselves. Both aspects of this aversion to the Liberal Party were not entirely without foundation. While many clergy could not defend the abuses and privileges targeted for elimination, they were reluctant to have reforms foisted upon them by the Government which funded the Church, based on their doctrine of the Church's "position as a divine society," and "reasserted the supernatural claims of the church to obedience" (Wirenius, "Not Charity" 286). Moreover, the Tractarians and the "High and Dry" defenders of the status quo distrusted the intentions of the Liberals, who "would substitute a vague theism, or even agnosticism, for dogmatic belief" (Wirenius, "Not Charity" 286–87; Kenyon 368–69).

Indeed, Tract 83 of the *Tracts for the Times*, attributed by Ruth Kenyon to John Keble, went further, declaring liberalism to be "a special effort made … to do without religion … an opinion avowed, and growing, that a nation has nothing to do with religion," and even equated Liberalism with the snares of Antichrist (Kenyon 370). Unsurprisingly, then, Newman avowed in his *Apologia Pro Vita Sua* that "my battle was with liberalism" (Wirenius, "Not Charity" 287).

According to Llewellyn Woodward, the Tractarians' essential Toryism, combined with a certain insulation from, and resultant lack of understanding of, the problems confronted by the working classes, effectively sidelined them from any practical engagement with those problems (Wirenius, "Not Charity" 286). Their inveterate opposition to all things liberal, and their tight focus on individual moral regeneration and the need to protect the Church's interests, left them counseling only resignation. For Keble, "faith and obedience seemed to him [as to Church and State] the duty of the subject," and "that absolute detachment from [temporal things] is demanded of the Christian; the sufferings of the poor in the hungry Forties, visitations of cholera, the Irish famine, the Crimean War, are met by the thought 'It is the Lord, the Lord Christ, let Him do what seemeth Him good'" (Kenyon 375).

In the days after the Oxford Movement went into eclipse—that is, after Newman's conversion—the members of the Movement found themselves viewed as potentially disloyal to the Established Church, and under a cloud of suspicion. As the Movement decayed into ritualism and borderline irrelevance, Pusey became much more active in addressing social problems, not only preaching against unfettered capitalism, but fostering pastoral outreach to the poor and working with reformers. His actions in this regard may have laid the foundation for the Anglo-Catholic revival of the late nineteenth century, with its emphasis on social justice as well as sacramental religion (Kenyon 384–89; Wirenius, "Not Charity" 288).

See also: *Barchester Towers*; *The Bertrams*; evangelical Christianity

Further Reading

Baker, Joseph Ellis. *The Novel and the Oxford Movement*. London: Russell & Russell, 1965, pp. 136–144.

Rodes, Robert E., Jr. *Law and Modernization in the Church of England: Charles II to the Welfare State*. Vol. 3: *This House I Have Built: A Study of the Legal History of Establishment in England*. Notre Dame, IN: University of Notre Dame Press, 1991, pp. 244–247.

Simpson, W.J.S. *The History of the Anglo-Catholic Revival from 1845*. London: Allen & Unwin, 1932.

Williams, N. P., and Charles Harris, eds. *Northern Catholicism: Centenary Studies in the Oxford and Parallel Movements*. London: SPCK, 1933.

Wirenius, John F. "Not Charity, But Justice: Charles Gore, Workers, and the Way." *Journal of Catholic Legal Studies*, vol. 50, 2011, pp. 279–96.

Pall Mall Gazette

The Pall Mall Gazette was started in 1865 by George Smith. Smith had worked with Thackeray and Trollope on the *Cornhill* and had published *Framley Parsonage*. Its initial offices were at 14 Salisbury Street in the Strand. The paper was edited by Frederick Greenwood and named after a fictional paper in Thackeray's novel *Pendennis*. The recently deceased Thackeray might have been said to have been the tutelary spirit of the creation of the paper. Unlike the other periodicals for which Trollope principally wrote, *The Pall Mall Gazette* was a daily newspaper, not a periodical, and is the ancestor of today's *Evening Standard*. Trollope's correspondence frequently took the form of (faux) letters to the editor. He commented on political scandals and particularly on the American Civil War, on which he took as strongly pro–Northern perspective. Later, however, he was critical about Reconstruction and not optimistic about the possibility of multiracial democracy in America. Trollope wrote his well-publicized eulogy for Abraham Lincoln for the *Gazette*.

Trollope also wrote *Travelling Sketches*, later collected into a book published by Chapman and Hall, for the *Gazette*. These were not descriptions of travel to particular places as much as evocations of the experience of traveling itself. The *Hunting Sketches* were similar, containing anecdotes serving as mock-instructive examples of the hunting life. These were meant to entertain both those who knew the scene and were yet designed to be titillating and intriguing for outsiders. The *Hunting Sketches* were also published by Chapman and Hall after first being written for the *Gazette*, in editions which specifically mentioned and in effect gave publicity to the *Gazette*. The same was true of Trollope's ecclesiastical writings for the paper, which were published in 1866 as *Clergymen of the Church of England*.

Gradually Trollope began to write less for the *Gazette* as he felt the pay rather low.

In addition, his time was taken up by his own periodical, *Saint Pauls*. Later, the *Gazette* published a negative review of Trollope's book on Thackeray in the English Men of Letters series because editors felt Trollope had been needlessly explicit about the income Thackeray left to his family.

The *Pall Mall Gazette* was a publication that had a distinct late–Victorian (as opposed to mid–Victorian) tinge. It featured notables of the latter part of the nineteenth century such as Robert Louis Stevenson who fused the literary and the popular in a new way. Trollope may be said to have helped form that climate of taste and pave the way for writers of a different idiom than his own.

See also: Fortnightly Review; Saint Pauls Monthly Magazine

Further Reading

Booth, Bradford A. "Trollope and the *Pall Mall Gazette*. Part One." *Nineteenth-Century Fiction*, vol. 4, no. 1 1949, pp. 51–69.
_____. "Trollope and the *Pall Mall Gazette*. Part Two." *Nineteenth-Century Fiction*, vol. 4, no. 2, 1949, pp. 137–158.
Scott, J.W. Robertson. *The Story of the Pall Mall Gazette. of its First Editor Frederick Greenwood, and of its Founder George Murray Smith*. London: Oxford University Press, 1950.

Palmerston (Lord)

Henry John Temple, third Earl of Palmerston (1784–1865), was Prime Minister for nearly ten years from 1855 to 1865, the years in which Trollope made his career both in the post office and as an author. But perhaps his most important role was in the years before that, in developing a British foreign policy of liberalism, free trade, and humanitarian intervention. As Lauren Goodlad (*Geopolitical*) has asserted, if Trollope had a foreign policy, the real-world foreign policy to which he was most inclined was Palmerston's. Though Palmerston's policy of advocating the self-determination of peoples had the pragmatic purpose discouraging any hegemony by a great power in Europe (something in line with British foreign policy as practiced by both parties), Palmerston made clear his enthusiastic endorsement of liberty for its own sake and as a cause worth advocating for intrinsic reasons. Palmerston had a distinct vision of Britain as a diplomatic power. He saw it as a prosperous nation with a vast empire, but not strong enough to dominate Europe and always on guard against a potential European hegemony. This vision is a determining background for how Trollope's characters navigate continental Europe, British settler colonies, and their suppositions of a cultural centrality not necessarily accompanied either by chauvinism or an air of absolute mastery. Furthermore, the everyday moral imperatives of characters Trollope portrays positively have inculcated in themselves are also manifest in policy practices of Palmerstonian idealism.

Palmerston's Anglo-Irish background, equipping him to be a character in Trollope novels such as *Castle Richmond* or *The Kellys and the O'Kellys,* did not make him sympathetic to Irish nationalism. But it did arguably give Palmerston that sense of the world as a place of cosmopolitan interactions of discrete interests. A good many of these were legitimate derivations of popular sentiment.

Trollope's book on Palmerston was his last book of nonfiction. *Lord Palmerston* was written between November 1881 and February 1882 and was published by W. Isbister and Company, publisher of *Good Words*, to which Trollope was a valued contributor. Trollope's book is in many ways an epitome of and commentary upon the existing biography of Palmerston by Palmerston's private secretary, Evelyn Ashley (1836–1907). Trollope's narrative goes through Palmerston's life and career step by step. Generally, Trollope demonstrates sympathy for Palmerston's work ethic and his liberal idealism. Indeed, though Trollope admired Gladstone more, Palmerston, with his industry, his literary talents, and his mood-swings from exuberance to surliness was more the sort to which Trollope would feel akin. This was so even though Palmerson's being of Trollope's father's generation meant his life-course was different in external contours. Gladstone was principled but Palmerston was idealistic. In Trollope's view, Palmerston at once succeeded in profiting British national interests abroad, but doing so in ways which conformed to ideals such as national self-expression and a balance of power in which no single European nation prevailed. Trollope depicts Palmerston urging the Austrians to withdraw from Italy, amidst a crisis depicted in several of the author's short stories. Trollope's passages on the years of the Crimean War alerts the reader that this conflict is the tacit background to novels such as *The Bertrams*. In discussing the Eastern Question, though, Trollope, mourns the perceived unreliability of the Turks as allies, definitely assuming his typical pro–Gladstone, anti–Disraeli position. Trollope understood challenges faced by a politician such as Palmerston. This was not just because he had run for office himself, but also because, as a high official in the post office, he understood the principles of administration and how to put idealistic instincts to practical use as policy.

Trollope praised Palmerston's honesty, industry, and courage. He did so as someone who had traversed many of the same institutions and faced some of the same obstacles and detractors.

See also: Disraeli, Benjamin; Gladstone, William Ewart

Further Reading

Goodlad, Lauren. *The Victorian Geopolitical Aesthetic: Realism, Sovereignty, and Transnational Experience*. London: Oxford University Press, 2017.

Halperin, John. *Trollope and Politics: A Study of the Pallisers and Others*. London: Macmillan, 1977.

the past

Trollope received a good classical education at Harrow and was proud of his abilities at Latin, although unlike most of those interested in the classics in Victorian England he did not have a university education. He did not rest on his schoolboy laurels, continuing to work hard and increase his knowledge of Latin as an adult. Trollope sprinkled a good deal of Latin and Greek into his books. This is exemplified by the title of the Duke of Omnium and the Katakirion line of clothes in *The Struggles of Brown, Jones, and Robinson*. He was asked to write two books on ancient Roman figures. Trollope's subjects, Cicero and the Commentaries of Julius Caesar, match the breadth and structure of Trollope's own interests. Cicero is famous as a writer but also engaged in politics. Caesar was a politician whose writings also achieved fame.

Trollope's book on Cicero (1880) shows him enjoying himself and sharing that enjoyment with the reader. He tells the story of Cicero in a tone not dissimilar to his fiction. Particularly Trollopian is the relation of Cicero's brief stint as governor of Cilicia and the provocative comparison of Cicero with Francis Bacon. Trollope points out that the term "First Triumvirate" is an *ex post facto* invention that was a back-formation of the later triumvirate of Octavian, Antony, and Lepidus, thus fostering a certain interpretation of the relationship of Caesar, Pompey, and Crassus. Trollope portrays both the moments when Cicero took decisive action, as in unmasking the conspiracy of Catiline, and those when he vacillated. He admires, and well conveys, the graceful informality of his writing style. Trollope defends Cicero from the charge of being capricious, though, arguing that, if Cicero seems inconsistent or insincere at times, modern humanity would be judged the same way.

Trollope's book on the commentaries of Julius Caesar on the Gallic Wars was published by Blackwood in 1870. It is not a biography of a man but a work of literary criticism on a given text. At the same time it conveys considerable biographical about Caesar, including a sense of how his interest in democracy was self-serving. Trollope refers to Caesar's account of his own involvement in the Gallic Wars as the first work of modern history, of a writer chronicling his own times. We inevitably think of Trollope's own oeuvre. Trollope neither lionizes nor demonizes Caesar. If anything he takes a slightly pro-republican, anti-imperial attitude. Trollope is thoroughly engaged in his material here both out of professionalism and out of genuine interest. He does not make parallels with his own day. But there is also no deep sense of why the past is important. This might be the basis for the accusation in Trollope's obituary in the December 1882 *Pall Mall Gazette* that the two classical books are worthless.

Although to later generations Trollope has appeared as indelibly a writer of the Victorian age, our "past," as a writer he seems to remain concerned with mainly that age,' his present.' He did write one historical novel, *La Vendée*. But in *The Vicar of Bullhampton*, when the Vicar appeals to Mrs. George Brattle's charitable impulses to get her to care for her distressed sister-in-law Carry by invoking Jesus' compassion for Mary Magdalene, she tells him that "them days and ours" are different. Though Trollope intends this episode to satirize Victorian realism by showing how a society nominally Christian can set aside that faith's core principles, he is also demonstrating that there is a past from which the present can be different. This sense of disparity also emerges with respect to the classical world. It shifts Fielding's famous dictum that the modern novel is a comic epic in prose over to the mock-epic. In *The Bertrams*, George Bertram's speaking of coming back from Jerusalem is compared to Aeneas speaking of returning to the living world from the other side of the River Styx. In *The Warden*, Eleanor Harding thinks of sacrificing herself as Iphigenia was sacrificed by Agamemnon in order to save her father from being vilified by her newspaper-reporter suitor. But the stakes are so much smaller that we laugh at the parallel. This mock-epic tendency is accentuated in Trollope's self-satire seen in Charley Tudor's story "Crinoline and Macassar" in *The Three Clerks*.

A few of Trollope's characters are interested in the distant past. Gregory Marrable in *The Vicar of Bullhampton* theorizes about Stonehenge. Lucius Mason in *Orley Farm* devotes himself to Indo-European philology. But both are depicted as dilettantes, and their interests as pedantic. There is little in Trollope of the palpable treasuring of the past in the work of Thomas Carlyle and John Ruskin.

Trollope was less at home in the Middle Ages than in the classical world. His short story "Gentle Euphemia" parodies medieval times rather than expressing nostalgia for them. In Trollope's discussion of the dream of Scipio in his book on Cicero, he barely alludes to its influential medieval afterlife. Though he told T.H.S. Escott that the surname "Trollope" derived from Normans who hunted in the New Forest, he had little further sense of the medieval, though there are stray references like the forename of Plantagenet Palliser (made fun of for its archaism by Isabel Boncassen in *The Duke's Children*), Alaric Tudor's first name in *The Three Clerks*, and the parallels between the heroine of *Miss Mackenzie* and patient Griselda in Boccaccio and Chaucer. The residues of distant English history—such as the provision for Hiram's Hospital that gave Mr. Harding his benefice in *The Warden*—are comical. Trollope was, however, an avid reader of Elizabethan and Jacobean drama. Though he found these plays not totally enjoyable, they nonetheless influenced his plots. In *An Autobiography*, he speaks of jotting down some notes on his copies of these texts, though there is no record of his ever having done so. Trollope was not ignorant of or incurious about the past, but his eye was firmly on the present.

See also: *The Bertrams*; *The Warden*

Further Reading

Epperly, Elizabeth R. "Trollope Reading Old Drama." *ESC: English Studies in Canada* vol. 13, no. 3, September 1987, pp. 281–303.

Nardin, Jane. *Trollope and Victorian Moral Philosophy*. Athens: Ohio University Press, 1996.

Resinski, Rebecca. "Trollope's Apollo: A Guide to the Uses of the Classics in Anthony Trollope." https://www.trollope-apollo.com/.

Rosner, Mary. "The Two Faces of Cicero: Trollope's Life in the Nineteenth Century." *Rhetoric Society Quarterly*, vol. 18, no. 3/4, Summer-Autumn, 1988, pp. 251–258.

Van Dam, Frederik, and Melanie Hacke. "Hellenising the Roman Past: Walter Pater's *Marius the Epicurean* and Anthony Trollope's *Life of Cicero*." *Reading Victorian Literature: Essays in Honour of J. Hillis Miller*, edited by Julian Wolfreys and Monica Szuba, Edinburgh: Edinburgh University Press, 2019, pp. 239–53.

Phineas Finn: The Irish Member

Phineas Finn was serialized 1867–1868 in *Saint Pauls Monthly Magazine* and published in book form by Virtue & Co. in 1869. Phineas Finn, a barrister and the son of an Irish doctor, is elected as the Member of Parliament for Loughshane, a pocket borough controlled by the Earl of Tulla, with the Earl's tacit support. From the beginning, however, Phineas shows signs of political independence.

Phineas's career progresses on three tracks: parliamentary, romantic, and financial. Only in the first does he enjoy steady success. After an initial failure, he soon learns how to speak effectively in the House of Commons. After Lord Tulla displaces Phineas, Lord Brentford, whose children are friendly with Phineas, installs him as the MP for his pocket borough, Loughton. When Loughton is abolished by a Reform Bill, Phineas once again is elected at Loughshane. Ultimately, he opposes his party on Irish tenant rights and resigns his seat, returning to Ireland as an Inspector of Poor Houses in Cork.

Financially, Phineas foolishly co-signs a bill (a loan) for his friend Laurence

Fitzgibbon, who defaults, leaving Phineas liable for the whole amount. Hounded by a collector, Phineas fears disgrace and bankruptcy, until Laurence's unmarried sister, Aspasia, pays off the debt. Romantically, Phineas falls in love with Lady Laura Standish, who returns his love, but rejects his proposal and marries Robert Kennedy to retrieve the ruined fortunes of her brother, Oswald, Lord Chiltern. When Phineas courts Violet Effingham, he finds the angry Oswald as his rival, and, after the two fight a duel, Violet rejects Phineas in favor of Oswald. Phineas is tempted by the beauty of the enigmatic and exotic "Madame Max" Goesler (who is quite wealthy), but determines to marry Mary Flood Jones, from his hometown of Killaloe.

Phineas Finn can be reasonably considered as a picaresque novel, in that it presents us with a realistic, episodic narrative that depicts the social rise of an outsider, in part through his amorous adventures (Ardillia 113, 121–24). However, although Phineas meets these criteria, he does not conform to the expectation that the protagonist, the *picaro*, be a rogue. Unlike his Spanish predecessors, and English predecessors such as Barry Lyndon, Roderick Ransom, or Tom Jones, Phineas Finn is too honor-bound to fully qualify. While he is swift to recover from romantic rejection, and facile in loving again, "he is false to no woman. He allows no prudential consideration to interfere with his loyalty to [the radical M.P. Joshua] Monk" (Wright 92). However, not all scholars reject Phineas as a *picaro*. He has been dismissively characterized as a "watered-down picaresque hero ... morally footloose, an adventurer whose fate it is to walk over volcanoes" (Edwards 154). *Phineas Finn* has some of the qualities of a picaresque novel, but also those of a bildungsroman, a novel depicting the education of a young protagonist, traditionally male.

In his early adventures Phineas has been sometimes likened to the typical Trollopean figure of the "hobbledehoy." Hobbledehoys are young men "generally pure of heart but handicapped by an innate ineptitude and a crushing lack of resources" who "stumble through life saying the wrong thing, wearing the wrong clothes, and cavorting with the wrong associates" (King 8–10). Unlike such classic examples as Charley Tudor (*The Three Clerks*), Tom Tringle (*Ayala's Angel*), and Johnny Eames (*Small House at Allington*), however, Phineas is too poised, too competent, and even too worldly wise to fall into that class. He enjoys quick social success: Lady Laura Standish, daughter of the Earl of Brentford, falls in love with him near the beginning of the novel; her great advantage over him in rank does not impede her in her passion. Furthermore, the artfully crafted letter he sends his father to justify his standing for election demonstrates that Phineas is far more adroit than the classic hobbledehoy. While he does lack resources, and does make the classic hobbledehoy error of signing a bill for a friend's debt, he is generally too graceful and clever to be so classed.

The novel is, formally speaking, hard to classify—a sort of hybrid of the picaresque and the *bildungsroman* in terms of Phineas's political education. But this story is wrapped around a core tragedy of the novel—the tragedy of Lady Laura Standish. Delineating the tragedy is quite simple. Lady Laura is herself quite aware of it, and in the sequel confesses to Phineas her irresistible love for him—and its disastrous effect on her rational decision to marry for money to restore her brother's position. "When I was young," she tells Phineas, "I did not credit myself with capacity for so much passion. I told myself that love after all should be a servant and not a master, and I married my husband fully intending to do my duty to him. Now we see what has come of it" (*Ph. Redux* Ch. XII). Later, near the end of the sequel, she is even more explicit: "When I was younger I did not understand how strong the heart can be. I should have known it, and I pay for my ignorance with the penalty of my whole life" (*Ph. Redux* Ch. LXXVIII). Lady Laura's bitter insight is too late, but also quite correct. Phineas and Laura are surprisingly compatible. Her recognition that her love for him will not leave her any peace, any place in his life, along with her guilt for rejecting his proposal, and embittering her husband to madness, are tragic, and psychologically well depicted.

Both Lady Laura and Phineas defy convention. She is tall, and not conventionally feminine. Laura "would lean forward when sitting, as a man does, and would use her arms in talking, and would put her hand over her face, and pass her fingers through her hair,—after the fashion of men rather than of women;—and she seemed to despise that soft quiescence of her sex in which are generally found so many charms. Her hands and feet were large,—as was her whole frame" (*Ph. Finn* Ch. IV). Lady Laura's striking nonconformity with feminine stereotypes does not prevent her "being considered a beauty," despite her red hair and large aquiline nose. Likewise, Phineas is an Irishman, and a Roman Catholic as well. Yet in an era in which the Irish were routinely stereotyped, Phineas avoids the stereotypes both as to his Irishness and his Catholicism (Heine 77).

Laura and Phineas are well-matched, and his soft manner, gentle bearing, and slight diffidence have been suggested to emphasize his feminine aspects to match Lady Laura's masculine nature (Heine 77–80). The age difference between them is frustratingly vague—when we first meet her, Phineas thinks of her as "some years older than himself" (*Ph. Finn* Ch. IV), but at the end of the novel we are told that she was 23 at the outset, while Phineas was 24; she is now 29—a year *younger* than Phineas, who is established as 30 years old by that point (*Ph. Finn* Ch. LXXV).

After Lady Laura, Phineas directs his romantic attentions to Violet Effingham, who loves, and is loved by, Lady Laura's brother, Oswald, Lord Chiltern. Violet refuses to marry Chiltern because of his violence and destabilizing anger, but rejects Phineas. Witheringly, she dismisses his suit to Lady Laura as a shallow exercise, saying, "He tried his 'prentice hand on you; and then he came to me. Let us watch him, and see who'll be the third. I too like him well enough to hope that he'll land himself safely at last" (*Ph. Finn* Ch. XLV).

And, indeed, there is a third candidate, the exotic, wealthy Viennese widow, Madame Max Goesler, "a woman probably something over thirty years of age," and thus some years older than Phineas, who is only thirty by the end of the novel (*Ph. Finn* Ch. XL). When she is first introduced to readers, Trollope's description of Madame Max is hardly flattering. She is "somewhat tall," as well as "so thin as to be almost meagre in her proportions." Additionally, she has thin lips and too perfect teeth, and "always wore her dress close up to her neck, and never showed the bareness of her arms." Likewise, her teeth, "which she endeavoured to show as little as possible, were perfect in form and colour" (*Ph. Finn* Ch. XL). In Trollope, a lady's perfect teeth which she nonetheless hides from view suggests that they are dentures (Glendinning xxi-xxii). In short, when we first meet her, Madame Max is an older woman whose skin can no longer be flaunted and whose charms are the result of artifice and intelligence.

In this first description Trollope describes Madame Max as "the familiar Oriental Jewess" of Victorian literature, who is characterized by her exoticness (in Madame Max's case, her dress) "her rampant sexuality" (Cheyette 31–32). In Madame Max's case, that rampant sexuality lies in her piercing dark blue eyes which "she seemed to intend that you should know that she employed them to conquer you" (*Ph. Finn* Ch. XL). Trollope's use of direct address is notable, as he seeks to instill in the reader the sense of being the object of Madame Max's spell—a spell that induces the arrogant Duke of Omnium, who never condescended to meet with his guests in *Doctor Thorne*, to plead with her to marry him.

Madame Max at first is tempted to grant his suit, if only to punish the too anxious Lady Glencora for using Madame Max's outsider status to argue that she is unworthy to be Duchess of Omnium. After leaving Lady Glencora in agonized suspense, Madame Max decides to reject the Duke for her own peace of mind. Madame Max knows very well that her power lies in not being too easily typed. As the Duchess of Omnium, she would be the foreigner who married an aging roué; as the woman who turns him down, she is Lady Glencora's and her son's benefactor, the magnanimous woman who did not stoop to conquer.

As the narrative impetus of the novel leads her to offer herself and her assets (both emotional and fiscal) to Phineas, his refusal in favor of returning to Mary Flood Jones is honorable, but a shock. Phineas's chemistry with Madame Max is palpable, and the badinage that demonstrates their mutual attraction is among Trollope's best dialogue. When she returns in the sequel, the frustrated narrative arc of *Phineas Finn* is finally fulfilled, and in Madame Max, Trollope depicts "a sexual and valorized midlife woman who achieves a liberated and companionate marriage in a serious plot with no hint of comedy" (Heath 117).

At the end of the novel, which is Phineas's first appearance in the Palliser series, Phineas finds himself thwarted. Rather than repining, he tries to adapt to his circumstances, constantly assuring himself that he is happy, and that he has decided well, as he tries to reconcile himself to a duller life than the one he enjoyed for five years in London. With all that Phineas has left behind, it is not surprising that Trollope resumed this aborted narrative in *Phineas Redux*.

See also: *The Eustace Diamonds*; Ireland; *Phineas Redux*

Further Reading

Ardila, J.A. Garrido. "The Picaresque Novel and the Rise of the English Novel, From Baldwin and Deloney to Defoe and Smollett." *The Picaresque Novel in Western Literature: From the Sixteenth Century to the Neopicaresque*, edited by Garrido Ardila. London: Cambridge University Press, 2015, pp. 113–39.

Cheyette, Bryan. *Constructions of the Jew in English Literature and Society: Racial Representations, 1875–1945.* London: Cambridge University Press, 1993.

Glendinning, Victoria. *Anthony Trollope.* New York: Knopf, 1992.

Grener, Adam. "The Language of Chance and the Form of *Phineas Finn.*" *Genre*, vol. 50, no. 1, 2017, pp. 77–95.

Heath, Kay. *Aging by the Book: The Emergence of Midlife in Victorian Britain.* New York: SUNY Press, 2009.

Heine, Jennifer. "Two Separate Persons: Ethnicity and Identity in Trollope's *Phineas Finn.*" *Elements*, vol. 12, no. 1, Spring 2016, pp. 75–81.

Noble, Christopher S. "Otherwise Occupied: Masculine Widows in Trollope's Novels." *The Politics of Gender in Anthony Trollope's Novels: New Readings for the Twenty-First Century*, edited by Margaret Markwick, Deborah Denenholz Morse, and Regina Gagnier, New York: Routledge, 2016.

Wright, Andrew. *Anthony Trollope: Dream and Art.* London: Macmillan, 1983.

Phineas Redux

Phineas Redux was originally serialized in the *Graphic: An Illustrated Weekly Newspaper* from July 1873 to January 1874 and was subsequently published by Chapman and Hall in 1874. The fourth novel in the series best known as the Palliser Novels, *Phineas Redux* is a direct sequel to *Phineas Finn* (1869); it also continues the storyline of Lizzie Eustace, the eponymous antihero of *The Eustace Diamonds* (1873). *Phineas Redux* begins with Phineas, a widower, yearning for the corridors of power and the political fray he so reluctantly abandoned. When he is offered a chance to stand as the Liberal candidate for the borough of Tankerville, he accepts, and, after losing the election, successfully challenges the result on the ground of fraud.

After this flash of his old luck, Phineas is beset by enemies old and new. The increasingly jealous and mentally unstable Robert Kennedy, estranged from his wife, Lady Laura, blames Phineas for her desertion of him. Kennedy threatens to publish a letter accusing Finn of having illicit relations with Lady Laura unless Finn promises never to see her again; when that threat fails, Kennedy shoots at Phineas.

Quintus Slide, the editor of *The People's Banner*, has received the letter from Kennedy, and publishes a lurid account of the events at the hotel, damaging Phineas's chances of obtaining office and the necessary income to continue in Parliament. Mr. Bonteen, another Member of Parliament, dislikes Phineas for his prior independence (as well as, seemingly, his Irishness and Roman Catholicism). Bonteen lobbies and uses his influence to thwart the efforts of Phineas's friends, particularly Lady Glencora, who becomes Duchess of Omnium, to see Finn restored to office. Failing to secure a place for Phineas, the Duchess thwarts Bonteen's own hopes for promotion to Palliser's old position as Chancellor of the Exchequer. Bonteen nonetheless receives promotion, and as President of the Board of Trade, finds himself acting as the champion of Lizzie Eustace in her efforts to divorce her husband, the shady clergyman Joseph Emilius. Bonteen's efforts to free Lady Eustace threaten to expose Emilius as a bigamist.

Bonteen and Finn break into an open quarrel on an evening at the club to which they both belong, the Universe. The arrival of "Royalty" (presumably the rakish Prince of Wales, later Edward VII) halts the quarrel, but Phineas, on his departure, jokes about killing Bonteen, brandishing the "life preserver" (a short, weighted club) he has carried since he rescued Robert Kennedy from garrotters some years before.

The next morning Bonteen is found dead, not far from the Universe, having been struck down by some form of club. The first suspect arrested is Emilius, but, apparently he could not have committed the crime as his landlady's house key was in her possession and the house locked at the time of the murder. Suspicion turns to Phineas, who is falsely identified by the obtuse Lord Fawn. Phineas is arrested and charged with murder. Lady Laura, now a widow since Kennedy's death, offers to pay for his defense, but her visit threatens to revive the scandal and prejudice any jury against him. While Lady Laura can only harm him, Madame Max Goesler investigates Emilius's alibi, first in London, and then following the trail to Prague.

Phineas is represented by the redoubtable defender Mr. Chaffanbrass, who has previously appeared in *The Three Clerks* (1858) and *Orley Farm* (1862). Chaffanbrass undermines Lord Fawn's testimony significantly, but the verdict is still in doubt until

Madame Max returns from Prague, where she has found the locksmith who copied the key for Emilius, voiding his alibi. A bludgeon, made in Paris, is also found; it might have been the murder weapon, but cannot be traced to Emilius. However, Emilius is convicted of bigamy and sentenced to five years hard labor.

On the seventh day of the trial, after the submission of the new evidence, Phineas is acquitted. In a state of exhaustion, Phineas resigns his seat—only to be reelected. He finds himself lionized as easily as he was condemned. After bringing himself to reenter the House of Commons, he accepts the Duchess's invitation to Matching Priory, where he meets Madame Max. To the Duchess's delight, he boldly kisses Madame Max. Later, he asks her to marry him, only for her to reply, "At last—at last."

Alongside the main plot, the old Duke of Omnium's final decline and death are depicted, including his deathbed proposal of marriage to Madame Max, who has been tending him since he fell ill (an incident depicted in *The Eustace Diamonds*). She refuses his entreaties, preferring to protect the interests of Glencora and her children. The novel also contains a comic-romantic plot, in which Adelaide Palliser, a cousin of Plantagenet's, is courted by the older, déclassé Tom Spooner (of Spoon Hall), and the languid, impecunious Gerard Maule. Upon the old Duke's death, Madame Max discovers that he has left her his jewelry, a legacy which she rejects, with the exception of one ring that the Duke regularly wore. Plantagenet, the new Duke, persists in urging her to accept the legacy. As both are obdurate, Glencora finds a compromise: the legacy goes to Adelaide, allowing her and Gerard to marry.

Trollope's subversive achievement in *Phineas Redux* is not generally recognized. An Irish Roman Catholic and a Viennese Jewish widow are the hero and heroine of the novel, published in an era in which anti–Irish, anti–Catholic, and anti–Semitic prejudice were rife. These two quintessential outsiders, the Irish Roman Catholic Phineas and the foreign-born Jewish adventuress are a couple that flout the normal criteria of social acceptability, and yet Trollope secures his readers' sympathy for them.

Madame Max (as we first meet her) is, like Phineas himself, a social climber, albeit one armed with a fortune inherited from her late husband, a Jewish banker from Vienna. Trollope equivocates as to her Jewishness by keeping her origins veiled in mystery; but as Paul Delany points out, far from hiding her Jewishness, Madame Max makes a performance of it, in her exotic style of dress, in her "Eastern" form of seating. As Delany further notes, "in two of the illustrations to *Phineas Finn* by Millais, Madame Goesler is given a stereotypically Semitic appearance with Oriental curls," and "Francis Holl represents her similarly in *Phineas Redux*" (Delany 6–9).

Likewise, Phineas is open about his Catholicism as well as his Irish identity. Indeed, the cause that leads to his initial resignation from office is his commitment to Irish tenant-right; in this he has anticipated his party's position by a year (Ch. I). Unlike Laurence Fitzgibbon, who flaunts his Irishness by playing the comic Irishman, Phineas treats his heritage as a given, but neither uses it nor denies it.

Another way in which the marriage of Phineas to Madame Max flouts literary convention is that Marie is some years older than Phineas, where novelistic and social conventions would dictate the reverse (Godfrey, *January–May*; Godfrey, "Victorian Cougar"; Hughes, "Gender roles"). It is unclear how much older than Phineas Marie actually is, but five to seven years seems about right. When first introduced at the midpoint of *Phineas Finn*, she is described as "probably something over thirty years of age," a phrase that suggests Trollope is being somewhat delicate (*PF*, Ch. XL). This first physical description of her similarly suggests that her beauty is enhanced by artifice. Moreover, in all their subsequent appearances, Phineas and Marie are well-suited, but remain childless, a rare fate for a happy marriage in Trollope, and suggestive here. As Deborah Denenholz Morse points out, "We know from other Trollope novels that children born quickly from a marriage are often a marker of the health of that union" ("Nothing" 52). The fact that Phineas and Marie are fiercely devoted to each other, as demonstrated in *The Duke's Children*, but have no children, suggests that by the time of their marriage, Marie may have been past safe child-bearing years.

Phineas, by contrast, is twenty-four when he is first elected to the House of Commons, and first meets Marie roughly two to three years into the action of the novel, as Phineas is described as having held the borough for which he sits "for two years" in June when he is asked to stand for Loughton (*PF*, Ch. XXXI), and some months pass between then and the introduction of Marie. (In the first chapter of *Phineas Redux*, set two years after the conclusion of the prior book, he is described as "not much over thirty.")

In his second appearance, Phineas is no longer susceptible of being thought of as a hobbledehoy. Where in *Phineas Finn* he is rather fickle in his romantic relationships (though always sincere at the moment), in the sequel, he is drawn only to Marie, he tries to be kind to Lady Laura, and he is friendly with the former Violet Effingham. He is nothing like the fickle, if charming, young man presented to readers in the first novel of the series. In fact, romance does not feature high in Phineas's list of priorities for most of *Phineas Redux*. He is uncomfortable with Marie, having turned down her offer of her fortune and her hand, and though they rebuild their friendship, there is a constraint between them. Association with his first friend and first love in London, Lady Laura, can only injure him here; Phineas tries to be loyal to his friendship with her, but his actions stem from duty, not passion.

The first half of the book depicts Phineas's struggle to re-establish his political career, and the slowly developing tension between Phineas and Bonteen. As a novel of political intrigue, *Phineas Redux* reaches its climax in a superb chapter, "The World Becomes Cold" (Ch. XXXII), in which Trollope masterfully depicts the inexorable way the Establishment can, with perfect politeness and seeming amicability, freeze out the outsider who is no longer desired. Phineas, having been invited to risk his small inheritance, is made painfully aware of his isolation and vulnerability.

From this point, the novel pivots to the quarrel between Phineas and Bonteen, Bonteen's murder, and Phineas's arrest and trial. The second half of the novel raises the stakes dramatically: Phineas's courage is tested even further by the ordeal of being widely believed to be guilty of the crime of which he is charged, and Marie is galvanized to take action on his behalf. Not only is Phineas's life in danger, so too is that of the Reverend Mr. Emilius, who is in fact guilty of the crime.

Trollope touches on some of his recurring themes in *Phineas Redux*. Kennedy's jealousy slowly building to madness is rather like that of Trevelyan in *He Knew he Was Right* (1869), except that, unlike Trevelyan, Kennedy is right to believe that his wife loves Phineas. He is only wrong in her belief that she has acted on her passion. Likewise, the novel also explores the danger of marrying for the wrong reasons, another recurring theme in Trollope. Lady Laura's suffering from her having married Kennedy for money builds on the relationship between them shown in the earlier novel. From Phineas's arrest through the end of the novel, her anxiety for him, and her realization that even though she is now free to marry, she has lost him to Marie, finally endows her with a bitter sort of wisdom. In her last words to Phineas she admits, "When I was younger I did not understand how strong the heart can be. I should have known it, and I pay for my ignorance with the penalty of my whole life" (Ch. LXXVIII).

Phineas's reaction to the ordeal of false accusation, imprisonment, and trial prompts much reflection on manliness—the question of how a man should behave in his social interactions and, especially, when in peril. In *Phineas Finn* and the sequel, Phineas displays physical courage—in his duel with Lord Chiltern, and then in rescuing Kennedy from the garrotters. In the sequel, however, Phineas displays both physical courage and honor under far more grueling circumstances—seven long days of trial, with the gallows awaiting him if he is convicted. In public, Phineas bears himself with courage until the last day of the trial. Only on the last day has the long imprisonment and suspense worn him down.

In private, the picture is more complex. While Phineas makes clear to his barrister, Mr. Chaffanbrass, that he "would be sooner hung for this,—with the certainty at my heart that all England on the next day would ring with the assurance of my innocence, than be acquitted and afterwards be looked upon as a murderer." Even the cynical Chaffanbrass is moved, and admits to Mr. Wickerby, the solicitor that "I never did,—and I never will,—express an opinion of my own as to the guilt or innocence of a client till after the trial is over. But I have sometimes felt as though I would give the blood out of my veins to save a man. I never felt in that way more strongly than I do now" (Ch. LX).

But in fact, Phineas's "long spell in solitary confinement demoralizes him"; he "fears the loss of reputation more than of life," and "dreads that he will be thought of as a base adventurer.'" During his imprisonment, Phineas "develops an almost extrasensory perception of the true feelings of his visitors," recognizing that Barrington Erle and Mr. Monk believe him to be guilty (Wall, *Trollope* 168, 167). Mr. and Mrs. Bunce, from whom Phineas rents his rooms, believe in his innocence, and he recognizes their sincerity.

When Phineas is released, he breaks under the long strain, and is reclusive to the point that his old pupil-master, Mr. Low, expresses perplexity, and his wife, like his anxious if rough friend Lord Chiltern, questions his manliness. As an outsider seeking admission to the inner circle, Phineas is far from alone in this novel. Marie has obtained her admission under the aegis of Lady Glencora, who becomes the Duchess of Omnium, by her repeated refusals to marry the Duke (behavior first described in *Phineas Finn*), which continues until the Duke's death. Glencora had feared that the Duke might have a son with Marie, ousting Plantagenet (and thus Glencora's children) from the succession. Marie's definite refusal wins Glencora's friendship. So does her care for the old Duke in his last days. By holding herself to an artificially high level of punctiliousness, and refusing even the legacy of the Duke's jewels, Marie reinforces her role as not just as a friend to the Pallisers, but as their benefactor.

When Phineas, still poor, offers himself to Marie, she knows it is with no mercenary motive. Her efforts on his behalf have cleared away the constraint between them, and revealed to him the depth of her love for him. Now, he can acknowledge his love of her. The courage he showed at the trial has earned the admiration of his peers in the House, and, the combination of that endurance and being brought into the orbit of the Duke and Duchess by marrying Glencora's closest friend solidify his place in society. Marie remains an independent businesswoman, while Phineas tends to his politics.

A third outsider—and, effectively, a fourth—figure prominently in the novel: the Rev. Joseph Emilius (or, as it may be, Yosef Mealyus) and his estranged wife, Lizzie Eustace. Steven Wall argues that Emilius is a parallel to Marie, writing that "Emilius's career is weirdly similar to Madame Goesler's—they are both central European adventurers trying to establish themselves in English high society" (Wall, *Trollope* 173). However, Emilius and Lizzie might better be deemed a dark mirror of Phineas and Marie. Both pairings involve a poorer but charming (especially to women) man whose profession requires oratory and persuasion married to a wealthy, strong-minded woman who is in Society, but with a catch—Lizzie, because of her demimondaine origins and the scandal regarding the theft of the Eustace Diamonds, and Marie because of her own origins, and the source of her wealth, the unspecified business interests of her first husband.

Phineas and Emilius further mirror each other in that they are both suspects in the murder of Mr. Bonteen, but also in their courage when under suspicion of that murder. Phineas bears himself manfully throughout his trial, although he flags on the last day—ironically, just as his innocence is established. But Emilius also bears himself coolly when interrogated and confronted with the evidence of the key, with the exception that he blushes.

Lizzie and Marie are likewise mirror images of each other. Where Marie knows Phineas to be innocent, and is impelled by her love of him to clear his name, Lizzie, though eager to be free of her husband, rather admires him for murdering Bonteen (as she is quick to realize), feeling "that the audacity of her husband in doing such a deed redeemed her from some of the ignominy to which she had subjected herself by her marriage with a runaway who had a wife still living" (Ch. LIX).

Lizzie erodes her place in Society by her greed in clinging to the Eustace family jewels, committing perjury to hide her possession of them when the strong box for the jewels is stolen, only to have them in fact stolen from her. Marie, by contrast, repeatedly renounces any form of gain from her relationship with the old Duke. Her last such act is, in contrast to Lizzie's greed, selflessly refusing the bequest of the old Duke's jewels. This earns both Glencora's and Plantagenet's admiration, and solidifies her place in their circle.

Yet Marie and Phineas in a way both remain outsiders, or at any rate, tenuous members of Society. In *The Duke's Children*, Plantagenet unjustly turns on Marie, and effectively exiles her, only to have to beg her pardon when she reproaches him. When asked by his son if he likes Finn, his first response is dismissive. In Trollope's world, highflying outsiders are never completely safe in their position.

In 1974, the BBC aired an adaptation of all six of the Parliamentary Novels in a 26-part series under the name *The Pallisers*. Written by novelist Simon Raven and produced by John Nathan-Turner, the adaptation starred Susan Hampshire as Lady Glencora and Philip Latham as Plantagenet. Parts 15 through 19 cover the events of *Phineas Redux*. Donal McCann portrayed Phineas Finn, Barbara Murray played Madame Max Goesler, Sarah Badel played Lizzie Eustace, and Anthony Ainley played the Reverend Mr. Emilius. The script hewed closely to the novel, though much of the Adelaide Palliser-Gerard Maule plot was cut. Additionally, Adelaide Palliser was transformed into a rather rubicund, comic figure.

Another significant difference is that Raven gives Plantagenet a more central role, depicting him as comforting Phineas after the trial, using some of the arguments Trollope gives to Mr. Low. Raven's script is unambiguous that "Expected Royalty" is the Prince of Wales, and adds a segment where, after his acquittal, Phineas dreams of Bonteen reproaching him for wanting to kill him, even though he was guiltless.

See also: *The Eustace Diamonds*; Ireland; *Phineas Finn*; Raven, Simon

Further Reading

Delany, Paul. "'This Half-Foreigner': Madame Goesler and Her Enemies." *Victorians: A Journal of Culture and Literature*, no. 128, September 2015, pp. 5–19.
Hughes, Kathryn. "Gender roles in the 19th century." *Discovering Literature: Romantics & Victorians*, British Library, May 15, 2014. *https://www.bl.uk/romantics-and-victorians/articles/gender-roles-in-the-19th-century*.
Morse, Deborah Denenholz. "'Nothing Will Make Me Distrust You': The Pastoral Transformed in Anthony Trollope's *The Small House at Allington* (1864)." *Victorian Transformations: Genre, Nationalism and Desire in Nineteenth-Century Literature*, edited by Bianca Tredennick, New York: Routledge, 2016, pp. 45–60.
Wall, Stephen. *Trollope and Character*. London: Faber & Faber, 1988.

post office

Trollope joined the postal service as a low-level clerk in November 1834, working for the meager salary of £90 a year at the London postal headquarters at St. Martin's le Grand. He obtained his job through his mother's acquaintance with Sir Francis Freeling, the long-entrenched General Secretary to the Post Office. The responsibilities were not exacting, but even so, the young Trollope proved indolent, incompetent, unimpressive, and disappointing to his supervisor, William Maberly. His career took off, though, in 1841 when he was appointed surveyor's clerk for the southern district of Ireland, where he worked for well over a decade until he secured a temporary transfer to the southwest of England. Trollope is credited with introducing the postal pillar box, first used in the Channel Islands in 1852. Because the island mail was collected by boat, using boxes avoided the issue of everybody who needed to send mail having to wait around for the boat. This was a very different idea than the organicist one deployed in *La Vendée*, during research for which he had seen the postal boxes in France. Trollope had the idea in late 1851. Upon his recommendation to his supervisor, G.H. Creswell, the boxes were introduced to St. Helier in Jersey in 1852 and to the neighboring island of Guernsey early in 1853. In this peripheral outpost of British rule not far from the French mainland, a locally marked sign of universal communication was introduced by Trollope. The post box, though, was soon seen as useful well beyond the highly specialized Channel Island context; it was introduced in London in 1855. The boxes allowed people much more freedom to send their letters when they wished and the privacy of not having to be seen visibly at the post office.

This work procured for Trollope a promotion to postal surveyor of the north of Ireland in 1854. He spent a good deal of his time during this period performing special missions for the post office in such exotic locations as the Caribbean and the Near East. In 1860, he returned permanently to England as Surveyor of the Eastern District, retiring from that position seven years later. By this time, the post office had not only grown in complexity due to the increase in population and better technology and communication. The agency now hired based on results of competitive civil service examinations (the Northcote-Trevelyan reforms, satirized in *The Three Clerks*) which Trollope opposed—and which he most likely he would not have passed at the age of nineteen when he first entered the postal service. A leading figure in the growth of the post office was Rowland Hill, Secretary to the Post Office from 1854 to 1964; he understood Trollope's merit but disliked him personally, a feeling which was reciprocated. When Hill retired, Trollope's brother-in-law, John Tilley, got Hill's job, and Trollope hoped for Tilley's. When the position went instead to Frank Scudamour, Trollope decided it was time to leave the post office.

Trollope's post office work, a job of bureaucratic routine and standardization which also involved travel to many different places, provided a combination of specificity and transposability that served him well as a pattern for his fictional employments. It immersed him in dull, pedestrian routine but also offered him public and social opportunities, as when he was presented at Court in 1868 before his third trip to North America. (The Queen was absent, so Trollope was received by the Prince of Wales.) More practically, by giving Trollope a steady salary without overly taxing his intellect and creativity, his work at the post office was the perfect practical base from which he could launch his career as a writer of fiction. Suggestively, his productivity actually decreased slightly once he gave up his day job in October 1867. Though he did so initially to run for Parliament, Trollope was in the end more the civil servant than the campaigner, as evidenced by the heroic portrait of the postal clerk Mr. Bagwax in *John Caldigate*, in his own way as exemplary a member of his vocational guild as Plantagenet Palliser was of his. In *Marion Fay*, Trollope has a postal clerk, George Rodden, revealed as being descended from an Italian aristocrat, both vindicating the profession and providing a kind of wish-fulfillment. It could be argued that the post office allowed Trollope space for a distinctive kind of masculinity, collegial and assiduous without relying on violence and force, disinterested, but hardly uninterested, in the affairs of the men and women around him which was part of his modern view of gender. This was something balanced later when women entered such jobs, as seen in the late story "The Telegraph Girl." Trollope by no means loved the post office. But he would not have been who he was as a writer without it.

See also: Australia; Ireland; short stories; travel

Further Reading

Martel, Michael. "Trollope and the State." *Routledge Research Companion to Anthony Trollope*, edited by Deborah Denenholz Morse, Margaret Markwick, and Mark Turner, New York: Routledge, 2017, pp. 36–48.

Menke, Richard. *Telegraphic Realism: Victorian Fiction and Other information Systems*. Stanford, CA: Stanford University Press, 2008.

Sullivan, Ceri. *Literature in The Public Service: Sublime Bureaucracy*. London: Palgrave Macmillan, 2013.

Super, R.H. *Trollope in the Post Office*. Ann Arbor: University of Michigan Press, 1981.

Thomas, Kate. *Postal Pleasures: Sex, Scandal, and Victorian*. London: Oxford University Press, 2012.

The Prime Minister

Published by Chapman and Hall, first in serial format (1875–1876) and then in book form (1876), *The Prime Minister* was a critical and financial failure by Trollope's standards (Sadleir 313). After three novels (*Ph F*, *ED*, and *Ph Redux*) in which Plantagenet and Lady Glencora Palliser have been ancillary figures, the main narrative turns again to them, with Palliser (now the Duke of Omnium, and barred from serving in his beloved House of Commons) becoming Prime Minister of a coalition Government. Palliser's efforts to make his Government useful and to grapple with the issues of the day are not successful; his is a caretaker Government, one that keeps things running while the two parties—Palliser's Liberals and the Tories—build up strength for the election that is to come. Glencora's efforts to heighten his prestige through lavish entertainments and charming the unlikely allies that make up the Omnium Government do not succeed either, nor does her effort to build up her newest and least likely protégé, the dubious Ferdinand Lopez.

Ironically, the novel was denounced by critics for the very fault with which Plantagenet charges Glencora in her efforts to support his Government: vulgarity (Berger 315–316). The hostile reception of the novel jars after Trollope's previous successes at rendering outsiders palatable and even sympathetic to his audience (as witness the popularity of the Irish Catholic Phineas Finn, and the acceptability to readers of his marriage to the exotic, older "Madame Max" Marie Goesler, who is strongly hinted to be Jewish). In *The Prime Minister*, however, the claimed vulgarity stems not from the outsider whose short career and death is one of the most sensationalistic plots in Trollope, but because the Duke of Omnium and his Duchess themselves are portrayed—as the contemporary critics thought—as descending into vulgarity.

What the critics have viewed as "vulgarity" in *The Prime Minister* has been argued to be a reflection of the novel's "eradication of formal distinctions both within the political arena as well as separating politics from the social world," which "precipitates a crisis of identity within the novel." That crisis becomes especially acute "under the guise of political 'unification'" (Berger 317). Put another way, when the two parties have no dramatic conflicts to wage, and by which to define their identities, all that is left is social commingling of the normally oil-and-water Liberals and Tories to pass the time and maintain a façade of normalcy. For Trollope, vulgarity "suggests a lack of distinction between one group and another, and ultimately between one person and another," in which pervasive sociality untethered from politics can have a similar effect, "subjecting everyone to the same rules of interaction, thereby doing away with the differences that help to formulate morals in the first place" (Berger 319). With Glencora's entertainment and busy socializing as part of the glue that binds the Coalition, we see how fragile and lacking cohesion it is, especially when the social whirl begins to pall, and old antagonisms reassert themselves, even absent any precipitating cause other than boredom and dislike (Berger 322).

The novel subverts the reader's expectation by perversely raising Plantagenet to the office representing the traditional pinnacle of political power in Great Britain while simultaneously stripping his premiership of any *actual* power under the highly unusual circumstances in which he was selected as Prime Minister—not to enact policy, but to maintain the day-to-day functioning of the Government and no more. Palliser's few efforts to break through the languor of the Coalition fail—his County Suffrage Bill dies, his surrender of the long-standing privilege of selecting the member of Parliament for his home borough of Silverbridge leads to a Conservative winning the seat, and in creating as a Knight of the Garter a "man of moderate means, no public stature, and a long record of selfless service to the poor," he "blunders into the error of Quixotism," souring both wings of the Coalition (Butte 224).

Palliser chafes against these restrictions, and also suffers from the conflict Trollope diagnosed in reviewing a book by his friend Charles Buxton, M.P., that a political actor must either "rid himself of his scruples and undertake the exigencies of public life … with a mind indifferent to its impurities and complexities; or else he must work forever in opposition, and must be fighting on small points against things which he knows to be good in the main" (Butte 213) The overly scrupulous, ambivalent Palliser, like Buxton, is afflicted with "enervation and hopelessness." The Duke's Government "is partly a reflection of his own condition. Its paralysis becomes a reflection of his paralysis" (Butte 224).

Surprisingly, then, Palliser and Phineas Finn engage in a debate over equality, with the staid, correct Duke energetically championing a gradualist diminishment of the differences between the ends of the social spectrum, while the former Irish firebrand is, highly uncharacteristically, almost contemptuous of the desirability of equality as a goal, even if only as an aspirational one (Ch. LXVII). Palliser's liberalism is never so clearly shown as in this, his most energetic manifesto of his own convictions. Phineas's skeptical response suggests a loss of the youthful idealism and of the convictions that drew him to political life in initially. However, when the Coalition falls, Phineas comforts Plantagenet by describing their time in office together as "a step towards the step … and in getting to a millennium even that is something" (Ch. LXXX).

The gradualism for which Palliser advocates represents Trollope's own views, as demonstrated in his exposition of his own political stance, that of "an advanced, but still a conservative Liberal" (*Autobiography* Ch. XVI). Trollope's elaboration of what that seemingly paradoxical phrase means is very reminiscent of Palliser's exposition of his views to Phineas. Despite that parallel, scholars have described Trollope's own politics as running the gamut from an "overriding liberalism"; a "cautious liberalism," which exposes the "cracks and contradictions of Victorian Imperialism"; to "having an essentially conservative temperament" and being a conflicted thinker whose "theoretical liberalism" contrasts to his "political conservatism"; and even having "a fractured and contradictory" outlook (Felber 421–422).

Palliser's politics are more easily characterized than those of his creator, perhaps, because Trollope is able to determine what tests Palliser must face. He is forced to reckon with his own thin skin and his romantic affection for the past, and he must reconcile these emotions with the pragmatic needs of the day. He may not be a politically effective Prime Minister, but Palliser's belief in service and in gradualism in social advancement is one he embraces in his life, as one witnesses in his genuine friendships with Madame Max Goesler and her husband, Phineas Finn.

In *The Prime Minister*, we see Glencora for once not viewing her husband with veiled, if affectionate, irony. When she discovers he is to be Prime Minister, her reaction is striking: "As she spoke she threw her arms up, and then rushed into his embrace. Never since their first union had she been so demonstrative either of love or admiration. 'Oh, Plantagenet,' she said, 'if I can only do anything I will slave for you.'" Palliser is moved by her enthusiasm; "he already felt the pleasantness of her altered way to him. She had never worshipped him yet, and therefore her worship when it did come had all the delight to him which it ordinarily has to the newly married hero" (Ch. VI).

The continuity in the characterization of Palliser and Glencora is pronounced. After some typical bickering, Plantagenet's great opportunity is announced. Suddenly. Glencora sees him in a brilliant light—but knows him well enough to know that she will have to supply the warmth that will hold the erstwhile foes together.

As Trollope himself noted, "The Duchess of Omnium, when she is playing the part of Prime Minister's wife, is the same woman as that Lady Glencora who almost longs to go off with Burgo Fitzgerald, but yet knows that she will never do so; and the Prime Minister Duke, with his wounded pride and sore spirit, is he who, for his wife's sake, left power and place when they were first offered to him;—but they have undergone the changes which a life so stirring as theirs would naturally produce" (*Autobiography* Ch. X).

Glencora's efforts to hold the Coalition together by dazzling its members with hospitality reflect a passionate loyalty toward her husband that she has never previously evinced. Her enthusiasm for Plantagenet's premiership represents a high-water mark in their relationship. For, quite possibly the only time in his life, Plantagenet is assured that his love for his wife is returned.

As always with Trollope, his characters are not allowed to remain on the summit of such emotional heights—Glencora's behavior begins to grate on Plantagenet, both in terms of the ostentation of her hospitality and in her greater ability to manage the disparate members of the Coalition (Berger 323–324). But it is Glencora's final protégé who opens up a breach between them.

Ferdinand Lopez, a trader in the City and friend of the younger, weaker Everett Wharton, is, like Phineas Finn and Marie Goesler before him, an unknown quantity of considerable charm but dubious provenance. Trollope opens the novel with an observation that quickly delineates Lopez's great disadvantage: "It is certainly of service to a man to know who were his grandfathers and who were his grandmothers if he entertains an ambition to move in the upper circles of society" (Ch. I). We know only three things about Lopez from the beginning of the novel: First, he is impecunious; second he is bold; and third, he is socially dubious, as his Portuguese names and his rumored Jewishness suggest.

His good looks and charm win him the affection of Emily Wharton, the daughter of a wealthy barrister, and the friendship of her brother; their father, barrister Abel Wharton, is suspicious of Lopez's speculative income, his origins, and his ethics. (As Lopez is beginning the process of ruining his unfortunate friend, Sextus ["Sexty"] Parker, Abel Wharton's instincts are clearly not entirely grounded in prejudice.) Lopez's early career mirrors that of the young Phineas Finn. Like Phineas, albeit more brazenly, he becomes the protégé of Glencora, who embraces him as the Duke's candidate for his old borough of Silverbridge. In an echo of Phineas's rescue of Robert Kennedy, Lopez recues Everett Wharton from a band of robbers who attack him late at night just outside St. James' Park, after leaving Everett because the younger man has petulantly picked a quarrel with him.

Unlike Phineas, who lost Lady Laura to Robert Kennedy, Lopez wins Emily away from a suitor more appropriate for her according to tradition, Arthur Fletcher. After their marriage, things begin to go against Lopez—his father-in-law will house, feed, and clothe him, but will not fund him. Likewise, Glencora's support of him is vetoed by Plantagenet, who will not assert the "right" to select the Member for Silverbridge as his uncle did. Lopez's complaints lead the Duke to pay his election expenses (which Abel Wharton has already done), and result in a question being raised in the House about the Duke's (really the Duchess's) conduct.

Phineas manages to shield Plantagenet and Glencora from the worst of the scandal by a fiery feat of oratory. Disgraced, and having lost his wife's affection by his callousness, Lopez tries to convince Lizzie Eustace to run away with him to Guatemala, quoting her old favorite Byron poem to her. "The Bride of Abydos," is, like "The Corsair," one of Byron's heroic poems. But now that Lizzie has drawn a Corsair-like suitor, she chooses to demonstrate that poetry is only a snare when she deploys it. She dismisses Lopez with stinging practicality, reflecting on her "£4000 a year and a balance at her banker's," saying simply "Mr. Lopez, I think you must be a fool."(Ch. LIV).

All hope lost, Lopez kills himself, in a startlingly grim and gritty chapter, "The Tenway Junction" (Ch. LX). Trollope creates of an ordinary railway junction a surreal hellscape which reflects the despair that has possessed Lopez. That despair is very much fueled by his outsider status. From the first chapter, the narrator "emphasizes Lopez's consciousness of this social reality and demonstrates that he is defeated both from without and within, by the social hierarchy and by his own consciousness of it" (Felber 439). Murray Baumgarten views Trollope as "a writer regarded as the author of mere Victorian entertainments hinting at the existence of that fierce subterranean phenomenon of Jewish self-hatred central to the explorations of contemporary writers such as Philip Roth and Rebecca Goldstein" (Baumgarten 56). Lopez's "self-loathing adds a complexity to his character that delves beyond a simplistic Jewish stereotype and adds further psychological insight to his eventual suicide at Tenway Junction—as well as a further layer of contradictions to Trollope's liberalism" (Felber 439).

As political normalcy begins to return, the Coalition dissolves, having fulfilled its purpose for three years. Plantagenet, sore at having held so high an office for so little effect, finds it hard to release the trappings of power. Glencora grieves the loss of her primacy, and of the unusual closeness she and her husband have shared (Chs. LXXIII, LXXX). The novel ends in striking an echo of *Can You Forgive Her?*—Plantagenet proposes to take Glencora to the Continent to ease her sorrow, and Emily Wharton, like Alice Vavasor before her, allows herself to be persuaded to marry Arthur Fletcher, of whom she feels terribly unworthy, as Alice did toward John Grey. The invocation of the closing chapters of *Can You Forgive Her?* seemingly brings the story of the Pallisers full circle. But as in life, so too in Trollope, such pleasing symmetry never lasts long.

See also: *Can You Forgive Her?*; novel series; *Phineas Finn*; Raven, Simon

Further Reading

Baumgarten, Murray. "Seeing Double: Jews in the Fiction of F. Scott Fitzgerald, Charles Dickens, Anthony Trollope, and George Eliot." *Between "Race" and Culture: Representations of "the Jew" in English and American Literature*, edited by Bryan Cheyette, Stanford, CA: Stanford University Press, 1996.

Berger, Courtney C. "Partying with the Opposition: Social Politics in the Prime Minister." *Texas Studies in Literature and Language*. Nineteenth-Century Quartet: Desire, Commodity, and Imperial Polity, vol. 45, no. 3, Fall 2003, pp. 313–336.

Butte, George. "Trollope's Duke of Omnium and 'The Pain of History': A Study of the Novelist's Politics." *Victorian Studies*, vol. 24, no. 2, Winter 1981, pp. 209–227.

Felber, Lynette. "The Advanced Conservative Liberal: Victorian Liberalism and the Aesthetics of Anthony Trollope's Palliser Novels." *Modern Philology*, vol. 107, no. 3, February 2010, pp. 421–446.

race

Whereas most Victorian novelists touched on race and empire only as they manifested themselves within England (such as the Norman/Saxon difference in English character, a theme rarely touched on by Trollope), Trollope's global travel gave him greater explicit exposure to racial differences. This did not exempt him from the racism that structurally infused all whites, even liberal whites, in the nineteenth century. This is most obvious in his early travel book, *The West Indies and the Spanish Main*: "the eye soon became accustomed to the back skin and thick lip," shows a characteristic mixture of othering and inclusiveness, distancing and identification.

Yet he could not incline his ear to "the broken patois which is the nearest approach to English" that he claims black Jamaicans make. In his vision of what Lauren Goodlad (*Geopolitical*) terms Colonial Man, Trollope was in favor of settler colonialism partially because he saw the English language disseminated worldwide. Unfortunately, he was not capable of hearing his own language in the English of the people of Jamaica. Trollope also was unable to recognize as Christianity the forms of that religion practiced by the population of Jamaica, which descended from African ancestors.

Trollope observed black Jamaicans had no country of their own. But he did not remotely foresee Jamaica becoming independent and sovereign as a black-majority state. He did see light-skinned black Jamaicans, the colored population, as eventually becoming the dominant people of the land, even surpassing the white settlers. But he saw distinctions between light- and dark-skinned black Jamaica as more rigid than they eventually became. He also saw colored people as still inferior to whites and denounced what he heard as their imperfect English. Trollope foresaw hybridity between African, Indian, and Chinese. But he was so negative about the African element that his vision of the future is not powerfully optimistic.

Trollope said, "No Englishman, no Anglo-Saxon, could be what he now is but for that portion of wild and savage energy" from their early medieval tribal forebears. Ironically, he did not understand that, like the early English who were themselves migrants, merely because black Jamaicans were not indigenous to Jamaica did not mean they did not see it as their home. Trollope understood that whites like the Anglo-Saxons who came from tribal societies could develop into modern societies. But he did not recognize this capacity in people of African descent.

He also was pessimistic about the resilience of conquered non-white races. Trollope wrote that it was apparent that Indigenous Australians would die out. He also thought that Māori in New Zealand had been successfully conquered, but warned that blacks in South Africa would never be quelled. Trollope saw people of color as mentally inferior to whites, though not perhaps as categorially as some of his peers did.

Trollope made clear in his book on South Africa that he believed whites can and should dominate blacks, while also calling for the races to be at roughly equal levels of employment and social satisfaction. How he thought the latter equilibrium could be achieved without disturbing racial hierarchies is unclear.

Racial intermarriage, which is at least contemplated if not delivered, by earlier nineteenth-century writers like James Fenimore Cooper, is unthinkable for Trollope (although his mother did contemplate it in at least one instance). Marriage between classes in Trollope is a way for white people to rise socially. But this avenue is not open to non-whites. Marriage between Christians and Jews depicted in *Nina Balatka* is as far as Trollope could go, although that was farther than many of his contemporaries wanted him to go.

Trollope's remarks about people of color, even though not totally negative, are still unquestionably racially tinged. Lines like this description of Bermuda from "Aaron Trow" underscore Trollope's sense of a universal humanity: "There are also here some six thousand white people and some six thousand black people, eating, drinking, sleeping, and dying" (*Tales of All Countries* 188).

Trollope regarded a Sinhalese-constituted parliament in Sri Lanka as inconceivable. He saw black majority rule in South Africa as something for a far horizon. In general, he did not see, under circumstances current at his time, non-whites as being capable of governing themselves responsibly. He did not say that this would be eternally so. Yet in some ways positioning the subject beyond the foreseeable future was a way of effectively negating it entirely.

Trollope was less racist than many of his contemporaries. Nevertheless, like many nineteenth century liberals, Trollope was at his least liberal in terms of race. He was undoubtedly a racist. But he did concede that people of color were destined to thrive and to hold power in the world to come.

Further Reading

Aguirre, Robert D. "'Affairs of State': Mobilities, Communication, and Race in Trollope's *The West Indies and the Spanish Main*." *Nineteenth-Century Contexts*, vol. 37, no. 1, 2015, pp. 1–20.
_____. *Mobility and Modernity: Panama in the Nineteenth Century*. Columbus: The Ohio State University Press, 2017.
Brantlinger, Patrick. *Dark Vanishings: Discourse on the Extinction of Primitive Races, 1800–1930*. Ithaca, NY: Cornell University Press, 2003.
Mouton, Michelle. "'Yams, salt pork, biscuit, and bad coffee': Food and Race in the *West Indies and the Spanish Main*." *Routledge Research Companion to Anthony Trollope*, edited by Deborah Denenholz Morse, Margaret Markwick, and Mark Turner, New York: Routledge, 2017, pp. 412–22.

Rachel Ray

Rachel Ray is set in remote southern Devon, in the town of Baslehurst and the even more parochial village of Cawston. The novel is one of Trollope's most rural and peripheral depictions of England. It features a more level and mixed treatment of social class than do Trollope's Barsetshire and Palliser novels. It was published in book form by Chapman and Hall in 1863 and was solicited by the Evangelical magazine *Good Words* in 1862, although the editors of the magazine were in the end dissatisfied with the manuscript. According to Trollope's *Autobiography*, they were upset because it contained a scene with dancing, although the mildly satiric portrait of the evangelical curate, Samuel Prong, might have also annoyed the magazine. In this respect, though, the Broad Church rector, Mr. Comfort, is parodied just as much. The entire tone of the novel, particularly the treatment of the beer-brewery, is lightly and deftly comic in mien.

The main plot concerns Luke Rowan, a young man from London who comes to Baslehurst in Devon. His great-aunt is the widow of Mr. Bungall, the deceased partner in the brewing firm of Bungall and Tappitt. The surviving partner, Mr. Tappitt, feels threatened by young Rowan's arrival. Rowan quickly becomes engaged to Rachel Ray of Bragg's End, being more drawn to her than to Mr. Tappitt's daughters, who are more sophisticated and well-appointed (for the locality, at least). Meanwhile, Mr. Prong is courting Rachel's elder sister, Dorothea Prime, a local power at charity meetings; however, Dorothea does not want to give up her financial independence. Trollope did not construct these oppositions moralistically. For instance, Mr. Prong supports the local parliamentary candidacy of Mr. Hart, a Jewish clothier from London, not so much out of evangelical philo-Semitism but because Hart's opponent, Mr. Butler Cornbury, is supported by Mr. Comfort and the Broad Church establishment. This issue is handled in a complicated way by the novel; Trollope wants to allow the possibility of a London clothier being elected over a local grandee and at the same time depicts a community which is not quite ready for that result. In the end, Luke marries Rachel and after honeymooning with her in Cornwall settles down in Devon to be a brewer. Hart loses to Butler Cornbury, and Mrs. Prime refuses to marry Mr. Prong, somewhat to the disappointment of her widowed mother, who wants her overbearing elder daughter off her hands. This combination of victory for the old order politically, integration of the newcomer socially, and the assertion of female autonomy in gender terms provides a mixed ending that largely but not unqualifiedly affirms the existing order.

Rachel Ray is written with a distinctive combination of lightness and tenderness, and has a place of definite distinction within Trollope's oeuvre. It was successfully adapted for the theater by Henry Ong in 2015.

See also: *Cousin Henry*; *Good Words*

Further Reading

Meckier, Jerome. "*The Three Clerks* and *Rachel Ray*: Trollope's Revaluation of Dickens Continued." *Dickens Quarterly*, vol. 25, no. 3, September 2008, pp. 162–171.

Nardin, Jane. "Comic Tradition in Trollope's *Rachel Ray*." *Papers on Language and Literature*, vol, 22, no. 1, Winter 1986, pp. 39–50.

Pollard, Arthur. "Trollope and the Evangelicals." *Nineteenth-Century Fiction*, vol. 37, no. 3, 1982, pp. 329–39.

Ralph the Heir

Ralph the Heir was published by 1871 by Hurst and Blackett (successor to one of Trollope's early publishers, Henry Colburn) and serialized as a supplement to *Saint Pauls* from January 1870 to July 1871. The book was illustrated by F.A. Fraser, who also illustrated *The Golden Lion of Granpere*; his skill at drawing local-color scenes aided him in illustrating the rural tableaux pictured in the book.

In *An Autobiography*, Trollope castigates *Ralph the Heir* as one of his worst novels. With *The Belton Estate*, in critical terms it is probably the least appreciated of his full-length works. If it is not major Trollope, though, the author's patented serenity, inventiveness, and sly humor are well evidenced in *Ralph the Heir*.

Sir Thomas Underwood is a moderately successful if solitary lawyer in his sixties who lives in Fulham at Popham Villa with his wife and his two daughters, Patience, the more intelligent, and Clarissa, the more beautiful. Each Underwood girl is in love with one of the Newton brothers: Ralph, his uncle's heir, and Gregory, a clergyman who has been given the local living by his uncle. Sir Thomas's niece, Mary Bonner, is in love with another Ralph, the illegitimate son of Gregory Newton, senior, who is the uncle of the Ralph and Gregory Newton who court the Underwood sisters. She stands by her affections even though the legitimate, propertied Ralph proposes to her. Sir Gregory Newton had planned to leave much of his fortune to his illegitimate son Ralph, but before he can arrange to buy from his nephew the rights to the estate (which is entailed), he is killed in a hunting accident. The estate thus passes to his nephew, Ralph the heir. As in *Doctor Thorne* the illegitimate child, in this case Ralph, is virtuous, while the legitimate Ralph is a moral weakling. The device of the two Ralphs, though not approaching the five Allan Armadales of Wilkie Collin's *Armadale*, did echo frequent sensation-novel devices. There is also a sense of the double here, as two men having the same name illustrate an abstract sense of the good and bad aspects of human character.

Did reviewers like *Ralph the Heir* (it was, contrary to Trollope's own assessment, one of the best-received of his novels) because the illegitimate son did not in fact inherit, thus in some ways justifying the English class structure? Ralph the heir loses the girl but still gets the property. There is a resolved marriage plot without any disturbance of the social order, the obverse of what Trollope was to chronicle in *Lady Anna*, written slightly later. The good Ralph secures a property in Norfolk, a farm near Swaffham, to which he eventually brings Mary as his wife. But Trollope had been a postal surveyor in this region when he had lived at Waltham Cross and made clear that it was not his favorite part of England. There is a sense of vindication of virtue over rank, but only a qualified sense.

The presence of two Ralph Newtons with a claim to being the heir was a sensation-novel element. There is also a fairy-tale element in Ralph, the heir, having aristocratic rights but being in fact common, as indicated by his willingness to marry the good-humored but lowly Polly Neefit, daughter of a stout tradesman who made breeches and until recently (a situation particularly damning in Victorian society) had lived over his shop. Ralph the heir wishes to marry Polly, who is decently beautiful, not for any romantic motives but because he is heavily in debt to her father. Like Mountjoy Scarborough in *Mr. Scarborough's Family* and George Hotspur in *Sir Harry Hotspur of Humblethwaite*, Ralph the heir is a man with every asset and privilege except the good character to live up to the station society had granted him.

A minor comic theme in the novel is Sir Thomas Underwood's project to write a life of the Renaissance thinker Sir Francis Bacon. While the action of the plot swirls around him, he doggedly is, or appears to be, at work on research, and at the end *Ralph the Heir* a wry, somewhat sardonic hope is expressed by the narrator that, as unlikely as it seems, Sir Thomas might one day finish his *magnum opus*. Somewhat like Casaubon in George Eliot's *Middlemarch*, Sir Thomas tacitly justifies his failure as a father, husband, and man of affairs (he loses in his contest to be MP for Percycross much as Trollope himself failed to be MP for Beverley) by his concentration on a great work that, the reader knows, has only a small chance of completion. In his suggestion that Sir Thomas could have just patched together a short biography of Bacon from other sources, Trollope might have been anticipatorily mocking his own biographies of Cicero and Palmerston.

Ralph the Heir is a rare Trollope novel whose immediate reception was as interesting (or more so) than its plot and characters. Charles Reade (1814–1884), the well-known sensation novelist, decided in 1872 to adapt the novel as *Shilly-Shally* and sell it to John Hollingshea to mount at the Gaiety Theatre. Reade was forthright with Trollope about his desire to adapt the work, but due to Trollope's being on his first trip to Australia word reached him later than it otherwise would have. Though no formal allegation of impropriety was ever made, relations between the two men, once warm, became virtually nonexistent for a number of years. Furthermore, the play was accused of being indecent, something very unusual for anything associated with the generally wholesome Trollope. The accusation could have impacted Trollope's sales to serializers and readers who considered themselves morally upright. In January 2020, the Trollope society in London mounted a production of Barbara Lauriat's dramatization of the falling-out between the two authors.

See also: *The Belton Estate*; Harry Hotspur in *Harry Hotspur of Humblethwaite*

Further Reading

Halperin, John. *Trollope and Politics: A Study of the Pallisers and Others.* London: Macmillan,1977.
Lauriat, Barbara. "Charles Reade's Roles in the Drama of Victorian Dramatic Copyright." *Columbia Journal of Law and the Arts*, vol. 33, no. 1, 2009, pp. 1–36.
_____. "*Shilly-Shally* Redux: Trollope, Reade, and Authorship." *The Princeton University Library Chronicle*, vol. 72, no. 3, 2011, pp. 713–732.
Taylor, Jenny Bourne. "Legitimacy and Illegitimacy." *Routledge Research Companion to Anthony Trollope*, edited by Deborah Denenholz Morse, Margaret Markwick, and Mark Turner, New York: Routledge, 2017, pp. 100–110.

Raven, Simon

Simon Raven (1927–2001) was a prolific novelist, memoirist, and writer for television and film, normally adapting the work of others. The author of 34 books, Raven wrote *romans fleuve*, the ten-volume *Alms for Oblivion* (published between 1964 and 1976), and the seven-volume *First Born in Egypt* (1984–1972). The two series are linked by two novels, *The Roses of Picardie* (1980) and *September Castle* (1983). The two linking novels feature supernatural elements reminiscent of Raven's early success *Doctors Wear Scarlet* (1960), and which figure in the later series. In her percipient appreciation of Raven's work, Brooke Allen acknowledges the quality of his novels, "as well as his many radio and television plays, essays, and reviews," but posits that "his reputation today rests almost entirely on his ten-volume *roman fleuve, Alms for Oblivion*" (9).

Raven did not, on the surface, take an exalted view of his career as a writer; as his fictional alter-ego Fielding Grey states, "I never said I was an artist. I am an enter-tainer.... I arrange words in pleasing patterns in order to make money. I try to give good value—to see that my patterns are well wrought—but I do not delude myself by inflating the nature of my function. I try to be neat, intelligent and lucid: let others be 'creative' or 'inspired'" (Raven, *Places* 196–97).

Ellen Moody, however, notes that Raven's adaptation of the six "political" or Pal-liser novels into twenty-six hour-long episodes is "a masterpiece of fascinating televi-sual art," and one which has "affected how Trollope's novels are read and Trollope novels are adapted ever since its first airing" (Moody, "Trollope on Television" 9–10). Together with the much shorter series, *The Barchester Chronicles* (1982; adapting *The Warden* and *Barchester Towers*), Raven's *Pallisers* is "among the more important ... sociological events to have happened to Trollope readerships, adaptations, and probably scholar-ship." Moody argues that these two series are "equivalent in influence to that of the much-discussed 1981 *Brideshead Revisited* and 1996 *Pride and Prejudice* on readerships and literary critical studies of Waugh and Austen" (Moody, "Trollope on Television" 1).

Moody notes that the adaptations of Trollope's novels that came after these two wa-tershed series, but especially Raven's *Pallisers*, are reactions to—and later against—his work. Thus, Moody traces Raven's influence through Andrew Davies's adaptations of *The Way We Live Now* (2001) and *He Knew He Was Right* (2004). Such reaction against Raven's adaptation was inevitable, in that his characters and worldview in many ways are less fully fleshed and more cynical than Trollope's. Characters that Trollope brought fully to life are mercilessly cut or flattened (Lady Dumbello, Lucy Morris, Lucinda Roanoke, Alice Vavasor), while Adelaide Palliser "becomes a comic, horsey woman" (Moody, "Trollope on Television" 7–8).

Other characters are surprisingly rehabilitated. Raven flips Trollope's sympathy for Lady Laura Standish and humanizes the perplexed, inarticulately lonely Robert Ken-nedy, while still delineating Lady Laura's agony at having married against her heart. Dolly Longestaffe, whose presence in the novels is fleeting and predominantly comic, is re-envisioned by Raven who "uses him for expository purposes, and occasionally to comment on the action" (Wirenius, *Phineas* 495). The casting of Donald Pickering as Dolly, visibly older than the other members of the Beargarden, allowed him to carry this additional Greek chorus-like role.

The most striking rehabilitation in Raven's script is that of Mrs. Carbuncle, who in Trollope is depicted as a "domineering mercenary obdurate bully who shatters her probably illegitimate daughter, Lucinda Roanoke's sanity." In Raven's hands she is "re-configured as a quick-witted, genial demi-mondaine who mothers Lizzie Eustace in a companionable bedroom scene where she gives Lizzie the good advice" that Lizzie "fails to profit by" (Moody, "Trollope on Television" 7). Raven seems to have recast Mrs. Carbuncle in the mold of the recurring character Masie, a good-natured prostitute who offers emotional support to the characters of his series as she does sexual gratification.

Raven's darker vision leads him to hint strongly that Phineas Finn has seduced Mary Flood Jones, a sharp departure from Trollope's novel, in which he marries Mary because, despite his other opportunities (and desires), he has given her his word, and she has waited faithfully for him. Likewise, the brief appearance of the murdered Bonteen to Phineas as he walks his neighborhood after his release invokes

Raven's supernatural flirtations. Like most of the supernatural moments in his fiction, Phineas's sighting of the reproachful shade of Bonteen could be interpreted as a manifestation of Phineas's guilt for his hatred of the dead man, or as a real apparition.

Raven's overall approach to the series is to bring a dynamic tension to the novels by focusing on two contrary impulses. Under his pen, "Trollope's novels become a filmic disillusioned political vision which justifies patriarchy in an ameliorated non-egalitarian society, and which is dependent on the self-erasure of women whose emotional and social support is needed to sustain it" (Moody, "Trollope on Television" 4).

Countervailing this seemingly smug endorsement of the Victorian status quo is Raven's acknowledgment that he "rewrote the five books so as to make all the stories he took over 'parts, large or small, of Glencora'" (Moody, "Trollope on Television" 4). By viewing Trollope's world predominantly through the eyes of Lady Glencora, Raven positions the restrictions and expectations placed by Victorian society at the heart of his adaptation. For all their bitterness and sharp satire, Raven's scripts show the costs and the psychic pain inflicted on women by the patriarchal society he treats as normative. That the central tragedy of the series is Glencora's loss of choice and autonomy rests on a humane vision that is far more empathetic than that of many of Raven's novels.

See also: *Can You Forgive Her?*; novel series; *Phineas Redux*

Further Reading

Allen, Brooke. "Who Was Simon Raven?" *New Criterion*, vol. 28, no. 8, April 2003, p. 9.

Barber, Michael. *The Captain: The Life and Times of Simon Raven*. London: Duckworth, 1996.

Moody, Ellen, "Trollope on Television: Intertextuality in the *Pallisers* and Other Trollope Films." *Victorian Literature and Film Adaptation*, edited by Abigail Burnham Bloom and Mary Sanders Pollock, Cambria Press, 2011, pp. 155-180.

Wirenius, John. *Phineas at Bay: A Novel*. New York: Monocle Press, 2014.

reception of Trollope

Some scholars such as Reginald Charles Terry (*Anthony Trollope*) deny that Trollope's reputation ever suffered, but the consensus is that Trollope's status in the canon dropped late in his life and for decades after his death, then was revived in the twentieth century. Trollope thought that Thomas Hay Sweet Escott would be the man initially responsible for his legacy. In his later years Trollope met, corresponded with, and encouraged Escott. Though Trollope correctly discerned Escott did not have the temperamental solidity to be a successful novelist himself, he felt the younger man knew him well and would be a faithful steward of his reputation. Escott's 1913 book *Anthony Trollope, His Work, Associates and Literary Originals* mostly made good on this promise, and was a part of a minor revival of Trollope in the1910s. Escott had a good sense of Trollope's character, as seen in his opening paragraph when he states that any pride Trollope had in his own ancestry was valued by him only as "social capital" for furthering his intellectual pursuits. But Escott was not always laudatory. He judges that the Barsetshire novels equal the achievement of Dickens only at their high points. Escott conveys Trollope's cosmopolitanism and global reach more than most critics would do for the next century. Escott also recognized what good work Trollope made of his travels not just in his nonfiction but in his fiction. But Escott does not always mark out Trollope's achievement as an author of memorable individual books. Nor, as seen in his denigration of *The Prime Minister*, is Escott comfortable with Trollope's darker material.

Trollope's own *Autobiography* was presumably intended to be a fillip to his posthumous reputation. But the book shadowed Trollope's legacy in the short run by talking of his own compositional habits and his frank desire to write for money. These revelations made him seem a commercial hack. Trollope's obituaries identified him as an upper second-rank writer—though the *Times* also put Jane Austen in this category. It was thought that Trollope was so tethered to his own times that his reputation would inevitably decline. Harsh criticism by Henry James and the rise first of naturalism and then an incipient modernism in the next two generations did little to dispel this.

Trollope never dropped out of the canon as much as did sensation novelists like Rhoda Broughton. In America, a certain fascination with his depiction of aristocrats kept him afloat among the literati. But the first critic to seriously rescue Trollope's reputation was the British bibliophile and collector Michael Sadleir. Sadleir's 1927 commentary on Trollope called attention to the novelist's psychological depth and ability to make the humdrum and ordinary into a mode of suspenseful entertainment. Sadleir did not defend Trollope in formal terms, though, which impeded appreciation of Trollope given that in the twentieth century criteria for evaluating literature were becoming formalist. The following year, Hugh Walpole, then quite popular as a novelist, wrote a small book on Trollope which was pointed in defending the Irish novels and some of the other non–Palliser, non–Barsetshire work.

Despite a lack of critical acclaim, Trollope remained stubbornly popular. During World War II, his works—available in the inexpensive and portable small blue hardcover editions published by Oxford University Press—became an iconic staple and rallying point for English readers for whom Trollope's relatively calm and orderly universe was both an escape from wartime tumult and an affirmation of English civility and decency.

These years also saw the founding of an American academic journal, *The Trollopian*. Though the journal's name was changed to *Nineteenth-Century Fiction* in 1949 and *Nineteenth-Century Literature* in 1986, its editors never forgot the centrality of Trollope to its mission. Critics such as Bradford Booth and A.O.J. Cockshut contributed to the journal and kept Trollope's reputation alive. Yet Trollope's wartime popularity got him no nearer the heights of the academic canon. The major theorists of the novel in that era—F. R. Leavis, Georg Lukács, and Erich Auerbach—either disliked Trollope or ignored him entirely. The New Critical concern for close reading and the continuing hegemony of the preference for the taut, compressed novel told from a limited third-person point of view in the style of Henry James, did not augur well for Trollope. Wayne Booth's *The Rhetoric of Fiction*, though not mentioning Trollope as much as it could have, did rehabilitate Trollope's garrulous, intrusive style. In the 1960s, a new generation of Victorianists open to Trollope's talent matured, including Ulrich Knoepflmacher, James Kincaid, Robert Polhemus, Ruth ap Roberts (sic), and David Skilton.

These critics wrote sensitively of Trollope's psychology and narrative technique, showing the reader not just that Trollope was pleasurable but why he was so. J. Hillis Miller, first from a phenomenological then a deconstructive perspective, kept Trollope at the center of his wide-ranging interests and showed that theoretical curiosity and a detailed interest in Trollopian nooks and crannies were not antithetical to current trends in critical inquiry. In a very different way, Shirley Letwin wrote of Trollope in a way that affirmed his quintessential Englishness but also showed how that Englishness was open to changes of climate, manners, and opinion.

Emulators also became explicators. Simon Raven, whose *Alms for Oblivion* series was, at least in its breadth if not its tone, modelled on Trollope, also adapted the Palliser novels for television in the 1970s. This led to many paperback reprints of Trollope, including the New York–based Dover Publications' reissuing many of Trollope's more obscure works. C.P. Snow, whose *Strangers and Brothers* was also Trollopian in its concern with daily English life and the corridors of power, published a biography of Trollope in 1975 and then in his 1978 study *The Realists* placed Trollope on a par with the gallery of writers he discussed, ranging from Pérez Galdós to Proust. Multiple academic books on Trollope appeared during the late 1970s. It could be argued that these years saw the Palliser books replace the Barchester novels as central to the Trollope canon (a shift explicitly announced in Cockshut's book, written well before the Palliser TV series). The earlier series, more distinctively English in its ecclesiastical and regional emphases, yielded to the series where questions of personal power and public politics were more applicable to contemporary cultural concerns. Yet British Prime Minister John Major, when he came out as a Trollopian in 1992, named a Barsetshire novel, *The Small House of Allington*, as his favorite book.

The 2000s saw Trollope fully accepted into the academic Victorian canon. Margaret Markwick and Deborah Denenholz Morse explored questions of gender in Trollope. Lauren Goodlad, Amanda Anderson, and Frederik van Dam examined Trollope in political and ethical terms in light of issues of liberalism and globalization. Steven Amarnick's textual study of the manuscript of *The Duke's Children* resulted in the publication of the expanded version in 2015, the year of the bicentenary of Trollope's birth. The book, and Trollope's anniversary, received wide media coverage. 2015 also saw an extensive global colloquium on Trollope in Leuven, Belgium. The success of Julian Fellowes' television adaptation of *Doctor Thorne* gave additional evidence that Trollope would be in the spotlight in the twenty-first century.

See also: *An Autobiography*; intrusive narrator

Further Reading

Dentith, Simon. *Nineteenth Century British Literature Then and Now, Reading with Hindsight.* New York: Routledge, 2016.
Hall, N. John. *The Trollope Critics.* London: Macmillan, 1981.
Terry, Reginald Charles. *Anthony Trollope: The Artist in Hiding.* London: Macmillan, 1977.

Rusden, G. W.

Rusden (1819–1903) was born in Surrey and emigrated to Australia at age sixteen when his father took up a clergy position there. He traveled briefly to China and then settled in the Australian colony of Victoria. There, he became a civil servant, helping set up education systems both in Victoria and Queensland. He later worked for the colonial office in Victoria and served as clerk of the Victorian Legislative Council. Rusden was thus in the middle of settler governance in the Australian colonies, and epitomized what Trollope himself envisioned in British colonies: a combination of British administrative procedure and the growing possibility of home rule. Rusden was also an *homme de lettres*, writing history, drama, and poetry; he also translated works from the French (his renditions of the verse of Gérard de Nerval were commended by Trollope).

When Trollope visited Australia in 1871, he found Rusden a congenial friend. They shared both literary and cultural interests as well as work in civil service. Like Trollope, Rusden observed the proprieties in his deportment and personal conduct, but was surprisingly liberal on some issues, especially, for his time, in those having to do with race. In Rusden, Trollope found a male social counterpart of the sort who sustained his public life in England. Trollope and Rusden continued to correspond after Trollope's trips to Australia ended. P.D. Edwards ("Trollope's Letters") comments that Trollope spoke to Rusden more candidly about his skeptical and latitudinarian beliefs than he did to his more socially conventional friends. Rusden was a true confidante for Trollope. Despite being a far more minor figure than Trollope, Rusden was trusted by him as a man of feeling and intellectual breadth. Because Rusden was so far away, Trollope's letters to him are among the most demonstrative of those to his friends.

In a turn that would fit very well in a Trollope novel such as *John Caldigate,* after Trollope's death Rusden returned to England, as if to reassume his British status. But he attempted to do so as an authoritative chronicler of Australia and New Zealand to the British public. This venture failed, partially due to inherent limits of Rusden's ability, partially because he spoke truths about the treatment of Australasian indigenous people that white settlers were unwilling to bear. Rusden returned to Australia. Here, he lived into the twentieth century, being one of Trollope's last intimates, his children aside, to die.

See also: Australia; *John Caldigate*; travel

Further Reading

Austin, Albert Gordon. *George William Rusden and National Education in Australia*. Melbourne: Melbourne University Press, 1958.
Edwards, P.D. "Trollope's Letters." *Sydney Studies in English Literature*, vol. 10, 1984, pp. 109–116.

Saint Pauls Monthly Magazine

Trollope founded *Saint Pauls Monthly Magazine* and edited it from 1867 to 1870. It was designed as a competitor to flourishing magazines such as *The Cornhill, Belgravia*, and *St James*. Its publisher, James Virtue, designed it as a personal vehicle for Trollope, originally hoping it would be called Anthony Trollope's Magazine, a name which Trollope vetoed. Trollope had earlier intimated that he might take over the editorship of the existing *Argosy*. But Virtue urged him to undertake an entirely new venture, one unimpeded by existing traditions or expectations. Trollope hoped it would be called *The Monthly Liberal*, but Virtue felt a name so political would alienate potential readers. The two men settled on *Saint Pauls* as a neutral London place name, complementing existing magazines such as *The Cornhill* and Mary Elizabeth Braddon's *Belgravia*, which used a generally known place-name as a kind of catch-all to engage a broad audience. Indeed Trollope's preface to the first issue assured readers that there was "no settled conviction" as to what a *Saint Pauls* article might be. This statement led the *Spectator* to accuse the magazine of being inoffensive to the point of blandness, and Trollope of being so modest an editor as to leave the journal without a flavor.

Trollope had supported *The Fortnightly Review*. But at *Saint Pauls* he actually edited the journal and attempted to read every submission. He also influenced the magazine's editorial policy, which aspired to have one major political article a month, and deemphasized book reviews. The journal ran monthly and was priced at a shilling.

Saint Pauls served as the site for serializing *Phineas Finn*, Trollope's most ambitious attempt to combine and synthesize his Irish and English subject matters. The magazine was also an arena for Trollope's short stories such as "The Turkish Bath" and "Mary Gresley" and essays such as his 1870 memorial of Dickens. He published women writers such as Margaret Oliphant, Marie Pauline Rose Blaze de Bury (whose *All for Greed* ran concurrently with *Phineas Finn*) and his sister-in-law Frances Eleanor Trollope, as well as writers very different from himself such as the fantasist George McDonald, from whom he solicited a Christmas story. Leslie Stephen, George Henry Lewes, and Eliza Linn Linton were among the nonfiction contributors. Virtue sold the magazine to Alexander Strahan in 1869, and Trollope was dismissed the following year. Never a true commercial success, *Saint Pauls* petered out in 1874.

Trollope's editorship of the magazine was made possible by his leaving the post office, and can be seen in the same vein as attempts to situate himself at the center of English life as his parliamentary run at Beverley. In both cases, Trollope found that he was more successful as a novelistic commentator on the London hubbub than a more direct participant in it. His experience as an editor also informed his portrayal of a struggling writer driven to madness in "The Turkish Bath"; indeed his 1869 collection *An Editor's Tales* is framed by his role as editor. The failure of *Saint Pauls* as a venture possibly informed Trollope's depictions of such noble attempts that fall short, such as the premiership of the Duke of Omnium in *The Prime Minister*.

See also: *The Fortnightly Review*; *Pall Mall Gazette*

Further Reading

Edwards, P.D. "Trollope's Working Papers as Evidence of His Contributions to *Saint Pauls*." *Victorian Periodicals Newsletter*, vol. 10, no. 2, June 1977, pp. 68–71.

Srebrnik, Patricia Thomas. "Trollope, James Virtue, and *Saint Pauls Magazine*." *Nineteenth-Century Fiction* Special Issue: Anthony Trollope, 1882–1982, vol. 37, no. 2, Dec. 1982, pp. 443–463.

Turner, Mark. "*St Pauls Magazine* and the Project of Masculinity." *Nineteenth-Century Media and the Construction of Identities*, edited by Laurel brake, Bill Bell, and David Finkelstein, London: Palgrave, 2000, pp. 232–252.

Scotland

Anthony Trollope did not particularly admire Scotland. This attitude contrasted with his view of Ireland, where, despite making some criticisms of the Irish, he was generally seen as an advocate of the country and an explainer of Ireland to the English. Trollope traveled in Scotland—he visited Broadford in the Isle of Skye in 1858—and was neither actively hostile nor deficient in knowledge about the country. But whereas Trollope's most famous Irishman is the charming, assimilable, and clubbable Phineas Finn, his most famous Scotsman is the dour, unfeeling, and vengeful Mr. Kennedy. Other antagonistic portraits of Scots in Trollope are Undecimus "Undy" Scott, the scheming parliamentarian (MP for Tillietudlem and scion of Lord Gaberlunzic of Cauld-Kale Castle in Aberdeenshire) who ruins the ambitions of Alaric Tudor in *The Three Clerks*, and Mr. Pessimist Anticant, the dour pundit in *The Warden* often thought to be modeled on Thomas Carlyle. That "Gaberlunzie" in the former story is a Scots word for licensed beggar indicates Trollope has a detailed knowledge of Scotland from which to launch his irony.

In *The Eustace Diamonds* Andy Gowran, the caretaker of Lady Eustace's estate, Portray, in Scotland is another character drawn from keen observation. Gowran understands Lizzie's criminal traits, though he is portrayed as opportunistic in his willingness to be used by her enemies. Glencora McCluskey, the wife of Plantagenet Palliser and later the Duchess of Omnium, is Scottish, the daughter of the Marquess of Auld Reekie and heiress of several unentailed Scottish properties. Mrs. Proudie, the bishop's wife in the Barsetshire novels, is also described as of Scots background. The most positive portrayal of Scotland in Trollope is probably in *Ayala's Angel,* where Glenbogie, the Tringle estate in Inverness-shire, is described as a pastoral, romantic haunt.

In nineteenth-century English literature, Scotland was often portrayed more positively than Ireland, as it was less "other," particularly less Catholic. Trollope's reevaluation of other Scotland-Ireland dyads is one of the inconspicuous ways he rebelled against a conventional system of hierarchies that in other places he often seemed to affirm. Part of his animadversion towards Scotland was his more general dislike of evangelical Protestantism, which, in its Presbyterian variety, often prevailed in Scotland. Mr. Kennedy's estate at Loughlinter is not only distasteful to Phineas Finn because it is there that Lady Laura Standish rejects him for Mr. Kennedy, but because of its owner's severe and joyless Calvinism. Trollope himself experienced some of this tendency, when he tried to write for the Scottish Christian periodical *Good Words*, only to have *Rachel Ray* castigated for its satire of a priggish (English) evangelical preacher. When in *Phineas Redux* Phineas tells Lady Laura he will not go to Loughlinter, he is not only rejecting her but saying he will not go to Scotland as the Irish lover of its English landlady who has inherited it from her late husband, a religious fanatic. Phineas realizes that Lady Laura is especially despised for how her personal life abrades the puritanical values of the estate's tenants. Phineas, as her prospective partner and an Irish Catholic to boot, would be even more tenuous in his position. He thus decides not to marry Laura. The way that the place names Loughton, Loughshane, Loughlinter occur in *Phineas Finn*— in Ireland, England, and Scotland respectively—shows Trollope having knowing fun with similarities and differences among the archipelagic peoples of the British Isles.

Scotland appears in numerous other works by Trollope. The country plays a supporting role in Trollope's travelogue "How the Mastiffs Went to Iceland." There is a hunting scene set in Scotland in *The Duke's Children*. Trollope was more generous to Scots in the colonies, nothing that they were instrumental in building the economies of the Antipodean countries. Trollope was happiest with Scots away from their religion. His literary relationship to Scotland was principally through his relationship to its greatest writer, Sir Walter Scott. Scott was important to Trollope because he represented a romanticism that, although set aside by Trollope's acquiescence to the demands of Victorian realism, was also, in another way, a part of it. Trollope made frequent reference in both his fiction and nonfiction to Scott's characters, from Richard Varney in *Kenilworth* to Dominie Simpson in *Guy Mannering* to Dugald Dalgetty in *The Legend of Montrose*. This shows not only that he had a sound knowledge of Scott's works, both major and minor, but that he expected his reader to do so as well.

For all Trollope's criticism of Scotland, there is also an essential good humor in his satire which telegraphs to his reader that they should not take his attitudes too seriously. After all, Trollope published several books and magazine articles with a Scottish publisher, Blackwood's.

See also: *The Eustace Diamonds*; "How the Mastiffs Went to Iceland"; *Phineas Redux*

Further Reading

Booth, Bradford. "Trollope on Scott: Some Unpublished Notes." *Nineteenth-Century Fiction*, vol. 5, no. 3, December 1950, pp. 223–230.

Pollard, Arthur. "Trollope and the Evangelicals." *Nineteenth-Century Fiction*, Special Issue: Anthony Trollope, 1882–1982, vol. 37, no. 3, December 1982, pp. 329–339.

Swingle, L.J. *Romanticism and Anthony Trollope: A Study in the Continuities of Nineteenth-Century Literary Thought*. Ann Arbor: University of Michigan Press, 1990.

short stories

Trollope's short stories are very different from the majority of his long fiction. Far from being set in the midst of English life, they often take place abroad or in unsettling situations at home. In "A Ride Across Palestine" a man becomes friendly with a younger male counterpart in unexplained trouble, only to find that "he" is a young woman disguising herself from the machinations of her uncle. The gay overtones in this story are evident, as they are in "The Turkish Bath" where a madman who aspires to publish in English magazines is able to gain the confidence of men who see him naked in a bath in a way he would not if they had seen his tatty clothes in the street. This story, about an Irishman who got some work in England but utterly finales in Dublin, is also an epic of disguised autobiographical anxiety. Before the success of the serialization of *Framley Parsonage* in 1860 Trollope could well have imagined himself as someone successful as a writer about Ireland but not in England.

The stories, in other words, serve as a way Trollope can look at the margins of English life the same way he looks so dedicatedly at the center of it in his long fiction. He is also much more autobiographical, whether it is his semi-satiric self-assertion as Archibald Green in "The Conors of Castle O'Conor," or the use of his maternal grandmother's surname in "Mary Gresley," a story about a young woman with literary aspirations and good looks but with little novelistic talent who abandons fiction when her dying preacher husband demands it. The story deals with one of Trollope's customary themes—a critique of evangelical Protestantism—put into a much more personal frame. Though Gordon Ray famously argued in 1968 that Trollope was best appreciated at full length, the shorter work has its own attractions. The short stories, in turn, are different from the short novels in form. In the short stories, plot and setting are roughly equal variables, whereas in the short novels, plot certainly prevails over setting. Though some of Trollope's shorter novels, such as *Nina Balatka*, *Linda Tressel*, and *The Golden Lion of Granpere* are also set internationally, they generally are like the longer fiction in making the reader at least superficially wonder about the outcome. This is rarely in doubt in a Trollope short story.

"Alice Dugdale" and "The Spotted Dog" are good ways of representing Trollope in a Victorian survey course without simply adding another long novel. Trollope contributed substantially to the form, and several of his stories are among his finest works. They are rarely suspenseful, indeed often less so than his longer fiction. His technique is very different from the intense, uncanny formula for the short story promoted by his contemporary Edgar Allan Poe.

But in his own way, Trollope concentrated his effects in a manner that Poe would approve. In "The Parson's Daughter of Oxley Colne" Trollope's narrator says, "there is no room for mystery within the limits of the short story." This is something generally, if not universally, true of his shorter fiction and less pertinent to his longer fiction. "Never, never—Never never" is referred to as a "condensed novel," which suggests another attempt on his part to fuse short and long forms. Trollope explicitly contrasts the two forms in "Crinoline and Macassar," the inset story supposedly written by Charley Tudor in *The Three Clerks.* This inset story provides Trollope an opportunity to send up an exaggerated version of his own style, although with much more dialogue and even some interpolated verse.

Some of the chapters in Trollope's long novels, such as Chapter 51 of *The Last Chronicle of Barset* where Maria Dobbs Broughton gives way to Clara Van Siever as the lover of Conway Dalrymple, could operate as self-contained short stories. In other words, although Trollope does not build the short story into his longer fiction the way Balzac did, it remains an important element of that imaginative realm.

See also: *An Editor's Tales*; *Good Words*; Ireland; *Lotta Schmidt and Other Stories*; *North America*; *Saint Pauls Monthly Magazine*; *Tales of All Countries*; *Why Frau Frohmann Raised Her Prices*

Further Reading

Eastwood, David R. "Romantic Elements and Aesthetic Distance in Trollope's Fiction." *Studies in Short Fiction*, vol. 18, 1981, pp. 395–405.
Garcia-Fernández, Erin. "The Way 'We' Died in Trollope's *Editor's Tales*." *Victorian Periodicals Review*, vol. 59, no. 3, Fall 2017, pp. 467–87.
Mouton, Michelle. "'Why Frau Frohmann Raised Her Prices': Anthony Trollope and the nineteenth-century global food system." *Victorians: A Journal of Culture and Literature*, no. 128, 2015, pp. 205–26.
Stone, Donald D. "Trollope as a Short Story Writer." *Nineteenth-Century Fiction*, vol. 31, no. 1 1976, pp. 26–47.
Wilkes, Joanne. "The Women of Anthony Trollope's *An Editor's Tales*." *Essays in Criticism*, vol. 67, no. 2, April 2017, pp. 136–153.

Sir Harry Hotspur of Humblethwaite see Harry Hotspur in Sir Harry *Hotspur of Humblethwaite*

The Small House at Allington

The Small House at Allington, the fifth of the six Barsetshire novels, was serialized in *The Cornhill* in 1862–1863 and published by George Smith in 1864. The novel was illustrated by John Everett Millais. The small house at Allington, where Mrs. Dale and her daughters live, is contrasted with the great house, where Squire Christopher Dale lives. Trollope keeps his focus squarely on the central class of the nineteenth-century English novel, not the titled aristocracy but the landed gentry who are more precarious and for whom decisions about marriage and career have more impact. The novel is only thinly connected to the previous Barsetshire novels, but Trollope folded the resolution of the plot into the sixth Barsetshire book, *The Last Chronicle*, to help suture it. With its pastoral but (unlike *Rachel Ray*) not remote setting, *The Small House at Allington* is set at the attitudinal pitch of the other Barsetshire books.

The action revolves around the two children of Mary and the late Philip Dale, Isabella ("Bell") and Lillian ("Lily"). Bell is beloved by her cousin Bernard; a union between them would be a great advantage to Bell, since Bernard is from the side of the family that has money, whereas her side lives in genteel poverty. But she prefers her other suitor, Dr. Crofts. Lily Dale is engaged to the charming Adolphus Crosbie. Crosbie forms an incorrect idea of Lily's wealth, and when the truth comes out Lily offers to absolve Adolphus of his obligation to her. Adolphus is undeterred, but begins to worry that he does not have enough money to support Lily. When Crosbie encounters Lady Alexandrina de Courcy, who is securely wealthy, he impulsively proposes to her and jilts Lily, writing Lily a letter breaking their engagement. But he instantly feels remorse, especially as he received a promotion at work which gave him more money. Though he marries Alexandrina, their relationship is unhappy. His wife and her mother soon leave for the Continent while Adolphus stays in England. Lily vows never to marry another man. Yet Johnny Eames, who had loved her from boyhood, persists in his suit.

Lily's wounded heart is juxtaposed with, and is not independent of, the precarious financial state of the two Dale sisters and their mother. Matthew Susman has called this novel Trollope's first fully psychological piece of fiction. The psychological dimension of the novel shows even in the portrayal of minor characters. One of the most affecting scenes in the book is when the sisters' uncle, the squire Christopher Dale, reveals himself intrinsically interested in the welfare of the girls, not just carrying out his duty as their financial guardian the way the girls and their mother had thought. The saga of Lily Dale and Johnny Eames is Trollope's unhappiest love story; Lily Dale is his most poignant heroine. Lily has a sublimity and a noble quality about her that remain even as her fate is tragically circumscribed and even as we recognize that Adolphus Crosbie is totally unworthy of her devotion.

There is an incongruity in the relationship of Johnny Eames and Lily Dale, partakers in a tragic love whose pathos almost exceeds the contours of conventional realistic fiction; nonetheless, they each exhibit the characteristic mundane preoccupations of their respective genders in the times in which they lived. Johnny Eames's London office life, something out of *The Three Clerks* or *The Struggles of Brown, Jones, and Robinson*, especially in the portrait of his eventual superior, Sir Raffle Buffle, provides a counterpoint to his selfless love for Lily. So does the squalor of Mrs. Roper's boarding-house where Eames resides before his promotion. A more disturbing side of Eames is the potentially excessive anger he has towards Crosbie. In their confrontation on a platform at Paddington Station, this emotion threatens to take Johnny's noble quest in Lily's defense into a darker desire for revenge.

Adolphus Crosbie is a ruthless portrait of an unprincipled social climber who does not even have backbone enough to be Machiavellian. So prominent is Crosbie in the narrative—and so much is the narrative from his point of view—that he is almost the antihero of the book. The moment when Adolphus Crosbie, having married Lady Alexandrina, realizes in the course of their honeymoon in Folkestone that he has nothing to say to her and does not enjoy her company yet is bound to her for a lifetime, is one of the most honest and affecting reflections on marriage in any Victorian novel. It also humanizes Crosbie and keeps him from being a pure villain, as the reader knows he regrets jilting Lily.

Nor is Eames a pure hero. For one, Lily is not really attracted to him physically. Eames's rather exploitative flirtations with Amelia Roper, in which he is the relatively naïve prey, and his later dalliance with Madalina Demolines, in which he is considerably more complicit, give Lily a rational basis upon which to reject him. Eames's friend and fellow clerk-hobbledehoy, Joseph Cradell, ends up marrying Amelia. As contrasted to Eames, Cradell is a wholly situational and expedient lover.

In Chapter 23, the introduction of Plantagenet Palliser as a minor character presented as paying court to the married Lady Dumbello (the former Griselda Grantly) is important in stitching together the two major series. It also presents Palliser, a man who in the Palliser series has to be taught to love as a husband and father, as a lover. This is striking even though Palliser's amours are conveyed only in a rhetorical sense; in his relation with Lady Dumbello, any actual sense of the erotic is soon quashed by propriety. Indeed, in resolving the Palliser-Dumbello relation Trollope previewed Palliser's marriage to Lady Glencora and a major plot line of *Can You Forgive Her?* That Plantagenet appears in the same book dominated by the lovelorn figure of Lily Dale shows the intimate braiding of public and personal space in Trollope.

See also: *Framley Parsonage;* hobbledehoy; *The Last Chronicle of Barest*

Further Reading

McMaster, Juliet. "'The Unfortunate Moth': Unifying Theme in *The Small House at Allington.*" *Nineteenth-Century Fiction*, vol. 26, no. 2, September 1971, pp. 127–144.

Morse, Deborah Denenholz. "The pastoral transformed in Anthony Trollope's *Small House at Allington.*" *Victorian Transformations: Genre, Nationalism and Desire in Nineteenth-Century Literature*, edited by Bianca Tredennick, London: Ashgate, 2011, pp. 45–60.

Sussman, Matthew. "Optative Form in Anthony Trollope's *The Small House at Allington.*" *Nineteenth-Century Literature*, vol. 71, no. 4, March 2017, pp. 485–515.

Turner, Mark W. "Gendered Issues: Intertextuality and the Small House at Allington in *Cornhill Magazine.*" *Victorian Periodicals Review*, vol. 26, no. 4, Winter, 1993, pp. 228–234.

South Africa

Trollope visited South Africa from 1877 to 1878 and his book on his travels, *South Africa*, was published by Chapman and Hall in 1878. Unlike his earlier great trips, which were on postal or family business, *South Africa* was done purely for literary purposes. Trollope wanted to complete what was in effect a series, in length nearly rivalling the Barsetshire and Palliser books, on English settler colonies and on what Lauren Goodlad (*Geopolitical*) terms Colonial Man. South Africa was, of course, demographically different, not just because of the colony's black African majority but because another substantial European nationality, the Dutch Afrikaans, were also there, and had been there before the British. Trollope avoided writing about a similar situation with respect to Québec, but he was captivated by the possibility of the two independent Boer (Afrikaans) republics in South Africa, the Orange Free State and the Transvaal, combining in a great union.

Trollope made clear to his reader that, outside the mostly coastal portions of the Cape Colony, South Africa had a black majority population that could not be imagined away as white settlers of Australia, and to a lesser extent New Zealand (fallaciously) imagined. Because of this potential resistance, British colonial society in South Africa was far more militaristic in nature than in the other colonies. Trollope was alternately curious and condescending about the black South Africans he meets, concluding they have potential as educated civilized people. He transcribed hymns and songs in Xhosa that he heard at the Lovedale mission station, but did not come to terms fundamentally with their culture, nor with the fact that, even though colonized, they possessed their own urbanity and modernity However, he did treat the Zulu chief Dingaan as a recognized political force.

Trollope provided little local color about the towns he visited. Trollope's eye was more trained on practicalities such as the state of the Cape Colony wool and liquor industry. At times, as in the opening of his chapter on Natal, he acts as historian. Trollope told the reader the British colonized the region basically to protect the Dutch and Zulu from each other. He traced the place's history to the Portuguese explorers who bestowed its name. Trollope gave a vivid, and quite derogatory, description of the diamond mines of Kimberley, in which life was too rough-eared and dog-eat-dog for him. Trollope was also aware of religious diversity in South Africa, noting both German Lutheran missions and Dutch Calvinist outposts along Anglicans, including maverick ones like John William Colenso, Bishop of Natal, the object of obloquy from the agnostic dogma-enforcement of Matthew Arnold.

Somewhat like Trollope's last Irish novel, *The Landleaguers*, *South Africa* is a narrative with the prediction of an unhappy ending. This is not just in the failed and unjust policy of racial separation. More immediately, the sense of future disappointment lies in how the English and Afrikaans could not resolve their differences peacefully; only a violent struggle, the Boer War of 1899 to 1902, brought about the union for which Trollope had so strenuously hoped. Trollope foresaw the impossibility of a black head of government in South Africa for at least the next century—a decade or so short of when one actually did come to power in the person of Nelson Mandela in 1994. At the time Trollope wrote, few British people were at all familiar with South Africa. *South Africa* did not do well commercially—as none of Trollope's travel books did—and was made outdated by the pressures leading up to the Boer War at the end of the century.

See also: Australia and New Zealand; travel; *The West Indies and the Spanish Main*

Further Reading

Davidson, J.H. "Anthony Trollope and the Colonies." *Victorian Studies*, vol. 12, no. 3, March 1969, pp. 305–330.
Morse, Deborah Denenholz, *Reforming Trollope: Race, Gender, and Englishness in the Novels of Anthony Trollope*. London: Ashgate, 2013.

The Struggles of Brown, Jones, and Robinson

This novel, whose full title is *The Struggles of Brown, Jones, and Robinson, By One of The Firm*, was serialized in the *Cornhill* 1861–62 and published (pirated) by Harper in New York in 1862 and in London by Smith, Elder in 1870. Trollope's usual publisher, Chapman and Hall, had earlier rejected it not out of any objection to its content but out of fear that Trollope's becoming too prolific would damage his brand name—a rather ironic response to a novel about advertising. *The Struggles of Brown, Jones, and Robinson* was Trollope's twelfth novel in order of publication. Trollope began writing it after finishing *The Three Clerks*, and it is similarly a tale of working life of young men in London, if a bit lighter and more deliberately amusing in tone. Trollope put down the novel for a while to work on some of the Barsetshire books, then finished it by 1861. In *An Autobiography*, Trollope described it as "a satire on the ways of trade" written in "a style for which I was certainly not qualified." It has received much opprobrium, and is frequently denounced for being a pale imitation of Thackeray, but has its moments of comic vigor and urbane social mockery.

As the full title indicates, *Struggles* is one of the few Trollope novels told in the first person, and one of the few with largely comic or even farcical intent. Yet it is also the novel which most centrally depicts the rising capitalist era, in which credit, promotion, and salesmanship are seen as ways to prosperity, and as such has some kinship with Baudelaire's reflections on the Paris arcades. The novel depicts what Richard Altick calls "the presence of the present" as Robinson, the narrator, realizes the power of advertising and of the general illusoriness of capitalism, even if he does not play the system to his advantage. The locale in which the story is set is called the Magenta House, because most houses in London have numbers rather than names, and its address, 81 Bishopsgate Street is blazoned as "nine times nine is 81." This promotion of image over reality makes Trollope a pioneer of the half-visionary, half-fraudulent imagination of capitalism. If Robinson's plans fail it is perhaps more because he understands the idea of the intersection of trade, advertisement, and modernity than he does their practical operation. The novel is prophetic in its realization of the lack of correspondence between advertising and truth, and how advertising is not just the description of a product but a lie in one sense, an enabling fiction in another.

Brown, Jones, and Robinson also is an early effort in portraying a workingman's but also white-collar London later seen in George and Weedon Grossmith's *Diary of a Nobody* (1892). Some of the novel's comic triumphs include the description of the Goose Club, the gentleman's club where Robinson is succored even after personal and professional humiliation, and its "perpetual chairman," styled "The Most Worthy Grand Goose." Robinson is a man, like Trollope himself, with not inconsiderable classical learning which he wears offhandedly. Robinson thus makes a brand of shirts that fit, calling them "Katakirion," Greek for "fitting."

The love plot of the story concerns Robinson's rivalry for the hand of Maryanne Brown, daughter of his partner, with the vulgar and voracious butcher William Brisket. Though Maryanne understands Robinson actually cares about her, the sheer force and Butcher's persistence, which she does not recognize as prompted by his desire for her money, make her waver. In the end, Maryanne rejects Robinson for Butcher, and Butcher rejects Maryanne as she has lost her money.

The failure of the firm is told in a mock-epic rather than tragic way. At the end, Robinson envisions running for Parliament—much as Trollope himself did in Beverley. Yet the denouement is nonetheless atypically downbeat for a Trollope novel. With all its broad satire of the inexact science of promotion and publicity, the novel is aware of the bitter end of most personal quests: "The gloss and gilding wear away, as they wear away also from the heart of the adventurer, and then the small aspirant sinks back into the mass of nothing from whom he had thought to arise. ... We see only the few who rise above the waves, and know nothing of the many who are drowned beneath the waters." Written when Trollope was still not completely secure in his novelistic vocation, *Brown, Jones, and Robinson* displays, beneath its whimsical veneer, a stark realism about success and failure in the Victorian public arena.

See also: *The Claverings*; clubs; *The Three Clerks*

Further Reading

Blake, Andrew. *Reading Victorian Fiction: The Cultural Context and Ideological Content of the Nineteenth-Century Novel*. London: Macmillan, 1989.

Titolo, Matthew. "Sincerity and Reflexive Satire in Anthony Trollope's *The Struggles of Brown, Jones and Robinson*." *Victorian Literature and Culture*, vol. 43, no. 1, March 2015, pp. 23–39.

Toadvine, April. "Catching the Elusive Consumer: Trollope's Adversarial Advertising." *Merchants, Barons, Sellers and Suits: The Changing Images of the Businessman Through Literature*, edited by Christina Mahalik, London: Cambridge Scholars Press, 2010, pp. 17–38.

Tales of All Countries, First Series

Tales of All Countries was published by Chapman and Hall in 1861. It was, aside from *The Bertrams*, the first instance of Trollope fusing his travel with his novelistic craft. With its successor volume published two years later, *Tales of All Countries* shows Trollope as not just the most well-travelled of the major Victorian writers but the most attitudinally cosmopolitan.

The first story, "La Mère Bauche," is set vividly in the Eastern Pyrenees. The title character, an innkeeper, inhibits her son from marrying Marie Calvert, his childhood sweetheart who is growing up in the inn alongside him. Mère Bauche thinks that better prospects will be found elsewhere for him in the great world. She thinks for her son to marry her ward will push her into "ignominy and disgrace." Marie is instead pushed by Mère Bauche into marriage with the elderly Capitaine; she flings herself off a cliff. This in another instance of Trollope's short stories having less happy endings than his novels. There, the young female protagonist's life would not end in suicide, although such an outcome is mooted in *Nina Balatka* and *Linda Tressel*.

The second story, "The O'Conors of Castle Conor, County Mayo" is more of a sketch of Irish life than a story, and is possibly Trollope's first piece of creative writing. Archibald Green, Trollope's alternate persona, is hosted by the fox-hunting Captain O'Conor. Green does not have the right shoes for the occasion, however, which causes embarrassment and disqualifies him from attracting the attention of O'Conor's pretty daughter. This equalizes any hierarchy between English visitor and Irish host, always an important theme in Trollope's Irish fiction.

"John Bull on the Guadalquivir" is narrated by John Pomfret in the first person. Pomfret's family has been in business for a generation with the Daguilars, a Spanish family. He has fallen in love with Maria Daguilar, who seems so much more restrained and serious than young Englishwomen of her age. Her father approves the marriage.

But Pomfret's own family is more reserved. They ask him to wait a year before he goes to Spain to press his suit. When that day finally comes, he sails to Cadiz; while aboard ship he taunts someone whom he believes to be a *torero* (bullfighter), twisting the button off the *torero*'s coat. When Pomfret lands, he finds that the "*torero*" is in fact the Marquis d'Almavivas, who is throwing a lavish party for the couple. John Pomfret is humiliated and apologizes. He thinks his prospects finished. But Maria forgives him and they marry. Two Trollopean themes, misunderstanding and cultural encounter, are brought together here.

The title character of "Miss Sarah Jack, of Spanish Town, Jamaica," is a matchmaker who presses for the union of her nephew, Maurice Cummings, and Marion Leslie. The story's somewhat neutral observation that the white society of Jamaica had gone down since the abolition of slavery does not make it Trollope's most attractive for twenty-first-century readers, though there is an admission that Jamaica did not have a future as a white-dominated society. Trollope at once shows an ability to conjure a setting and also braid a plausible plot into that setting.

"The Courtship of Susan Bell" has the exotic setting of upstate New York: Albany, Saratoga Springs, and even a stray reference to Ballston figure in the story. Susan Bell is a young woman living with her widowed mother. When the engineer Aaron Dunn, an acquaintance of Susan's uncle in New York City, comes to lodge with them while working on upstate railroads, Susan's mother immediately recognizes the romantic potential between the two young people. Susan's more demure sister, Hetta, is engaged and married to the low-church Phineas Beckard. Beckard is a local man, whereas Aaron is not only from the big city but also an Episcopalian. These differences, and Aaron's lack of a remunerative permanent position on the railroad, pose roadblocks for this relationship with Susan. But when Aaron procures just such a position, both the Beckards and Susan's mother come to accept him as one of the family.

"The Relics of General Chassé" is set in Antwerp. It reflects on Belgium during the first years of its independence, a place where Trollope and his family had spent a good deal of time. General Chassé was, despite his French-sounding name, a Dutch general who fought against Belgian independence. The narrator is in the company of an English clergyman, Augustus Horne. In a rogue moment while touring General Chassé's house, Horne decides to switch his trousers with the general's. After he does this, a group of five Englishwomen discover what they think to be the general's trousers, which are in fact Horne's. Though only an anecdote, the story does bring home the contingent nature of nineteenth-century nationhood, in this case the still-new nation of Belgium. The story also, at a distance, alludes to the far more consequential defeat of Napoleon at Waterloo, also in Belgium.

"An Unprotected Female at the Pyramids" begins by describing the construction of the Suez Canal, and the frequency of Egypt as a crossing point from travel from Europe to India and Australia. This encourages the arrival of western customs including single women, who come as tourists. One of these, a Miss Dawkins, loudly proclaims that she is unprotected and emancipated, although this is largely a tactic to procure a husband for herself, or at least to fasten herself onto a group of people. She does so on a trip to the pyramids with the Damer family and Miss Damer's beau, Mr. Ingram. Yet she is gently pried away from the entourage once the trip is over, to seek further, and in the end, futile, social gratification in Constantinople. The story takes a satiric perspective on tourism, unattached women, and how the exotic quickly becomes routine.

The collection concludes with "The Château of Prince Polignac." This story is set in the village of le Puy amid a picturesque volcanic formation in the French province of Auvergne. It is something of a miniature French version of Trollope's novel *Lady Anna*. Mrs. Thompson, a widow with two daughters who are being educated in France, is first seen at the morning table d'hôte. She ends up falling in love with Monsieur Lecordaire, a tailor who she had thought to be a banker. The title comes from the local château where Lecordaire takes Mrs. Thompson in the course of wooing her. But it is also ironic, juxtaposing the vista of the old aristocracy with the reality of the present-day working-class male. Trollope depicts English people abroad and how life is changing, worldwide, in the nineteenth century.

See also: *The Golden Lion of Granpere*; short stories; travel

Further Reading

Buzard, James. "Portable Boundaries: Trollope, Race, and Travel." *Nineteenth-Century Contexts*, vol. 32, no.1, March 2010, pp. 1–18.

Tales of All Countries, Second Series

Tales of All Countries, second series, was published by Chapman and Hall in 1863. The volume continues the strand of short fiction based on Trollope's travels. The first story, "Aaron Trow" is set in Bermuda, and is both part of Trollope's Caribbean body of work and, in its evocation of Bermuda as a prison colony, reflects on his Australian stories. Trollope's narrator refers to Bermuda as the possible setting of Shakespeare's *Tempest*, then goes on to relate the story of Aaron Trow, a charismatic convict who leads a rebellion; when the revolt is quelled, Trow is punished further, but then escapes. Caleb Morton, a Nova Scotian missionary, becomes engaged to Anastasia Bergen, a young white Bermudian woman managing her father's modest cedar-wood trading estate. Anastasia is wondering how to overcome her father's opposition to the marriage when Trow bursts in on her, demanding food and threatening her. She gives Trow food. But when Trow demands money and is rebuffed he physically assaults Anastasia, his aim being to damage and disfigure her. She screams for aid, and Trow is disturbed by the sound of footsteps. Eventually, Morton arrives and attacks Trow. The two are locked in mortal single combat, and Morton is about to die when two allies in a boat kill Trow. Morton and Anastasia then live in married happiness. "Aaron Trow" is one of Trollope's most exciting and violent stories. In its portrayal of the condition of convicts, race, and Christianity, one of his most Atlantic-centered works.

"Mrs. General Talboys" is set in Rome just before the Risorgimento. A married woman, Ida Talboys, takes up an *amitié amoroeuse* with a young Irish sculptor, Charles O'Brien. Ida is surprised when Charles takes her attentions too literally. She then unequivocally rejects him. This story's suggestion of even the possibility of extramarital sex and its mention of illegitimate children was thought potentially scandalous by no less a critic than Thackeray.

"The Parson's Daughter at Oxney Colne" is set in Devonshire, lauded for its beauty in a descriptive paragraph at the beginning of the story. Patience Woolsworthy grows up the daughter of a widowed father, under the semi-benevolent watch of the only prominent local landowner, Miss Le Smyrger. When Miss Le Smyrger's wealthy, London-based nephew, Captain John Broughton, comes to Oxney Colne, they fall in love. For Miss Le Smyrger, though, this presents a complex sort of gratification. She had intended to disinherit her family with respect to her Oxney Colne property and leave the estate to Patience Woolsworthy. The story seems set for a happy, pastoral ending when Captain Broughton asks Patience to recognize what a leap upward socially marriage to him would be. Realizing that the Captain thinks his social standing of more value than her heart, Patience declines to proceed with the marriage. The Captain, in turn, realizes that to renounce love for money is as irreparable and drastic a choice as to renounce money for love. In parabolic terms, it is the same message as *The Small House at Allington*; a woman loses a man who does not deserve her. But the story form makes it more abstract, more categorical. Patience, presumably, still inherits the Oxney Colne property from Miss Le Smyrger. Thus, in a story of male turpitude, patriarchy and primogeniture are rebuked.

"George Walker at Suez" concerns a man, George Walker of Friday Street in London, who visits the area of the Suez Canal in the years of its construction. Walker is unenthusiastic both about the place, which he regards as boring and anticlimactic, and the project, which he regards as unimportant. His friend Robinson is transiting to Australia, but Walker is bound to stay at Suez. Suddenly, though, an Arab man, Mahmoud al Ackbar, ill-translated by an Italian from Trieste who speaks little English (the French did most of the work in constructing the Canal, and the Arab is surprised Walker speaks no French), invites George Walker on a boat trip down the Red Sea to see the Well of Moses. Walker is exhilarated at being seen as important and that something is finally happening to make his trip worthwhile. He prepares for departure the next morning, only to find that there had been a misunderstanding. Another older and more important George Walker—a man going out to govern part of Burma for the Queen—has arrived. It turns out the other Walker was the one sent to visit the Well of Moses. "Our" George Walker stays at Suez, grateful for even the fleeting bit of glamour and adventure he experienced.

"The Mistletoe Bough," published in 1861 in *The Illustrated London News*, is one of Trollope's Christmas stories. It is set in Cumberland. As he does almost always in his representation of the area, Trollope uses the name or suffix "Thwaite," calling the residence where the Garrow family lives Thwaite Hall. The premise of the story is that Elizabeth Garrow objects to her mother's hanging mistletoe bough because she fears loose young women will kiss their beaux under it. Her attitude reflects the more strict mores of Victorian women than the more permissive customs of their elders, and also displays some Puritanical influence. In fact, Elizabeth is in love with a neighboring man, Geoffrey Holmes. She is both repressing her own amorous ardor and trying to define herself as a woman outside the boundaries of love and marriage. The story ends with Elizabeth and Geoffrey entering the room where the mistletoe has been hung. This is an unusual ending for Trollope as it implies a resolution without fully stating it. The minor characters in this story—Geoffrey's sister Isabella and the Coverdale sisters—are as engaging as the principal protagonists. As a Christmas story, "The

Mistletoe Bough" makes the connection between the festivity of Christmas and a less evangelical churchmanship.

"Returning Home" concerns an Englishman, Harry Arkwright, and his wife, returning back to England from Costa Rica. They are excited at the prospect of their homecoming. Being on the Central American isthmus, they have the choice of going via the Caribbean or the Pacific, and Mrs. Arkwright chooses the Caribbean as more picturesque, but soon afterwards feels a premonition that she will not return to England. As the journey proceeds, though, she becomes more optimistic, only to die in a canoeing accident just before they have reached their goal. Harry Arkwright then decides not to go back to England himself, as he cannot face his dead wife's mother. The title is thus ironic, and indeed, both in its transnational setting and its laconic sense of tragedy, "Returning Home" is anticipatory of the short fiction of Joseph Conrad. The sense that, if they had chosen the Pacific route, this way, though further from England, would have been ultimately better, is also Conradian.

"A Ride Across Palestine" is narrated by a middle-aged Englishman who calls himself Jones. He comes across a younger man, John Smith, and they agree to travel together westward across Palestine from Jerusalem to the sea. Jones finds himself being solicitous of Smith's wellbeing and trying to make the younger man comfortable. Smith alludes to some unspecified trouble from which he is on the run. At the end of their story in Jaffa, Jones is confronted by an irate baronet, Sir William Weston. Weston explains that Jones must marry his niece since he had lived with her in very intimate conditions. Smith, it turns out, is a young woman, Julia Weston. Jones eventually convinces Sir William that nothing untoward transpired between Smith and his niece. But the reader is left with not just the visible specter of transvestism but the latent presence of homosexuality. All this occurs amid the Biblical and Orientalist backdrop of the Holy Land. The story is, in a much slighter and more comic vein, comparable to Melville's 1876 poem *Clarel*, also involving a visit to the Holy Land and inarticulable same-sex desire.

"The House of Heine Brothers in Munich" concerns an oddly frequent subject for Trollope: German capitalism. The Heine brothers, unlike the figureheads of other business concerns, actually run their own businessmen even though they are elderly; they have their premises on the Schrannanplatz in Munich. Trollope's narrator remarks on the cultural strangeness of Germany, and says that, in terms of manners, an Englishman might find himself more at home in Central America than among the Teutons, offering a kind of warning about the racist Anglo-Saxonism prevalent in Victorian England. This statement is particularly addressed, though, with respect to Isa Heine, the daughter of the younger of the brothers, who is presented as sturdy, but not glamorous. When her cousin Herbert Onslow arrives in Munich to learn the business, he falls in love with Isa. But neither her father nor his are willing to provide them with money they need to marry. Isa's father promises it within four years. But Isa doubts Herbert has the patience to persevere for that long. Isa, though, asks the elder Heine brother, her bachelor uncle, for the money. After initial resistance, he provides the funds. The story ends happily, but also serves to dislodge the trope of the German cousin from the realm of ethnic kinship to that of affective relationship.

"The Man Who Kept His Money in a Box" is set in northern Italy in the resort areas of Bellagio and Lake Como. An Englishman given the name Mr. Greene insists on carrying his money in a box, and inevitably loses it. Another man named Robinson, who is attracted to Mr. Greene's pretty, eighteen-year-old daughter, offers to help, only to have the box turn up in his own luggage a few days later. The story has the same orientation around misunderstandings while in transit that characterizes the later "Christmas at Thompson Hall." As so often in Trollope's travel fiction, travel intensifies the potential for miscommunication and brings English people abroad into unexpected juxtapositions.

See also: *Nina Balatka*; short stories; travel

Further Reading

Buzard, James. "Portable Boundaries: Trollope, Race, and Travel." *Nineteenth-Century Contexts*, March 2010, vol. 32, no. 1, pp. 1–18.

Thackeray, William Makepeace

Thackeray (1811–1863) was revered by Trollope as a master, but he was a very different kind of novelist. He privileged empathy much more and sarcasm and irony much less than Trollope. Upon becoming editor of the new publication *The Cornhill*, Thackeray serialized Trollope's *Framley Parsonage*. Trollope was grateful for this as well as for the general example proffered by Thackeray, who wrote of English society with humor, brio, and a grasp of human nature. Trollope wrote extensively on Thackeray both in *An Autobiography* and in *Thackeray* (1879) published in the English Men of Letters series.

But Trollope's view of Thackeray was one of differentiation as well as emulation. Trollope recognized that Thackeray had talents in drawing and light verse which Trollope himself did not have. Inferentially, he conceded that what he considered Thackeray's greatest work, *Henry Esmond*, was an achievement in a genre, the historical novel, in which Trollope failed abysmally with *La Vendée*. But Trollope depicted Thackeray as lacking self-confidence and being prematurely aged by the traumas of his domestic life—a mentally ill wife who had him seek comfort elsewhere and thus forsake his place in polite, urbane society. Trollope also remarked that Thackeray, his benefactor at *The Cornhill*, was not a good editor. Trollope thought it was good Thackeray lost in his race for Parliament and failed to gain the civil service job he sought because he would have been unsuccessful at both. These comments, involving areas in which Trollope did succeed (civil service) and almost succeeded (politics), reveal a rivalry with Thackeray as much as admiring emulation.

There were also differences in narrative technique and psychology. Other than in a very few instances, Trollope eschewed the first-person narrator that Thackeray used in *Barry Lyndon* and *Denis Duval*. Trollope did not portray the antagonistic mothers-in-law who bedevil Thackeray's characters in *Barry Lyndon*, *Pendennis*, and *Lovel the Widower*. Thackeray's comment in the preface to *Pendennis*, that the decorum of English fiction does not permit depiction of a man in all his variety, could well be used to target Trollope's approach to fiction. Thackeray may be judged to have put more into individual novels than the more prolific Trollope. Only *Orley Farm* or *Mr. Scarborough's Family* among the non-series novels can be compared to the multi-generational social chronicle of *The Newcomes*. The fate of Lady Alexandrina De Courcy in *The Small House at Allington* is, in a more minor and pathetic key, analogous to that of Becky Sharp in *Vanity Fair*.

Trollope saw *Vanity Fair*, along with *Henry Esmond,* as being Thackeray's best work. He judged Thackeray's later work a falling off from the high standard set in these two novels. He called attention to the fact *The Newcomes* and *Pendennis* were intertwined by Arthur Pendennis narrating the former. He remarked on how morally inadequate and unexemplary their young male protagonists were. In his fiction Trollope abstains from the sentimentality of Dickens. But there is a lack of idealism in Thackeray that made Trollope actually lean more in the direction of Dickens's wholesome humanism. Thackeray delights in scoundrels while excoriating them. In Trollope the emphasis is reversed. But Trollope says Thackeray, even the Thackeray of *Barry Lyndon,* is safe for the young female reader. Indeed, the fate of Colonel Newcome in *The Newcomes* epitomizes a pathos that Trollope rarely attained.

The Irish canvas of Thackeray's *Barry Lyndon* can be seen as an inspiration for Trollope's Irish fiction, though by the time Thackeray's book appeared Trollope had already published short stories set in Ireland. Trollope, by saying that Thackeray emulated Lever's humor, implies that Trollope's vision of Ireland went deeper and was more socially probing. Trollope liked Ireland more, and possessed a greater interest in the country. His view stemmed in part from the fact that he was simply more prone to like things than Thackeray was. Nevertheless, Trollope recognized the intellect that went into *Barry Lyndon*. He praised the skill in Thackeray's ability to make readers identify with a scoundrel who is openly depicted as such. Thus the novel manages at once to be both scandalous and comforting.

The two writers also had different views of Empire. What Lauren Goodlad (Geopolitical) terms Trollope's Colonial Man was interested primarily in settler colonies such as Australia. Trollope never visited India, whereas Thackeray's Indian experiences were key to both *Vanity Fair* and *The Newcomes*. Trollope, in turn, was mainly interested in the United States through the prism of his mother's experiences there and as a source for contrasting manners and mores. Not only in *The Virginians* but *Denis Duval* and *Barry Lyndon* Thackeray saw the historical experience of American colonialization and revolution as constitutive of the British present. That these distinctions can be made so readily, though, points to the underlying similarities and shared approaches in their fiction, which Trollope very much appreciated and broadcast.

See also: Dickens, Charles; Eliot, George

Further Reading

Knoepflmacher, U.C. *Laughter and Despair: Readings in Ten Novels of the Victorian Era.* Berkeley: University of California Press, 1971.

Markwick, Margaret. *New Men in Trollope's Novels: Rewriting the Victorian Male.* London: Ashgate, 2013.

Miller, J. Hillis. "Trollope's Thackeray." *Nineteenth-Century Fiction*, vol. 37, no. 3, December 1982, pp. 350–357.

Super, R.H. "Trollope's Vanity Fair." *The Journal of Narrative Technique,* vol. 9, no. 1, Winter, 1979, pp. 12–20.

Thomas, George Housman

Thomas (1824–1868) worked as a court painter for Queen Victoria and an engraver of bank notes for the United States government, but these state-commissioned achievements garnered him little fame either in his own time or in the eyes of posterity. He was educated in Trowbridge, Wiltshire, and then trained in Paris as an engraver. Thomas's highly topical painting of Garibaldi at the siege of Rome was exhibited at the Royal Academy, then in Trafalgar Square in 1849, and he continued to show there through his paintings *Apple-Blossom* and *Masterless* which were shown there in 1867. Thomas's first major book illustration was for Harriet Beecher Stowe's *Uncle Tom's Cabin* in 1855, although he was not the only illustrator for that book's British edition. Thomas first crossed path with Trollope when he was chosen to illustrate *The Last Chronicle of Barset*. He was at a disadvantage, in that the ecclesiastical characters in the books, such as Mr. Septimus Harding, Archdeacon Theophilus Grantly, and Mrs. Proudie, were already well known and people had their own mental images of them. Furthermore, some of the other characters—Lily Dale, Johnny Eames, Adolphus Crosbie—had been handsomely illustrated by John Everett Millais in *The Small House at Allington*. One could view this either as setting a high bar for Thomas or as inhibiting his creativity, but either way he faced a formidable challenge. Trollope found Thomas's illustration of Grace Crawley's cheeks too fat and insisted on revision.

Nonetheless, and despite occasional critical demurrals, Thomas's achievement in his illustrations is substantial, particularly in capturing the slight otherworldliness of Mr. Crawley and Lily Dale. These qualities are seen in drawings of Crawley trying to defend himself and Lily Dale firmly yet compassionately rejecting the suit of the ever-ardent Johnny Eames. Thomas's work in America in his early twenties gave him a slightly foreign perspective on England. This aided him in his rendering of English types and allowed him to realize the universality of Trollope's locally situated fictional shire.

Thomas took on a heavy workload analogous to Trollope's own and, similarly, used his art to support his family. But he lacked the novelist's stamina. Griped by ill health, he took his wife and children to Boulogne-Sur-Mer in France where he thought he might recuperate, but died there in 1868.

See also: Fawkes, Lionel Grimston; Millais, John Everett; Small, William

Further Reading

Hall, N. John. *Trollope and His Illustrators.* London: Macmillan, 1980.

The Three Clerks

The Three Clerks was published by Richard Bentley in 1858, though the book actually appeared in December 1857. It was never serialized in a periodical. The novel draws from Trollope's experience of modern bureaucracy in his life at the post office, while generating its plot from the activities of the eponymous three clerks in the Weights and Measures department headquartered in Somerset House. The middle-class Alaric Tudor, his younger cousin Charley, and the more genteel Harry Norman, all develop romantic attachments to the three Woodward daughters. The combination of this fairytale aspect with the most up-to-date description of advanced administrative life yet rendered in fiction attests to Trollope's peculiar mixture of traditional entertainment and clear-eyed observation of the developing differentiated work activities around him.

If in terms of his sense of manners and romance Trollope hearkens back to Jane

Austen here, in his crisp registering of the rapid transformation of the modern world Trollope's London is the same London, if observed differently, as that of Karl Marx. In other works of his—*The Struggles of Brown, Jones, and Robinson* and stories such as "Why Frau Frohmann Raised Her Prices"—Trollope portrays the world of mid–Victorian capitalism as directly and even clairvoyantly as any writer of his time. *The Three Clerks* is arguably Trollope's central work in this direct, matter-of-fact observational mode of a world which was, in James Taylor's phrase, characterized by creative capitalism.

The three opening chapters of the novel set the scene, with the delineation of Somerset House as a space more glamorous than the post office but less so than Westminster, and of the Weights and Measures Bureau as a tenebrous and obscure aspect of Somerset House. The Tudor cousins and Norman are servants of the Queen, yet live amid the humdrum of statistics and regulations. They lead a dull office life, but have easy access to the active social life, and courtship opportunities, of convivial, genteel London. They court Harry's cousins, the Misses Woodward of Hampton (Gertrude and Linda), but are not seen as having enough money to be suitable suitors for either. Linda is in love with Alaric, but he proposes and is accepted by Gertrude after Harry has proposed to Gertrude and (to the chagrin of Gertrude's mother Susan) been refused by her. Alaric is ambitious, whereas Harry has a good heart, leading Alaric to fall for the trap set for him by the unscrupulous Undecimus "Undy" Scott. Harry has his more sensitive feelings bruised, and his friendship with Alaric damaged, by Gertrude's rejection of him. Scott manipulates Alaric into investing in the Wheal Mary Jane tin mine in Cornwall, initiating the novel's curious antithesis: that Alaric is more efficient and ambitious within the civil service than Harry, but it is Alaric who also feels that the slow climb up the bureaucratic ladder is not enough, that he has to accelerate his advancement through investments and intrigue. Whereas a higher-level bureaucrat like Sir Gregory Hardlines, the Chief Clerk of the Weights and Measures office, wants nothing but bureaucratic excellence, for Alaric, who comes from money, more overt signs of social advancement are needed as a fillip.

Thus the necessity of Alaric's involvement with Undy Scott, a sign of insecurity and disequilibrium that leads to trouble in his marriage, public indebtedness, and disgrace, make him the first of Trollope's heroes to emigrate to Australia. Alaric and Harry are well-balanced, as Alaric has more gumption but the more passive Harry has the steadier heart. The contrast could have simply one of class—with the names clearly revealing a dichotomy, less Norman and Saxon as usual in the Victorian era after Sir Walter Scott than Norman and Goth. But it is also one of temperament, with Harry being allowed to stay in England and marry the nicest of the sisters, Linda; his good fortune stems not merely from his being more of a gentleman simply because he is on a higher social level than the Tudors (whose last name, after all, clearly recalls a royal dynasty).

Similarly, Trollope's satire of the civil service also reveals his understanding that civil-service jobs have an important governmental function. Trollope's opposition to the Northcote-Trevelyan reforms, reflected in the novel, is sometimes seen as a genteel resistance to bourgeois professionalism. But the reforms, by privileging those who had the best education, also posed the danger of an artificial meritocracy centered on Oxford and Cambridge graduates. This was something Trollope, who had not attended these universities, wanted to avoid. Trollope valued the work the civil service did, but he wanted it to be open to people with talent.

The work of politics in the Palliser books or the church in the Barsetshire saga is essentially a satiric backdrop for the novels' love and domestic plots. But work is taken very seriously in *The Three Clerks*. The novel, though, contrasts the mundane reality of bureaucratic life with a high-spirited satire. Indeed, *The Three Clerks* is one of Trollope's sunniest books, one whose portrait of the administrative state is marked far more by bemusement than righteous indignation. As Lauren Goodlad (*Victorian Literature*) points out, the characters seem to aspire to a more genteel alternative to the bureaucratic world they are in. But the book does not reveal any respite from Victorian social market economy. Even Charley, the most creative of the three young men, does not escape the market. Though he evades his cousin's initial attempt to inveigle him into a romance with Undy Scott's sister-in-law Miss Clementina Golightly, and his unlikely but ultimately successful courtship of the youngest Woodward sister, Katie, Charley achieves only moderate success in both his public and creative lives. Charley wants to rise higher, to fulfill the motto of "Excelsior" so often uttered in the book. Though he stays within the conventions and also tries to express himself truthfully in art, as Trollope himself did when he was a government worker, and does not exceed his bounds the way Alaric and so many of Trollope's less admirable characters, the trajectory is not entirely dissimilar. In Charley's literary ambitions, Trollope satirizes a figure ensconced in both the civil-service and publishing world—in other words, someone like himself' Though Charley's first attempt at a romance, "Crinoline and Macassar," is a more fanciful and contrived work than anything Trollope ever wrote, the skeptical portrayal of newspaper reviews of Charley's book in the Conclusion comes straight from Trollope's own feelings of being misunderstood by the reviewing press.

The strand of London satire seen in *The Three Clerks* led immediately to *The Struggles of Brown, Jones, and Robinson*, begun just afterward and published a few years later. After that, this strand lay dormant in Trollope as a dominant motif. But it contributed in a minor way to many of his works, from the office-worker hobbledehoys of *The Small House at Allington* and *The Claverings* to John Neverbend, the intransigent social reformer in the 1980-set *The Fixed Period*, who well may have been a great-grandson of the adamantly honest Fidus Neverbend, one of the three clerks' co-workers in the Somerset House of the 1850s. Trollope's early portrayal of modern urban life and work, rendered with flair but also brutal honesty, was a resource he continued to draw upon for the rest of his long career.

See also: hobbledehoy; post office; *The Struggles of Brown, Jones, and Robinson*

Further Reading

Archibald, Diana C. *Domesticity, Imperialism, and Emigration in the Victorian Novel*. Columbia: University of Missouri Press, 2002.

Goodlad, Lauren. *Victorian Literature and the Victorian State*. Baltimore: Johns Hopkins University Press, 2004.

Meckier, Jerome. "*The Three Clerks* and *Rachel Ray*: Trollope's Revaluation of Dickens Continued." *Dickens Quarterly*, vol. 25, no. 3, September 2008, pp. 162–171.

Ruth, Jennifer. *Novel Professions: Interested Disinterestedness in the Victorian Novel*. Columbus: Ohio State University Press, 2006.

Taylor, James. *Creating Capitalism: Joint-Stock Enterprises in British Politics and Culture, 1800–1870*. London: Royal Historical Society, 2014.

travel

Anthony Trollope was a world traveler. Far more than any of his Victorian contemporaries, he went outside the accustomed route of the grand tour and not only, like Dickens, visited America but set foot on every continent but Antarctica. To illustrate the range of his travel, he was in Fiji in 1875 and Iceland in 1879. Only the most inveterate and cosmopolitan travelers even in the twenty-first century could say that in only four years they had visited Fiji and Iceland. Trollope's stamina as a traveler may be likened to his productivity as a novelist, showing an ability to dilate himself in space, without appreciable exhaustion and with an ability both to absorb external stimuli and maintain his sense of self.

Even though Trollope lived well before the age of air travel, improvements in transportation and logistics crucially aided his journeys. The age of steam had replaced the age of sail. The Suez Canal, which he wrote about in the short story "George Walker at Suez," had become the artery of the Old World. Trollope thus could travel on a large scale without relinquishing his identity as an Englishman or carving a huge part out of his personal and professional life in England.

Trollope travelled mainly for work. At the beginning, this was work for the post office. Later, by the time he went to South Africa in 1877, it was work for his books. His Australian trips were at least partially personal in nature, given that his son was trying to make a living in Australia.

By necessity, Trollope traveled far more within England than outside it, and much of that was both for work and to gather materials for his fiction. Trollope, though, never wrote up his English travels, or produced a book like Richard Ayton's 1814 account of his voyage around Britain. Trollope's visit to the Channel Islands in 1852 gave him the idea of propagating the postal pillar box in England. More broadly, however, his trips to Devon, Somerset, Cumberland, Westmoreland, and other fairly remote shires helped inform novels set there, and gave his fiction of daily English life an internal cosmopolitanism, a differentiated sense of society not just in class but in regional terms, which served his art richly and well. The Traveling Sketches he published for the *Pall Mall Gazette* in the mid–1860s also display this interface between the phenomenology of traveling and the social customs of observed places.

As Lauren Goodlad points out, Trollope never visited or wrote about India. Indeed, in *Australia and New Zealand* Trollope makes a categorical distinction which excludes India—where in his day there were still very few people of English descent—from the category of colony. For Trollope, a colony was only a place populated largely by white English-speakers and foreseeable as a future, independent, white-dominated country.

Part of the course of Trollope's travels was determined by the post office, which sent him either to lands under British supervision or governed along analogous principles, such as the United States. But even after he stopped working for the post office, Trollope emphasized the settler colony in his travels. Trollope's emphasis on the colonies, and, to a lesser degree, Central Europe in his travel writings avoided to a certain degree the traditional emphasis on the Grand Tour and its privileged locales of France and Italy. Part of this might have been that Trollope's brother, Thomas Adolphus, lived in Italy and wrote extensively about both Italy and France. Trollope's travelogues are geographic and educational in intent, and, in an era where coverage of the world was less intense and immediate then it later became, he was writing as much to introduce the places he was writing about to the British public than to entertain or to make money off his books. In turn, his travel books were never either popular or lucrative, though they were always published, reviewed, and gained some sort of audience.

Though Trollope's characters did not travel as much as their author did—for one, that would not have been realistic—they do travel. Sometimes that travel is involuntary, when characters do things or make choices that render them temporarily or permanently beyond the pale of English society. In *Phineas Finn,* Lord Chiltern and Phineas must duel in Belgium. In *Phineas Redux,* Lady Laura moves to Dresden to separate from her husband, echoing Lady Alexandrina Crosbie's exile to Baden-Baden in *The Last Chronicle of Barset* after her separation from Adolphus. But voluntary travel can register changes in relationships. In *Can You Forgive Her?,* Glencora and Plantagenet Palliser build a firm foundation for their marriage when Plantagenet sacrificially turns down promotion to take Glendora to the Continent. In *The Duke's Children,* Palliser takes his daughter, Lady Mary, to Europe so that she will get over her love for Frank Tregear, offering to take her even further afield, to the Western States of the United States or cities in China if that is what will do the job. The Chinese reference is probably only a rhetorical excursus, but raises before the reader the very real, and very new, availability of world travel in that era. Trollope took full advantage of this in both his travel books and his fiction, not only writing about many different lands but making the most parochial place in England, such as the small Devon community in *Rachel Ray,* feel connected to wider spaces as well as being a travel destination in its own right.

See also: Australia; Ireland; *Nina Balatka*

Further Reading

Buzard, James. *Disorienting Fiction: The Autoethnographic Work of Nineteenth-Century British Novels.* Princeton, NJ: Princeton University Press, 2005.
Davidson, J.H. "Anthony Trollope and the Colonies." *Victorian Studies*, vol. 12, no. 3, March 1969, pp. 305–330.
Goodlad, Lauren M.E. *The Victorian Geopolitical Aesthetic.* London: Oxford University Press, 2018.

Trollope, Frances Milton

Anthony Trollope's mother was born in 1780 in Bristol, where she lived for the first few years of her life. Though she used her formal name "Frances" in all her published writings, her family always called her "Fanny." Frances was the daughter of William Milton, who became vicar of Heckfield in Hampshire, and Mary Gresley, after whom Anthony Trollope named one of his short stories. Mary Gresley Trollope died in childbirth in 1784. William Milton remarried Sarah Partington, with whom Frances had an adversarial relationship. The Hellicars, a Bristol-based family related to Frances on her mother's side, were important to her. According to the memoir of Frances written by her daughter-in-law, Frances Eleanor Trollope, she continued to correspond and stay in touch with her Hellicar relatives throughout her life. In 1808, Frances met Thomas Anthony Trollope, a lawyer six years her senior. They had an engaging epistolary courtship, full of good humor and references to books and manners of the day. Thomas

Anthony tried to reassure his intended about his financial situation, an issue which was to prove a trial in their subsequent marriage. Frances married Thomas Anthony in May 1809. Their marriage was not ideal; her husband lived a far more financially precarious life than she anticipated. Though they remained married until Thomas Anthony's death, Frances in many ways lived her own life and spent considerable time apart from her husband.

Following her husband's sojourn to Europe in search of a livelihood, Frances Trollope became friendly with the reformer Frances Wright. Frances Trollope came to know Frenchmen of a liberal-aristocratic variety, ranging from the Marquis de Lafayette to King Louis Philippe himself (whose rule was praised by Anthony Trollope in *The Bertrams* as affording relative freedom). Frances's social views, insofar as they can be categorized, may be called Orléanist, a tendency not far from her son's heralded advanced conservative-liberalism.

In many Anthony ways felt himself an afterthought to Frances. When Frances took her other children to America to Wright's Nashoba Commune in Tennessee (dedicated not just to communal living but to abolition and including people of color) she did not take Anthony. After the commune foundered, Frances moved to Cincinnati. Here she attempted to support herself by various artistic and entrepreneurial ventures; these also failed. But they left her with an embittered sense of the flaws of American democracy. She distilled this sense in her first and breakthrough book, *Domestic Manners of the Americans* (1832). This is still the most famous critique of the United States by a foreigner. It is the negative counterpart to Alexis de Tocqueville's extolling of democracy in America. *Domestic Manners of the Americans* not only established Frances's reputation but set the tone for a stance of fascinated British critique of American vulgarity that continued into the twentieth century in the work of commentators such as Evelyn Waugh and Martin Amis. Frances Trollope is often thought to have been uniformly hostile to Americans. But the volume shows that she was observant and open to the sights and sounds of American experience from North to South, Atlantic to Mississippi. But she could not get over the American habit of boastfulness, which violated the ideals of cosmopolitanism she felt had been dominant in Europe since Waterloo. The book was a success, titillating the English and infuriating the Americans. From then on, Frances Trollope copiously published both novels and travel books. Often she wrote a novel and a travel book both on the same subject (the United States, Austria), a practice intermittently followed by her son.

Frances wrote to support herself and her family and established the principle followed by her son that writing was at once an art, a craft, and a trade. Trollope admired his mother's industriousness, was proud of and grateful for her success, and took her late vocation as a novelist as a role model. But he found her approach to life in her fiction to be too exaggerated, sensational, and moralistic. Trollope took an active role in his mother's publishing career, engaging in correspondence with her major publisher, Richard Bentley, as early as the mid–1830s. His acquaintance with Henry Colburn, publisher of his second and third novels, was due to his mother's having published hackwork with Colburn's firm. As the subtitle of her daughter-in-law Frances Eleanor's biography, *From George III to Victoria*, indicates, Frances Trollope's life extended through the Romantic, Regency, and Victorian periods, and her novels fill a gap in a period after Walter Scott had died and when Dickens and Bulwer-Lytton were beginning their careers.

As a novelist, Frances Trollope was social and representational, in a way carried on by both her novel-writing sons, Anthony and Thomas Adolphus. To a certain extent this marked off the Trollope family oeuvre from other nineteenth-century writers who were more pure storytellers. The twentieth-century consensus, codified by Norman Gardiner in his 1969 University of London dissertation, was that most of her novels were artificial and contrived; but she was at her rare best when she wrote in a representational, realistic mode. More recent critics, though, have seen more value in Frances's social concern, writing of women's lives, and adept handling of multiple genres.

Anthony not only inherited professional connections from his mother but also a ferocious productivity which could resonate as either professionalism or hackwork in the eye of the beholder. Frances's most ambitious effort as a novelist may well be the tetralogy of *Martha Barnaby*, *The Widow Barnaby*, *The Widow Married*, and *The Barnabys in America*. These can be seen as a direct precursor to the novel series of her son, particularly the Phineas diptych which features, in a modified way, the same characters and situations. Though Trollope's mother was certainly not the only source for Trollope's aesthetic vision of the novel—as opposed to his trade as a novelist—Frances Trollope's use of a secluded rural spot to examine broader social mores in *Jessie Phillips* (1844) and her representation of Devon in *The Widow Barnaby* definitely lie behind the Barsetshire novels and *Rachel Ray*.

Frances's portrait of ecclesiastics in *The Vicar of Wrexhill* (1838) is not far different from her son's in *Barchester Towers*. Frances's *A Romance in Vienna* (1838) influenced her son's "Lotta Schmidt" and *Nina Balatka*. The America-set *Jonathan Jefferson Whitlaw* (1836) and *The Old World and the New* (1849) sketches settler-colonial contours similar to those in Anthony's *John Caldigate*. Anthony saw much more potential in Britain's colonies and former colonies, although Frances in *The Old World* did represent an Indigenous character, Watawanga, something her son never really attempted—although Watawanga's fate, to become assimilated, marry a white woman of impeccable social respectability, and take the name Ferdinand Fitzclarendon, is much more Trollopean. In other areas though, Anthony Trollope did not take up his mother's baton. Her *Michael Armstrong. Factory Boy* is an industrial novel in the genre later taken up by Dickens and Gaskell, but never by her son. Her *One Fault* (1840) depicts marital discord and the predicament of women abused by their husbands. Frances Trollope wrote two anti–Catholic novels, *The Abbess* (1833) and *Father Eustace* (1847). But Anthony, in his Irish novels and in the *Phineas* diptych, was always fair to Catholicism. Part of this difference was generational, in response to the reality of Catholic emancipation. Part of it had to do with how Anthony's soul as a novelist was formed by his sojourn in Ireland. On the other hand, T.H.S. Escott suggested that perhaps the greatest continuity of emphasis between mother and son lay in their shared disdain for the more evangelical tendencies in the established Anglican Church. That the Trollopes made this critique from a position of impeccable social respectability made it all the more trenchant.

Though Frances moved to Italy and saw her other literary son, Thomas Adolphus Trollope, much more often, Frances and Anthony were closer toward the end of her life than they had been before. When she died, Anthony Trollope noted her achievement of eighty-five years and her late-in-life emergence as a successful novelist. He commended the eulogy for her by John Doran.

See also: old age; Trollope, Thomas Adolphus; women

Further Reading

Griffin, Susan M. "Revising the Popish Plot: Frances Trollope's *The Abbess and Father Eustace.*" *Victorian Literature and Culture*, vol. 31, no. 1, 2003, pp. 279–293.

Heineman, Helen. *Mrs. Trollope: The Triumphant Feminine in the Nineteenth Century.* Athens: Ohio University Press, 1979.

Kissel, Susan. *In Common Cause: The "Conservative" Frances Trollope and the "Radical" Frances Wright.* London: Popular Press, 1993.

Lambert, Carolyn. "Frances Trollope and the Picaresque Marriage." *For Better, For Worse: Marriage in Victorian Novels by Women*, edited by Carolyn Lambert and Marion Shaw, New York: Routledge, 2018, pp. 18–33.

Michie, Elsie. "Frances Trollope's *One Fault* and the Evolution of the Novel." *Women's Writing*, vol. 18, no. 2, May 2011, pp. 167–181.

Wagner, Tamara S., ed. *Frances Trollope: Beyond "Domestic Manners."* New York: Routledge, 2013.

Trollope, Thomas Adolphus

Thomas Adolphus Trollope (1810–1892) had a childhood similar to that of his brother. He witnessed his father's penury and his mother's attempt to secure a living for the family. In September 1828, he boarded the ship *Corinthian* to accompany his father on a transatlantic voyage to New York and then Cincinnati, where his mother was living. Unlike his mother, he showed no disdain for Americans, praising the sweetness and appeal of the American girl, even forgiving them their habit of boasting about their nation's achievements, and he spoke admiringly of the sculptor Hiram Powers (whom he later knew in Italy) and the banker and vintner Nicholas Longworth. These associations were monied, Northern in tincture (an important variable considering Cincinnati's location on the Ohio River) and anti-slavery in mien, which indicates the socio-political milieu in which the Trollope family fell during their American sojourn.

Thomas had expected to go to Oxford University's New College, to which his public school, Winchester College, served as a feeder. Unfortunately, there were no vacancies there so he had to use the scholarship Winchester had afforded him in a different arm of the university. At St. Alban Hall (later amalgamated with Merton College) he came under the tutelage of the college's principal, Richard Whately, the great logician and later Archbishop of Dublin, and Samuel Hinds, later Bishop of Norwich. These were broad-to-high churchmen. They confirmed Trollope in the family's natural non-evangelical inclination in terms of churchmanship. Trollope's career at Oxford was an undistinguished one. He joined his family in Bruges, first making a visit to Paris, where he met such political eminences as François Guizot and the young Adolphe Thiers, and then traveled to Austria. Thomas Adolphus fell in love with the Continent and, though he went back to England for a short time to serve as a master at King Edward's School, Birmingham, his life and vocation were on the Continent.

After the death of Thomas Anthony Trollope, Frances Trollope took Thomas Adolphus as a kind of junior partner in her writing. This began a career which saw the production of over fifty books of fiction, biography, and travelogue. Although Thomas Adolphus did not achieve nearly the fame or success of his younger brother, he became notable as a novelist and writer, largely on Italian matters, at a time when the Risorgimento and the romantic cause of Italian unification made Italy the lodestone of liberal hopes in the English-speaking world. Next to Robert Browning and Elizabeth Barrett Browning (the latter a friend of his first wife, Theodosia Garrow), Thomas Adolphus probably did more to arouse interest in Italy in the literary world than any other Anglophone writer. For these efforts, in 1862 Victor Emmanuel II, the first king of the newly united country of Italy, bestowed upon him the Order of St. Maurice and St. Lazarus by Victor Emmanuel II. Suitably appreciative, Thomas Adolphus proposed a biography of Victor Emmanuel. But English publishers were skeptical whether a life of the *re galantuomo* would generate enough interest on British shores. The hesitancy on the part of these publishers demonstrates that, for all the currency Italy had as a mid–Victorian cause and vogue, those writers who explored it were contending with a deep xenophobia and lack of curiosity on the part of the British reading public.

Indeed, there was a double valence to Thomas Adolphus's advocacy of Italy. He promoted the liberalism of the Risorgimento which in some ways was exporting Britain's view of its own polity. Yet in a deeper sense, though in line with the anti-clerical tendencies of Italian unification, he provided an image of the people of Italy which sees them as having the potential to be modern, autonomous, and enlightened. Thomas Adolphus Trollope undeniably favored the nascent Italian state over the clergy

Thomas Adolphus's novel *Beppo the Conscript* (1865) is set in Romagna, a region formerly controlled by the papacy. In this novel, Trollope makes clear his disdain for the clergy who encouraged the young men of the province to avoid conscription into the new Italian army. But he is also understanding of why these people would not be overly enthusiastic about fighting for an abstract and still incipient national concept. The first volume of the novel takes place in the small Romagna town of Bella Luce. Beppo Vanni falls in love with his orphaned cousin Giulia, even though his father wants him to marry the wealthy Lisa Bertoldi. Don Evandro, the local priest, encourages the union with Lisa, which will increase his power, and dispatches Giulia to a menial job in in the unprepossessing maritime city of Fano on the Adriatic. The second volume takes place largely in Fano, and revolves around Don Evandro's false promise that if Beppo avoids conscription (which Don Evandro, as a priest loyal to Pope Pius IX, wants to prevent), the priest will protect Giulia from the rival attentions of a Corporal Tenda. After a heated rivalry with Tenda and an equally intense reconciliation with Giulia, Beppo is pardoned by King Victor Emmanuel for avoiding conscription and he and Giulia marry. *Beppo the Conscript* was serialized in *Once a Week,* the rival of Dickens's *All the Year Round,* in which Anthony Trollope frequently published.

Thomas Adolphus's nonfiction *Life of Pius IX* (1877) actually has much in common with *Beppo the Conscript,* as the Pope who resisted unification and proclaimed himself infallible was also from the Adriatic coast; the first chapter chronicling the youth of Giovanni Mastai-Ferretti (the future Pius IX) as chronicled by Trollope has a similar atmosphere to the novel. Furthermore, Trollope, who was writing while the Pope was still alive and was anticipating that the Pope would publish his own autobiography, freely speculates as to the Pope's motives and feelings—the way, he admits, a novelist might. Thomas Adolphus's portrait of the Pope is not complimentary. He accuses Pius IX of being vain, hungry for adulation, and superstitious. Despite this bias, Trollope gives an able, if polemical, account of a man who vigorously resisted the liberalism, modernity, and anticlericalism that were Thomas Adolphus's core convictions (though, as he makes clear at the end of his autobiography, he himself was no radical). Anthony Trollope, who wrote in implicit support of German and Italian unification, would have sympathized with his brother's basic views. But in his own fiction his attitude towards Catholicism was less hostile than either his brother or his mother.

Though Anthony Trollope was often accused of being inartistic, when compared to both his mother and brother he wrote more out of an artistic imperative and less as a provider of information. Thomas Adolphus's fictions were basically imaginative extensions of his nonfictional oeuvre. Another way of putting it is that Thomas Adolphus was more his mother's son as a writer. This was made explicit in the books in which Thomas Adolphus took an apprentice role. Frances put her name to one of Thomas's works, as she appears on the cover of Thomas's *A Summer in Brittany* (1840) as its editor, a sales tactic designed to draw some of the mother's notoriety onto the son as well as to establish the son's own name as an author. The exact amount of work mother and son each did on the volumes is unknown. The work resembles much of his mother's work, as it is a French travel book, and Thomas soon produced a second volume, *A Summer in Western France* (1841). This marked the closest connection with Anthony's oeuvre, as the rambles of the elder brother were set in the same region where his younger sibling situated his novel *La Vendée*. Thomas Adolphus, a vigorous walker who remained fit into his eighties, experienced by foot the hidden corners of *la France profonde*. His France is a place of deep regional distinctions, unlike the shires of England as portrayed by his brother Anthony as places becoming more and more interchangeable. Thomas Adolphus's travel books show a real love of place and of the slower pace of life in continental Europe. This was, paradoxically, of considerable appeal to a British reading public living in an ever more urban and modernized world.

Thomas Adolphus lived for many years in Florence. Here he met his first wife, Theodosia Garrow. His mother moved there and lived with him until her death in 1863. After Theodosia's death in 1865 he remarried and moved to Rome, where he lived at 367 Via Nazionale. He corresponded with Anthony frequently. The brothers visited as much as distance allowed.

The brothers had different literary casts of mind and some evident differences in the way they viewed their lives. For instance, Thomas Adolphus did not see the family's time on the Weald as being as horrific as Anthony did. But the brothers fundamentally got along well. Whether or not Anthony Trollope was making a comment on his brother by having the less-than-noble character of Crosbie in the last two Barsetshire novels bear the Christians name of Adolphus remains an open question.

Thomas Adolphus's first wife, Theodosia Garrow (1816–1865), was also a writer. She was primarily a poet but was also a woman of letters, and she shared her husband's love for, knowledge about, and advocacy of Italy. Theodosia's mother, Theodosia Abrams Fisher, was Jewish; her father, Joseph Garrow, was born in India, where his father worked for the East India Company. It is easy to see Thomas Adolphus's enthusiasm for Italy as a romantic enthusiasm, but Theodosia's highly multicultural ancestry made her husband's Italophilic proclivities more a part of a complex international engagement of the Trollope family that included both Frances Trollope's life in

France and America and Anthony Trollope's ability to write stories set in numerous countries.

Thomas Adolphus called Theodosia his "Angel in the House" and was devastated by her loss. The year after Theodosia's death, Thomas Adolphus married Frances Eleanor Ternan, on October 23, 1866. Frances Eleanor was the sister of Ellen Ternan, famous as Dickens's mistress, and the daughter of the actress Frances Eleanor Jarman. Frances Eleanor Trollope was twenty-five years her husband's junior and outlived him by twenty-one years, dying in 1913.

See also: *Tales of All Countries;* Trollope, Frances Milton

Further Reading

D'Alfonso, Francesca. "...a people so chained up: Frances Trollope and Italy." *Journal of Anglo-Italian Studies,* vol. 13–14, 2014, pp. 197–204.
Poston, Lawrence. "Thomas Adolphus Trollope: A Victorian Anglo-Florentine." *Bulletin of the John Rylands Library of Manchester,* vol. 49, 1966, pp. 133–164.
Trollope, Frances Eleanor. *Frances Trollope, Her Life and Work from George III to Victoria.* London: Bentley, 1895.
Trollope, Thomas Adolphus. *What I Remember.* London: Richard Bentley, 1887.

uncollected short stories

Toward the end of his life, Trollope wrote and published short stories which he did not live to collect in a volume. "Gentle Euphemia," published in the *Fortnightly Review* in 1866, is set in a parodied medieval world where the diction of the characters is deliberately and laughably archaic. Euphemia is the daughter of Count Grandnostrel and is loved by Mountfidget. Euphemia discourages his attentions. She prefers to study with her tutor Alasco and devote herself to learning. Mountfidget prepares to present his suit by showing off the large amount to livestock he has to prove his eligibility. But his livestock is confiscated, and he arrives at the castle alone. He is assailed by the castle's defenders and wounded with a poisoned arrow. But he is cured with a mixture prepared by Alasco, who is skilled in the learned arts. Euphemia's father consents to her marriage with Mountfidget. Trollope here parodies both the Middle Ages in a way reminiscent of Cervantes' *Don Quixote* and, to a degree, also makes fun of the fairytale quality of his own domestic plots.

"Katchen's Caprices" was published anonymously in the US magazine *Harper's Weekly* in 1866; some critics, including Ellen Moody, have argued that Trollope did not write the work. Like "Frau Frohmann," it is set in an Austrian inn. It features a love plot. Katchen is an innkeeper's daughter who loves Fritz, who is accused falsely of stealing money. Katchen sells her golden hair to pay off what people thought Fritz had stolen. (It was in fact taken by a man named Heinrich Amsel, who used it to buy passage to America.) As moving as the love plot is, the story ends with the renunciation of Casper Ebner, the rich man who had hoped to marry Katchen; it turns out that Casper bought Katchen's hair so that she can marry Fritz. This playful version of something close to the sacrifice of Sydney Carton in Charles Dickens' *Tale of Two Cities* has an ending that is morally equivocal, in that someone outside the married couple is proven to be good and worthy.

"Never, Never–Never, Never" has the best and most original title of all of Trollope's stories. It was first published in December 1875 in an American magazine, *Sheets for the Candle*. It is almost an auto-pastiche of *The Small House at Allington,* as it tells a similar story in miniature, though has a much more comic tone, with characters having preposterous names such as Fitzapplejohn, Mount Energy, and Pieponder. Trollope referred to it as a "condensed novel" after those written by the American writer Bret Harte; it is composed of short paragraphs that read almost like plot summaries for a novel never fully written. The title comes from the actions of Mary Tompkins, a central character, who refuses a proposal from John Thomas' and also from the Rev. Abraham Dribble, one of Trollope's low church opportunists. Like Lily Dale in *The Small House at Allington*, Tompkins styles herself an Old Maid. As in the novel, the important result is not just the reality of her being an old maid, but that she knows she is one and is willing to accept that part of her identity as necessary for the autonomy that leads her to speak the words of rejection embodied in the story's title.

"Catherine Carmichael, or, Three Years Running," a New Zealand Christmas story published in the Christmas number of *Masonic* magazine for 1878, relates the saga of Catherine Baird, a young woman married to Peter Carmichael a harsh, cruel, and unyielding older man, a friend and contemporary of her gold-mining father. Catherine eventually finds solace, after Carmichael's death, in the arms of his more presentable younger relative. Part of the drama is how John, the new Carmichael husband, leads Catherine to accept the bequest from her husband despite her loathing of him. John Carmichael does not pressure Catherine into marriage but helps foster her emotional reparation. The story is also an allegory of the replacement of the rougher men who had helped make white settlement possible in New Zealand with more urbane and compassionate men, who nonetheless had not done the hard work of their predecessors.

"Two Heroines of Plumplington," published in 1882 in the evangelical magazine *Good Words*, is set in the Barchester universe at about the same time as the events depicted in *The Warden*. Emily Greenmantle is in love with Philip Hughes, a lowly clerk at the bank managed by her father. The father forbids their marriage. A structurally analogous situation occurs when the brewer's daughter, Polly Peppercorn, is infatuated with the malt salesman Jack Hollycombe. Both young women seek counsel from Dr. Freeborn, the rector of the church in Plumplington, Freeborn advocates for the cause of the two young men, even though in doing so he risks being accused of exceeding his role and with interfering with the families of the two fathers. The tale is Shakespearean in its division between upper-class and lower-class protagonists and in the slight contempt evidenced for Harry Gresham, the idle layabout once thought more suitable for Emily but who ends up left in the cold.

"Christmas at Kirkby Cottage," was published in 1880 in *Routledge's Christmas Annual*. Isabel Lownd, the daughter of a clergyman, is courted by Maurice Archer, the son of a friend of her father's. When Archer says Christmas Day is a bore, Isabel misunderstands him as referring to the religious celebration, not the customs and festivities of the day. She turns against him, thinking him a radical agnostic. By the time Christmas is over, the two young lovers have worked out their misunderstandings and are on the path towards marriage.

"Not If I Know It" was Trollope's final Christmas story. It was published in 1882 in *The Life Christmas Annual.* George Wade and Wilfred Horton have been brothers-in-law for three years. During Christmas season at the Wade home of Hallam Hall, Wilfred asks George to sign a letter for him. Thinking it to be a financial obligation, Wilfred retorts "not if I know it." Wilfred means the comment in a jocular way. In his own mind, he feels he would sign it if it were really urgent. But George takes notable offense. In one of the most religious turns in Trollope's Christmas stories, celebrating the sacrament in church brings the two men closer to forgiveness. But they do not know how reconcile, having each taken umbrage. The signature, in the end, was meant to be a general affirmation that Wilfred was a man of property. Thus it had vaguely to do with money. But it did not put the signer under a specific fiduciary obligation. George, who is widowed, reveals there is a new lady in is life. Amid this celebratory mood, the two men reconcile. The story ends with Wilfred, this time in mock-irony, uttering the title phrase. The phrase "not if I know it" had in fact been used by Trollope in several of his previous novels. The story is a meditation on the microtonal shifts and linguistic semantics of utterance. Despite his propensity to work on large-scale canvases, Trollope was fascinated with these linguistic anomalies.

See also: *An Editor's Tales*; short stories; *Tales of All Countries*; *Why Frau Frohmann Raised Her Prices*

Further Reading

Birns, Nicholas. "Trollope and the Antipodes." *The Cambridge Companion to Anthony Trollope,* edited by Carolyn Dever and Lisa Niles. London: Cambridge University Press, 2010, pp. 181–195.

Blythe, Helen Lucy. "The Rough and the Beautiful in Trollope's 'Catherine Carmichael': Class and Gender in Trollope's Colonial Aesthetic." *The Politics of Gender in Anthony Trollope's Novels*, edited by Margaret Markwick, Deborah Denenholz Morse, and Regenia Gagnier, London: Ashgate, 2009.

Valsopolos, Anca. "The Weight of Religion and History: Women Dying of Virtue in Trollope's Later Short Fiction" *The Politics of Gender in Anthony Trollope's Novels*, edited by Margaret Markwick, Deborah Denenholz Morse, and Regenia Gagnier, London: Ashgate, 2009, pp. 221–34.

La Vendée

Trollope's lone historical novel, written as his first venture about Ireland, was a misfire in the opinions of most, including its author. *La Vendée* concerns the revolt of rural French peasants in Brittany, led by aristocratic officers against the new French revolutionary government in 1793. It was published in 1850 by Henry Colburn, who paid £20 for it. Apparently the book received no contemporary reviews or notices. Why Trollope chose the subject was unclear. He knew little about the region—his brother Thomas Adolphus Trollope, who had published *A Summer in Western France* in 1841, knew more—and never at his height achieved the kind of success in the genre of the historical novel that his contemporaries Dickens, Eliot, Balzac (on the related subject of the Chouans), and certainly Thackeray did. Although Trollope assiduously read Thomas Carlyle, Archibald Alison, and novelists such as Bulwer-Lytton on related subjects, the book does not come alive—even his nonfiction works on Thackeray and Cicero seem more vibrant. Perhaps Trollope felt that, having written with sympathy of the Catholic rural peasantry and fading aristocracy of rural Ireland, the west of France—especially Celtic Brittany—would offer a similar purview. If so, this overlap was foiled not just because of Trollope's lack of familiarity with France but because the French rural rebels had an ideology perceived as reactionary, which was not true of the more politically active Irish Catholics. Another reason Trollope may have thought a novel on the subject of revolution would appeal to readers was that at the time of its publication, the political turmoil in France after the Revolutions of 1848 was fresh in readers' minds. The recent events across the Channel renewed British interest in France and spurred fear of the radical left coming to power in Britain; hence, *La Vendée*'s clear critique of the French Revolution might have gratified readers.

Unfortunately, Trollope failed to exploit these parallels, not simply because of lack of public interest but because Trollope was not willing or able to provide a hero or standard-bearer of the Right. The madman, Denot, is quite the reverse. Nor does Trollope mechanically link his insanity to being a traitor to the cause, as there is an equally strong hint that it was the cause that drove him crazy. As Hugh Walpole points out, Denot is an instance of how Trollope was able to depart from his source—the *Memoirs of the Marquise de Lacorchejaquelin* (translated by Sir Walter Scott) and generate autonomous characters. Although the young Larochejaquelin, the honorable Lescure and Cathelineau—notable because he was from the peasant classes himself—are presented more positively, their modest charisma is not enough to save their cause from doom. Trollope insisted that, even though the Vendean rebels had much of the air of the rebel and revolutionary, men like Cathelineau were not to be considered as such because in their mind they were fighting for their king and the legitimate order.

La Vendée is unusual for Trollope not just in its historical but for being stagy. Trollope wrote his most ambitious theatrical piece, *The Noble Jilt*, at about this time, and *La Vendée* is festooned with set pieces, especially ekphrases (verbal descriptions of works of art or furnished rooms) and prolonged deathbed scenes. These contain some outstanding writing, as does Trollope's hostile but not biased portrait of the revolutionary leader, Maximilien Robespierre, but are more set pieces than parts of a cumulative story. Yet the novel showcases Trollope's ability to paint a broad social canvas and to juggle multiple plots. His next, and far more successful novel, *The Warden*, similarly portrays heedless reform attacking long-held traditions, but does so at once on a more subtle scale and with more mastery.

See also: Ireland; travel; Trollope, Thomas Adolphus; *The Warden*

Further Reading

Birns, Nicholas. "Place and Topicality: *La Vendée* and Anthony Trollope's Novels of Regional Change." *Routledge Research Companion to Anthony Trollope*, edited by Deborah Denenholz Morse, Margaret Marwick, and Mark Turner, New York: Routledge, 2017, pp. 378–87.
Cove, Patricia. "The Blood of Our Poor People: 1848, Incipient National Identity, and the French Revolution in Anthony Trollope's *La Vendée*." *Victorian Literature and Culture*, vol. 44, no. 1, March 2016, pp. 59–76.

The Vicar of Bullhampton

The Vicar of Bullhampton was originally to be published in *Once a Week*, then edited by the Victorian man of letters Eneas Sweetland Dallas. But Dallas tried to renege when a new novel by Victor Hugo became available, instead offering Trollope serialization in the *Gentleman's Magazine*, which Trollope considered inferior. Trollope refused, but *Once a Week* then went out of business, forcing its parent company, Bradbury and Evans, of Bouverie Street, London, to issue *The Vicar* serially themselves and then bring it out in book form in 1870. The novel was serialized in America, by *Lippincott* magazine in Philadelphia.

The narrative focuses on the Brattles, a working-class milling family who are tenants of Harry Gilmore. Gilmore holds a lease within the larger estate of John Augustus Stowe, Marquis (not the usual English spelling of "Marquess") of Trowbridge. When the miller's son, Sam, is falsely accused of murdering a tenant of Gilmore's, and his daughter, Carry, bears a child out of wedlock, the Marquis tries to force Gilmore to evict the Brattles, but Gilmore refuses. Frank Fenwick, the Vicar of Bullhampton, becomes Carry's great advocate, searching for her after she goes into hiding and, after he has located her, trying to find a home for her with either her father, Jacob, or her more genteel farmer brother, George.

Upset at his inability to expel the Brattles because Gilmore actually has the legal right to decide, Lord Trowbridge rents the plot across from the Vicar's Anglican church to a group of Primitive Methodists. This act of promoting an evangelical sect, and its odious leader, The Rev. Puddleham, shows Lord Trowbridge's excessive petulance, since out of spite he disentangles the customary bond between an English country gentleman and the local Anglican vicar. The Vicar's reaction, though, is in turn also excessive, as he seeks revenge on Lord Trowbridge to an extent unseemly for a clergyman. The land turns out to be glebe land, i.e., land historically owned by the church, so the Primitive Methodist congregation has to decamp. After Carry's sister, Fanny, advocates persistently for Carry's cause, their father Jacob brings himself to forgive Carry and takes her—however limited her future prospects—back into the family fold. Jacob Brattle is both a hard-hearted man and a religious skeptic, and his decision to re-embrace Carry is linked to a slight spiritual opening on his part. Characteristically, however, Trollope seems to take less umbrage at Brattles' skepticism than at Puddleham's evangelical insistence.

In a subplot, the rector tries to match up Harry Gilmore, his ally against Lord Trowbridge, with Mary Lowther, a close friend of the Vicar's wife Janet. Mary respects Gilmore's gentlemanliness and high moral qualities, but she makes clear she is not physically attracted to him. Pressure increases on her to marry Gilmore, though, especially as a potential rival, her second cousin Walter Marrable, an army officer returned from India, has been disinherited by his vindictive father. This plot is resolved happily, though, as Marrable inherits money from an uncle, Gilmore gallantly yields, and Walter and Mary find happiness in marriage.

The novel is most known for Trollope's portrait of Carry Brattle, a troubled woman who society judges to have fallen. Unusual for him, Trollope wrote a preface for *The Vicar* focusing on this character, in which he called her a "castaway" and explained that, unlike his usual practice in his novels, he could not rescue Carry by marrying her to a man, although he does not entirely close off hope for some improvement in her condition. Trollope is unable to evade the reality that a male hobbledehoy in his world might be able to morally earn his way out of sowing his wild oats, perhaps even if he had sired an illegitimate child, but for a young women to earn her way into moral respectability after bearing a child out of wedlock would be too much for the most strenuous female good works to countermand. Trollope said his aim in not giving Carry a happy ending was both to warn his readers against emulating her and asking that they have compassion on people in similar straits. For all her sins, Carry Brattle ends up an old maid within the family circle, arriving at the same destiny that is also that of the virtuous Lily Dale in *The Small House at Allington*. Trollope was very aware he was encroaching on socially risky territory and, in *An Autobiography*, revisits the subject, understanding both the severity with which society responds to Carry's conduct and the very real need for compassion. Trollope rejects any sense that, for young women to know they must not behave this way, there must be the deterrent that would keep them from being shunned and disgraced. He pleaded for a more compassionate response, one stressing admonition more than chastisement, of sympathy over ostracism. Some critics, such as David Heddendorf, have seen the influence of Nathaniel Hawthorne's *The Scarlet Letter* on Trollope's portrait of Carry, and certainly the theme of a fallen women in a puritanical culture is similar.

For all the stress *The Vicar of Bullhampton* inevitably places on Carry Brattle, its overall tone is different from what at that point seemed standard Trollope fare. As Escott points out, Barchester names are "conspicuous by their absence" (Escott 240) in the book. The portraits of both the clergy and local life is darker. As compared to the Barchester series, *The Vicar of Bullhampton* represents, like *Cousin Henry* and *The American Senator*, a different sort of regionalism. In the opening paragraph, for instance, the town of Bullhampton, though fictional, is situated very precisely in Wiltshire, and the novel contains references to the real town of Westbury. This is appropriate for a novel that is far less pastoral and more naturalistic than the Barsetshire novels.

The Vicar of Bullhampton was a financial success for Trollope, making him £2000, which was more than he earned for most of his non-series books. The scandalous subject matter might perhaps be credited for this greater revenue.

See also: *Barchester Towers*; *The Bertrams*; women

Further Reading

Gibson, Richard Hughes. *Forgiveness in Victorian Literature: Grammar, Narrative, and Community*. Chicago: Bloomsbury, 2015.
Heddendorf, David. "Anthony Trollope's Scarlet Letter." *Sewanee Review*, vol. 121, no. 3, 2013, pp. 368–75.
Watt, George. *The Fallen Woman in the Nineteenth Century Novel*. New York: Routledge, 1984.

The Warden

The Warden, published by Longman in 1855, was conceived as a small, comic character study. It was nonetheless the portal for Trollope to undertake his first great novel series. *The Warden* is a work of unusual delicacy and grace for Trollope. In its compression and tact, it resembles *Cranford* by Elizabeth Gaskell, published just two years before. It functions perfectly as the antechamber for the larger Barsetshire series. The final scene of the book, where the elderly Bishop Grantly marries Eleanor Harding to John Bold, flows seamlessly into the beginning of the succeeding novel, *Barchester Towers*, which starts with the election of a new bishop to replace the deceased Grantly. Yet *The Warden* is self-contained. Septimus Harding is the warden of Hiram's Hospital, an almshouse that is a haven for twelve elderly men who are provided for by a fifteenth-century will and testament. Under the terms of that will, the Warden receives an annual stipend far exceeding his responsibilities. This has not been a problem for many decades. But with the newly assertive press of the nineteenth century seeking stories of scandal, the newspaper soon lear of it. The muckraking newspaper in the book, the *Jupiter*, is based on the London *Times,* nicknamed "the Thunderer," and Trollope was writing at the height of this newspaper's influence and of its reformist zeal. Its editor, Tom Towers, is portrayed as crusading and self-righteous, carrying originally laudable principles of reform to a self-promoting extreme. The force behind the exposure of the scandal is the young surgeon John Bold, who paradoxically is also in love with Harding's daughter Eleanor.

This is not the only intimate connection between Harding and his opponents. Most of the old men of the hospital—the bedesmen—also launch a lawsuit against Harding. This is spurred by the misapprehension that they will get the money if he does not. Harding, though, has powerful forces in the church defending him. This is particularly so since his other daughter is married to Archdeacon Grantly, the son of the diocesan bishop of Barchester and himself a powerful man in the church. The elder Grantly is described as a kind man if past his prime. But the younger Grantly is more morally ambiguous. His house, Plumstead Episcopi, is described as unfriendly.

This helps balance out our sympathy among the disputants. The Grantlys engage for Mr. Harding the services of the prestigious barrister Sir Abraham Haphazard. Haphazard is as much a satiric portrait as Towers, as Haphazard is portrayed as a self-made and (and thereby) a consummately self-centered man. A lawsuit is about to ensue when Bold, spurred by love of Eleanor and recognition of Harding's true spiritual qualities, has a crisis of conscience and reconsiders his attack on the warden. But Towers, armed with information from Bold, has already launched his own vituperative attack.

With his position now public knowledge, Harding resigns, giving up a stable income. The arrangements are made to give him another benefice (and he never renounced his supplementary duties as precentor). Harding is perceived to have made a gesture of renunciation and acquires an even greater air of holiness about him. Bold and Eleanor marry. But the bedesmen themselves are not provided for. They slowly age and die. This note of bitter realism nimbly combines with the broader satire of Tom Towers and Mr. Popular Sentiment—a sardonic rendering of Dickens—and Mr. Pessimist Anticant—a sour portrait of Thomas Carlyle—to provide a balanced novel with many small pleasures, including an early commentary on the pre–Raphaelite painters.

The novel has very overt, pointed satire of journalism and Victorian pundits. But it also has some subtler, more ironic humorous passages, as when the intrusive narrator comments that Plumstead Episcopi is not really very pleasant. There are some moments of downright hilarity, as when Mr. Harding paranoically searches the Bradshaw railway tables to make sure there is no way Archdeacon Grantly can get down to London while he is there, or when he patronizes a sleazy London chophouse just to evade Grantly's pursuit, even though Harding and Grantly are in a partisan sense on the same side. Grantly is so partisan that he seeks to constrain Harding against the Warden's own conscience. In *The Warden* Trollope excels at portraying different vantage points, as several characters presume themselves moral; readers delight in their comic clash. But there is not necessarily a stable midpoint between any of these clashing moral positions.

As Lauren Goodlad points out, the various practitioners of law and journalism in the novel do not give confidence as to the establishment of a disinterested public sphere. *The Warden* gives a convincing portrait of the worlds of both Victorian journalism and the mid-nineteenth century Church. Yet in *An Autobiography* Trollope claimed to have done minimal research and, given he was living in Ireland for most of the 1850s, claimed that at the time he knew virtually no English journalists or clergymen. Trollope, necessarily, was closer to being a journalist than a clergyman. But in this book he is far more sympathetic to the representatives of the Church and negative about the print culture of which he was so indispensable an aspect.

See also: *Barchester Towers*; novel series; *La Vendee*

Further Reading

Goodlad, Lauren. *The Victorian Geopolitical Aesthetic*. London: Oxford University Press, 2015.

Langford, Thomas. "Trollope's Satire in *The Warden*." *Studies in the Novel*, vol. 19, no. 4, Winter 1987, pp. 435–447.

Meckier, Jerome. "The Cant of Reform: Trollope Rewrites Dickens in *The Warden*." *Studies in the Novel*, vol. 15, no. 3, Fall 1983, pp. 202–223.

Voyles, Katherine. "Trollope Through the Window-Pane." *Victorian Literature and Culture,* vol. 41, no. 2, 2013, pp. 283–296.

The Way We Live Now

The Way We Live Now was serialized by Chapman and Hall from 1873 to 1875 and published by that firm in 1875. The novel is unique among Trollope's novels in that it is full-throated satire, an indictment of the era in which it was published. In his *Autobiography*, Trollope explained that he was motivated by his desire to deplore "a certain class of dishonesty, dishonesty magnificent in its proportions, and climbing into high places, [which] has become at the same time so rampant and so splendid that there seems to be reason for fearing that men and women will be taught to feel that dishonesty, if it can become splendid, will cease to be abominable" (Trollope, *Autobiography* Ch. XX). In particular, Trollope "went beyond the iniquities of the great speculator who robs everybody, and made an onslaught also on other vices,—on the intrigues of girls who want to get married, on the luxury of young men who prefer to remain single, and on the puffing propensities of authors who desire to cheat the public into buying their volumes" (Trollope, *Autobiography* Ch. XX).

Despite its unpopularity in its own day, *The Way We Live Now* has come to be viewed among novels in the Trollope canon as "the one that many [modern] readers consider the most attuned to their own concerns" (Hall 384). Trollope's satirical purpose in *The Way We Live Now* does not diminish his characteristic interest in the psychology of his characters. However, this hallmark of his writing jockeys for primacy with an unaccustomedly comprehensive—and scathing—portrait of the morals of England in 1873. The "complexity of Trollope's vision in this novel has invited fundamentally deconstructive or Foucauldian-style readings that stress the ways in which his seeming ideals are always compromised by the inescapability of the negative forces which pervade all social behavior." Particularly, "dishonesty defines even the so-called respectable spheres of life, which all rely on ambitious self-interest and misrepresentation" (Anderson 526).

The corruption of commerce is key to the novel, with swindlers large (Augustus Melmotte) and small (Hamilton K. Fisker) burrowing their way into the highest ranks of society. Melmotte is nothing but a swindler on an epic scale, but the greed of the gentry gives him entry to the highest circles of society, and he becomes so celebrated that he is elected to Parliament. Fisker operates on a much smaller scale, but he manages to embroil, among others, Paul Montague, Miles Grendall, Lord Nidderdale, and Mr. Adolphus Longestaffe *père* in his fraudulent railroad venture.

The pervasive dishonesty extends to family relationships and the "marriage market" which, underneath the trappings of romance and love, has been coopted by the financial needs of impecunious would-be bridegrooms (such as Lord Nidderdale, Sir Felix Carbury, and Dolly Longestaffe) seeking the wealth of Marie Melmotte, and brides (Georgiana Longestaffe and, if her mother had her way, Hetta Carbury). Lady Carbury pressures both her dutiful daughter Hetta and her scapegrace son Sir Felix to marry to obtain financial security. In "Lady Carbury's desire that her daughter participate in the same marriage market in which she made her own bad marriage bargain, Trollope examines a part of the way we lived then that is as devoid of emotional content as the materialistic alliances he describes in *The Way We Live Now*" (Morse, "The Way"). Lady Carbury "suffered terribly in her own abusive marriage, yet she sees her daughter as an object of exchange in a similar business transaction," ruminating that: "A woman … without wealth of her own, must give up everything, her body, her heart—her very soul if she were that way troubled—to the procuring of a fitting maintenance for herself" (Morse, "The Way," quoting Ch. XCI). Morse notes that "Trollope's choice of the word 'procuring' could scarcely more pointedly compare marriages of convenience to prostitution" (Morse, "The Way.")

Lady Carbury pushes Felix to court Marie Melmotte, and Hetta to marry the older Sir Roger Carbury, who is "not much short of forty years of age and [is] still unmarried" (Ch. VI). Roger loves Hetta, but Hetta is drawn to his younger friend Paul Montague. Trollope does not satirize the lovers but treats them with his typical insight into the emotional states of his characters.

Unusually, there is not a love triangle in *The Way We Live Now*, but rather a quadrilateral, or even a pentagon: Paul Montague is sexually involved with, and in fact engaged to, the beautiful widowed American, Winifred Hurtle, but loves Hetta. Roger also loves Hetta, and falls out with Paul over his courtship of her, though he helps him untangle himself from Mrs. Hurtle. Hetta is stalwart in clinging to her love of Montague until she is aware of Mrs. Hurtle and believes her honor requires her to end their engagement. In a brilliant move born of desperation, Paul sends her to Mrs. Hurtle, who truthfully bears witness to his abandonment of her in favor of his love for Hetta.

Near the end of the novel, Mrs. Hurtle discovers that her "late" husband is in fact alive and disputes the validity of the divorce she obtained in the United States (Ch. XCVII). Mrs. Hurtle, who is almost a decade older than Paul, has an outsize presence in the novel. She pursues Paul to England, striving to rekindle their love affair from two years earlier. Mrs. Hurtle is strong willed, intelligent—she recognizes "the inferiority of his [Paul's] intellect" to her own—and wrathful when betrayed (Ch. XCVII). In responding to Paul's letter announcing his engagement to Hetta, and asking to be excused from his promise to go to Mrs. Hurtle, the American writes three letters in reply. Her first draft is a noble, self-sacrificing letter. She then pens a furious letter commanding him to honor his promise to go to her, and "find me with a horsewhip in my hand," prepared to "whip [him] until I have not a breath in my body." She finally sends a letter reading simply "Yes, come." When he arrives, she shows him all three letters, and when he weeps upon reading the forgiving letter, she in fact forgives him. In a wonderful bit of comic relief, Paul deplores the horsewhip threat as unfitting a woman and Mrs. Hurtle wryly responds, "It is certainly more comfortable for gentlemen—who amuse themselves—that women should have that opinion" (Ch. XCVII).

Mrs. Hurtle also plays a pivotal role in Felix Carbury's descent, as she becomes the self-appointed protector of the young rural Ruby Ruggles, whom Carbury debauches. Mrs. Hurtle not only ensures that Felix is thoroughly punished, she picks as Ruby's avenger the young farmhand who loves her, engineering a reconciliation and sealing them in matrimony. The virago flouts the conventions of British society, but, as Trollope acknowledges "Mrs. Hurtle, for all her faults, was a good natured woman" (Ch. XCVII).

A critical subplot involves the banker Ezekiel Breghert and his courtship of the shallow and desperate Georgiana Longestaffe, who decides that Breghert's wealth outweighs her repulsion at his age, his Jewishness, and his uncouth (to her mind) appearance. Her family opposes the engagement, but offers no other hope for Georgiana than a frustrated spinsterhood. (The similarly placed, but more pragmatic Lady Julia Start succeeds in marrying the young Lionel Goldsheiner, in part because her mother arranges an elopement. After the deed is done, the family makes a place for their Jewish son-in-law.) When Breghert's finances are adversely impacted by the interlocking set of schemes in which Melmotte features, Georgiana drops her pretensions to liberalism and rebuffs him when he candidly tells her that he cannot yet support two households for her. By contrast, Breghert "is depicted as honest and entirely forthright: he steadily confronts the objections of Mr. Longestaffe and also is singled out for his direct communications with Georgiana, who is exposed as unequal to recognizing his worth" (Anderson 526). Breghert clarifies that "Trollope does not absolutely associate Jewishness with a corrupt form of rootless cosmopolitan finance," as Melmotte, who is probably Jewish, could be taken as signifying (Anderson; Wall, 385–86).

The weight of this courtship is that Breghert, like Roger Carbury, is never anything less than honest. Where Breghert excels Roger Carbury is in his generosity of spirit. He is kind to Georgiana despite her callous and mercenary approach to him. Roger Carbury repeatedly does the right thing, but must force himself to do so. He is honest to Hetta and to Paul, but his honesty is grudging and reluctant. Roger's discipline makes him live up to his ideals, and he softens toward Paul at the end of the novel, but Breghert's heart is gentle throughout.

As is so often the case with Trollope, the outsider, the liminal character on the margins, lives out the ideals to which corrupt society pays lip service. Breghert joins a long list of outsiders—Anty Lynch from *The Kellys and the O'Kellys*, Phineas Finn, Marie ("Madame Max") Goesler, Miss Dunstable from the Barchester books, and Isabel Boncassen in *The Duke's Children*, to name but a few—who are at first viewed with suspicion, but ultimately serve the ideals of the society they join (Edwards 195).

Lady Carbury's own story, her efforts to support herself by vapid literary works made to sell by "puffery," and her ultimate marriage to the publisher who sees through her machinations but loves her nevertheless, which Trollope had originally seen as the central plotline of the novel, fades almost entirely into the background (Wall 370–71). The novel's center of gravity inevitably is Augustus Melmotte, whose conspicuous consumption, brusque manner of conferring a favor by extracting one's money, and shady reputation bring all the lords and ladies to gape, and in a strange way to admire.

In his palmy days, Melmotte effortlessly dominates his social "betters." Lord Alfred Grendall and his son Miles "willingly submit to being patronized by and run errands for the great financier for the sake of what they hope to get from him" (Wall 373). Mr. Longestaffe, proud of his "lineage and gentility," becomes a supplicant to Melmotte and "acts as a dummy director on the board of Melmotte's greatest enterprise," the entirely fraudulent South Central Pacific and Mexican Railway, originated by the sharp American Hamilton K. Fisker (Wall 373). Most of the aristocrats in the novel "are only too eager to associate themselves with such an unprincipled venture" (Wall).

The "investors in the share market have no way of knowing that Augustus Melmotte's South Central Pacific and Mexican Railway exists purely to profit its directors, as the narrator remarks, 'not by the construction of the railway, but by the floating of the railway shares'" (Lovett 693). In Trollope's jaundiced view of the markets he surveys, "the market mechanism seems to have run amok: social status, titles, and reputations circulate like commodities in a sea of new money that swamps traditional distinctions between creditworthiness, social capital, investment and speculation, and commerce and graft" (Lovett 691).

The pervasive sense that "everything has its price extends to intimate social relations, including courtship and marriage. Penniless, pretty women of good families, such as Julia Triplex (later Lady Monogram) and Lady Carbury, much like penniless, titled men such as Lord Nidderdale and Lady Carbury's handsome son Felix, recognize that, for them, marriage is a business arrangement in which the pretense of sentiment between the parties is little more than a social convention" (Lovett 691). But the novel "also suggests that the frenzy that free-for-all market forces have unleashed will exhaust itself, just as the speculative price bubble in railway shares central to the narrative eventually collapses" (Lovett 691). Trollope's satire of the excesses of capitalism offers as an alternative to the madness of unfettered speculation a more hopeful vision of "the imposition of standards of behavior that foster honest commerce" (Lovett 691).

Trollope takes his time in sharpening the point of his satire. Melmotte is at first presented only from the exterior—his words and actions alone are presented. But as the narrative progresses, his consciousness comes under increasingly close scrutiny. Melmotte is a cool player until his downfall is inevitable. Only then do the few hints of desperation he has previously displayed (such as his panicked fury when Marie refuses to sign over the money he has placed in her name) begin to erode his control. When he stands up drunk in the House of Commons, his effrontery is no longer supported by sufficient force of will to command his circumstances. Even then, there is something to Melmotte beyond a thwarted villain. Melmotte "is treated in part sympathetically, as an outsider who tries to enter the upper reaches of English society by appealing to its greed" (Morse, "The Way"). We are at length finally granted access to Melmotte's own thoughts, and his mix of courage and braggadocio as all collapses around him touches a chord of pity as he chooses death by poison rather than life in disgrace and prison.

The Way We Live Now is not entirely bleak in its depiction of a profoundly cor-
rupted world. Rather, the good and the bad exist together, the light piercing the veils
of darkness and transmuting the dark satire and finding pockets of redemption. For so
severe a satire, *The Way We Live Now* shows considerable mercy to its characters: Lady
Carbury finds in Mr. Broune a man who loves her despite knowing her foibles, and
dispatches the troublesome Felix to the Continent; Georgiana finds a lover from among
the clergy; Roger forgives Paul, and receives him "quite in the old way" of friendship
(Ch. C); and a hardened Marie Melmotte marries the rascally Fisker, only after making
sure that her money will remain her own. Even Melmotte's common-law widow finds
a husband in his clerk Croll, whose qualms had earlier led him to desert his employer.

See also: *He Knew He Was Right; The Prime Minister*

Further Reading

Anderson, Amanda. "Trollope's Modernity." *ELH,* vol. 74, no. 3, Fall, 2007, pp. 509–534.
Edwards, Owen Dudley. "Anthony Trollope, the Irish Writer." *Nineteenth-Century Fiction*, vol. 38, no. 1, June
    1983, pp. 1–42.
Hall, N. John. *Trollope: A Biography*. Clarendon Press, 1991.
Lovett, Denise. "The Socially-Embedded Market and The Future of English Capitalism in Anthony Trollope's
    The Way We Live Now." Victorian Literature and Culture, vol. 42, no. 4, 2014, pp. 691–707.
Morse, Deborah Denenholz. "The Way He Thought Then: Modernity and the Retreat of the Public Liberal
    in Anthony Trollope's *The Way We Live Now*, 1873" (July 2014). *BRANCH: Britain, Representation and
    Nineteenth-Century History*, July 2014. http://www.branchcollective.org/?ps_articles=deborah-denenholz-
    morse-the-way-he-thought-then-modernity-and-the-retreat-of-the-public-liberal-in-anthony-trollopes-the-
    way-we-live-now-1873
Wall, Stephen. *Trollope and Character*. London: Faber & Faber, 1988.

The West Indies and the Spanish Main

The West Indies and the Spanish Main was published by Chapman and Hall in
1859. Trollope began the book by stating he was writing it as he was making the trip
around the region. Though the book is nonfiction, it is comparable in length to that of
Trollope's recently published novel *Doctor Thorne*, and his skill as shaping narratives
informed the scope and organization of his travel writing. He travelled for work, on a
special postal mission to the West Indies. The usual gap between experience and narrative in travel writing is gone. The text is contemporaneous with the journey itself,
giving the narrative both a hyper-journalistic feel and a resistance to certain shaping
tendencies normally associated with constructed narrative. Unlike the technique he
employs in *Australia and New Zealand*, in *The West Indies and the Spanish Main* Trollope often expresses himself in the first person and shares his own personal opinions;
Trollope himself concluded that the earlier book was more readable. He was travelling
alone—unlike his trips to North America and Australia, where he travelled with his
wife Rose—and this perhaps gave him a better opportunity to achieve a personal perspective. The book opens in Jamaica, where, as in the short story "Miss Sarah Jack of
Spanish Town," Trollope describes how prosperity on the island has decreased since
the abolition of slavery (and from the era of earlier narratives such as J.W. Orderson's
Creoleana). While writing before the Governor Eyre trial and the Morant Bay rebellion—events which dominated Jamaican history in the 1860s—Trollope registers the
quantum change in the West Indies from prized economic possessions to the period

after abolition when the area became a backwater; there seemed to be no future unless self-determination by the black majority was to be welcomed. Whereas, by the end of the century, the British writer James Anthony Froude and the white Antiguan novelist Frieda Cassin would adopt a pessimistic view of a white future in the Caribbean, Trollope was more equivocal. But he realized that the area he was describing had been of less concern to the British public since abolition both removed the moral stain from the region and made it no longer a source of wealth.

Trollope treated every island he visited individually. He let empirical impressions take their course rather than foisting generalizations about the region on each locality. He found Cuba extravagant and a bit overwhelming, and thought that the best course for the island would be its immediate annexation by the United States—upbraiding his fellow Britons for being envious of the increase of American power and territory. Though his conviction that Cuba would be under the Stars and Stripes was misplaced, it does, by reflection, explain the importance, in the following century, of Cuban nationalism. Trollope spoke of Barbados as pleasant but lacking touristic appeal. He admired the natural beauty of Dominica but wondered at the island's poverty, which he attributed partially to the baleful effects of its former French colonizers. Trollope notes both that Antigua had handled emancipation quickly and efficiency and also boasted of its own Anglican bishop.

Grenada offered Trollope gustatory delight—mangoes beyond compare and pineapples and oranges reaching nearly that standard—and a capital, St. George's, that resembled a good English town. St. Lucia charmed Trollope with its French-speaking ways and the prosperity of Castries, St. Vincent offered the writer little but gratification that the island's indigenous population had been conquered and exiled. He did not visit Tobago. British Guiana—present-day Guyana—was a land Trollope found particularly pleasant, saying he would gladly have spent a prolonged amount of time there. He recorded the growing role of transplanted workers from India and China (and, to a lesser extent, Madeira) whose use he defended though without particular regard for their political rights and social aspirations. Trollope wrote stories concerning only Caribbean whites, such as "Miss Sarah Jack of Spanish Town" and "Aaron Trow," leaving it to later white novelists to write stories of the non-white population such as Edward Jenkins's 1877 Guyana-set *Lutchmee and Dilloo*. The Guyana chapter contains a detailed description of sugar harvesting, a process Trollope found aesthetically unappealing, though he respected its economic necessity.

Once Trollope leaves the British colonial sphere to the already-independent Spanish-speaking nations of the mainland, his narrative opens up even further, conscious that he is now addressing a polity in which his readers will not feel any sort of stake. Trollope then sailed to the mainland, touring northern Colombia, in which modern-day Panama was then included. This is territory later to be famously explored by Joseph Conrad in *Nostromo,* and Trollope gives a sense of the material circumstances which Conrad would explore. He gives the reader a brief history of Colombia and the life and career of Simón Bolívar. Trollope tolerated the intense tropical heat and recorded his awe at first seeing the Pacific. He then moved on to Costa Rica, which he found a pleasant country, and gave detailed descriptions of the coffee plantations there. He ascended the volcanic rise of Mount Irazu, without sublimity, though encountering, along the way, a Miss Ouseley. He then diverted to Nicaragua, going into the country's great central lake, and encountering the English-speaking population along the Mosquito Coast.

Trollope foresaw a Central American canal (more so in Nicaragua than what was to become Panama) but was less than sanguine that it could be built in the foreseeable future. So much of Trollope's writing is a diagnosis of the prospective future of the places he visits, so the reader lodged in that future reads the book retrospectively, while his original readers saw it as a prognosis of what would be.

Trollope's final island visit was to Bermuda. Given that by the time Trollope visited Australia even Tasmania, the last convict colony, no longer had a convict population, Bermuda was Trollope's only encounter with such, a situation brilliantly rendered in his short story "Aaron Trow." Whereas Trollope feared republican government in Jamaica because of the potential black majority, in Bermuda he thought not only the mixed-race nature of the population but its small scale militated that it be governed as a strategic fortress along the line of Malta and Gibraltar—this of course being more important in an era where American friendship or stability was not assured. The book ends with brief accounts of Trollope's visits to New York, Saratoga Springs, and Montréal, which he visited on his way back to England.

See also: *Australia and New Zealand*; *South Africa*; *Tales of All Countries*; travel

Further Reading

Aguirre, Robert D. "'Affairs of State': Mobilities, Communication, and Race in Trollope's *The West Indies and the Spanish Main*." *Nineteenth-Century Contexts*, vol. 37, number 1, 2015, pp. 1–20.

Mouton, Michelle. "Food and Race in the *West Indies and the Spanish Main*." *Routledge Research Companion to Anthony Trollope*, edited by Deborah Denenholz Morse, Margaret Markwick, and Mark Turner, New York: Routledge, 2017.

Why Frau Frohmann Raised Her Prices and Other Stories

The title story of Trollope's 1880 volume *Why Frau Frohmann Raised Her Prices and Other Stories*, "Why Frau Frohmann Raised Her Prices," is as close to a play-by-play chronicling of the rise of capitalism as can be found in English literature outside the fiction of Elizabeth Gaskell. The story is almost the paradigm of a shift from an agrarian to a capitalist economy, a society characterized by fixed monetary values to one in which value is flexible and mobile. Frau Frohmann, proprietress of the Peacock Inn in the Alps west of Innsbruck, is told by her lawyer, Fritz Schlessen, that she needs to raise her prices, as prices are rising everywhere. But, reluctant to disturb what had worked well for her, she insists on keeping things the same, even though the farmers who supply her food learn there is a market further away in Innsbruck and work to sell their goods there. Importantly, even though Frau Frohmann is persuaded to raise her prices, she makes sure not to disturb her traditional relationships in the community, covertly giving some close friends lower prices so she may survive but not at the expense of her near neighbors. That an Englishman, Mr. Cartwright, convinces the Frau to raise her prices and explains to her that salaries are generally going up, is both a self-representation on the part of Trollope and a reflection of the British association with liberal capitalism and a way to allow readers to see the Frau as a woman who is open to changing new relationships but who also values the existing connections that have sustained her life in business for so many years.

"Why Frau Frohmann Raised Her Prices" is not only set in Austria; it is perhaps Trollope's most paradigmatic story of political economy. The "Tory"—Trollope's use of this very English term transnationally is itself suggestive—Frau Frohmann does not want to raise her prices and change with the economic times. In tandem with growing tourist patronage from England and other foreign parts, this indicates that she knows it is a convulsive paradigm shift. Frau Frohmann even considers shutting the inn down or taking a loss on the food and services. The plot resolves everything happily. The Frau's daughter Amelia marries the lawyer Schlessen. There is a corollary sense that prosperity is universal, that a rising tide lifts all boats. Yet this does not diminish the story's sense of this shift not just being a microeconomic but a macroeconomic one. The story was published in February 1877 in *Good Words*, a religious periodical in which Trollope achieved a fragile entente with the precautions and sensitivies of low-Anglican taste, which in this instance did not find a moral objection to capitalist enterprise.

"The Lady of Launay" was first published in the United States by *Harper's* in 1878. The story concerns a young man, Philip Miles, of the Launay estate, who, unusually, has inherited his surname and eventually his property from his mother. When Philip is an adolescent, he meets Bessy Pryor, a ward much like Fanny Price in Jane Austen's *Mansfield Park*. Bessy is intended for the parson, Mr. Morrison, but does not love him. Bessy comes to perceive that Philip loves her and regards herself as engaged, but Philips' mother objects and turns Bessy out of the house. In the guardianship of her governess, Mrs. Knowl, Bessy is banished to Normandy. Philip persists in his suit. His mother, who is tender at heart, is eventually brought round. By the story's end, Bessy becomes the "Lady of Launay" of the title. This renders the title, like that of "Catherine Carmichael," slightly an in-joke.

In "Christmas at Thompson Hall," the Browns live in France. But for the first time in almost a decade they have been lured back to spend Christmas at Thompson Hall, the English country home of Mrs. Brown's family. While staying in Paris, Mrs. Brown perpetuates a comic incident: while trying to give her husband a mustard treatment to salve his sore throat, gives it to the wrong man. The man, baffled by this turn of events, turns out to be betrothed to Mrs. Brown's sister, and also bound for Thomson Hall, at which point the confusion is resolved and everyone is happy. The story's reference to Dickens's *Barnaby Rudge*, and that the Christmas tale as a genre is so dominated by Dickens, raises the specter of Dickens's own writing on transactions between France and England.

Like Henry James's later short story "In the Cage," "The Telegraph Girl" has as its heroine a young woman working in a menial way at the frontiers of communication. Lucy Graham works for the National Telegraph Office at the same building where Anthony Trollope had worked for the post office in St. Martin's-Le-Grand. She is an independent single woman living with her married brother, and is both steeped in English literature and acquainted with foreign languages. After her brother dies and the rest of her family moves away, she is left alone at twenty-six, and moves in with her best friend, Sophia Wilson. Lucy and Sophia's relationship is highly companionate, and shows how the new space of the telegraph office encourages a new sense of gendered relations. Lucy and Sophia live together in Clerkenwell in a relationship that at one point is compared to marriage. But there is a fundamental incompatibility, as Sophia wants to do light and amusing activities whereas Lucy wants to devote herself to her work and high-minded interests. Sophia and Lucy encounter a man, the engineer Abraham Hall, who is a widower with a young son. Lucy thinks Abraham is interested in Sophia, especially when he tries to give her money, a gesture rejected by Lucy as unseemly. But he is in fact interested in Lucy. They marry and live a happy domestic life in Gloucestershire, while Sophia marries a hairdresser, Mr. Brown. The story has attracted much recent attention for the lesbian overtones of Lucy and Sophia's relationship as well as for its portrait of working women.

In "Alice Dugdale" a poor but virtuous girl, Alice Dugdale, wins the heart of Major John Rossiter over the haughty and superficial Georgina Wanless. It is not a melodramatic opposition. Georgiana Wanless is given positive attributes, such as being of great beauty. But Trollope makes clear that she is better fit to a suitor like Burmeston the brewer. In some ways Major Rossiter's ultimate choice of Alice Dugdale reverses the plot of Jane Austen's *Persuasion*, where a military man gains the prestige necessary to marry into an aristocratic family; Trollope depicts a comparable figure choosing the girl next door over someone with more exalted connections. The length of "Alice Dugdale" is notable. Indeed, it is almost a short novel. But the length provides Alice an opportunity to undertake a psychological self-examination to decide that she could live on her own, without the Major. This paradoxically exemplifies the strength of character which ends up winning his heart. "Alice Dugdale," like the other stories in the *Frau Frohmann* book, has internal chapters and is of such length that only its appearance in a book with other short stories distinguishes it from Trollope's short novels. "Alice Dugdale" is almost the reverse of "The Parson's Daughter at Oxney Colne" in which the urbane military officer, Captain Broughton, jilts Patience Woolsworthy. He reveals that he values more metropolitan connections over the virtue of the simple Devon girl whose heart he has won.

See also: *An Editor's Tales*; short stories

Further Reading

Mouton, Michelle. "'Why Frau Frohmann Raised Her Prices': Anthony Trollope and the nineteenth-century global food system." *Victorians: A Journal of Culture and Literature*, no. 128, 2015, pp. 204–218.
Valsopolos, Anca. "The Weight of Religion and History: Women Dying of Virtue in Trollope's Later Short Fiction." *The Politics of Gender in Anthony Trollope's Novels*, edited by Margaret Markwick, Deborah Denenholz Morse, and Regenia Gagnier, London: Ashgate, 2009, pp. 221–234.

women

Trollope is one of the male novelists most applauded for his portraits of women. (Two of the others, Henry James and Leo Tolstoy, were both influenced by Trollope.) Thomas Chandler Halliburton, the Nova Scotian sketch-writer and statesman, said in 1858 that Trollope was the leading delineator of female character in the present era. Yet today a similar sort of appreciation has come from female critics such as Margaret Markwick and Deborah Denenholz Morse, as well as male critics like Robert Polhemus. Though some have dissented—the narrator of Anthony Powell's *Dance to the Music of*

Time refers to Trollope's women as not being able to analyze their own predicaments—the consensus is that Trollope's depiction of women is effective. Himself the son of a prominent and successful woman who represented women as empowering themselves through philanthropy in her fiction, Trollope in his adulthood was friends with such successful and independent women as Kate Field and George Eliot. Trollope nonetheless depicted women most often in domestic roles or in the process of courtship. But this did not mean that he deliberately avoided complexity. In *The Claverings*, Harry Clavering's vacillation between the girl-next-door type in Florence Burton and the passionate temptress in Julia Ongar is not just a contrast between two personality types. It depicts women as having diverse temperaments. Trollope concedes that, if it were socially possible, Glencora would make as good a Prime Minister as her husband, who actually holds the position.

Despite his reformist position on other issues, Trollope was always opposed to women having the vote. He was aware of movements of female suffrage in England and America. Yet he ruled this prospect out from the start and did not even think it worth serious debate. Although slightly less skeptical of women working in the same professions as men did, he thought this was an abnormal state. As detailed in *North America*, Trollope was horrified at the thought of women aiming for any goals other than marriage. His response to any sort of organized feminism is nearly always satiric. But Trollope's recognition that society was organized in a way that systematically was unequal to women is displayed throughout his work. Women were relegated to domestic space, expected to be, in Coventry Patmore's phrase, the Angel in the House, revered but granted little agency, and ultimately expected to obey men. However, women can have power in courtship. Trollope celebrated such power by his stirring depictions of female beauty, which he always managed to make meaningfully individual, such as his description of the fetching but idiosyncratic Madeline Staveley in *Orley Farm* (in this, he was aided by his illustrators, especially John Everett Millais). But in most aspects of life men have more power because they have both the public status and the money. It is almost impossible in Trollope's world to gain the former since private and public space are so gendered. But it is possible for women to have the latter. Mrs. Prime in *Rachel Ray* refuses to marry a man who will not let her retain control over her money. Martha Dunstable, who marries Doctor Thorne in *Framley Parsonage* only after being reassured she will maintain control, and Madame Max Goesler in *Phineas Redux* who is willing to use her money to benefit the man he loves confident he will respect her, are examples of women who control their own funds. This was made much more systematically possible with the passage of the 1882 Married Women's Property Act, ratified the year Trollope died. Trollope's women named above have this right *ad hoc*, not by law. They have the freedom to act because they have money that they control. Otherwise, women can exercise indirect power by knowing how much money and status men have. They then have the freedom to make decisions in light of that knowledge, i. e., marrying the poorer man over the richer should they so wish. Anna Lovel in *Lady Anna* renounces both money and class privilege in marrying the tailor Daniel Thwaite. But she retains her autonomy. On the other hand, many women in Trollope are either targets or victims of financial opportunists. Miss Mackenzie in the novel titled after her is an example of the former and Emily Wharton in *The Prime Minister* epitomizes the latter.

Another way for women to retain autonomy is to have an artistic identity. Rachel O'Mahony in *The Landleaguers*, is an opera singer. Clara Van Siever, in *The Last Chronicle of Barset*, and Ayala Dormer, in *Ayala's Angel,* gain more social capital in their courtship situations because of their associations with art, the first as a sitter for a portrait, the second as an artist's daughter and sister-in-law. Sometimes women engage in professionalism by proxy, as in the Barsetshire books when both of Septimus Harding's daughters follow his vocation by marrying clergymen even if they cannot be clergy themselves. In general, though, the power of women is exercised through their physical beauty, gender-appropriate temperament, and eligibility of status, concentrated in one temporal moment in their life-trajectory—courtship and marriage; after marriage such autonomy is sparse. Caroline Waddington in *The Bertrams* is both conscious of the power of her beauty, and aware that one rash move will dissipate this power. Men also make consequential decisions in courtship—witness Adolphus Crosbie in The *Small House at Allington* or Phineas Finn in *Phineas Redux*. Yet women cast the die much more decisively at that stage in their lives. But the power women have in the courtship process is witness to their limited power elsewhere. The awareness of this precarious state is why women in Trollope put so much into their choice of a husband; for many it is the only meaningfully autonomous act in which they will engage. In different ways, Clara Desmond in *Castle Richmond*, Linda Tressel in Trollope's work by that name, and Clara Amedroz in *The Belton Estate* all exert their wills forcefully in choosing a marriage partner. The process leads to various ends of triumph, tragedy, or autonomous accommodation. Trollope's young women are the paradigm of his depiction of meaningful human will.

Wallachia Petrie in *He Knew He Was Right* is an American feminist poet who does not want her friend Caroline Spaulding to marry, a position denounced in the narrative. Women in Trollope's world are vulnerable, though, and can, like Carry Brattle in *The Vicar of Bullhampton* or Kate O'Hara in *An Eye for an Eye,* fall to a socially unacceptable position, or, like Lady Laura Kennedy in *Phineas Redux* or Lady Alexandrina de Courcy in *The Small House at Allington*, have to leave the country out of disgrace or marital discord. Trollope also depicts women on the social boundaries, the governess or companion figure. Miss Casseway in *The Duke's Children,* Miss Todd and Miss Baker in *The Bertrams*, are formally or informally employed by women of greater privilege in whose orbit they precariously hover. Some relationships between women, as Sharon Marcus has argued, take on overtones of a same-sex partnership, such as the friendship of Glencora and Alice in *Can You Forgive Her*?

Older women are less of a presence in Trollope than in Thackeray and Dickens, although one of his greatest characters, Mrs. Proudie in the Barsetshire novels, is an older woman who exercises substantial power through her prominent but passive husband. There is also a certain power in Trollopian widowhood. Lady Lufton in *Framley Parsonage* exercises a certain agency on behalf of political conservatism in Barsetshire that she would not have been able to do in the same way had her husband still been alive. Older women young enough to still hanker after courtship situations, such as Lady Mabel Grex in *The Duke's Children* and Lady Alexandrina de Courcy in *The Small House at Allington,* have very limited options, despite their high rank.

In *The Small House at Allington,* Trollope recognizes women in courtship situations had "so many points in their favor" in terms of power. But he knew that, despite his rich and varied portrait of them, women were still disempowered within larger Victorian society.

See also: *The Duke's Children*; homosexuality; *Orley Farm*

Further Reading

Elliott, Dorice Williams. *The Angel Out of the House: Philanthropy and Gender in Nineteenth-Century England.* Charlottesville: University Press of Virginia, 2002.
Markwick, Margaret. *Trollope and Women.* Hambledon, 1987.
Markwick, Margaret, Deborah Denenholz Morse, Regenia Gagnier, eds. *The Politics of Gender in Anthony Trollope's Novels.* London: Ashgate, 2009.
Nardin, Jane Baron. *He Knew She Was Right: The Independent Woman in the Novels of Anthony Trollope.* Carbondale: Southern Illinois University Press, 1989.
Polhemus, Robert. *The Changing World of Anthony Trollope.* Berkeley: University of California Press, 1968.
Watt, George. *The Fallen Woman in the Nineteenth Century Novel.* New York: Routledge, 1984.

Appendix:
General Secondary Bibliography of Anthony Trollope

Biographies

Escott, T.H.S. *Anthony Trollope, His Work, Associates and Literary Originals.* London: Bodley Head, 1913.

Glendinning, Victoria. *Anthony Trollope: A Biography.* New York: Knopf, 1993.

Hall, N. John. *Trollope: A Biography.* London: Clarendon Press, 1991.

Mullen, Richard. *Anthony Trollope, A Victorian in His World.* London: Duckworth. 1990).

Snow, C.P. *Trollope: His Life and Art.* London: Macmillan, 1975.

Super, R.W. *The Chronicler of Barsetshire.* Ann Arbor: University of Michigan Press, 1990.

Bibliographies

Irwin, Mary Leslie. *Anthony Trollope: A Bibliography.* London: Wilson, 1926.

Kincaid, James. *Bibliography of Anthony Trollope. Victorian Web.* http://www.victorianweb.org/authors/trollope/kincaid/primarybibl.html.

Lyons, Anne Kearns. *Anthony Trollope, an Annotated Bibliography of Periodical Works by and about Him in the United States and Great Britain to 1900.* London: Tankevill, 1985.

Sadlier, Michael. *Trollope: A Bibliography.* London: Constable, 1928.

Reference Works and Online Resources

Daniels, Mary L. *Trollope-to-Reader: A Topical Guide to Digressions in the Novels of Anthony Trollope.* London: Greenwood, 1987.

Gerould, James Thayer, and Winifred Gerould. *Guide to Trollope.* Princeton, NJ: Princeton University Press, 1948.

Newlin, George. *Everyone and Everything in Trollope.* Armonk, NY: M.E. Sharpe, 2005.

Terry. R.C. *A Trollope Chronology.* London: Palgrave, 1989.

Tingay, Lance. *The Bedside Barsetshire.* London: Faber & Faber, 1949.

The website maintained by the Trollope Society at *http://www.trollopesociety.org* is an invaluable resource, as are Ellen Moody's Trollope commentary at *https://ellenandjim.wordpress.com/tag/anthony-trollope/* and the Trollope resources of the Victorian Web: *http://www.victorianweb.org/authors/trollope/index.html.*

Companions

Dever, Carolyn, and Lisa Niles, eds. *The Cambridge Companion to Anthony Trollope.* London: Cambridge University Press, 2010.

Morse, Deborah Denenholz, Margaret Markwick, and Mark Turner, eds. *Routledge Research Companion to Anthony Trollope.* New York: Routledge, 2017.

Terry, R.C. *The Oxford Reader's Companion to Trollope.* London: Oxford University Press, 1999.

Van Dam, Frederik, David Skilton, and Ortwin de Graef, eds. *The Edinburgh Companion to Anthony Trollope.* Edinburgh: Edinburgh University Press, 2018.

Anthologies of Classic Trollope Criticism

Hall, N. John, ed. *The Trollope Critics.* London: Palgrave, 1981.

Smalley, Donald, ed. *Anthony Trollope: The Critical Heritage*. New York: Routledge, 2013.

Secondary Critical Works

Anderson, Amanda. "Trollope's Modernity." *ELH*, vol. 74, no. 3, Fall, 2007, pp. 509–534.

ApRoberts, Ruth. *The Moral Trollope*. Ohio University Press, 1971.

Ben-Yishai, Ayelet. *Common Precedents: The Presentness of the Past in Victorian Law and Fiction*. London: Oxford University Press, 2013.

Black, Barbara. *A Room of His Own: A Literary-Historical Study of Victorian Clubland*. Athens: Ohio University Press, 2012.

Bloomfield, Morton. "Trollope's Use of Canadian History." *Nineteenth-Century Literature*, vol. 5, no. 1, June 1960, pp. 67–74.

Booth, Bradford. *Anthony Trollope: Aspects of His Life and Art*. London: Greenwood, 1978.

Bowen, Elizabeth. *Anthony Trollope: A New Judgment*. London: Oxford University Press, 1946.

Cameron, Lauren. "Infertility and Darwinian Anthropology in Anthony Trollope's Phineas Novels." *SEL: Studies in English Literature 1500–1900*, vol. 59, no. 4, Autumn 2019, pp. 893–912.

Cecil, Lord David. *Early Victorian Novelists*. Harmondsworth: Penguin, 1948.

Clark, John Williams. *The Language and Style of Anthony Trollope*. London: Deutsch, 1975.

Cockshut, A.O.J. *Anthony Trollope: A Critical Study*. New York: New York University Press, 1968.

Cotsell, Michael. "Anthony Trollope: The International Theme." *English Literature and the Wider World, Vol. 3, Creditable Warriors, 1830–1876*, edited by Michael Cotsell, London: Ashfield, 1990, pp. 243–256.

Dames, Nicholas. "Trollope and the Career: Vocational Trajectories and the Management of Ambition." *Victorian Studies*, vol. 45, no. 2, Winter 2003, pp. 247–278.

Dentith, Simon. *Nineteenth Century British Literature Then and Now: Reading with Hindsight*. New York: Routledge, 2016.

Durey, Jill Felicity. "*An Eye for an Eye*: Trollope's Warning for Future Relations between England and Ireland." *Victorian Review,* vol. 32, no. 2, 2006, pp. 26–39.

_____. *Trollope and the Church of England*. London: Palgrave Macmillan, 2002.

Edwards, P.D. *Anthony Trollope: His Art and Scope*. London: Harvester, 1978.

Farina, Jonathan. *Everyday Words and the Character of Prose in Nineteenth Century Britain*. London: Cambridge University Press, 2018.

Felber, Lynette. "The Advanced Conservative Liberal: Victorian Liberalism and the Aesthetics of Anthony Trollope's Palliser Novels." *Modern Philology*, vol. 107, no. 3, February 2010, pp. 421–446.

_____. *Gender and Genre in Novels Without End: The British Roman-fleuve*. Gainesville: University Press of Florida, 1995.

Frank, Cathrine O. "Trial Separations: Divorce, Dis-establishment, and Home Rule in *Phineas Redux*." *College Literature,* vol. 35, no. 3, Summer 2008, pp. 30–56.

Franklin, J. Jeffrey. "Anthony Trollope Meets Pierre Bourdieu: The Conversion of Capital as Plot in the Mid-Victorian British Novel." *Victorian Literature and Culture*, vol. 31, no. 2, 2003, pp. 501–521.

Gagnier, Regenia. *Literatures of Liberalization: Global Circulation and the Long Nineteenth Century*. London: Palgrave Macmillan, 2018.

Garrett, Peter. *The Victorian Multiplot Novel: Studies in Dialogical Form*. New Haven, CT: Yale University Press, 1980.

Gilmour, Robin. *The Victorian Period: The Intellectual and Cultural Context of English Literature, 1830–1890*. New York: Routledge, 1993.

Goodlad, Lauren. *The Victorian Geopolitical Aesthetic: Realism, Sovereignty, and Transnational Experience*. London: Oxford University Press, 2017.

_____. *The Victorian Novel and the Victorian State: Character and Governance in a Liberal Society*. Baltimore: Johns Hopkins University Press, 2004.

Gopnik, Adam. "Why Anthony Trollope Is Trending." *New Yorker*, April 27, 2015. https://www.newyorker.com/magazine/2015/05/04/trollope-trending.

Hall, N. John. *Trollope and His Illustrators*. London: Macmillan, 1980.

Halperin, John. *Trollope and Politics: A Study of the Pallisers and Others*. London: Macmillan, 1977.

Hennedy, Hugh L. *Unity in Barsetshire*. London: Mouton, 1971.

Henry, Nancy. *Women, Literature, and Finance in Victorian Britain: Cultures of Investment*. London: Cambridge University Press, 2018.

Herbert, Christopher. *Culture and Anomie: The Ethnographic Imagination in the Nineteenth Century*. Chicago: University of Chicago, 1991.

_____. "*He Knew He Was Right*, Mrs. Lynn Linton, and the Duplicities of Victorian Marriage." *Texas Studies in Literature and Language,* vol. 25, no. 3, Fall 1983, pp. 448–469.

Hewitt. Margaret. "Anthony Trollope: Historian and Sociologist." *The British Journal of Sociology*, vol. 14, no. 3, September 1963, pp. 226–39.

Humphreys, Susan L. "Trollope on the Sublime and Beautiful." *Nineteenth-Century Fiction*, vol. 33 no. 2, September 1978; pp. 194–214.

Jarvis, Claire. *Exquisite Masochism: Sex, Marriage, and the Novel Form*. Baltimore: Johns Hopkins University Press, 2016.

Jones, Anna Maria. *Problem Novels: Victorian Fiction Theorizes the Sensational Self*. Columbus: Ohio State University Press, 2007.

Kendrick, Walter. *The Novel Machine: The Theory and Fiction of Anthony Trollope*. Baltimore: Johns Hopkins University Press, 1980.

Kincaid, James. *The Novels of Anthony Trollope*. London: Clarendon: 1977.

King, Margaret. "The Place of Lucius Mason in Trollope's Studies of Perversity." *South Atlantic Bulletin*, vol. 45, no. 4, November 1980, pp. 43–54.

Lansbury, Coral. *The Reasonable Man: Trollope's*

Legal Fiction. Princeton, NJ: Princeton University Press, 1991.

Letwin, Shirley. *The Gentleman in Trollope: Individuality and Moral Conduct.* Cambridge, MA: Harvard University Press, 1982.

Levine, George. *The Realistic Imagination: English Fiction from Frankenstein to Lady Chatterley.* Chicago: University of Chicago, 1983.

Markwick, Margaret. *New Men in Trollope's Novels: Rewriting the Victorian Male.* London: Ashgate, 2013.

Maurer, Sara L. *The Dispossessed State: Narratives of Ownership in Nineteenth-Century Britain and Ireland.* Baltimore: Johns Hopkins University Press, 2012.

McCourt, John. "Anthony Trollope: An Irish Writer." *http://blog.oup.com/2015/04/anthony-trollope-irish-writer/.*

_____. *Writing the Frontier: Anthony Trollope Between Britain and Ireland.* London: Oxford University Press, 2015.

McDonald, Susan P. *Anthony Trollope.* London: Twayne, 1987.

McMaster, Juliet. *Trollope's Palliser Novels: Theme and Pattern.* Oxford: Oxford University Press, 1978.

Michie, Elsie. *The Vulgar Question of Money: Heiresses, Materialism, and The Novel of Manners from Jane Austen to Henry James.* Baltimore: Johns Hopkins University Press, 2011.

Miller, J. Hillis. *The Form of Victorian Fiction.* Notre Dame: University of Notre Dame Press, 1968.

Mizener, Arthur. "Anthony Trollope: The Palliser Novels." *From Jane Austen to Joseph Conrad: Essays in Memory of James T. Hillhouse,* edited by Robert C. Rathbun and Martin Steinmann, Minneapolis: University of Minnesota Press, 1958, pp. 160–176.

Moody, Ellen. *Trollope on the Net.* London: Hambledon, 1999.

Morse, Deborah Denenholz. *Reforming Trollope: Race, Gender, and Englishness in the Novels of Anthony Trollope.* London: Ashgate, 2013.

_____. *Women in Trollope's Palliser Novels.* University of Rochester Press, 1987.

Morse, Deborah Denenholz, Margaret Markwick, and Regenia Gagnier, eds. *The Politics of Gender in Anthony Trollope's Novels: New Readings for the Twenty-First Century.* London: Ashgate, 2009.

Park, Clara Claiborne. "Grease, Balance, and Point of View in the Work of Anthony Trollope." *Hudson Review,* Autumn 2007, pp. 435–444.

Polhemus, Robert. *The Changing World of Anthony Trollope.* Berkeley: University of California Press, 1978.

Pollard, Arthur. *Anthony Trollope.* London: Henley, 1978.

Pope-Hennessey, James. *Anthony Trollope.* London: Cape, 1971.

Psomiades, Kathy. "Heterosexual Exchange and Other Victorian Fictions: *The Eustace Diamonds* and Victorian Anthropology." *Novel: A Forum on Fiction,* vol. 33, October 1999, pp. 93–118.

Ray, Gordon. "Trollope at Full Length." *Huntington Library Quarterly,* vol. 31, no. 4, August 1968, pp. 313–340.

Sadleir, Michael, *Anthony Trollope: A Commentary.* Boston: Houghton Mifflin, 1927.

Sanders, Andrew. *Anthony Trollope.* Liverpool: Liverpool University Press, 1998.

Schaffer, Talia. *Romance's Rival: Familiar Marriage in Victorian Fiction.* Oxford: Oxford University Press, 2017.

Shelangoskie, Susan. "Anthony Trollope and the Social Discourse of Telegraphy After Nationalisation." *Journal of Victorian Culture,* vol. 14, no. 1, 2009, pp. 72–93.

Skilton, David. *Anthony Trollope and His Contemporaries: A Study in the Theory and Conventions of Mid-Victorian Fiction.* London: St. Martin's, 1972.

Slakey, Roger. "Trollope's Case for Moral Imperative." *Nineteenth-Century Fiction,* vol. 28, no. 3, November 1973, pp. 305–320.

Small, Helen. "Against Self-Interest: Trollope and Realism." *Essays in Criticism,* vol. 62, no. 4, October 2012, pp. 396–416.

Super, R.H. "Trollope at the Royal Literary Fund." *Nineteenth-Century Fiction,* vol. 37, no. 3, November 1982, pp. 316–328.

Sutherland, John. *The Secret Trollope: Anthony Trollope Uncovered.* London: Edward Everett Root, 2019.

Thale, Jerome. "The Problem of Structure in Trollope." *Nineteenth-Century Fiction,* vol. 15, no. 2, September 1960, pp. 147–157.

Tillotson, Geoffrey, and Kathleen Tillotson. *Mid-Victorian Studies.* London: Athlone Press, 1965.

Tingay, Lance. "Trollope's Popularity: A Statistical Approach." *Nineteenth-Century Fiction,* vol. 11, no. 3, December 1956, pp. 223–229.

Tracy. Robert. *Trollope's Later Novels.* Berkeley: University of California Press, 1978.

Turner, Mark. *Trollope and The Magazines: Gendered Issues in Mid-Victorian Britain.* London: Palgrave, 1989.

Voyles, Katherine. "Trollope Through the Window-Pane." *Victorian Literature and Culture,* vol. 41, no. 2, 2013, pp. 283–296.

Wall, Stephen. *Trollope and Character and Other Essays on Victorian Literature.* Ed. Seamus Perry. London: Anthem, 2018.

_____. "Trollope, Balzac, and the Reappearing Character." *Essays in Criticism,* vol. 25, no. 1, January 1975, pp. 123–144.

Walpole, Hugh. *Anthony Trollope.* London: Macmillan, 1928.

Walton, Priscilla L. *Patriarchal Desire and Victorian Discourse: A Lacanian Reading of Trollope's Palliser Novels.* Toronto: University of Toronto Press, 1995.

White, Lisa. "Mrs. Proudie and the Bed Post: Anthony Trollope's Insights Into Victorian Furnishing." *Furniture History,* vol. 51, 2015, pp. 211–221.

Wilson, Cheryl A. *Fashioning the Silver-Fork Novel.* London: Routledge, 2015.

Wolfreys, Julian. *Being English: Narratives, Idioms, and Performances of National Identity from Coleridge to Trollope.* New York: SUNY Press, 1994.

Wright, Daniel. "Because I Do: Trollope, Tautology, and Desire." *ELH,* vol. 80, no. 4, 2003, pp. 1121–1143.

Works Cited

Abelove, Henry. "The Bar and the Board: for Eve Kosofsky Sedgwick." *Glq,* vol. 17, no. 4, 2011, pp. 483–486.

Allen, Brooke. "Who Was Simon Raven?" *The New Criterion,* vol. 28, no. 8, April 2003. https://newcriterion.com/issues/2003/4/who-was-simon-raven.

Altick, Richard. *The Presence of the Present: Topics of the Day in the Victorian Novel.* Columbus: Ohio State University Press, 1991.

Amarnick, Steven, Robert F. Wiseman, Susan Lowell Humphreys, and Michael G. Williamson. *Commentary to the First Complete Edition of the Duke's Children by Anthony Trollope.* London: Folio Society, 2015.

Anderson, Amanda. "Trollope's Modernity." *Elh,* vol. 74, no. 3, Fall, 2007, pp. 509–534.

Ardila, J.A. Garrido. "The Picaresque Novel and the Rise of the English Novel, from Baldwin and Deloney to Defoe and Smollett." *The Picaresque Novel in Western Literature: from the Sixteenth Century to the Neopicaresque,* edited by Ardila, London: Cambridge University Press, 2015, pp. 113–39.

Baker, Joseph Ellis. *The Novel and the Oxford Movement.* London: Russell & Russell, 1965.

Bakhtin, Mikhail. *The Dialogic Imagination: Four Essays.* Ed. Michael Holquist. Trans. Caryl Emerson and Michael Holquist. Austin: University of Texas Press, 1981.

Barber, Michael. *The Captain: The Life and Times of Simon Raven.* Duckworth, 1996.

Ben-Yishai, Ayelet. "The Fact of a Rumor: Anthony Trollope's the *Eustace Diamonds.*" *Nineteenth-Century Literature,* vol. 68, no. 1, 2007, pp. 88–120.

Bentley, David. *English Criminal Justice in the Nineteenth Century.* London: Hambledon, 1998.

Blackstone, Sir William. *Commentaries on the Laws of England.* 4 vols. London: Collins & Hannay, 1832.

Boddice, Rob. "Madness and the 'Morality of Field Sports': E.A. Freeman and Anthony Trollope, 1869–1871." *The Historian,* vol. 70, 2008, pp. 1–29.

Booth, Bradford A. *Anthony Trollope: Aspects of His Life and Work.* London: Edward Hulton, 1958.

Buzard, James. *Disorienting Fiction: The Autoethnographic Work of Nineteenth-Century British Novels.* Princeton, NJ: Princeton University Press, 2005.

Cheyette, Bryan. *Constructions of the Jew in English Literature and Society: Racial Representations, 1875–1945.* London: Cambridge University Press, 1993.

Clarke, C.P.S. "The Genesis of the Movement." *Northern Catholicism: Centenary Studies in the Oxford and Parallel Movements,* edited by N.P. Williams and Charles Harris, London: SPCK, 1933, pp. 12–16.

Cockshut, A.O.J. *Anthony Trollope: A Critical Study.* New York: New York University Press, 1968.

Cora, Gina. "The Bad and the Good: How the *Eustace Diamonds* Changes Representations of Femininity in *Vanity Fair.*" Trollope Prize, First Prize 2003. Archived at https://sites.fas.harvard.edu/~trollope/2003.htm.

Delany, Paul. "'This Half-Foreigner': Madame Goesler and Her Enemies." *Victorians: A Journal of Culture and Literature,* no. 128, September 2015, pp. 5–19.

Durey, Jill Felicity. *Trollope and the Church of England.* London: Palgrave Macmillan, 2002.

Edwards, Owen Dudley. "Anthony Trollope, the Irish Writer." *Nineteenth-Century Fiction,* vol. 38, no. 1, June 1983, pp. 1–42.

Edwards, P.D. *Anthony Trollope: His Art and Scope.* St. Lucia: University of Queensland Press, 1977.

_____. "Trollope's Letters." *Sydney Studies in English Literature,* 2008, pp. 109–116.

Escott, T.H.S. *Anthony Trollope, His Work, Associates and Literary Originals.* London: Bodley Head, 1913.

Felber, Lynette. "The Advanced Conservative Liberal: Victorian Liberalism and the Aesthetics of Anthony Trollope's Palliser Novels." *Modern Philology,* vol. 107, no. 3, February 2010, pp. 421–446.

Fisichelli, Glyn-Ellen. "The Language of Law and Love: Anthony Trollope's *Orley Farm.*" *Elh,* vol. 61, no. 3, Autumn 1994, pp. 635–53.

Freedman, Monroe H. "Brougham and Zeal." *Hofstra Law Review,* vol. 34, no. 4, Summer 2006, pp. 1319–1324.

Gest, John Marshall. "The Law and Lawyers of Charles Dickens." *American Law Register,* vol. 53/44, no. 7, July 1905, pp. 401–428.

Glendinning, Victoria. *Anthony Trollope.* New York: Knopf, 1992.

Godfrey, Esther. *The January-May Marriage in*

Nineteenth-Century British Literature. Basingtoke: Palgrave Macmillan, 2009.

_____. "Victorian Cougar: H. Rider Haggard's *She,* Ageing and Sexual Selection in Marriage." *Victorian Network,* vol. 4, no. 2, Winter 2012, pp. 72–84.

Goodlad, Lauren M.E. *The Victorian Geopolitical Aesthetic.* London: Oxford University Press, 2018.

_____. *Victorian Literature and the Victorian State.* Baltimore: Johns Hopkins University Press, 2004.

Hagan, John H. "*The Duke's Children*: Trollope's Psychological Masterpiece." *Nineteenth-Century Fiction,* vol. 13, no. 1, June 1958, pp. 1–21.

Hall, N. John. *Trollope: A Biography.* London: Clarendon Press, 1991, pp. 384–388.

Halperin, John. "Trollope, James, and 'The Retribution of Time.'" *Southern Humanities Review,* vol. 19, 1985, pp. 301–308.

Heath, Kay. *Aging by the Book: The Emergence of Midlife in Victorian Britain.* New York: SUNY Press, 2009.

_____. "Trollope and Aging." *The Routledge Research Companion to Anthony Trollope,* edited by Margaret Markwick, and Mark W. Turner, London: Routledge, 2017, pp. 295–305.

Heine, Jennifer. "Two Separate Persons: Ethnicity and Identity in Trollope's *Phineas Finn.*" *Elements,* vol. 12, no. 1, Spring 2016, pp. 75–81.

Hughes, Kathryn. "Gender Roles in the 19th Century." *Discovering Literature: Romantics & Victorians.* British Library, 15 May 2014. https://www.bl.uk/romantics-and-victorians/articles/gender-roles-in-the-19th-century.

Humphreys, Susan L. "Order—Method: Trollope Learns to Write." *Dickens Studies Annual,* vol. 8, 1980, pp. 251–271.

Jarvis, Claire. *Exquisite Masochism: Sex, Marriage, and the Novel Form.* Baltimore: Johns Hopkins University Press, 2016.

_____. *Making Scenes: Supersensual Masochism and Victorian Literature.* Dissertation. UMI Dissertation Publishing, 2008.

Jones, Wendy. "Feminism, Fiction and Contract Theory: Trollope's *He Knew He Was Right.*" *Criticism,* vol. 36, no. 3, Summer, 1994, pp. 401–414.

Kendrick, Walter M. "*The Eustace Diamonds*: The Truth of Trollope's Fiction." *Elh,* vol. 46, no. 1, Spring 1979, pp. 136–57.

_____. *The Novel-Machine: The Theory and Fiction of Anthony Trollope.* Baltimore: Johns Hopkins University Press, 1980.

Kenyon, Ruth. "The Social Aspect of the Catholic Revival." *Northern Catholicism: Centenary Studies in the Oxford and Parallel Movements,* edited by N.P. Williams and Charles Harris. London: SPCK, 1933, pp. 367–384.

King, Mark. *The Hobbledehoy's Choice: Anthony Trollope's Awkward Young Men and Their Road to Gentlemanliness.* ProQuest Dissertation Publishing, 2005.

Lansbury, Coral. *The Reasonable Man: Trollope's Legal Fiction.* Princeton, NJ: Princeton University Press, 1981.

Locke, John. *Two Treatises of Government.* Ed. Peter Laslett. London: Cambridge University Press, 1987.

Lovett, Denise. "The Socially-Embedded Market and the Future of English Capitalism in Anthony Trollope's the *Way We Live Now.*" *Victorian Literature and Culture,* vol. 42, no. 4, December 2014, pp, 691–707.

Markwick, Margaret. *New Men in Trollope's Novels: Rewriting the Victorian Male.* London: Ashgate, 2013.

Maurer, Sara. "The Nation's Wife: England's Vicarious Enjoyment in Anthony Trollope's Palliser Novels." *Troubled Legacies: Narrative and Inheritance,* edited by Allan Hepburn, Toronto: University of Toronto Press, 2007, pp. 58–65.

McMaster, R.D. "Trollope and the Terrible Meshes of the Law: *Mr. Scarborough's Family.*" *Nineteenth-Century Fiction,* vol. 36, no. 2, September 1981, pp. 135–156.

Miner, Heather. "Trollope and the Hunt for West Country Identity." *Victoriographies,* vol. 1, no. 2, 2011, pp. 221–242.

Moody, Ellen. "Trollope on Television: Intertextuality in the *Pallisers* and Other Trollope Films," *Victorian Literature and Film Adaptation,* edited by Abigaim Burnham Bloom and Mary Sanders Pollock, Amherst, NY: Cambria Press, 2011, pp. 155–180; archived at https://www.academia.edu/6438191/Trollope_on_TV_Simon_Ravens_adaptation_of_Anthony_Trollopes_Parliamentary_novels_as_the_Pallisers.

_____. *Trollope on the Net.* London: Hambledon, 1999.

Morse, Deborah Denenholz. "'Nothing Will Make Me Distrust You': the Pastoral Transformed in Anthony Trollope's the *Small House at Allington* (1864)." *Victorian Transformations: Genre, Nationalism and Desire in Nineteenth-Century Literature,* edited by Bianca Tredennick, London: Routledge, 2016, pp. 45–60.

_____. *Reforming Trollope, Race, Gender, and Englishness in the Fiction of Anthony Trollope.* London: Routledge, 2016.

_____. "The Way He Thought Then: Modernity and the Retreat of the Public Liberal in Anthony Trollope's the *Way We Live Now, 1873.*" *BRANCH: Britain, Representation and Nineteenth-Century History,* July 2014. http://www.branchcollective.org/?ps_articles=deborah-denenholz-morse-the-way-he-thought-then-modernity-and-the-retreat-of-the-public-liberal-in-anthony-trollopes-the-way-we-live-now-1873.

Murray, James A.H., ed. *The Oxford English Dictionary,* Vol. IV. Oxford: Oxford University Press, 1901.

Oberhelman, David D. "Trollope's Insanity Defense: Narrative Alienation in *He Knew He Was Right.*" *Studies in English Literature, 1500–1900,* vol. 35, no. 4, Autumn 1995, pp. 789–806.

Raven, Simon. *Places Where They Sing.* London: Anthony Blond, 1970.

Riffaterre, Michael. "Trollope's Metonymies." *Nineteenth-Century Fiction,* vol. 37 no. 3, December 1982, pp. 272–292.

Rodes, Robert E., Jr. *Law and Modernization in the Church of England: Charles II to the Welfare State.*

Vol. 3: *This House I Have Built: A Study of the Legal History of the Establishment in England.* Notre Dame, IN: University of Notre Dame Press, 1991.

Roth, Alan. "He Thought He Was Right (But Wasn't): Property Law in Anthony Trollope's the *Eustace Diamonds.*" *Stanford Law Review,* vol. 44, no. 4, April 1992, pp. 879–897.

Sadleir, Michael. *Trollope: A Commentary.* London: Constable, 1945.

Schneider, Wendie Ellen. *Engines of Truth: Producing Veracity in the Victorian Courtroom.* New Haven, CT: Yale University Press, 2015.

Sedgwick, Eve Kosofsky. "Selections from 'The Warm Decembers.'" *Raritan,* vol. 6, no. 2, Fall 1986, pp. 51–62.

Shaw, George Bernard. *Pygmalion.* London: Oldhams, 1934.

Sheingold, Leonard. *Is There Life Without Mother? Psychoanalysis, Biography, Creativity.* Hillsdale, NJ: Analytic Press, 2000.

Smalley, Donald, ed. *Trollope: The Critical Heritage.* London: Routledge, 1969.

Snow, C.P. *The Masters.* London: Macmillan, 1951.

———. *The Realists.* London: Macmillan, 1978.

———. *Trollope: His Life and Art.* London: Macmillan, 1975.

Stevens, Wallace. "The Emperor of Ice-Cream." *The Collected Poetry of Wallace Stevens.* New York: Alfred A. Knopf, 2000, p. 64.

———. *Harmonium.* New York: Knopf, 1932.

Sussman, Matthew. "Optative Form in Anthony Trollope's the *Small House at Allington.*" *Nineteenth-Century Literature,* vol. 71, no. 4, March 2017, pp. 485–515.

Taylor, James. *Creating Capitalism: Joint-Stock Enterprises in British Politics and Culture, 1800–1870.* London: Royal Historical Society, 2014.

Terry, Reginald Charles. *Anthony Trollope: The Artist in Hiding.* London: Macmillan, 1977.

Thomas, Kate. *Postal Pleasures: Sex, Scandal, and Victorian Letters.* Oxford: Oxford University Press, 2012.

Tracy, Robert. *Trollope's Later Novels.* Berkeley: University of California Press, 1978.

Trollope, Anthony. *Can You Forgive Her?* London: Oxford University Press, 2011.

———. *The Duke's Children.* London: Oxford University Press, 2011.

———. *The Eustace Diamonds.* London: Oxford University Press, 2011.

———. *Framley Parsonage.* Leipzig: Tauchnitz, 1861.

———. *He Knew He Was Right.* London: Strahan, 1869.

———. *The Macdermots of Ballycloran.* London: Chapman and Hall 1880.

———. *Mr. Scarborough's Family.* London: Chapman and Hall, 1883.

———. *Phineas Finn.* London: Oxford University Press, 2011.

———. *Phineas Redux.* London: Oxford University Press, 2011.

———. *The Prime Minister.* London: Oxford University Press, 2011.

———. *Tales of All Countries.* London: Chapman and Hall, 1864.

———. *The Way We Live Now.* London: Chapman and Hall, 1875.

Van Dam, Frederik. *Anthony Trollope's Late Style: Victorian Liberalism and Literary Form.* Edinburgh: Edinburgh University Press, 2016.

Wall, Stephen. *Trollope and Character.* London: Faber & Faber, 1988.

Wiesenthal, Christine S. "The Body Melancholy: Trollope's *He Knew He Was Right.*" *Dickens Studies Annual,* vol. 23, 1994, pp. 227–258.

Williams, N.P. "The Theology of the Catholic Revival." *Northern Catholicism: Centenary Studies in the Oxford and Parallel Movements,* edited by N.P. Williams and Charles Harris, London: SPCK, 1933, pp. 130–35.

Williamson, Michael. "Contextual Notes." *Commentary to the First Complete Edition of* The Duke's Children *By Anthony Trollope,* edited by Steven Amarnick et al., London: Folio Society, 2015.

Wirenius, John F. "Not Charity, but Justice: Charles Gore, Workers, and the Way." *Journal of Catholic Legal Studies,* vol. 50, 2011, pp. 279, 284–288.

Woodward, Llewellyn. *The Age of Reform: 1815–1870.* London: Oxford University Press, 1962.

Wright, Andrew. *Anthony Trollope: Dream and Art.* London: Macmillan, 1983.

Index

"Aaron Trow" 171, 190, 217–8
"The Adventures of Fred Picker-
  ing" 117–8
alcoholism 32, 52–3, 60–1, 213
"Alice Dugdale" 220
All the Year Round 19–20, 41, 44,
  49, 54, 95, 130, 203
Amarnick, Steven 49, 55, 100
The American Senator 20–1, 28,
  89–90, i2, 137, 140, 210
Anglicanism 50, 67; *see also*
  Church of England
Anglo-Saxon racialism 170, 192
apRoberts, Ruth 177
Arnold, Matthew 33, 43, 69, 186
Australia 6, 12, 21–25, 48, 78–80,
  81, 89, 91, 95, 101–2, 105–7, 121,
  124, 125, 128, 135, 138, 142–3,
  170, 174, 178–9, 186, 188, 190,
  194, 198, 218
Austria 117–8, 133, 200, 202, 213
An Autobiography 1, 2, 5, 12, 20,
  25–6, 48, 69, 76, 90, 11, 119,
  143, 155, 172, 177, 193, 204,
  210, 212
Ayala's Angel 12, 27–8, 70, 86, 90.
  104, 140, 156, 181, 222

Bakhtin, Mikhail 92
Balzac, Honoré de 139–40, 183,
  207–9
Banim, John 84
Barchester Towers 5, 29–31, 51,
  67, 82, 86, 88, 92, 109, 139–40,
  149, 175, 201, 210, 212
Barsetshire novels 1, 4, 11–12, 28,
  44, 51, 52, 54, 82, 93, 109, 126,
  139–45, 171, 176–8, 181, 183–4,
  185, 187, 197, 200–1, 204, 210,
  222
Belgium 4, 9, 133, 178, 189
Bermuda 171, 190
The Bertrams 22, 29, 31, 33–35,
  50, 52, 67, 83, 85–6, 88, 92, 125,
  129, 140, 143, 153–4, 188, 200,
  210, 222
Bible 33–4, 67
Boers 186

Booth, Wayne C. 92
Brontë, Charlotte 25, 142
Brontë, Emily 121, 142
Browne, Hablot K. 36, 41

Caesar, Gaius Julius 87, 115,
  153–4
Cakobau (king) 23
Can You Forgive Her 5, 24, 35–9,
  41, 55–6, 66, 81, 88, 128, 141,
  169, 199, 222
Canada 22–23, 69, 85, 135, 138
Capitalism 40, 151, 187, 192, 196,
  216, 218
Caribbean 11, 49, 69, 135, 190–
  92, 216–18
Carleton, William 93
Caroline, Queen 147
Castle Richmond 11, 39–41, 45,
  81, 87, 94–5, 106, 116, 125, 128,
  145, 152, 222
"Catherine Carmichael" 22, 24,
  206, 219
Cetewayo (king) 23
Chapman and Hall 27, 31, 41, 45,
  51, 53, 54, 59, 63, 68, 89, 95,
  101, 105, 121, 128 135, 145, 151,
  155, 172, 185, 187, 190, 212, 216
"The Chateau of Prince Polignac" 190
childhood 26, 48, 108, 202
Christmas 49, 67, 79, 128, 180,
  191–2, 206, 219
"Christmas at Thompson Hall"
  193, 219
Church of England 67, 71, 98,
  131, 141, 146, 150; *see also* Anglicanism
Cicero, Marcus Tullius 5, 25,
  153–5, 174
Cincinnati 10, 12, 200, 202
civil service 10, 165, 179, 193,
  196–7
The Claverings 26, 41–43, 49, 67,
  125, 197, 221
Colenso, John William 67, 186
Cooper, James Fenimore 3, 136,
  139

Cornhill 11, 12, 41, 44–5, 72, 115,
  151, 179, 183, 193
Cornwall 118
"The Courtship of Susan Bell"
  70, 137, 189
Cousin Henry 5, 45–7, 88, 92,
  114, 124, 125, 143, 210
crime 45–7, 110, 146, 159–60
Crimean War 43, 136, 150, 152
Crittenden, John J. 135–6
Cuba 217
Cumberland 80, 90, 105, 191, 198

dance 28, 96–7
Dickens, Charles 3, 10, 19, 25–6,
  36, 39, 41`, 43–4, 46, 48–9, 52,
  60, 67, 69, 94, 98–9, 109, 112,
  136–7, 139, 123, 128, 142, 176,
  180, 194, 205, 207, 211, 219, 222
Dickens, Charles, Jr. 49, 198,
  201, 203
Disraeli, Benjamin (Earl of Bea-
  consfield) 6, 23, 35, 50–1, 62,
  75–6, 99, 103
Divorce 159, 213
Doctor Thorne 5, 47, 51–3, 82,
  100, 109, 111, 124, 126, 139–40,
  158, 173, 178, 216
Dr. Wortle's School 12, 32, 53–4,
  67, 70, 121, 126, 137
Dostoyevsky, Fyodor Mihai-
  lovich 46, 110, 133
dueling 94, 134 156, 162, 199
The Duke's Children 5, 12, 19,
  21, 27, 54–59, 70, 87, 95, 96,
  98, 119, 124, 129, 137–8, 140–1,
  155, 161, 163, 168, 178, 181, 199,
  214, 222

Eastern Question 50, 62, 75, 153
Edgeworth, Maria 93–4, 103
Egypt 33, 174, 189
Eliot, George 3, 4, 8, 12, 29, 44,
  48, 50, 53, 61–2, 70, 75, 91, 98–
  9, 115, 142, 207, 221
England 50–53, 62, 68, 71, 79,
  80, 81, 88, 95, 98, 100–102, 105,
  121, 122, 135–6, 155–6, 167

Escott, T.H.S. 43, 72, 114, 155, 176, 177, 201, 210

The Eustace Diamonds 47, 63–6, 71–2, 86–8, 99, 11–12, 113, 128, 14–1, 146, 159–60, 163, 181

Evangelical Christianity 66–8

An Eye for an Eye 40, 68–9, 124, 222

farming 79, 128, 135, 173

"Father Giles of Ballymoy" 118

Fawkes, Lionel Grimston 69

feminism 7, 39, 62, 63, 211

Field, Kate 54, 61, 69–70, 119, 137, 144, 221

Fiji 23, 198

Fildes, Luke 69

Fish, Hamilton 136

fishing 73

The Fixed Period 13, 22–3, 70–1, 102, 127, 143, 145, 187

food 108, 190, 218–9

Fortnightly Review 12, 31, 41, 45, 47, 59 63, 71–2, 196, 105, 115, 140, 152, 205

Framley Parsonage 28, 32, 44–5, 72–4, 110–1, 124, 126, 128, 140–1, 149, 182, 193, 221–2

France 76, 133, 164, 180, 190, 204, 207–8

French Revolution 5, 207–8

futurity 12, 22–5, 59, 71, 89, 107–8, 127, 133–4, 137–8, 143, 170, 186, 189, 217–18

Galsworthy, John 140

"Gentle Euphemia" 155, 295

"George Walker at Suez" 191, 198

Germany 10, 43, 61, 73, 76, 97, 117, 119, 125, 133–4, 142, 186, 192, 104

Gladstone, William Ewart 23, 43, 50, 62, 74–6, 95, 142–3, 153

The Golden Lion of Granpere 76–8, 104, 124–5, 134, 173

Good Words 67, 76, 78, 118, 128, 153, 172, 206, 219

Goodlad, Lauren M. E. 152, 170, 178, 185, 194, 197–8, 211

Gresley family 9, 80, 199

Guizot, Francois 202

Gunn, Mrs. Aeneas 24

Guyana 217

Harrow School 10, 51, 87, 127, 138, 153

Harry Heathcote of Gangoil 22, 44, 49, 78–80, 125

Hawthorne, Nathanael 81–2, 136, 210

He Knew He Was Right 25, 44, 47, 78, 83–85, 104, 112, 136, 175, 222

Hellicar family 9, 199

Hervieu, Auguste 129

higher criticism 33–4

Hobbledehoy 26, 28, 42, 47, 59, 85–87, 156, 161, 185, 197, 209

Holl, Frank Montague 86–7, 160

homosexuality 59, 87–8, 192

horse racing 98, 103

"How the Mastiffs Went to Iceland" 5, 88–9

humor 42, 53, 57, 97, 131, 173, 193–4, 211

Iceland 5, 88–9, 106, 181, 198

illustration 27, 68, 74, 83, 109, 128–9, 160, 195

India 4, 28, 95, 109, 189, 194, 198, 204, 209, 217

Indigenous Australians 170

inheritance 36, 43, 45–6, 48, 55, 61, 103, 130–3, 141, 161

intrusive narrator 28, 30, 32, 68, 91–3, 177, 211

Ireland 4, 6, 11–13, 23, 26, 40, 47, 68, 70, 89, 93–96, 103, 107–8, 118, 120–1, 127, 137, 142, 150, 155, 1645, 180–2, 194, 201, 207, 212

Is He Popenjoy? 4, 18, 46–7, 67, 95–7, 99, 101, 123

Italy 30, 69, 95, 105, 119, 133, 153, 192, 198, 202–5

Jenkins, Edward 217

Jews 39, 50, 99–101, 108, 134–35, 160, 166, 169, 171, 172, 204, 214

"John Bull on the Guadalquivir" 188

John Caldigate 22, 47, 54, 101–2, 125, 165, 179, 201

"Josephine de Montmonerci" 60

"A Journey to Panama" 119

"Katchen's Caprices" 205

The Kellys and the O'Kellys 49, 50, 68, 93, 95, 102–4, 126, 152, 214

Kept in the Dark 78, 92, 104–5, 125, 128

Kincaid, James, *177*

Knoepflmacher, Ulrich 177

Lady Anna 5, 22, 27, 32, 59, 71–2, 80, 86, 95, 105–7, 124, 173, 190, 221

"The Lady of Launay" 219

The Landleaguers 13, 40, 47, 49, 76, 93, 95, 98, 100, 103, 107–9, 137, 186, 222

"The Last Austrian Who left Venice" 78, 118–9

The Last Chronicle of Barset 11, 29, 33, 36, 44–6, 74, 109–12, 127–8, 140–3, 149, 183–4, 105, 199, 222

law 70–71, 83–84, 112–115, 125, 126, 110, 131, 133, 136, 211

Lawless, Emily 107

Leavis, F.R. 62, 177

Letwin, Shirley 6, 178

Lever, Charles 94

Lewes, George Henry 12, 61, 115

Lincoln, Abraham 119

Linda Tressel 10, 73, 76, 88, 115–17, 134, 182, 188, 222

localities 20–21, 46, 79, 80, 105, 139–40, 164, 172–3, 186, 195, 210, 217

London 9–13, 18, 40, 41, 44, 46, 83, 85, 88, 94, 96–7, 103, 106, 114, 151, 156, 159, 161, 164, 172, 174, 180, 184, 187, 191, 196–7, 211

Longworth, Nicholas 202

"Lotta Schmidt" 117, 201

Louis Philippe, King 52, 200

Lukács, Georg 177

The Macdermots of Ballycloran 11, 47, 49, 94, 102–3, 120–1

Major, John 178

"Malachi's Cove" 118

Māori 24, 171

Marcus, Sharon 222

Marion Fay 20, 25, 27, 45, 47, 52, 54, 67, 90, 96, 104, 105, 121–3, 165

marriage plot 31, 68, 71, 81, 86, 102, 110, 123–6, 129–30, 173

Marx, Karl 40, 196

Marxism 62

"Mary Gresley" 59–60, 180, 182, 199

Meetkerke family 9 10, 32

"La Mère Bauche" 188

Merivale, John Lewis 127–8

Millais, John Everett 36, 41, 44, 74, 78, 128–9, 160, 183, 195–6, 222

Miller, J. Hillis 7, 123, 177

Milton, Henry 9

Milton, John 118

Milton family 9, 106, 199

Miss Mackenzie 60, 67, 125, 129–30, 140, 155, 223

"Miss Ophelia Gledd" 119

"Miss Sarah Jack of Spanish Town" 189, 216

Mr. Scarborough's Family 6, 13, 19, 29, 47, 99, 112, 130–33. 142–3, 173, 193

"The Mistletoe Bough" 191–2

"Mrs. Brumby" 61

"Mrs General Talboys" 190

music 3, 108, 117

Napoleon I 189

Napoleon III 76

"Never, Never-Never, Never" 137, 183, 205–6

New Zealand 12, 22–5, 62, 89, 138, 171, 179, 186, 206
The New Zealander 20, 22
Nina Balatka 76–7, 100, 106, 133–5, 171, 182, 186
The Noble Jilt 208
"Not If I Know It" 206–7

"The O'Conors of Castle Conor" 120, 182, 186
Old Man's Love, A 86, 117, 143–4
opera *3, 34, 222*
Orley Farm 1, 9, 11, 34, 40, 47, 50, 61, 65, 79, 82, 100, 105, 112–4, 128–9, 143–4, 145–48, 154, 159, 193, 221
Owenson, Sydney 93
Oxford movement 4, 30, 67, 148–51

Palestine 6, 75, 182
Pall Mall Gazette 12, 47, 75, 89, 151–2, 154, 198
Palliser novels 6, 19, 36, 58, 67, 71, 128, 139–41, 159, 170–1, 175, 177–8
Palmerston, Lord 75, 152–3
Panama 119, 217–8
"The Panjandrum" 60
"The Parson's Daughter of Oxney Colne" 183, 190–1
Patmore, Coventry 28, 221
Phineas Finn 25, 35, 47–8, 57, 71, 83, 89, 94–5, 100, 112, 124, 125, 126, 128, 138–9, 141, 155–8, 275, 181, 189, 214, 220
Phineas Redux 9, 42–4, 46–7, 54, 86–7, 99, 106, 112–3, 124–25, 140–3, 159–65, 181, 199, 221–2
Polhemus, Robert 177
post office 10–12, 26, 61, 85, 90, 93, 114, 135–6, 144, 152, 164–5, 180, 195–6, 198, 219
Powell, Anthony 6, 91, 140, 220
Powers, Hiram 202
Prague 159
The Prime Minister 19, 33, 44, 55, 99, 141, 166–70, 180, 221

Québec 138, 185

Ralph the Heir 90, 96, 172–4
Raven, Simon 5, 6, 140, 174–6
Ray, Gordon 5–6, 80, 182
"Relics of General Chassé" 189
"A Ride Across Palestine" 87, 182, 192
Riffaterre, Michael 93
Risorgimento 190, 203

Roman Catholicism 49, 56, 68, 95, 126, 148–9, 157, 159–60
Rusden, G.W. 12, 143, 178–9

Sadleir, Michael 177
Saint Pauls 12, 50, 59–61, 152, 155, 172, 179–80
Satchell, William 24
satire 12, 49, 51, 54, 60, 69, 90, 120, 154, 176, 181–2, 187–8, 196–7, 211–2, 215–6
Scotland 88, 95, 108 150, 180–82
sensation novel 34, 54, 102, 104, 131, 173, 177
serialization 12, 19–20, 25, 27, 31, 35, 41, 44–5, 49, 53, 63, 68, 70–2, 76, 78, 80, 83, 95, 101, 104–5, 109, 115, 121, 122, 130, 133, 137, 141, 156, 159, 172, 174, 180, 182, 186, 193, 195, 203, 208–9, 212
settler colonies 7, 12, 22, 24–5, 71 89, 138, 145, 152, 170–1, 185, 194, 198, 200
Shakespeare, William 3, 64, 122, 123, 190
silver-fork novel 5, 146
Sir Harry Hotspur of Humblethwaite 1, 32, 47, 80–1, 105, 173
Skilton, David 177
The Small House at Allington 26, 45, 85, 109, 126, 128–9, 137, 140, 156, 178, 182–4, 191, 193–4, 197, 206, 210, 222
Snow, C.P. 140, 178
Somerville and Ross 93
South Africa 101, 145, 171, 185–6
Spain 189
"The Spotted Dog" 60–1
Stephen, Leslie 45
The Struggles of Brown, Jones, and Robinson 49, 70, 97, 100, 153, 184, 186–8, 196–7

Tauchnitz editions 117
"The Telegraph Girl" 86, 165, 219
television adaptations of Trollope 4, 6, 62, 98, 111, 128, 176, 178
Thackeray, William Makepeace 5, 11, 25–6, 39–40, 42–4, 48, 63, 66–7, 72, 84, 91, 94, 98, 128, 137, 139, 142, 151–2, 187, 190, 193–4, 207, 222
theatrical adaptations of Trollope 107, 172, 174
Thiers, Adolphe 202
third plots 28, 39, 111, 123
Thirkell, Angela 4
Thomas, George Housman 109, 128, 194–5

The Three Clerks 195–7
Tolstoy, Leo 3, 46, 91, 220
Trollope, Frances Eleanor 180, 199, 205
Trollope, Frances Milton 9–10, 48, 54, 102, 106, 135–9, 199–202
Trollope, Henry Marivale 11–12, 41, 54, 128
Trollope, Rose Heseltine 11, 13, 89, 93
Trollope, Theodosia Garrow 100, 202–5
Trollope, Thomas Adolphus 27, 69, 104, 114, 119, 133, 198, 200–5
Trollope, Thomas Anthony 9–10, 199–200, 207
"The Two Generals" 118
"The Two Heroines of Plumplington" 140, 206

United States of America 6, 8, 11, 23–4, 49, 54, 118, 126, 129, 135–8, 142, 194, 198–200, 213, 217, 219
"An Unprotected Female at the Pyramids" 189

La Vendée 15, 50, 61, 39, 82, 105, 154, 164, 193, 204, 207–8
The Vicar of Bullhampton 123, 154, 208–9, 222
Victoria, Princess Royal 62
Victoria, Queen 4, 45, 48, 50 121, 142, 165, 194

Wales 45–6, 150
The Warden 5, 11, 49, 621, 102, 109, 126, 128, 139, 149, 154–5, 175, 181, 206, 208, 210–2
Waugh, Alec 41
Waugh, Arthur 51
Waugh, Evelyn 41, 91, 175, 200
The Way We Live Now 1, 28, 33, 35, 47–8, 50, 57, 69, 10, 110, 112, 136, 140, 175, 212–6
"Why Frau Frohmann Raised Her Prices" 10, 100, 112, 196, 205, 218–9
Wodehouse, P.G. 57
women 4, 23, 28, 39, 44, 77, 81, 86–9, 201, 210, 220–3
Woolf, Virginia 45, 126
work 42–3, 59, 79, 86–7, 102, 137–8, 153, 164–5, 173–4, 186–8, 195–7
Wright, Frances 200

Young, Brigham 137

Zulus 23, 186